W9-AFK-826

Bette Midler

BOOKS BY MARK BEGO

The Captain & Tennille (1977)

Barry Manilow (1977)

The Doobie Brothers (1980)

Michael! [Jackson] (1984)

On the Road with Michael! [Jackson] (1984)

Rock Hudson: Public & Private (1986)

Sade! (1986)

Julian Lennon! (1986)

The Best of "Modern Screen" (1986)

Whitney! [Houston] (1986)

The Linda Gray Story (1988)

TV Rock (1988)

Between the Lines [with Debbie Gibson] (1990)

Linda Ronstadt: It's So Easy (1990)

Ice Ice Ice: The Extraordinary Vanilla Ice Story (1991)

One Is the Loneliest Number [with Jimmy Greenspoon of Three Dog Night] (1991)

I'm a Believer: My Life of Music, Monkees and Madness [with Micky Dolenz of the Monkees] (1993)

Country Hunks (1994)

Country Gals (1994)

Dancing in the Street: Confessions of a Motown Diva [with Martha Reeves of Martha & the Vandellas] (1994)

I Fall to Pieces: The Music & the Life of Patsy Cline (1995)

Rock & Roll Almanac (1996)

Alan Jackson: Gone Country (1996)

Raised on Rock: The Autobiography of Elvis Presley's Step Brother [with David Stanley] (1996)

George Strait: The Story of Country's Living Legend (1997)

Leonardo DiCaprio: Romantic Hero (1998)

LeAnn Rimes (1998)

Jewel (1998, Music Sales Press)

Matt Damon: Chasing a Dream (1998)

Will Smith: The Freshest Prince (1998)

Vince Gill (2000)

Madonna: Blonde Ambition (2000, Cooper Square Press)

Aretha Franklin: Queen of Soul (2001)

The Marx Brothers (2001)

Cher: If You Believe (2001)

Bette Midler: Still Divine (2002, Cooper Square Press)

Bonnie Raitt: Still in the Nick of Time (2003, Cooper Square Press)

Tina Turner (2003, Cooper Square Press)

STILL DIVINE

MARK BEGO

INTRODUCTION BY RITA COOLIDGE

Cooper Square Press

First Cooper Square Press edition 2002

This Cooper Square Press hardcover edition of *Bette Midler: Still Divine* is an original publication. A portion (now greatly revised and expanded) of the material contained herein appeared in a work by the author entitled *Bette Midler: Outrageously Divine*, first published as a mass market original paperback in New York in 1987. *Bette Midler: Still Divine* is published by arrangement with the author.

Published by Cooper Square Press
A Member of the Rowman & Littlefield Publishing Group
200 Park Avenue South, Suite 1109
New York, New York 10003-1503
www.coopersquarepress.com

Distributed by National Book Network

Library of Congress Cataloging-in-Publication Data

Bego, Mark.
    Bette Midler : still divine / Mark Bego ; introduction by Rita Coolidge.—
1st Cooper Square Press ed.
        p.   cm.
    Revised and expanded edition of Bette Midler: outrageously divine, 1987.
    Includes bibliographical references and index.
    Discography: p. 327
    Filmography: p. 346
    ISBN 0-8154-1232-0 (cloth : alk. paper)
    1. Midler, Bette.   2. Singers—United States—Biography.   I. Coolidge, Rita.
II. Title.

ML420.M43 B4   2002
782.42164′092—dc   212002009347

∞ ™ The paper used in this publication meets the minimum requirements of American National Standard for Information Sciences—Permanence of Paper for Printed Library Materials, ANSI/NISO Z39.48–1992.
Manufactured in the United States of America.

To Glenn Hughes:

Fans around the world
will always remember you
as the "Leather Man" from the Village People.
I will always remember you
as a dear and caring friend.
You were the original
"Knight in Black Leather."

CONTENTS

ACKNOWLEDGMENTS

The author would like to thank the following people for their help and encouragement with this book: Joseph Amaral, David Andrew, Bart Andrews, Brooks Arthur, Marilyn Arthur, Ann Bego, Angela Bowie, Peter Brown, Joe Canale, Rita Coolidge, Trippy Cunningham, John Deeg, Hector DeJean, Baby Jane Dexter, Michael Dorr, Howard Einbinder, Luke Falby, Terry Fischer, Dr. Clark Fuller, Sasha Goodman, Gary Herb, Tom Hill, Jan Kalajian, Dr. Kamran Kalpari, John Klinger, Sally Kirkland, Moogy Klingman, Buzzy Linhart, Virginia Lohle, Walter McBride, Michael Messina, Keven Mulroy, Jim Pinkston, Ross Plotkin, Bobby Reed, Debby Regiani, Sherry Robb, Richie Rothenstein, David Salidor, Barbara Shelley, Don Siegel, Andy Skurow, Mark Sokoloff, Dr. Steven Tay, George Vissichelli, Beth Wernick, and Dr. Robert Wolfe.

INTRODUCTION

I just love Bette Midler: her music, her personality, and everything she stands for. I released my first solo album around the same time that her *Divine Miss M* album was released. It was an era of female singer/songwriters like Carly Simon and Carole King, and I was very aware of what kind of music everyone else was making at that time.

While, personally, my music was more folk– and country–based, hers seemed to intersect all sorts of styles. Naturally, Bette really got my attention with her raucous and humorous songs of this era. However, what impressed me the most about her, initially, was her ability to really sell a ballad. She seemed to completely connect with the songwriter's lyrics and become a part of the song. What she did with John Prine's "Hello in There" was a great example of how she was able to set a mood with her voice.

After hearing Bette do her rendition of the classic blues song "Am I Blue?" I, too, wanted to record an album of jazz and pop standards. I liked what she did with that song so much that in 1975 I recorded it as well, for my *It's Only Love* album.

In 1969, when I was on Joe Cocker's "Maddogs and Englishmen" tour, I debuted a song called "Superstar." Although I never did get co-writing credit for my contributions to this composition, it was a song that Bonnie Bramlett and I wrote with Leon Russell. Bonnie and I had first written down the lyrics to it during the "Delaney & Bonnie & Friends" tour of 1969, and the guitarist that we were singing about was Eric Clapton. After I was heard singing the song on the *Maddogs and Englishmen* album, it was always one of my trademark songs. I loved what Bette did with this song on her first album. She put her heart into this song, and it will always be one of my favorite Midler recordings.

I love Bette Midler in the movies as well. She has created some of the most memorable film roles of the last thirty years. Her portrayal of a rock singer in *The Rose* really captured the essence of what it was like to be on 1960s rock shows. She was great in *Beaches* and so funny in *First Wives' Club*. I am certain that there are many more movie roles to come for the Divine Miss M.

Another thing that I admire her for is her charitable work over the years. When the AIDS crisis began, Bette Midler was right there to lend a hand and sing her songs for the cause to find a cure. Her recent involvement in cleaning up the environment is really admirable. It takes a lot of courage for one person to spearhead cleaning up New York City, but if any diva can accomplish the task, it's Bette Midler.

I love Bette Midler. She is a clever, funny, and brilliant performer. Her life story is a fascinating tale of determination, creativity, and survival.

—RITA COOLIDGE, 2002

PROLOGUE

In 1972, when I was in college at Central Michigan University, a friend of mine played an album for me that he had just purchased, called *The Divine Miss M.* It was by a new singer I had never heard of: Bette Midler. I couldn't believe how much I loved it. She seemed to hit every musical emotion on it, from rock to camp to swing, and back again. After I had heard it only once, I got in my car and went to the local record shop and bought my own copy, I loved it so much.

Since that day, I have also owned the 8-track tape of *The Divine Miss M,* the cassette, and finally the compact disc. Every time I thought of compiling my all-time Top 10 list of albums, this particular disc is always on it.

The following year, I was thrilled to discover that Bette Midler was going to be appearing in Detroit at the Masonic Auditorium. I couldn't wait to see her in concert. I had seen a lot of concerts, but I had never seen anyone quite like Bette Midler. She was flashy, she was trashy, and she expended so much energy on stage, neither my friends nor I had ever witnessed a performer quite like Miss Midler. What I saw that night in Detroit made me a lifelong fan of Bette's.

The first time I ever wrote about her was in my college newspaper—*Central Michigan Life*—when I reviewed her 1973 album *Bette Midler.* By 1975 I had moved to New York City to pursue my writing career. In the spring of that year I was one of the rabid fans who stood in line in the freezing rain to buy tickets to her amazing *Clams on the Half Shell* show on Broadway.

In the fall of 1975 I was doing freelance writing for a short-lived Manhattan newspaper called *51 Newsmagazine.* I was interviewing celebrities for the publication, and one of the people I interviewed was Barry Manilow. I spent over an hour in his apartment on East 27th Street, talking to him about his newly established solo recording career and about his relationship with Bette Midler. In fact, I have remained friendly with Barry, and on occasion I have run into him at different music industry events. When I wrote my first two books—which were published in 1977—they were *The Captain & Tennille* and *Barry Manilow.*

I continued to follow both Bette's and Barry's careers through the years. By the 1980s, my writing career blossomed when I wrote three million-selling books in a row and became a *New York Times* best-selling author. Suddenly, I had a new platform in which to write about all of my favorite media stars.

In 1987 New American Library published my paperback biography *Bette Midler: Outrageously Divine.* It was one of my favorite books, and since I was in New York City, I had access to many of Bette's friends and co-workers. Much of the interview information from my 1987 book is included in this book. That same year, I ran into Barry Manilow at the annual ABA (American Book Association) Convention, where I was promoting one of my books, and he was promoting his own memoir, *Sweet Life.*

We chatted for a few minutes, and during our conversation he paid me a great compliment by telling me, "I loved the book you wrote about Bette." I was highly flattered and happy to hear that, since I rarely get feedback from the subjects of my books—even though I presently have well over forty books in print.

I was always a little disappointed that 1987's *Bette Midler: Outrageously Divine* didn't have a longer run in bookstores, as I had so much fun writing it. However, I had a fabulous party to celebrate its publication, and it was excerpted in *Cosmopolitan* magazine.

In the fifteen years since it was published, so much had happened in Bette's life and career, and I avidly followed every move, bought every record, watched every movie, and became friendly with so many more of the key people in Midler's life. I met Harlette Sharon Redd at a benefit at the Palladium in 1989, having been introduced to her by my close friend Glenn Hughes of the Village People. I hosted and sang (yes—sang!) on a nightclub show along with Ula Hedwig of the Harlettes. I met Midler musical director Marc Shaiman in New York City and in Los Angeles. And the list goes on and on.

When I was approached by Cooper Square Press in the year 2000 about doing this new book on the life and career of Bette Midler, I was ecstatic to have the opportunity to turn all of this material into a brand new book about her. Her story had grown so much, and her body of work had more than doubled since 1987. Furthermore, I was able to look at her early years with a new perspective and add several pages of new material and new interviews to the years that I had previously written about. Among the new material in this book are fresh interviews with Midler record producers Moogy Klingman and Brooks Arthur.

Bette Midler is wonderful, talented, dazzling, shocking, outrageous, exciting, entertaining, touching, and so is this book!

Not only is Miss M "still divine"—to paraphrase her own words: She's beautiful, damn it!

—MARK BEGO, 2002

BETTE MIDLER: THE ULTIMATE DIVA

She stands only five-foot one-and-a-half-inches tall, but in the black high heel shoes she wears, she looks much taller as she struts across the stage. She is wearing a fashionable black designer pant suit, with a rhinestone-studded top. Her hair is exquisitely coiffed into a mass of champagne blonde curls atop her head. She looks glamorous, and she is more svelte than audiences are used to seeing lately. She is on stage at the MGM Grand Hotel in Las Vegas, in a concert performance called *Diva Las Vegas*. Known for her chameleon-like quality for singing songs from many different genres, she launches into a number sung to the tune of "Everything's Coming Up Roses," from the Broadway show *Gypsy*. However, instead of singing the familiar opening line of "I had a dream," she sings new lyrics to the song to signify her present stature in the show business world: "I'm in a hit! A big *FUCKING* hit, BABY!" The crowd roars with delight, but before the song is over, she lyrically commands people to "blow some smoke up my ass!" Are they insulted? Hell no—they love it! Is there any doubt who the diva in question might be? Only one person can carry on in such a way and have the crowd begging for more. It could only be Bette Midler.

It is January of 1997, and in Midleresque terms, everything truly *IS* coming up roses for her at the moment. She has just starred in the biggest box-office hit of her film career, *First Wives Club;* her greatest hits album—*Experience the Divine*—has been certified Platinum in America; and she is on a highly touted concert tour that is selling out wherever she goes. Even the TV special that this performance is being filmed for is destined to win her both an Emmy Award and a Cable ACE Award.

During the performance, she tells filthy jokes, salutes strippers, lampoons lounge singers, sings songs about her breasts, and even heckles audience members from the stage. There is nothing she won't do or say to titillate the audience or to get a laugh. However, when she slows down the pace of the show to sing a sentimental song, she has the audience in the palm of her hand. As the familiar opening piano notes sound, with metronome-like repetition, this tiny-but-bawdy blonde begins to sing what has become her signature song. She has the audience mesmerized and totally in her spell as she intently sings "The Rose."

For Bette, roses have always held a special significance in her career. It seems that everything she names after the fabled flower somehow creatively blossoms. Her first film, *The Rose,* netted her an Academy Award nomination and a Golden Globe Award. The song "The Rose" became her first million-selling single—which won her a Grammy Award. Her soundtrack album, *The Rose,* became the first Triple Platinum disc of her career. When she tackled the role of Mama Rose in the 1993 film *Gypsy,* she won another Golden Globe and another Emmy. When she recorded a 1995 LP called *Bette of Roses,* it became her fifth million-selling album, further solidifying her reputation as one of the most highly acclaimed vocal stylists and accomplished actresses in show business.

However, the rose is also a flower with painfully sharp thorns. Like the rose, Midler's career has had more than its share of thorns along the way. Hers has been a career filled with extreme peaks and valleys. Some of Bette's projects are wildly successful, and others have been disappointing failures. Very often, the projects Bette really puts her heart into come up short.

The years following 1997 have brought both highs and lows to Bette. In 1998 she released a new album called *Bathhouse Betty,* which became her highly anticipated return to her *Divine Miss M* formula of combining bawdy, trashy, and humorous songs with sensitive ballads. It became a big hit and was quickly certified "Gold." Yet her next album, *Bette* (2000), while finely crafted, failed to find an audience. After the success of *First Wives Club,* it would have seemed that anything Midler touched would turn to box-office magic. However, her next three starring roles found her in one onscreen miscalculation after another: *That Old Feeling* (1997), *Drowning Mona* (2000), and *Isn't She Great?* (2000).

Frustrated and despondent over her ability to find a successful movie project, in the year 2000 she decided that the future of her acting career was going to be in television. She had great success in the past with TV specials—why not a series? With that, she threw herself into the production of her own half-hour situation comedy, entitled *Bette.* It proved to be one of biggest mistakes of her entire career.

She knew that she was taking a risk by bringing her bigger-than-life persona to the small screen. According to her at the time, "It has been suggested to me by friends that I should be more careful about this as a career move. But I say, 'What are you talking about? I've had a great career. They can't take thirty years away from me.' What can they do— put you in jail because you've done a lousy sitcom?—Maybe they should!" (1).

The show drew a great opening episode audience, but by midseason was performing so poorly in the ratings that the network pulled the plug on it and chose not to air all of the episodes filmed—or to put it into reruns. Midler, at the time, was crushed. She even threatened to write a tell-all exposé about her infuriating network nightmare, in a book entitled *Canceled.* Other than an unbilled one-scene role in the film *What Women Want,* for over a year she launched no new projects; her only public performances were at charity or special events.

But this is nothing new for Bette. She has been through these slow eras before, and she has always emerged stronger than ever. There have been great disappointments for her along the way—but her quiet periods never last long. Like water off a duck's back, misfortune never keeps a good diva down. To quote a phrase often used by the bawdy and outspoken Midler herself: "Fuck 'em if they can't take a joke!"

For the last four decades, the self-proclaimed "Divine Miss M" has forged a unique career, peerlessly unmatched in the sheer outrageousness of it. She has the unique ability to switch from drama to comedy, from silly to sentimental, and from tasteful to raunchy, within the blink of an eye. Even her looks, her weight, and her hair color constantly vary. But whether she is a blonde, a redhead, or a brunette—and she has been them all—she cannot disguise the incredible talent that she possesses.

There is no one quite like Bette. Singer, actress, TV star, movie star, stand-up comedian, best-selling author, media goddess, and charitable humanitarian. Her career has been one of great variety. Her songs are sometimes comically outlandish, sometimes sexually risqué, and sometimes they can bring an audience to tears. On one hand, she has scored her biggest musical successes with the sentimental ballads "The Rose," "The Wind beneath My Wings," and "From a Distance." Yet on the other hand, she has simultaneously built herself a wild reputation for lewd, bawdy, and blue songs like "Doctor Long John," "Pretty Legs and Great Big Knockers," "My Knight in Black Leather," "Drinking Again," "Marahuana," and "Empty Bed Blues." She has proved time and time again that there are few legends quite like her in the history of the music business.

In the mid-'70s, when Midler was the toast of Broadway and records, she dreamed of becoming a movie star. At the time it seemed like such a natural move, since her elaborate stage shows and dramatic story-songs featured such varied role-playing. Although the path has at times been bumpy, she has produced a body of filmed and recorded work that is awesome in breadth and impressive in scope. How incredible to think that since that time she has starred in well over twenty films and has recorded and released over eighteen albums!

She has also had some of the most memorable movie roles in the last thirty years of cinema. Her dramatic film debut as a drugged-out rock star-on-a-collision-course in *The Rose* won her an Academy Award nomination in the Best Actress category. Her back-to-back hits *Down and Out in Beverly Hills, Ruthless People,* and *Outrageous Fortune* made her the biggest movie star at Disney Studios in the mid-'80s. Her tearjerker film *Beaches* was another huge box-office hit for Midler and a feather in her cap for her own company, All Girls Productions. Her over-the-top turn as a witch in *Hocus Pocus* has become a perennial favorite Halloween-season family film. Her gutsy role in the film *Gypsy* brought Broadway excitement back to both large and small screens around the world, winning more awards and accolades for the diva. Unfortunately, not all of Bette's movies are financial successes. Some of her best work on the screen is in films that don't become huge, but are greatly entertaining, like her tour de force as a U.S.O. entertainer in *For the Boys.* Or, simultaneously arguing and shopping with Wood Allen in

Scenes from a Mall. Or, playing a pair of mismatched twins opposite a Lily Tomlin duo in *Big Business.*

Bette Midler wasn't a shrinking violet when it came to launching her career while cementing her wild reputation. She virtually exploded onto the America show business scene in 1972, with her schizophrenically varied repertoire of songs and her acid-tongued humor. Her inexhaustible and outrageous onstage and off-stage performances quickly established her as one of the true music industry originals of the 1970s. Her initial legion of fans found her eclectic singing and her onstage mugging a bizarre combination of the Shangri-Las, Ethel Waters, the Andrews Sisters, Janis Joplin, and Mae West.

She called herself a "diva," and she described her singing style as "sleaze with ease." *Cash Box* magazine called her "a really great star" (2). *Rolling Stone* called her "One hell of a talent" (3). *Record World* called her "a superstar of superstars" (3). The gay population—whom she openly courted—called her their own personal discovery. *Newsweek* called her "the reigning cult figure of New York's restless underground" (4). And once in Buffalo someone called the vice squad—and busted her band!

Throughout the 1970s Bette did everything that she could to attain the kind of stardom that was predicted for her. She set high standards for herself. She stopped at nothing to endear herself to her fans. One night onstage in St. Louis she even flashed her breasts. She "mooned" an audience in Massachusetts and once hatched an elaborate plot to tape rolled marijuana "joints" to the bottom of each audience member's seat as a midconcert "treat" from "Divine." Midler caused a scandal in Chicago when she closed her show by announcing to the audience, "I thought you were wonderful. . . . And to this band, I'd like to say one thing: FUCK YOU!" (5). It seemed there was no end to what she would do for attention. She not only became a star, she became a sensation!

~~~

Prizes, trophies, and awards? Her living-room mantel is littered with nearly every form of gilded statuette imaginable. She won the first of her four Grammy Awards in 1974 as "Best New Artist," following it up a month later by winning a special Tony Award for her record-breaking three-week run at the Palace Theater on Broadway. In 1975 she set a new Broadway box-office record for first-day ticket sales to her *Clams on the Half-Shell Revue* at the Minskoff Theater. Her 1979 TV special *Ol' Red Hair Is Back* was awarded an Emmy. In 1980 she received an Academy Award nomination and two Golden Globe Awards for her dramatic film debut in *The Rose.* That same year she was entered into the *Guinness Book of World Records* for autographing 1,500 copies of her best-selling book *A View from a Broad* in a mere six hours. Also in 1980, Bette won her second Grammy Award for her song "The Rose" and a third one for her contribution to the children's album *In Harmony.* She broke box-office records at New York City's famed Radio City Music Hall for ticket sales of her "De Tour" shows in 1983. In 1980 she was nominated for an Academy Award and won a Golden Globe for her performance in *The Rose.* Her hit "The Wind beneath My Wings" in 1990 won her a fourth Grammy Award. In 1993 she received another Academy Award nomination and another Golden Globe for her dream project *For the Boys.* And the list goes on and on.

Tornado of energy that she is, her stardom has also catapulted several members of her musical entourage to fame. In the early 1970s her musical director was a then-unknown piano player named Barry Manilow. He coproduced her first two hit albums and launched his own career as an incredibly successful solo superstar. When Bette made her Carnegie Hall debut, one of her first background-singing Harlettes was an aspiring songwriter named Melissa Manchester. She has also become a huge singing star. Another trio of Harlettes left her to record their own successful album. In the 1990s former Harlette Katie Sagal became a TV star when she portrayed the role of Peg Bundy on the hit series *Married with Children.* And both Jenifer Lewis and Linda Hart have gone on to successful acting careers in films and TV since their Harlette days with Midler.

In addition to her dazzling career glories, Bette Midler's bizarre road to fame is dotted with personal heartbreak and tragedy. For a large part of her career, it seemed that every time she attained one of her creative goals, she suffered a personal loss.

Born the youngest of three daughters to a house painter and his wife, Bette grew up the only Caucasian in her school class in Honolulu, Hawaii. She remembers, "It wasn't easy being a Jewish kid in a Samoan neighborhood" (6). Having always felt like a misfit in school, Bette eventually gained self-confidence when she discovered that she had the ability to make people laugh at her jokes and her comedic singing. She studied drama at the University of Hawaii and earned money by packing pineapples in a canning plant. Not exactly glamorous. But when there was an "extra" casting call for the film *Hawaii*, Bette landed a featured role as a seasick missionary, and suddenly she was in show business.

With the earnings from her role in *Hawaii*, Bette left home and headed for New York City, attracted by the lure of Broadway. It wasn't long before she landed a part in the hit show *Fiddler on the Roof*. During her three-year run in the show, her sister Judy came to visit her in New York City. In a freak accident, Judy was struck by a moving car, pinned against a wall, and killed.

After three years in *Fiddler*, Bette began to develop her own signature sound in small nightclubs like Hilly's in Greenwich Village and the Improvisation. It wasn't long before she started performing her act for men dressed in bath towels at the Continental Baths. Next came television, records, and her own triumphant Broadway revue.

At the height of her initial success, Bette suffered a near collapse from nervous exhaustion. Just as Midler was about to celebrate the popularity of her first film, her mother, Ruth, died of cancer. Like the character called "The Rose," throughout her life Bette had always had an odd relationship with her parents. While her mother loved her career, her father was distant. Finally, by 1986, Bette made peace with her father when she discovered she was pregnant. Fred Midler had long refused to see his "foul-mouthed" daughter perform in concert, but they at last learned to deal with each other's opposing viewpoints. Just as she was enjoying her newfound film success, however, her father died, leaving much of the responsibility for taking care of her retarded younger brother, Danny, on Bette's shoulders. Hers has not always been an easy life.

⌒⌒

Bette Midler has had a wildly erratic career, only further accentuated by the reviews she receives in the press. Critics either love her projects or viciously hate them. However, Bette's career has never been fueled or destroyed by good or bad reviews. Her true fans flock to her movies and her concerts or purchase her record albums regardless of what the critics have to say. And if she releases an occasional "turkey," she has the ability and the drive to simply go back to the drawing board and invent a new winning formula.

Cinematically, she has stood at the fork of many roads. Often she heads down the right path to success (*The Rose, Down & Out in Beverly Hills, Outrageous Fortune, Beaches, First Wives Club*), and occasionally she unwittingly heads in a completely opposite direction (*Isn't She Great?, Stella, Drowning Mona*). When she was a huge hit in her first film role as *The Rose,* it seemed as if every time she would get in front of the movie cameras, it would turn into gold. Unfortunately, the movie business isn't like that at all. Some of the best blueprints look great on paper, but, once constructed, are less than architectural feats. Back-to-back box-office bombs—*Divine Madness* and *Jinxed*—nearly drove her to a nervous breakdown and right out of Hollywood in the early '80s.

Work on television has likewise proved "hit" and "miss" for Miss M. She has won an Emmy Award and Golden Globe Awards for her most successful forays into broadcast and cable television (*Ol' Redhair Is Back, The Tonight Show* finale, *Gypsy*). Yet on the other hand, she has also misguidedly stumbled into what is destined to be remembered as the worst quagmire of her entire career—her disappointing TV sitcom. *Bette* was perhaps the worst TV series ever overproduced for a major multimedia star. Joyless, forced, and decidedly unfunny, it sent her in a complete downward spin. However, for Midler, it merely meant she was ripe for yet another comeback.

⌣

Bette has been captured on film and on record many times over the past four decades, but to really understand and appreciate her as a performer, one must see her live in concert. Few stars expend so much energy and share so much of themselves with an audience as she does. In her ever-changing stage show she has invented several different personas to bring to life her most outrageous antics. First and foremost, there is her bawdy and trashy diva, "the Divine Miss M." When she tells dirty jokes, she is Soph, the sluttish vaudeville-like comedienne, who was originally modeled after Sophie Tucker. There is Vickie Eydie, the cheesy lounge singer who is trapped in a tacky nightclub act not of her own design. There's the Magic Lady—also known as Nanette, the forlorn shopping bag woman who turns despair into optimism. Bette's screaming rock & roll blues-singer persona is clearly an extension of the fictional character she portrayed in *The Rose*. And last but not least: Dolores De Lago, the Toast of Chicago, the schmaltzy songstress in a mermaid suit.

Bette has always held the great female vocalists in high esteem. Her long-time favorites include Aretha Franklin, Edith Piaf, and Bessie Smith. However, there are also a few singers of whom she has never been too fond. This list includes Helen Reddy—"She *should* be singing 'I am Woman.' Who could tell?" (6); the Carpenters: "I can't believe I'm on the same stage where Karen Carpenter got her drums banged!" (6); and Madonna: "The only thing that girl will ever do like a virgin is have a baby in a stable!" (7). In 1999 Midler scored her first Number 1 dance hit, by singing the celebratory song of self-deification "I'm Beautiful." In other words: Don't cross this diva!

~~

"In your young life, you rebel against values you think are square. After you've lived awhile, you realize they are good values, and there's a reason they've been around for thousands of years" (8). Wait a minute, Bette said that? She couldn't have possibly said that . . . not "the Divine Miss Midler!" Oddly enough, she did. Although she certainly had her "wild" phase, underneath the profanity-spewing surface she is a very moral person, with a steadfast work ethic. She has made her way up the ladder of success due to her hard work and single-minded determination. She once proclaimed that what she most wanted to become was "a legend." It is a goal she has amply accomplished.

In addition to being the number one "taste-free" purveyor of "trash with flash," Bette Midler is also a devoted wife and mother, as well as a passionate activist when it comes to human rights issues. In the 1980s, when the AIDS epidemic ran like the "black plague" through the gay population, Midler became one of the few stars in Hollywood to give open, compassionate, and undying support to the community. In the 1990s she turned her focus from "trashy" songs to helping the environment by cleaning up real trash in the parks and highways of America. When the World Trade Center was destroyed by terrorists in September of 2001, Midler toured Ground Zero and sang her poignant anthem "The Wind beneath My Wings" at the memorial service, which was held in Yankee Stadium that same month.

Has movie stardom changed Bette Midler? Is she still the mud-flinging woman who insults public figures, or is she now a tasteful housewife whose fashionable home has been featured on the pages of *Architectural Digest?* What was the reason for her sudden move from Coldwater Canyon in Los Angeles back to New York City in the '90s? Has Bette Midler really killed off her wild alter ego, the Divine Miss M, and become a full-fledged adult? Unthinkable!

In the mid-1980s, after a decade of divine madness and outlandish behavior, Bette announced, "I've sown all my wild oats. . . . I'm prepared to settle down and be a mom, because I've had twenty years of real nuttiness" (9). Oh my God . . . had too much avocado dip at too many Hollywood parties mellowed her out to the point of no return? The sarcastic no-holds-barred Bette once said, "What I want is to be a bisexual fantasy. I want to be the most loved, the most desired loved woman on this earth" (6). Is she still the multisexual Peter Pan–like diva for all seasons? Or, has she forsaken her convention-defying silliness to become one of *The Stepford Wives?*

Has time tamed the outrageous Bette? Or is the calmer, more contained side of Miss M simply another facet of this original show-business gem? Predictability has never even entered the mind of this divine queen of camp. There are many sides to Bette Midler and always have been. Has the role as mother and wife changed her forever? "Do you mean am I going to remain *vul-gah* and crass?" she laughingly counter-questions (10).

These and several other mysteries in the vivid life of Bette Midler beg to be answered. How did she end up in an all-male gay bathhouse? Why did Paul Simon strip off her vocals on his recording of "Gone at Last" and replace her with Phoebe Snow? What is the truth about her clashes with Bruce Springsteen? Who did Ken Wahl have to pretend to be kissing to get through the filmed love scenes with her on camera? Did she jinx *Jinxed,* or was she set up as the "fall girl" for a picture that was doomed from the start? What compelled her to become one of the first entertainers to openly rally to raise money for the AIDS epidemic? Was she devastated when her 1991 film *For the Boys* received strong critical reviews only to go "bust" at the box-office? Did the huge success of *Gypsy* signal a new Broadway career for her? What is the truth about her long-running feud with Cher? What's up with her supposed "affair" with journalist Geraldo Rivera? What's up with that? What the hell was Midler thinking when she produced that dreadful network television series—*Bette?* And how on Earth did she get the nickname "Bathhouse Betty?"

To solve the riddle of Miss M, one must go back into her turbulent and colorful past. Back to the days where she used to sit in school and daydream of becoming a sarong-clad movie star like Debra Paget in *Bird of Paradise*. It began in Honolulu, the land of hibiscus leis, grass skirts, and bright floral shirts. The real-life saga of the divine Miss Midler all started with a little girl who had an unhappy childhood and who dared to dream that one day she would become a truly divine star. . . .

ALOHA, HONOLULU

World War II had been over for only four months when Fred and Ruth Midler's third child was born on December 1, 1945, in Honolulu, Hawaii. Like her two sisters before her, she was named after one of her mother's favorite movie stars. Judy's name had been chosen for Judy Garland, and Susan's namesake was Susan Hayward. When it came time to pick the new baby's name, Ruth decide on Bette, in honor of Bette Davis. Ruth, however, believed the actress pronounced her name "bet," and the name stuck.

Years later, when she was questioned about her name, Bette Midler laughingly explained, "That's my real name. You don't think I'd pick that out of a hat? My dear, if I were looking for a name . . ." (11).

The Midlers were one of the few Caucasian families living in the area of Honolulu known as Aiea. Fred worked as a house painter for the United States Navy at the base in Honolulu. The muscular body he had developed working out with weights at the local YMCA in his home-town of Patterson, New Jersey, earned him the nickname "Chesty." He met and married a girl named Ruth Schindel from nearby Passaic, New Jersey, and together they emigrated to Hawaii in the early 1940s in search of a tropical paradise.

Ruth and Fred's first home in Hawaii was a converted military bar-racks near a vast expanse of sugar-cane fields. While Fred worked at naval house painting and other civilian jobs with the navy's ordinance detail, Ruth passed her time reading movie fan magazines and sewing. After their three daughters, a son named Danny was born.

"We lived in a fabulous place called Halauua Housing—poor people's housing," recalls Bette disdainfully (12). One of her first memories is of the sweet scent of oleander blossoms from the bushes that surrounded their apartment building and wafted through the warm tropical air like perfume.

In time the Midlers moved into their own home. Bette explains, "We lived in a really funky house, just like the one in that play *The Effect of Gamma Rays*. My father had machinery all over the place—he had twenty-seven lawn mowers—and my mother always had a stack of sewing up to the ceiling" (4).

According to Bette, "Eventually, she and my father bought a couple of houses and fixed them up and had tenants. They were small-time landlords. My mother was extremely talented at it and got a real kick out of that, yet she did it all from her own house. She never had the nerve to go out and get a job; she was TOTALLY house-bound. She wanted to be in the world the way other people were in the world. She was just a housewife, but she wanted to take part" (13).

Bette never remembers the atmosphere at home as being happy, in any sense of the word. She describes her dad as "a major tyrant, he would scream and carry on. He thrived on it" (13).

She also recalls, "My father was a bellower. To get a word in, you had to bellow back. He loved a good argument, he loved the adrenaline rush" (14).

Fred Midler later said of Bette, "The only times she talked back were when I jumped on her. Like most parents, I tended to yell a lot and regret it afterwards. . . . She was rather bossy. She liked to take charge of things and she was *always* talking. Our Bette, she was always a yenta" (15).

According to Bette, "My mother was the most negative woman. Hypertense. I saw this misery, this incredible misery that she could not force her way out of, this loneliness and bitterness. But I adored her because I saw in her this somebody who was trying to get out, who had a dream that unfortunately never came true" (16).

As a result of a postnatal illness, Bette's younger brother Danny was left mentally handicapped. This became a source of aggravation for Fred Midler; he was mad that he couldn't do anything to change his son's condition, and he found his attempts to teach the boy extremely frustrating.

"The public health authorities, the social workers wanted to put Danny away, but my parents wouldn't hear of it," explains Bette. "This doctor told my mom that Danny's tongue was too long, and he would have to cut it a bit in surgery. And because the doctor cut it, Danny lost the power of movement there. In other words, the doctor severed some nerves, so Danny wasn't able to move his tongue anymore. So now he can't chew, he doesn't talk quite right. At that time they didn't have public-school classes for retarded children, so my father taught him. He used to come home from work at about four o'clock every day and sit him down in the rocking chair to teach him to talk, read, write, and add" (13).

Bette distinctly remembers her father's sessions with Danny. "Pa would start off quietly, but by the time four-thirty rolled around, he was screaming at the top of his lungs out of frustration, and Daniel would be crying. He's not so retarded that he doesn't know it. But eventually Danny did learn. It took a lot of love for my father to do that. Or some heavy guilt" (13).

"I think there are certain things you have to pass through in life in order to come out of the other side," she concludes (13).

Bette recalls that her parents set an example with what they did with their lives, and they instilled a strong work ethic within her. According to her, "We were really poor, and my mother made sacrifices that I can't even dream of making. My brother was mentally handicapped and they raised him at home. That was a real struggle. They succeeded, but they sacrificed their entire life for it. When you have that example, you never really forget it" (17).

With the children in the area, Bette felt like an outcast from an early age. "The kids in the neighborhood were Hawaiians, part Hawaiians, Samoans, and Filipinos" (12). She describes her feelings of inadequacy: "At the time I really hated it—I was an alien, a foreigner even though I was born there" (8).

Recalls Bette with residual pain, "I remember children being so cruel. You don't forget these things" (18).

She found Aiea to be "equivalent to any of the tough neighborhoods in Harlem or Brooklyn, except from a different perspective. You rarely saw blacks. What you would see were the Japanese, Chinese, Samoans, or Filipinos—heavy on the Filipinos—the Filipinos were always the toughest. The Portuguese were very tough. See, they always took me for a Portuguese because in Hawaii there's a distinction between them and whites, even though they're both Caucasian. The Portuguese used to work in the fields, and 'hacles'—white people—were the overseers. I wasn't Portuguese, but I let them think it because it was easier than anything else. Because Portuguese people were accepted, Jews were not" (11).

"I thought of myself as a poor kid, poorer than any of them because they always seemed to spend money and I never had any to spend. It was the fashion among the kids not to speak good English—they spoke *pidgin* English. It was a put-on, but I didn't realize it at the time" (12).

Unhappy with her home life and her social life with the local kids, Bette found it easy to bury herself in her schoolwork. In the first grade she had her first real taste of show business when she sang "Silent Night" in front of her class. She won a prize for her performance, but she couldn't even share her glory at home, "I was afraid to tell my mother, because I was Jewish and we weren't supposed to sing Christmas carols" (19).

According to her, "After that, you couldn't stop me from singing. I'd sing 'Lullaby of Broadway' at the top of my lungs in the tin shower—it had a really good reverb. People used to gather outside to call up requests or yell that I was lousy" (20).

"The Midlers were the only white family for blocks and blocks around . . . [and] we were Jewish, which was even weirder. We didn't even have a Christmas tree, which would have made us normal in the eyes of the neighbors. They were all Christians, and they had Christmas trees which they decorated to death. No matter how poor a family was, they would scrape together money and give their children the most wonderful Christmases" (21).

Bette recalls that her first cinematic dreams came from watching MGM's most famous swimming movie star and her opulent musical numbers. "I wasn't really smitten with show business until I saw Esther Williams. Technicolor killed me. You felt like you were in paradise when you saw those pictures" (22).

At the age of twelve, she saw a touring production of *Carousel*, and she went Broadway-crazy. "I couldn't get over how beautiful it was. I fell so in love with it. Everything else in my life receded once I discovered theater, and my mother was all for my starting on the journey and going full speed ahead. When I was the lead in the junior-class play, she brought a bouquet of roses and presented them to me over the foot-lights" (20).

As a little girl Bette took hula-dancing lessons, and when she turned twelve, her mother taught her how to sew. "On Saturdays," she remembers, "from the time I was six years old to the time I was eighteen, my father would take me and my sister to town and go to the library. My parents would go off shopping at the local John's Bargain Store, and my sister and I would either stay in the library or walk around town. When I was young, I would rush in and read about French courtesans till it was all rushing out of my ears. Later, when I got very brave, I'd go out to the red-light district and walk around. All the sailors and people in the armed forces would go there to see a dirty movie or a bawdy show or pick up a girl. It was a REAL red-light district and it was so wonderful!" It wasn't bullshit Forty-Second Street or bullshit Eighth Avenue [New York City]. It was for real—opium dens and lots of Orientals" (21).

According to Bette, her parents never knew what she was up to when she was supposedly perusing books at the library. "They never knew. They went out shopping. I never had any misadventures except for one at this movie house when I was thirteen. This guy put the make on me and that was scary. Usually, it was a great thrill for a child to walk around in that environment. You must remember that even though I was in Hawaii, I had a very, very strict lower-middle-class Jewish upbringing, so it was quite mind-boggling to be in the midst of all this Orientalia, and still be in New Jersey at the same time" (21).

Her parents clearly would have flipped out if they'd had any inkling of what their daughter was up to. "My mother was always trying to make sure I wasn't exposed to any of the seamier aspects of life. Consequently, I was always fascinated by the seamier aspects of life. That was the biggest influence in my life. She was trying to keep me away from the seamy type of life and I just thought it was the best, I wanted to be with seamy people and be in seamy places," she explains (23). And so began the bawdy side of Bette Midler, even though at the time she had no outlet to express herself.

When Bette and her sisters were in their teens, they began experimenting with makeup and hair coloring. According to her, her first foray into hair dye was a total disaster. "I've been dyeing my hair religiously since I was thirteen. I started out with what I thought was going to be ash-blonde, but which turned out green!" (24).

Bette's sister Susan remembers how violent their father would get at the idea that they were becoming painted women. "He didn't like us wearing makeup and we had a curfew: some ridiculous hour like ten o'clock, and if you weren't in the house, you usually got locked out. Us sisters were always sticking up for each other, and sneaking each other in the window at night" (13).

"My sister Susan and Pa, they'd have terrible riles. She used to call the cops on him! He used to piss her off," says Bette. "My father was always right, never wrong. It was simple: he was the loudest and the oldest, and the heaviest. It was usually him against us. My mother tried to be a soothing influence, but she wasn't very successful at it. There was that kind of passion" (13).

When she was in the fifth grade, Bette teamed up with a classmate and presented a skit in front of the class. "Me and this girl, Barbara Nagy—I remember *everybody*—we decided to put on a skit for the class. She was the man, I was the woman: Herman and Oysterbee. I don't know where the *hell* that name came from" (16). They both forgot the script that they had worked out and ended up improvising the dialogue. When the class laughed at the skit, Bette discovered a whole new kind of love that comes to a performer on stage when the audience laughs and applauds.

In the sixth grade Bette entered a school talent show and won first prize for her rendition of "Lullaby of Broadway." She convinced herself that what she wanted to be when she grew up was an actress. "As I grew older, all the best times in my life were when I was standing in front of an audience performing," she remembers (24). "I learned that I could be popular by making people laugh. I became a clown to win people's acceptance, and I think that's when I decided that I wanted to be in show business" (25).

"I was an ugly, fat little Jewish girl with problems. I kept trying to be like everybody else, but on me nothing worked," says Bette of her years at Radford High School (26). "The school I went to was just like any high school anywhere, like a high school in Brooklyn or Cleveland. We had rock & roll, sock hops, *American Bandstand,* the same as anywhere else. The only thing different was that all the kids were Japanese, Chinese, Filipino, Samoan, and all the girls hated me because I had such big boobs" (25).

Bette was titillated by the audacity of street-wise girls in Honolulu. According to her, "I was always fascinated by the local bad girls. And we were surrounded by these JDs—juvenile delinquents—and listen, I LOVED them! I used to follow them even though they wouldn't take me with them or anything. I'd go after them on their adventures like shoplifting. I always liked that other side of life, you see" (21).

Remarking about her short-lived life of crime, Bette later explained, "Once my friend and I were shoplifting at a Woolworth's or Piggly-Wiggly's; we were carrying those great big purses women were using then and we were loaded with stuff we'd taken. As we were leaving the store it was pouring rain, approaching a hurricane. My girlfriend had a cold, and she got down on her knees in the middle of this deserted road and repented. She cried, 'Oh God, if I don't catch pneumonia, I swear I'll never shoplift again!' And she didn't, so after that I had to shoplift by myself—I didn't get down on my knees, see. *Never!*" (16).

"I was a little chubbier than I am now. I had gigantic tits, and I was very plain. I wore harlequin glasses—you know, those hideous glasses that ruined a lot of people's lives. I was fairly bright. I had a terrific sense of humor," she recalls (21).

The fact that she developed a bust early in puberty was one issue that bedeviled her, and the fact that she developed such a *big bust* so early in life compounded the problem. "I'll never forget eighth grade," she recalled. "My mother wouldn't buy me a bra. I used to get teased, and I remember coming home weeping, so she broke down and got me one for my birthday. Oh, I was so relieved. Oh my dear, sooooo relieved" (16).

Of her painful years as a teenager, says Bette, "I had to go to phys ed class with all these Oriental girls who had brassieres that were holding up nothing. It was horrible. They teased me incessantly because I would, like, bobble on my way home" (27).

One of her classmates, Penny Sellers, later commented, "When I first met Bette—she spelled her name Betti and we pronounced it 'Betty'—she was a quiet and serious student. She wore harlequin-shaped glasses, thin shirt-waist dresses, and had sandy blonde hair that frizzed in the Honolulu humidity. In our junior year, although she made the requirement of the National Honor Society, she seemed less studious. Her raucous laugh made us all giggle, and her witty remarks were—well—*bawdy*" (16).

During her junior year in high school, Bette became best friends with a girl named Beth Ellen Childers. She remembers Beth as "hysterically loud and loved noise and a good time. I fell in love with her. She was the most adorable thing. She made me feel okay to be who I was, enjoyable, good to have around. My family never made me feel this way. She drew me out of myself" (14).

According to Bette, her life started to change for the better. "I came into glory in high school. I *bullossomed*. I blossomed into a D-cup and there were finally white kids in my school. I was even popular. It was a real surprise. . . . in high school I became a person. That was when I began to realize I wasn't as bad as I thought" (16).

"I never had boyfriends until high school, and then I found myself mainly with military kids, because a lot of them were nice and smart. But I never really fit it—even though I was elected senior-class president. I won that by default: you should have seen the other candidate! The truth is that I was just about the only white in an all-Oriental school, and most of those kids never said two words to me. So I got buried in studying. I was always the best in English. I had to be the best, because it was all I had" (4).

Bette graduated from high school in 1963. The school newspaper's graduation edition exuded the kind of confidence in her that her previous seventeen years didn't substantiate. According to the newspaper, "Bette Midler, who is considered to be one of Radford's greatest dramatists, is the president. Unknown to many is her scrawny soprano warble, which can be heard while taking her Saturday night bath. . . . Her ambition is to join the Peace Corps and, perhaps, someday become another Bette Davis" (28).

Her theatrical experience at that time was limited to her appearance in the school's production of *When Our Hearts Were Young and Gay*, yet she felt that she had found her calling in life . . . as a thespian. Being declared class valedictorian didn't mean half as much to her as the prospect of pursuing a life in the theater. "I was always perfectly sure. I couldn't think of anything else to be," remembers Bette (24). By the end of her senior year in high school Bette was crazy to be an actress: "I had entrenched myself into performing very heavily—a lot of speech festivals; they have a huge speech problem in that state—and I was always working on a show or some kind of presentation. . . . I really liked the theater better than anything else" (11).

Of the music that Bette was exposed to at that time, she remembers mostly what she heard on the radio airwaves. "I used to listen to the radio a lot," she recalls, "but always AM. Before rock & roll it was mostly white music. I didn't get into rhythm and blues until later on in rock &

roll like the early sixties. I loved the girl groups and I loved straight ahead rock & roll: the Coasters, and the Del Vikings, and the Skyliners. I wasn't a collector" (6). At that point her only musical experience came as part of an all-girl trio. They sang folk songs, and they called themselves the Pieridine Three ("It means 'like a butterfly'") (13).

Like so many people who have lonely, unhappy childhoods and teenage years, Bette had a powerful drive toward making something of herself. She had felt so much like an ugly duckling that she was determined to prove to all of the classmates who'd snubbed her, to her strict parents who'd disciplined her, and, more important, to herself, that she could make her dreams a reality and become the envy of them all.

According to Bette, "When you're an outcast, your imagination works, becomes honed a little sharper. You learn to rely on yourself more. It readies you for what life is really about: Life isn't all camaraderie and games. I guess it's better to have a miserable childhood and a terrific adulthood than to live the other way around" (21).

The summer after she graduated from high school, Bette landed a job in a local pineapple canning factory. It was her job to select the uniform pieces of freshly sliced pineapple off the assembly line as the pieces went by, leaving the core and rind behind. She sat there, hour after hour, in her rubber gloves and dreamed of how she was going to find stardom as an actress one day.

That fall, Bette entered the University of Hawaii and began realizing her fantasies by majoring in drama. It was during her first and only college year that her first major personal tragedy came. Her best friend, Beth Ellen Childers, was killed in a car accident. According to Bette, she carried on so much at hearing of the death of her friend that "My mom thought we must have been lesbians" (16). Bette mourned the loss of her best friend for months.

In 1965 Bette's big break came. She discovered that several sequences of the film version of James Michener's epic novel *Hawaii* were going to be filmed on location, and that extras from the local community were to be used. She literally jumped at the opportunity to be cast in the film and managed to land a tiny part. She played the role of a missionary's wife aboard the ship that Julie Andrews and Max Von Sydow sailed to the islands.

Bette is first seen in the movie when Von Sydow is preaching to the travelers on the voyage from New England. The waves are heaving, the boat is pitching back and forth, and several of the travelers are seasick.

A young brunette Bette is seen looking queasy, while Von Sydow spouts biblical rhetoric. When the ship lands on Maui, Bette can be spotted aboard the main deck if you watch closely. In the final print of the film she has no lines of dialogue.

Much more footage of film is generally shot than ever reaches the screen. When the production company was finished shooting on location in Hawaii, several of the local actors and actresses were flown to Los Angeles to complete some of the scenes. Much to her excitement, Bette was asked to return to L.A. with the company.

As far as she was concerned, that trip to Hollywood was to be her big break, and she wasn't going to blow it. The money that Bette made on the movie wasn't going to be squandered on frivolous possessions. Her earnings from *Hawaii* represented her ticket to New York City to break into the theater. "I thought that if I had to have a career in the theater, the way to do it was to get a job on the New York stage. I mean, they don't have much theater in Chicago or Cleveland. See, I figured it was the only place to go" (6).

When she was filming *Hawaii* in L.A., Bette hoarded every penny she made. She recalls, "I was paid three hundred dollars a week and seventy dollars per diem, and I lived on two dollars a day. When it was over, I took my money—my little savings pot with a thousand dollars—and I came to New York at the end of 1965. I left fifteen hundred at home, just in case I had to go back, or in case they had to send it to me. I was really frightened. I had to go out and get a job. I wanted the money to last. I think I still have that original thousand!" (12).

Back in Hawaii, after filming her movie debut, Midler began to hatch her New York City plan. By this point, Bette had already moved out of her parents' house. "I was living with a guy and I didn't want my ma to know, so I had to move out of the house. I was nineteen—it was the right time to do it" (12). Her move to Manhattan represented an even bigger step toward realizing her career ambitions.

Bette distinctly remembers that day in November of 1965 when her family drove her to the Honolulu airport. She wore a plaid dress, a girdle with a garter belt, nylons, and a pair of bright red high heels. Sad—but resolved—she said her tearful good-byes to her family, and even her stern father had a tear in his eye. It was the end of an era for teenage Bette Midler. She said "aloha" to Hawaii—and off she flew for New York City to become a star of the theater. Everybody has dreams, but few people really put them into action. However, Bette was determined to make sure that hers came true.

3

FROM PINEAPPLES TO THE BIG APPLE

When Bette Midler arrived in New York City, she wanted to live right in the middle of the theater district. Times Square, the Great White Way, the home of Broadway shows, opening nights, dinners at Sardi's, limousines, and the stars of stage and screen. Unfortunately, at that point in time it was also the home of prostitutes, hustlers, drug dealers, seedy porno theaters, pickpockets, and thieves. Right in the center of the profane and the sacred, that's where she headed.

Her first stop was a seedy, rundown hotel amid all of the action. It was dirty, in a dangerous neighborhood, and completely affordable.

Despite the sleaze and potential danger, Bette couldn't care less. All she could think of was the magnetic glitter of Broadway. "I was very anxious to get to the city. I didn't notice that there was anything wrong with it," she remembers, seeing it all through rose-colored glasses. "I didn't even notice the place. All I saw was a line of theaters: Forty-Fourth Street, Forty-Sixth Street. I didn't even KNOW Forty-Seventh Street! All I knew was that there were theaters there and real people onstage, and that was all I could think of" (21).

"I really blossomed out when I came here. I never felt I was home till I came here, I became all the things I wanted to be. It was like I was finally free" (12).

Bette remembers the Broadway Central Hotel quite distinctly: the huge hole in the mattress, the seedy communal bathroom down the hall, the winos passed out in the hallway, and the lesbian bar downstairs.

According to her, "I developed a lot of wind, running from all manner of strange people . . . fighting the dykes off with a club!" (16).

However, after being under the watchful eyes of her parents in Honolulu, Bette found New York City to be one big adventure after another. "The first month that I was here was when they had the blackout. I thought it was fabulous. And right after that, in January, the subway went on strike. And, I was living down here and I had to go up to 119th Street to get to work every day. I was working at Columbia University—typing. So it was like this incredible hassle. But I just thought it was a lark!" she recalls (6).

According to her, she was mesmerized by the everyday people she encountered while living in the Times Square neighborhood. "I'm fascinated by people whom I guess most people consider bad. People outside the pale, Tennessee Williams characters. People who have found themselves—through no fault of their own—in certain positions in life . . . alcoholics, junkies, prostitutes and Bowery bums. I like people who live lives outside the ordinary" (29).

Almost immediately, she began focusing on her acting career. "I figured that the best way to get into the theater was in a musical comedy, because it was the easiest nut to crack. I mean, if you don't have a lot of credit in serious or classical acting, they won't even look at you. And I didn't have training when I came to the city. It was all instinct and guts. I mean, I wasn't disciplined or trained or anything like that. I mean, I had no idea of what I was doing. I was just elbowing my way into the wing. I was so in love with it. So I figured I'd get a job to support myself and learn while I earn" (6).

Her file-clerk job at Columbia University was just one in a long succession that she took to pay the rent while she pursued acting parts in the theater. During those initial months in Manhattan, Bette also found work selling gloves at Stern's department store and as a hat-check girl in a restaurant. Those jobs were all short-lived. She would end up quitting, after waiting on grouchy customers who complained of receiving the wrong hat or fussy women who couldn't decide on what pair of gloves to buy.

One of Bette's most bizarre part-time jobs came in Union City, New Jersey, where she found herself working as a go-go dancer. The most shocking aspect of that job was seeing the part of New Jersey that lies right across the Hudson River from New York City. Her parents had always spoken of their lovely native state, but Bette was horrified when she saw how gray and industrial it all was.

"They were living in paradise [in Hawaii], yet they always talked about how beautiful New Jersey was, and how they missed their family here. So I always wanted to come to New Jersey," she explains. "When I got here I almost died, it's the tackiest, dirtiest place in the world. No one seems to even try to keep it clean!" (23).

Eventually, she made some friends, and she often went out exploring in Manhattan. One of her favorite pastimes was wandering around Greenwich Village in hopes that she would run into Bob Dylan—as he was one of her musical idols. But through it all, it was theater that was on her mind.

Coming to New York City with little more than boundless energy and blind ambition, Bette constantly made the rounds of all the casting agencies and "open calls" for stage shows. Ninety percent of the time, the reception she received was less than warm, but that did not discourage her one bit.

"It didn't faze me, though," she claims of her usual rejection by agents and directors. "'Okay,' I'd think to myself, 'go ahead, shut the door in my face! Be out to lunch! Hang up on me! I don't care: I'll be back!' I kept looking at all those casting directors and thinking, 'You should never wear plaid.' I was never intimidated by that kind of garbage, because I knew I was as good as anything else coming down the pike. I could sing. I could read lines" (21).

In New York City there are all kinds of theatrical opportunities. Bette soon found herself investigating some of the more avant-garde theater that was happening in Greenwich Village and other parts of the city. "There were a lot of people doing exciting things then," she remembers. "I got a great deal of my early inspiration from Charles Ludlam. The first thing I ever saw him do was *Turds in Hell,* which blew me away. It was the most incredible piece of theater I had ever seen. And there was this chick in the show who was really terrific. Her name was Black-Eyed Susan. She really inspired me" (25). In the production Black-Eyed Susan was totally outrageous, and in one scene she appeared onstage as the Statue of Liberty, wrapped in toilet paper and dollar bills. When Susan opened her mouth and began singing the song "Wheel of Fortune," Bette was convinced that she could get up on stage and do a much better job vocally. Without abandoning her dream of breaking into Broadway productions, she began investigating the possibility of working in Off-Broadway shows and experimental theater productions, strictly for experience.

Eventually, she landed a part in Tom Eyen's production of *Miss Nefertiti Regrets* at the Cafe La Mama. She originally appeared in the chorus of the show in its initial run, but when the director saw Bette come alive onstage during a performance, she became Miss Nefertiti in the revival. She was quite a sight in her blonde wig, high heels, and a bikini!

The summer of 1966 was spent in what is known as the Borscht Belt, in the Catskill Mountains in upstate New York. It was there that she appeared in stage shows in resort hotels, including Brickman's. When she returned to New York City in the fall, she was cast in Eyen's next production, *Cinderella Revisited.* During the afternoon the cast would perform the fairy tale classic *Cinderella,* and in the evening they would spice it up for the adults and call it *Sinderella.* Again, Bette had the title role—playing an "ugly duckling" whose wildest dreams came true. It wasn't long before life was due to imitate art for her.

During this same time period, one of the hottest shows on Broadway was *Fiddler on the Roof.* It opened in 1964 and ran for seven years. In fact, at one point, when it hit 3,242 performances, it was the longest-running show on Broadway at that time. Due to the large cast and chorus, there were constant cast changes and periodic "open calls" where anyone could audition, whether they were members of Actor's Equity or not. Bette went to several of the open auditions in an attempt to break into Broadway and become the big star of stage that she longed to be.

Finally, after several auditions, in 1966 she landed a small part in *Fiddler on the Roof,* in the chorus. According to Bette, "EVENTU-ALLY, I got into *Fiddler* as a chorus girl, after about a whole year of auditioning on and off." Although she didn't have a specific role all her own, she was ecstatic: "I was actually on stage!" (25).

Set in turn-of-the-twentieth-century Russia, *Fiddler on the Roof* centers around a poor Jewish milkman named Tevya; his wife, Golde; and their daughters. His eldest daughter, Tzeitel, falls in love with a poor tailor named Motel. She wants to marry him instead of having an arranged marriage to someone else. The second daughter, Hodel, announces that she is going to marry Perchik, an idealistic revolutionary—without permission. And the third daughter, Chava, scandalously takes up with a man named Fyedka, who is a Christian. In the context of the musical, Tevya has several comical conversations with God, about his family and the decisions he is called upon to make. The story is about anti-Semitism, tradition, and how the world happens to be changing around them—all set to music.

"When I was in the chorus," Bette explains, "I understudied the part of Tzeitel, and when the part opened, [director] Jerry Robbins had to see all the girls up for it, but the lady who was casting didn't want me to have the job. She called me up two hours before the audition, and said I didn't have a prayer. But if I didn't go in, she said, I could have the chorus job back" (11).

Bette, who had found the original chorus job to be a temporary assignment, was dying to get back into the show, so she decided to gamble. According to her, "I at least wanted to get a look at Robbins—I worship the ground he dances upon—so I said, 'I'm sorry, I'm taking the audition!'" (11). She was cast in the part, and she stayed in *Fiddler on the Roof* for three years as Tzeitel, the eldest of the three daughters in the family. During those three years, the roles of the other two sisters were played by several actresses who also had their sights on bigger things. Among the girls to play Bette's sisters were Adrienne Barbeau and Pia Zadora.

"I was really good in *Fiddler* for the first two years," says Bette. "But in the third year I came to a screeching halt. There I was in the third year, working for the same money I made in the first, breaking my ass, and feeling miserable because I couldn't get into agents' offices. And when they would send me out for auditions, the people wouldn't like the way I looked, or the way I sounded. I couldn't make them understand that there was really something there" (25).

"I saw it wasn't going to be the way I thought it was going to be," she continues. "I wanted to work a lot, to grow, and the theater is a closed market. I couldn't get anything else, and the way I was brought up, I was taught you must work. But I came to New York to have a career, not to be in one show, so at the end of the second year, I thought, 'Time to move,' and I had a bunch of experiences that related to that move. I was getting very high, and I was with people who were brilliant, and they were flashing things across my brain. I was getting freaked out on everything that was going on" (3).

When tragedies strike, weak people often crumble, while strong people look inside themselves for courage and emerge with an even stronger will to survive. It was during Bette's third year in *Fiddler on the Roof* that the Midler family suffered a horrible loss, and it was Bette who had to remain a tower of strength.

Bette's eldest sister, Judy, like Bette before her, had left Honolulu to pursue her career aspirations. Judy moved to San Francisco, where, according to Bette, "She was studying to become a moviemaker" (14). That year Judy came to New York City to see Bette—her younger sister, the Broadway star. In a bizarre twist-of-fate accident, Judy was in the heart of the theater district when she was hit by a speeding car and killed.

It was Bette who had to telephone Hawaii to notify her family. Her sister Susan remembers answering the call. "I gave the phone to my father," she recalls. "Bette spoke to him first, and then it was passed around to all of us. It was a nightmare. I don't think my mother ever got over it" (13).

"It was very bad losing Judy," Fred Midler recalled. "As I understand it, an auto came out of one of these indoor garages and smashed her right up against the wall. Mutilated her completely. The funeral directors wouldn't even permit us to view the body" (13).

Judy's death had a profound effect on Bette's life. She realized how short life can be, and she felt that hers was passing by, and she was not moving quickly enough. She realized that it was time to get out of the Broadway show she felt stuck in and to move on to new experiences.

She explains, "See, by that time, *Fiddler* wasn't where it was at; it was the Beatles and marijuana, and *Hair* and Janis Joplin. All of a sudden people my age were happening, and I just wanted to see where, and IF, I could fit in" (13).

When her sister Judy was killed, Bette took off only a week and a half and then returned to the show to ponder her future. During her time away from *Fiddler*, the role of Tzeitel was played by her understudy, Marta Heflin.

Heflin recalled lending her support to Bette when Judy died. "It was a terrible, terrible thing. I was there at her house for sitting *shiva*. I was very impressed with her then. Because it was a terrible tragedy. But she is very strong. You could tell that she was very upset, but she was very strong. She's a very strong lady, you know. You saw those guts coming through. I'll never forget that. There was no self-pity, no breast beating. I did the role for a week and a half, and then she was back" (5). It was Marta who threw a much-needed life preserver to a creatively drowning Bette.

In Greenwich Village there were several small "showcase" nightclubs where an aspiring singer could arrive on specified nights with sheet music in hand and perform. Marta was already going down to a club called Hilly's and trying out her own material in front of the audiences on "open mike" nights. Marta invited Bette to go down to Hilly's on one such night, to try her hand at cabaret singing.

"She wasn't making [any] money at it," Bette recalls of Marta's ventures to Hilly's, "but she was having a good time. So, the next time she went down there, I went along" (19).

Bette will never forget her first night of performing at Hilly's. Up until this point, she had never considered becoming a singer—apart from the musical theater stage. "I always sang, but never seriously," she remembers. "I got up in front of this little audience and just sang. The first two songs weren't anything special, but the third—something just happened to me—something happened to my head and my body and it was just the most wonderful sensation I'd ever been through. It was not like me singing. It was like something else!" (25).

"I sang 'God Bless the Child,' which I don't sing. I never sang it. I sang it once and that was all, because it frightened me so. It really freaked me out. I was screaming at the end of it. The song had a life of its own that imposed itself on me and I don't even know what happened. I was just this instrument for what was going on. Bizzzzzarre . . . so I decided that was a nice change. I decided to just do it for a while, and I did" (25).

Bette suddenly found herself wrapped up in discovering all sorts of old songs that she had not previously been aware of, and she would test them on audiences at Hilly's and other small nightclubs and cabarets in the city. She spent several hours each week at the Lincoln Center Library, listening to old albums and getting turned on to the music of Bessie Smith, Ethel Waters, and the Harry Warren tunes from the famous 1930s Busby Berkeley musicals. Suddenly, a whole new world of music and performing opened up to her. She had been so obsessed with the idea of being a Broadway actress that she didn't even consider that every song could become an act, a mood, an emotion, and a characterization all its own. She fell in love with singing and with breathing a unique life into each song she sang.

According to her, "I love Bessie Smith. I love Aretha Franklin. Gospel is some of the most wonderful music around. You get up and you can't stop. I makes you vibrate. I like torch songs and torch singers that make you cry. Ethel Waters used to kill me when I first started listening" (25).

"I heard the stories these women were telling, they were laying incredible stuff down, their lives were fabulous lives, and it was in their voices and their songs, and I was fascinated by that. And there were some things I had to say about where I've been and who I've been with, and the pain I know" (3). She was especially enamored of torch songs, and all of a sudden she was singing all sorts of classic blues numbers like "What a Difference a Day Makes," "My Forgotten Man," "Ten Cents a Dance," and "Am I Blue?"

At the time, Bette was dating one of the other cast members from *Fiddler on the Roof*, Ben Gillespie. She would go over to Ben's apartment, and the two of them would listen to old records. It was Gillespie who introduced her to Aretha Franklin's early recordings from the era when Aretha was a young blues singer, years before she was dubbed "Lady Soul." Bette still recalls the night he put on Aretha's *Unforgettable* album, and she sang at the top of her lungs to the album. "A real awakening" is what she called the music on that particular Aretha Franklin album, which was recorded as a tribute to Franklin's singing idol, Dinah Washington. One of the performances on that classic Aretha album was a torch number that would later become one of Midler's earliest signature songs: "Drinking Again." According to her, "It was like I had no idea what music was all about until I heard her sing. It opened up the whole world" (5).

"My mentor was a man named Ben Gillespie," Bette later recalled. "Ben was a dancer I met when I was doing *Fiddler on the Roof* on Broadway. He opened up the world for me. . . . I was crazy for him. He really opened up my eyes. He taught me about music and dance and drama and poetry and light and color and sound and movement. He was an artist with great vision of what the stage could provide. He taught me a grandeur I had never known before. He inspired me not to be afraid and to understand what the [music of the] past had to offer me. I never lost the lessons he taught me" (30).

William Hennessey was another of her friends from that same era. She had met him when he was one of the hairdressers who worked on *Fiddler*. Hennessey remembered, "She had another friend then, a dancer named Ben Gillespie, who was a thirties and forties freak, and the three of us used to hang around all the old movie houses in New York. Afterward Bette would do takeoffs of Charlotte Greenwood, Martha Raye, and Joan Davis" (4). Bette's "Divine Miss M" persona was born from her interpretation of these famous Hollywood crazy ladies of the 1940s.

Bette and Marta began to go regularly to Hilly's on West Ninth Street and to a club on West Forty-Fourth Street called the Improvisation. Also singing at Hilly's during this same period was an aspiring blues and rock singer with a powerful voice, named Baby Jane Dexter. "There were a lot of us back then," Dexter recalls. "We were just kids, and we were trying our hands at singing in front of an audience, and trying out new material. There was a woman who ran the showcase, and she made a big deal out of Bette coming in from *Fiddler on the Roof*" (31).

"Bette sang 'Am I Blue?' and she sang 'Happiness Is a Thing Called Joe,'" explains Baby Jane. "She sang only slow songs—nothing fast—all slow ballads, and she would fondle her tits while she was singing and emoting. I gave her the worst advice that there ever was—which was to put a bra on!" she laughs (31).

"She used to wear this red velvet dress, and a guy named John Foster played the piano. She wore this red velvet dress until it wore into air— disintegrated. She was into old antique clothing, and she wanted to be a Helen Morgan type. She had dark brown hair, which she pulled back real tight, and made a thing that looked like Jane Eyre, on the side of her head—a snood. It was not that flattering, but I only know that it was not that flattering because later she got a more flattering look" (31).

According to Dexter, "People used to look at her rubbing her tits and not know what to think. She was always doing this stuff, and she was never boring. I thought her voice was strong then. Her voice hadn't been rock & roll-ized—it hadn't been harmed. I thought she sounded good, and I liked listening to her singing these songs. She was very emotional. It wasn't that she was doing something so incredible, but there was something about her—she was totally driven!" (31).

Of her days at the Improv, Midler remembers, "Originally, in my velvet dress with my hair pulled back and my eyelashes waxed, I was convinced I was a torch singer. Because the Improv was a comedy club, you had to be a little bit funny, so I added chatter between songs. There I was, singing my ballads and crying the mascara off my eyes, and in the next breath telling whatever lame joke I'd just heard" (20).

While Bette was still in her third year of *Fiddler*, both she and Marta began to venture into other theater projects. Bette played the Red Queen in a children's production of *Alice through the Looking Glass*, and Marta left *Fiddler* to appear in a rock musical Off-Broadway, called *Salvation.* In the play, Marta played the part of a comic nymphomaniac. When she was offered the opportunity to play the same part in the Los Angeles company of *Salvation,* she recommended Bette as her replacement in New York. Bette landed the part of Betty Lou and joined the cast of *Salvation* in 1969.

Meanwhile, Bette's performances at the Improvisation brought her to still another level. It was there that she met the owner of the club, Bud Friedman, who was to become her first manager.

At this time, Bette and Marta were regularly performing their material at the showcase clubs, and Bette was heavily into her torch-song and blues trip. Friedman distinctly remembers that Bette's selections tended toward the maudlin—songs from *Three Penny Opera* and several sad blues numbers. He wasn't particularly into her singing—and neither was the audience.

According to Baby Jane Dexter, a man named Frankie Darrow came down to Hilly's one night and wanted several of the performers to come uptown to West Forty-Fourth Street, to a club he was managing called the African Room. "He wanted all of these people to come up to a big showcase he had," says Dexter. "People like David Brenner, Irene Cara—she was eleven or twelve at the time—Jimmy Walker, Bette Midler, and me. Frankie had these Monday night showcases and they picked someone out of this showcase to be the opening act for a Caribbean singer named Johnny Barracuda. It was between two girls that Frankie was going to hire. Who was going to get this big gig, and get paid fifty dollars to open for Johnny? It was between Melba Moore and Bette. He went with Bette, and this was her first paying gig as a singer" (31).

A couple of months passed, and Bud Friedman from the Improvisation showed up at the Africa Room one night to see a girl named Roz Harris. At the time he was considering managing Harris, and who should be on stage that same evening but Bette Midler? Through all of her work in the clubs, she had really polished her singing style on all of her favorite numbers. When she sang "Am I Blue?" that night, Friedman remembers being knocked out by her performance. Bud invited her to return to the Improvisation, and this time around he was quite taken by her singing and her stage presence; he signed her to a one-year management contract.

One of Bette's strengths has always been her ability to see or hear something that she likes in someone else's act and to adapt it for use in her own performances. All of her songs were taken from old recordings she'd heard, recordings she would then reinterpret. One night at the Improvisation, Bette used a funny line that she had heard a comedian at the club use. The female comedian went screaming through the club while Bette was onstage, accusing Midler of ripping off her material. Although Bette never did that again, she began to feel that she wanted to develop her own comic patter to use between songs. This marked the beginning of an important evolution in Bette's act.

Another trademark of her stage act came from her use of vintage clothing that visually emulated the mood of the songs she was singing. The whole idea of wearing the old velvet gowns came from a Helen Morgan album cover that she had seen. Bette decided that she needed something extra to complete her own chanteuse image. In addition to the red velvet gown, which by now was falling apart, she found a long beaded black velvet gown, for which she paid ten dollars at a second-hand clothing store.

The dresses were more than clothes, more than costumes; they visually represented her complete transformation into her concept of a torch-singing diva. The velvet dresses helped Bette feel like something more than an aspiring actress who occasionally sang. Wearing them, she was beginning to step outside of herself onstage and become a distinctive character of her own creation.

4

STEAMING UP THE CONTINENTAL BATHS

Only the "sexual revolution" climate of the 1970s could have given birth to an establishment like the Continental Baths. Never before—or, for that matter, since—has an emporium been so open about being a public meeting place for on-premises all-male sexual activities. By 1970 the changing sexual mores encouraged individuals to pursue whatever sexual expression they chose. The Continental Baths could not have existed before that time because of the moral attitude toward homosexual activity. It clearly could not continue to exist after the early 1980s because of the advent of AIDS. The bathhouse was indeed as unique as the era that gave birth to it.

It was neither morality nor health concerns that ultimately finished off the Continental Baths. As America's attitude toward homosexuality became more liberal, the bathhouse as a place for sexual encounters became less and less necessary. By the middle of the 1970s the Continental Baths closed, changed hands, and became the short-lived heterosexual swinging singles sex-on-the-premises club called Plato's Retreat.

For the brief couple of years that the Continental Baths did exist, it was, by all reports, something unique. Located in the basement of Manhattan's Ansonia Hotel, at West Seventy-Fourth Street and Broadway, the baths' proprietor, Steve Ostrow, set out to make it the ultimate gay bathhouse—complete with snack bar, dance floor, video screens, steam room, swimming pool, private "massage" rooms, and finally, the added attraction: live entertainment.

"The Continental Baths was a huge loft-like space, with tons of white tiles everywhere," explains one of the regular customers. "You would walk in, and to the left there was a huge Olympic-size pool and platforms where you could sit. The feeling was one of huge space, and there was music playing. Everyone wore white towels" (32).

"To the right they would have a small private seating area, where people would come in and see the shows, and that's where Bette Midler performed. The steam rooms were off to the right. There was an upstairs . . . and you could see patrons going upstairs, and there were rooms where you could do whatever you wanted to do. But the atmosphere downstairs was one of a loft space. It was not someplace where you would say, 'Let's stop off for a drink.' You had to be into the whole baths scene" (32).

Ostrow initiated his live musical entertainment policy by booking a folk-singing duo to perform. They were a husband-and-wife team, Lowell and Rosalie Mark. The Marks' contract called for them to perform one show a week, and their engagement lasted for three months. However, Ostrow wanted something a bit more "special" than the duo's pleasant little musical set.

Bette's progression to the Baths was a simple case of being at the right place at exactly the right time. Between her theatrical performances and her showcase club engagements, Midler was simultaneously taking singing and acting lessons. One of her teachers was Bob Ellston, who taught at the Herbert Berghof Studio. Ellston knew Steve Ostrow and suggested that Ostrow catch Bette's act at the Improvisation. Ostrow did, liked her singing, and, according to Bette, "There was a teacher here [Herbert Berghof Studio] named Bob Ellston, and he called me up one day and said, 'Listen, I know this guy that owns this homosexual bath, and he needs someone to sing'" (3).

Ostrow offered her $50 to do two shows each weekend—one show each Friday and Saturday night at 1:00 a.m. *Salvation* had closed on April 19, 1970, and Bette was looking for a regular-paying gig, so she jumped at the opportunity. Even at $50 a weekend it was an improvement, especially since she was singing for free at the Improvisation.

Bette Midler's first engagement at the Continental Baths began in July of 1970. She was booked for an eight-week run, which was extended off and on over the next couple of years. At first, her personal confidence level was low, and her initial reception at the Baths was lukewarm. Slowly and tentatively, she tried out her wings onstage, and once she began, she just kept on growing. Over the next twenty-eight months, she made the Continental Baths famous, and her appearances there shaped and molded her into the "Bette Midler" who was a star.

As she later recalled, "My career took off when I sang at the Continental Baths in New York. Those 'tubs' became the showplace of the nation!" (8).

For her debut at the bathhouse, Bette engaged the services of a piano player named Billy Cunningham, whom she had met at the Improvisation. Together, they faced the towel-clad crowd at the Continental Baths that first night, not knowing quite what to expect. That first night's show at 1:00 a.m. could hardly be called a roaring success. She opened her set with the lamenting ballad "Am I Blue?" and continued the show in a very bluesy, "down" sort of a vein. The reception from the twenty to thirty people who comprised that first audience was very polite. Before the show, Bette had felt very nervous and insecure about the whole event—her songs, her singing, the baths, everything.

As she sang her all-ballad set, she quickly realized that the most terrifying thing that could possibly happen was that no one was going to pay any attention to her. After all, she would have be pretty damn entertaining to ever hope to compete with the "steamy" goings-on in those private "massage" rooms. In essence, she had to be *better than sex* to make anyone even notice her torch song act that night.

After the show, her friends—Bill Hennessey, Billy Cunningham, and Ben Gillespie—encouraged her to become wilder on stage. They wanted her to let out that side of her they saw when she acted silly and did impersonations of other actresses. When she did that, she was funny and flamboyant and campy. That side of her would get much more attention onstage at the Continental Baths than her serious Helen Morgan side. Bette thought back to all of those woman who played their singing and their routines strictly for laughs: Charlotte Greenwood kicking her legs up over her head and laughing wildly, Martha Raye making goofy facial expressions midsong, Joan Davis gawking and looking stunned during her double takes, and that crazy Black-Eyed Susan swathed in toilet paper while belting out "Wheel of Fortune."

Bette was afraid of falling flat on her face and afraid of not being taken seriously as a singer. She had to invent another personality to house her wild side. She had to come up with a character who wasn't afraid to be brazen, tacky, bawdy, and completely off-the-wall. This character became known as the Divine Miss M, the ultimate over-the-top fearless diva.

Bette later analyzed the birth of Miss M: "At the Continental Baths I was playing to people who are always on the outside looking in. To create the semblance of someone like that can be wonderful. And so, I created the character of the Divine Miss M. She's just a fantasy, but she's useful at showing people what that outsider's perspective is" (4).

"I was dying to make it big," she later admitted. "You know why? Because I wanted to be somebody else. I didn't know who. . . . Edith Piaf perhaps" (4).

Her transformation started out slowly, and once begun, it all just seemed to mushroom. First her attitude changed, then her material, and then her recognition from the audience at the Continental Baths. She began to say outrageous things on stage—about herself, the bathhouse, the audience—and to relate her own crazy experiences.

Her appearance started to change as well. Turbans, halter tops, and 1940s gowns she had found at thrift shops were among her favorite clothing choices on stage. At some point during this era, her hair color went from brown to bright red. Her new flame-colored mane made her seem even bigger-than-life than she already was.

Bette and Ben continued their exploration into the music of the bygone eras, and Bill wrote her some gag lines to use onstage. It wasn't long before Bette began adding rock & roll and pop tunes to set off her slower blues numbers. Steve Ostrow was quite vocal about pointing out that her act had too many depressing "dirges" in it. Soon, songs like "Honky Tonk Woman, " "Lady Madonna," and "Sha-Boom Sha-Boom" loosened her up on stage and gave her show more balance.

After the end of her first eight-week engagement at the Continental Baths, her run was extended for another eight weeks. The only change was that the Friday night shows were eliminated. Considering that the same men came to the baths week after week, she ended up playing to many repeat customers. With once-a-week performances she was able to learn new songs, try out different material, and eliminate weak numbers.

"Whose idea was it to play this dump?" she would sarcastically quip onstage (4). "Oh! Oh! You're all mad. M-aa-d I say! Gawd, it's steamier than usual tonight. Wait till Marlo Thomas and her sister Terry play this room. Way-i-t!" (33).

Before long, she developed a wildly campy sense of onstage humor that became as important as her singing. Trashy, silly girl-group songs from the fifties and the sixties became a staple of her act even before she had a background group to sing with. "Remember the bouffant BMT subway hairdo of the 1950s?" she would shout to her audience. "Remember AM radio? Oh, my dears, AM. That's where it was all at. You didn't have to think, just listen. What fabulous trash! Remember girl groups? The Shirelles, Gladys Knight & the Pips? Okay. I'll be the leader and you be the Dixie Cups" (33). With that, she would swing into "Chapel of Love."

Something wonderful was beginning to happen on the tiny makeshift stage at the Continental Baths. That shy, insecure, homely little girl from Hawaii, with big dreams, was transforming herself into someone who was attractive because of the genuine "fun" image that she was creating before her unconventional, liberated audience. The sheer outrageousness of the whole atmosphere encouraged her to be much freer and more controversial than any other crowd would allow.

She referred to the Continental Baths as "the tubs" and described its ambiance as "the pits." Her frizzy mass of henna-red hair she accredited to her gay hairdresser, whom she claimed had created her coiffure with an eggbeater. She pranced around the stage in platform shoes, with a towel wrapped turban-like around her head, pretending she was Carmen Miranda on speed. Bette Midler was discovering herself, and her audience was discovering her ability to make them laugh at her crazy behavior and eclectic choice of songs. Just as she had done years before in grammar school, Bette was learning to bury her feelings of insecurity and unattractiveness in the laughter of others.

As she explained her amazing metamorphosis: "I was an ugly, fat, little Jewish girl who had problems, I was miserable. I kept trying to be like everyone else, but on me nothing worked. One day I just decided to be myself. So I became this freak who sings in the tubs" (33).

It wasn't long before the word-of-mouth reviews on Bette spread through the gay community in New York City. It wasn't long before men who would never have dreamed of venturing to the baths were showing up at the Continental just to see this short Jewish red-headed singer everyone was talking about. With justification, one of the happiest people in town was Steve Ostrow, who was packing people into his bathhouse on Saturday nights. "It was just something I felt, something live happening on that stage," he later said of the magic little lady who referred to herself as the Divine Miss M (4).

During this same time period, her new manager, Bud Friedman, began to book Bette's initial national television appearances on *The David Frost Show* and *Merv Griffin*. In the early summer of 1970 she made her debut on *The Tonight Show* with Johnny Carson. This was back in the days when the show was still being broadcast from New York City. Her appearance on the show resulted from her work at the Improvisation, when a talent scout was looking for up-and-coming entertainers to appear on *The Tonight Show*. She auditioned for the show's producers, and they ended up loving her. True to comedy-of-errors form, on her way to the audition Midler caught her dress in a taxi-cab door and ripped it all the way up to her rear end. In classic "the show must go on" tradition, she fastened the torn garment together with a paper clip and went ahead with the audition. Torn dress or not, they loved her and booked her for an appearance on the program.

On that first *Tonight Show* performance, Bette sang two songs, but was not invited to be interviewed on the set by Carson. The songs that she sang that night were "Am I Blue?" and the vampy Mae West number "Come Up and See Me Sometime." Her appearance on the show was quite a success, and it was unique because there were few young performers at that time who were breathing new life into songs of the 1930s and 1940s.

Johnny Carson recalls, "When I first saw her on the show, I saw a quality that reminded me very much of Streisand. Bette really grabbed the audience. There was an empathy, a rapport that was hard to equal" (4).

From 1970 to 1972 Bette made seven guest appearances on *The Tonight Show*. She became one of Carson's favorite guests, and the more outrageous she became during those developmental years, the more her popularity grew on a national level.

Her second visit to *The Tonight Show* came in October of 1970, while she was busy steaming up the Continental Baths. Bette sang the Depression-era Joan Blondell production number "My Forgotten Man," from the film *Gold Diggers of 1933*. In the interview segment that followed, she revealed, "I'm probably the only female singer in America who sings in a Turkish bath. It's a health club. . . . it's called the Continental Baths and it's a HAPPY place," she said, discreetly substituting the word *happy* for *gay*. Amid the laughter that ensued, she said of the baths' audience, "They all sit in front of me, and when they love me, they throw their towels at me!" (34).

The fact that Bette Midler's phenomenal initial success came at the Continental Baths—and gave her an exclusively gay following—later proved to be both a blessing and a curse. It was the surreal and totally liberated atmosphere of the Baths that allowed her to be outrageous and to emerge from her own shell of insecurity. What was it that made her attractive to the gay crowd and unattractive to the Broadway producers whom she had once longed to impress? "I don't know," she admitted. "Maybe the gays see something in me. Maybe they see that poor *schlump* from Radford High School just trying to make it through. You know that's a very hard row to hoe, being gay. That's a tough one" (21).

"I'm a strong lady—I think they like that. I think they like to see independence. Who knows? Maybe they like the clothes I wear? I mean, it's more than that, though. It's People—PEOPLE! Everybody has a little bit of everyone else in them . . . a little bit of man, a little bit of woman in them" (21).

She later explained, "The Baths is a male health club in New York. It's sort of kitschy, decorated to death. And on Friday and Saturday nights, they have the distinction of being one of the only health clubs in the world that has entertainment. It's like a lounge. They pack these guys in, on the floor, in chairs, in their bathrobes or towels or whatever, and they just watch the show and enjoy themselves. Working at the Baths allowed me a chance to really stretch out and grow in a way I had not been able to before. I was able to work with a piano player and drummer every week and I didn't have to pay for it. And I had a big, built-in captive audience. I mean, where were they going to go? They were practically naked!" (19).

Each time she went back to the Baths, her repertoire grew. "I used to throw in a couple of odd numbers like 'Boogie Woogie Bugle Boy' and 'Marahuana,' which is a 1930s song, and 'Love Potion No. 9' and 'Great Balls of Fire.' Songs that make people laugh" (19).

"I got a lot of inspiration from Mae West. When I first started working, a friend brought one of her records over. It was in the early pot days, you know, when we were all smoking [marijuana], and everyone was seeing their fantasies come to life," recalled Bette (21).

For Midler, her own dreams and fantasies were beginning to come true. In the short span of four months, from June to October of 1970, she had grown from a hopeful unknown actress who sang on the side to an up-and-coming singing sensation with national television appearances and a strong legion of gay fans in New York City. But she wanted more. She wanted to be something more than a "freak who sings in the tubs" (8). She wanted to grow and to reach a much larger audience. However, as with everything else in the world, with growth comes change.

ENTER: THE DIVINE MISS M

Bette Midler's past is populated with dozens and dozens of friends, acquaintances, musicians, employees, background singers, and assistants. A few of the key people in her life have remained loyal to her, with mutually beneficial results. There are several more who crossed paths with Bette, worked with her for a time, contributed to her success, and afterward went off on their own.

Pianist Billy Cunningham was the first to make his exit. Playing piano at the Continental Baths wasn't paying him very much money, so when a higher-paying gig came along, he moved on. Before he left, he suggested a replacement. According to one of Bette's former employees, Cunningham was friends with another unknown piano player who had found some degree of success writing jingles for television commercials. At the time, the other pianist had hit it big with a jingle for MacDonald's hamburgers and was doing some vocal coaching on the side. The other pianist's name was Barry Manilow.

"He [Billy] had to give up the gig," says the former Midler employee, "so he asked Barry if he'd be interested in filling in for him. So Barry said, 'Do I have to take my clothes off?' And Billy said, 'No, no!' Barry said, 'All right,' and Billy said, 'You'll be hearing from Bette Midler, this singer.' So, Bette calls up and the first thing she says is that she wants two rehearsals, which no one had ever done. So Barry said, 'Well, all right, fine.' She comes to see him in his apartment, which was on Twenty-Seventh Street on the East Side at that time. Barry said, 'It was hate at first sight,' and he said that she 'walked through the rehearsals.' But he did the gig. He said, when she did 'Chattanooga Choo Choo,' he suddenly couldn't restrain himself from laughing, and he completely went mad for her—she brought down the house" (35).

"Afterwards Bette said to Barry, 'Do you want to be my musical director?' And he said, 'No, but I'll work with you until you can find a musical director.' Of course, she never found a musical director, at that time, so their relationship developed as it went along" (35).

According to Barry, he had his doubts about their chemistry onstage. However, the first time they performed together at the Continental Baths, somehow magic was created. "I played and she sang. But then we did it in front of an audience. She came downstairs in this turban and an outfit that could have come from my grandmother's closet. She was a tornado of energy and talent. I was six feet away, and this vision was one of the thunderbolts in my life" (20).

Manilow later recounted, "Somehow it seemed like Bette and I were not going to get along. We could not understand what the other was into. But of course, later we worked together on the stage act and in the studio, and we connected beautifully. She chose the tunes, I arranged them" (25).

It was during this same era that Bette met a lifelong friend, Buzzy Linhart—and not long afterward, his writing partner, Moogy Klingman. Through them, she was given one of the most significant songs of her career: "Friends." Linhart was known as a folk and rock singer, and Klingman had worked with Jimi Hendrix and Eric Clapton. On Carly Simon's successful debut album, Linhart contributed his song "The Love's Still Growing," and Klingman contributed "Just a Sinner."

"I co-wrote 'Friends' with Buzzy Linhart in 1970," recalls Klingman. "When we brought it to my publisher, he wanted to get Tiny Tim to do it. He was all excited about Tiny Tim using it as his follow-up to 'Tip-Toe through the Tulips.' We thought Tiny Tim was going to do it" (36).

That was before Buzzy met Bette. By a twist of fate, Buzzy Linhart and Bette Midler were both asked to portray the lead characters at the backer's audition for a new Broadway-hopeful show called *Uprise*.

"A slightly odd couple of artists, who claimed to have written a new musical, a new chapter to *Hair*, spiritually speaking," says Linhart of the playwrights. "Kirk Newrock, who is famous for doing strange often avant garde improvisational group music, with audiences performing. And his partner, Jill—I think it was Jill Gorham, a lady who wore shades day and night, even though she claimed to be totally straight. They had written a musical called *Uprise*, and it was really quite good. In a nutshell, it was two couples: the black couple and the white couple; of course, they all stayed with their own kind. And they were activistic, and eventually they got so many kids and disenfranchised street people behind them, and everything, that it became almost its own city. And eventually what happens in the end is the government comes and builds a fence. They think it's to separate them from the people they don't like, and eventually they realized that they have been fenced in, and they're in this big cage, and they're climbing up the wall" (37).

"Anyhow, there was a need for there to be white leads and black leads, male and female. It was kind of in the style of the old-styled musicals, but with this almost kind of horror movie twinge, [like] *Rocky Horror Show*. . . . Bette was performing at the Baths. I was hired to sing the two male leads at the backer's auditions, including our big one, [which] would be for David Merrick. . . . I rehearsed in private with the two writers, learning just the male part of the song, and Kirk squeaking out the female things, while I waited to meet the female who had been picked to do the backer's audition with me—a lady who they said was really dynamic, and would be able to do both the white female and the black female, in the backer's audition. We actually wouldn't get paid for anything, but David Merrick would see us singing the things first, and of course, and we would be first choice for the roles" (37).

"After I spent quite a few weeks working on this—and personally I loved the music. . . . I was anxious to meet this great lady who had apparently played a supporting role in *Fiddler on the Roof,* and was some sort of a wild lady. One afternoon, when it was time to meet her, and us to sing these songs together for the first time, I came to the rehearsal and I brought my acoustic guitar, so when I met her . . . When I met a new female—I wanted to show people what I did right away" (37).

So, he serenaded her with his song "Friends," right then and there. Recalls Buzzy, "And she said, 'That's great!' Either on that day, or very shortly thereafter, she asked me if she could sing that song at her shows at the Continental Baths; on Fridays and Saturday evenings she was doing a midnight show" (37).

According to Moogy Klingman, "Ultimately, it became Bette's theme song early on. Before her first album, it caught on as her opening and closing number—and just innocently became her theme song, and was just an overnight sensation" (36).

Buzzy Linhart and Bette had an instant friendship. After she told him about her gig at the Continental Baths, Linhart said that he could sure use a paying gig. "I was so hungry, and so underpaid and starving—even though I was doing gigs—that I asked her if she could possibly get me a gig at the Baths to make some money. So she got me a gig to sing at the buffet on Sunday afternoons as a soloist" (37).

He recalls the audition at the Continental Baths that day: "She introduced me to these people. It was a weekday afternoon, and there were people cleaning up the club around me. And I sang a couple of songs to them, and they said, 'Oh, that's great'" (37). With that, he landed the brunch job at the Baths.

At the time, Bette was dating a drummer by the name of Luther. According to Linhart, "Luther Rix had just been in the St. Louis or Chicago Symphony, or something like that and he got out and came to New York, and was doing some session work and stuff. . . . he was the great love of her life at one point" (37).

Recalls Buzzy, "Bette said to me, 'You know, Luther is just such a perfect drummer for you, because he just plays every style, and he's schooled, and he can read and can write charts, and you guys—you just gotta meet him. I know you are gonna play together.' And I got on the subway to go home, and I went one stop, and the door opened on this subway going down to the Village from up at the Baths, which is 74th and Broadway. And the door opens and here comes this dude wearing a cape, with a cane, with a serpent's head on it, and some kind of a funny hat. And he comes and sits down beside me, and he says, 'Oh man, I see you got a guitar case. You know, the greatest guitarist in the world is playing tonight in the Village, you really should catch him.' THIS was Luther, her boyfriend, and we didn't separate for a year and a half after that" (37).

Linhart's working relationship with Luther and friendship with Bette were both long-lived. However, his gig at the Baths was not. It was just Buzzy and his guitar and a bunch of gay boys in towels, making eyes at each other. According to Linhart, "It was fun, but it just wasn't me. Somebody could have done showtunes, it would have been perfect for someone else. I did two weeks. They were all in towels, and I've grown up in the theater, which is a very special place to be. I got the gig because she got me a job 'cuz I needed some money. For the right audition pianist, it would have been heaven, for someone who knew every showtune ever written. So, we decided after a couple of weeks that it wasn't for me" (37).

In a very real sense, Bette's initial gigs at the Continental Baths were limiting. She was making only $50 a week herself, and Steve Ostrow was paying Manilow. Not convinced that she was going to find the end of the rainbow at the Baths, she continued to attend theater auditions, and, thanks to Bud Friedman, she was beginning to get some legitimate nightclub work outside of New York City.

The first of her major gigs outside of Manhattan came in October of 1970, in Chicago, at a club called Mr. Kelly's. The engagement was as the opening act for Borscht Belt comedian Jackie Vernon. She was paid so little, there was no way that she could bring along her own piano player, only her musical arrangements. However, this was her big chance to see if she could hold her own onstage with a "straight" crowd. She had to delete her Carmen Miranda camping, her Mae West routines, and her Fire Island/gay hairdresser jokes, but she managed to garner laughs by spontaneously reeling out a whole routine about her lifelong fascination with Frederick's of Hollywood's sleazy lingerie.

For her Mr. Kelly's gig, Bette wore a bright purple dress—without a bra. There was Bette, shaking her ample breasts on stage to her raucous opening number, the ever-tasteful "Sha-Boom Sha-Boom." Her two opening act shows a night at Mr. Kelly's were a successful mix of 1950s rock and several blues numbers. Jackie Vernon came across like a corpse after Bette's energetic set.

After she returned to New York City, Bette continued to do research for her act. She began singing a mix of new material, including rockers like "C. C. Rider," theatrical pieces like Kurt Weil's "Surabaya Johnny," and the lewd and bawdy "Long John Blues," which is about a dentist who satisfies his female patients by filling their "cavities" with his big, long "drill." Only Midler would go out of her way to unearth such material—and have the nerve to perform it.

Bette was beginning to feel much more comfortable with her new role in show business—as an interpreter of classic songs. "That's really my thing, " she admitted, "I watch things, then I twist it around to get another view, then give it back to them and make them see it in another way that they never saw before 'cause they were so busy taking it seriously. I can't take any of it seriously. You work as hard as you can, but no matter how brilliant you think it is, there is always going to be someone that's going to look at it cockeyed and turn it around for you. That's what I get from the Theater of the Ridiculous—the sardonic side of it. What good is it if you can't giggle at it? 'Cause in the long run that's all it is" (6). Finally, Bette was beginning to step outside of herself and laugh at the paradoxes in her life.

Her next stint at the Continental Baths in late 1970 took her through to the following year. The past year had proved quite successful for her and was most notable for the entrance of the Divine Miss M. Her arrival on the scene represented a liberation from her past anxieties and insecurities.

Says Midler of Miss M: "She was a tortured torch singer on the foggy waterfront, wrapped up in her sorrow and a fur neckpiece." As Midler grew, so did Miss M: "My natural tendency to poke fun at myself and others came out, and the bedraggled torch singer became a little broader, a little funnier." Miss M allowed Bette to separate her personal life from her stage act: "I never remember her until she shows up. She has a life all her own, and that's very nice—as long as she doesn't mix in when I'm talking to the grocer or the taxi driver. I don't let her into my regular life" (24).

During her beginnings as a performer at the Continental Baths, Bette lived right around the corner, on West Seventy-Fifth Street. Eventually, she took up residence in a brownstone apartment in Greenwich Village, on Barrow Street, which was to remain her home for the next several years.

"The place likes me," explained Bette at the time of her move to her new Village residence. "I knew as soon as I walked in the door, it was glad to have someone here. The guy before me didn't do a thing, it was filthy and ugly and hadn't been painted in twenty-five years. But I'm trying to make it comfortable, like a home. I've never really had a home. I lived in one place for five years, but I had no furniture. I had a rug on the floor and I had some mattresses" (3).

Still uncertain about cabaret singing as a lifelong career choice, in May of 1971 Bette did her final theatrical engagement before stardom found her. She went to the state of Washington to appear in the Seattle Opera Company's production of the rock opera *Tommy*. Bette played two parts in the show: Mrs. Walker and the Acid Queen. Naturally, the part of the Acid Queen was the one that she had the most fun with. Singing the song "The Acid Queen" was like playing an even more liberated version of the Divine Miss M.

"I really loved that number," said Bette after the run of the show. "As we visualized it, it had nothing to do with drugs but was about the pervasiveness of female sexuality in American life. This Acid Queen was like the negative forces of female sexuality, all the things that drive boys to be homosexuals and to frighten men and make them run away. Larger-than-life female sexuality: suffocating" (19).

"She jumps out of a box, out of a carnival wagon, and has a G-string on with fringe and this little brassiere with little red rubies on it. And it looks like I have nothing on from where you're sitting. I'd never done anything like that before. I wanted to know what it felt like, and it didn't hurt me. Except I got bruised a lot jumping out of that box. I had to put makeup all over my legs because I was black and blue for three weeks. Anyway, I jumped out and started shrieking, 'I'm the gypsy, the Acid Queen, pay before you start. The Gypsy, I'm guaranteed to tear your soul apart.' And of course, all she does is just freak poor Tommy out" (19).

July of 1971 found Bette back in Chicago, for her return engagement at Mr. Kelly's. After playing the Acid Queen, she was loosened up, revved up, and ready for anything. This time around, she was the opening act for another comedian, Mort Sahl.

Bette was moving up the ladder, and she felt that she could begin to ask club owners for favors. For this stint at Mr. Kelly's she was being paid $750 a week, for two weeks. Before she arrived in Chicago, Bette telephoned the club's owner, Norman Kean, and informed him that she wanted to bring her new pianist, Barry Manilow, with her. She explained that she didn't mind paying Manilow out of her wages, but she couldn't afford the airfare. Would Norman pay for Barry's ticket to Chicago?

Kean complied with the request, sensing that Bette would give a better show if she felt comfortable with her own accompanist. As Barry explained it, "We knew we were good for each other, I guess. What she didn't have were arrangements and pacing. I tried to give her a musical stamp all her own" (38). When Midler and Manilow arrived in town, Norman Kean found that was exactly what Barry gave her act. It had improved vastly since her last appearance at Mr. Kelly's.

However, at first sight, Manilow also asked Kean a favor. He inquired if he could have three copies of the Chicago phone book. Startled, Kean asked Barry what he wanted three phone books for? Did he have friends in the Windy City he wanted to look up? No, answered Manilow: he wanted to sit on them while playing the piano!

Nowadays, Midler is famous for her devotion to cleaning up America. However, this is not a new passion of hers. According to Barry, she first demonstrated her civic duty when they were together in the Windy City. "Once we were walking on a Chicago beach, deep in conversation. She kept picking up bottles and caps, all this crap in the middle of our heavy talk, dumping it into the garbage pail," he recalls (20).

The show at Mr. Kelly's went fabulously. With Manilow's restructuring of Bette's show to get the most out of her material, Bette was a big hit. Many felt that poor Mort Sahl had a real problem trying to follow an opening act that totally eclipsed his own.

It was during this Chicago engagement that Bette caused her four-letter-word scandal. Talkshow host and local columnist Irv Kupcinet held an annual charity event to benefit the veterans' hospitals, called the Purple Heart Cruise. The event was heavily covered by the press, and the entertainment on the day-long voyage in Lake Michigan was provided voluntarily by whoever was appearing in Chicago at the time. Bette gladly agreed to sing a set for the cause. However, the musicians that were provided for her were also volunteers—all of the musicians from the local musicians' union who happened to be free that day.

Bette had become quite a perfectionist, a quality that she borrowed from Barry. After a brief rehearsal, the band was still doing everything wrong, much to the frustration of Midler. She tried again and again to put them on the right tempo and in the right key, with no luck. When the show began, they got it all wrong again.

Bette smiled sweetly to the audience, turned around to the musicians, who were obviously unenthusiastic and not terribly adept, and she instructed them what to do—while the crowd looked on. Song after song, they got it all wrong, but somehow she muddled through to the confused conclusion.

At the end of the set, she again smiled sweetly to the audience of war veterans and said, "I want to thank you all for being such a patient audience. I thought you were wonderful. I'm glad you're having such a wonderful time. And to this band, I'd only like to say one thing: 'FUCK YOU!'" Needless to say, she was never invited back on that charity cruise again.

While appearing on another television talkshow in town called *The Sig Sakowitz Show,* Bette was introduced to someone who was visiting the station. His name was Michael Federal, and he was immediately attracted to Bette. In fact, he asked her out on a date right then and there. He came to see her show at Mr. Kelly's, loved what he saw, and the two of them began an affair that would last for the next two years. Coincidentally, Michael was an actor and a bass player. It was Bette's intention, especially after the debacle of the Purple Heart Cruise, to put together her own band. So, she invited him back to New York City as her bass player, and he enthusiastically accepted.

While she was in town, Bette had told a reporter for the *Chicago Sun Times* about her plan to have her own band. "I'm not worried about how good the band is," she explained. "All I'm worried about is how good we are together. Because with [Janis] Joplin, I remember, I used to think Big Brother & the Holding Company was one of the worst bands in the world. But playing with her: 'dynamite,' 'great!' It's all in the vibrations going with some musicians who really love me. . . . Either it's going to be the highlight of my life, or it's going to be a total bust. In that case, I will know what direction to go in" (19).

Upon her return to New York City, Bette located a drummer for her newfound band and was now ready to expand. With Barry Manilow on piano, Michael Federal on bass, and Kevin Ellman on drums, she was prepared for bigger and better things. It wasn't long before she got just that. September of 1971 found Bette and her new band back at her old stomping ground, the Continental Baths, for a short engagement. The demand for Bette Midler at this point was so overwhelming that Steve Ostrow made special concessions so that women could come to the Baths to see her show. A special area was set up, and all women had to exit immediately following Bette's set. A sign was clearly posted that read: "Ladies Requested to Leave after the Show." Even celebrities were coming in to catch her act. There were all of the "regulars," in their terrycloth towels, standing next to such notables as Mick Jagger, Andy Warhol, and Helen Gurley Brown!

Entertainment writer Marie Morreale remembers being one of the first women to venture into the Continental Baths to see Bette Midler. "I had friends who used to go there," she explains. "They had seen her show, and it was just sort of like underground talk about how hysterical and terrific she was, and they invited me to go with them one night. It was a strange scene. I guess I had envisioned some sort of a Roman orgy, but it wasn't like that at all. It was just lots of people hanging around. No one was running around naked or anything like that, but you knew that there was sex on the premises" (39).

"There was a decadent feeling about it, because it was a new policy—letting women in there. It was like entering into a taboo area. You felt like you were on the cutting edge of something new—and then all of a sudden to see that sort of bosomy, crazy, campy kind of person. She was different than anyone I had ever seen before, and she had a different kind of in-the-know, sarcastic, cutting humor. At that time, the humor everyone was used to was more political rather than sexual innuendo. Her act was total fun for fun's sake: Just enjoy everything, and don't take anything too seriously. She was something special. The minute she came on and started singing and camping around, people were hysterical laughing. She was unbelievable. The only thing that I could think of was, here is a Sophie Tucker in the making. Here is someone who didn't give a shit about the rules. She was breaking the rules with her material, and you were breaking the rules by being there" (39).

In late September of 1971 came an engagement that would really advance her career. It was going to snag her the one thing that could spell tangible stardom for her: a record deal.

The supper club known as Downstairs at the Upstairs was located on West Fifth-Sixth Street. It was a very important gig for Bette because it was her first legitimate New York City booking. Here was her big chance, and she was mortified that something would go wrong and she would blow it. Just to make certain that she looked right, in the eleventh hour she pleaded with Laura Nyro's lighting man to come into the club and light her show; it had to be perfect. The lighting man was Peter Dallas, and he came immediately to one of her rehearsals to draw up a lighting scheme.

Opening night was September 20, 1971—Rosh Hashanah—and to top it all off, the night of a huge hurricane in New York. Talk about the kiss of death! Bette made her grand entrance that night, only to find that the audience consisted of eight people.

On the second night there was no improvement; and on the third night there were only five people in the audience. Here she was the hit of a gay bathhouse, and she couldn't even get arrested by straight New Yorkers! This called for drastic measures.

Bette hustled her buns down to West Fourteenth Street, to the tacky offices of the controversial swinging-sex-scene tabloid *Screw* magazine. She plunked down her own money and took out a big ad with her picture on it that carried the headline "Bette from the Baths—At the Downstairs!" and all of the details.

Talk about amazing intuition: By the sixth night of her engagement, the place was crowded with patrons. And the following night, it was "standing room only." The next thing Bette knew, her two-week engagement was extended to ten weeks, to accommodate the demand for reservations, and people like Johnny Carson, Karen Black, and Truman Capote were showing up to see Miss M perform.

Peter Dallas was certain that a recording contract was what Bette needed, and he was going to help her get it. Laura Nyro was recording for Columbia Records at the time, and through working with her, he knew several people who worked for the company. He invited one of his friends from Columbia to the Downstairs, and the friend flipped out when he saw Midler's act. Dallas urged him to get the president of Columbia Records, Clive Davis, to see the show. Davis accepted the invitation, but was totally unimpressed by the act and left the club without a word to anyone. Bette and the band were very disappointed.

By some odd turn of fate, however, the next night Ahmet Ertegun, president of Atlantic Records, was in the audience. Ertegun recalls, "I went there after a ball at the Plaza Hotel. I told my wife that I had to go hear a singer I had been told about" (40).

Strangely enough, a troupe of Bette's biggest fans from the Baths, an outrageous contingent of hairdressers from Brooklyn, showed up that same night—in rare form. They screamed and carried on throughout the show, and when it was over, they stood on the tops of their tables and threw confetti at her. The crowd was so wild that night that Bette was literally carried off the stage by fans, like a victorious gladiator who had just slain an arena full of lions. There sat Ertegun in a tuxedo— totally unrecognized and completely knocked out by what he had just witnessed.

"She had done the Baths and made a few Carson appearances when friends told me to catch her at the Downstairs at the Upstairs," says Ertegun, who vividly recalls that particular evening (4).

"She was unlike anybody I'd seen before. People of all types— grandmothers, couples, drag queens—everyone was screaming and jumping up and down on tables for this woman. She was doing everything: fifties greaseball stuff, swing era nostalgia, current ballads. You could discern a great wit there—she was trying to seem raunchy and tasteless AND exude a certain elegance, and she pulled it off. What she had was STYLE" (15).

"She was overwhelming. I couldn't believe that a young person like her could not only understand those old musical styles so well but capture the flavor of the periods and make them a part of herself. It was the wittiest musical performance I'd ever seen. It was striking to see such innate elegance and good taste in someone who superficially appeared not to have elegance or good taste. You know, she never EMBARRASSED onstage" (4).

So much for taste and elegance—Ertegun was blown away by what he saw on the stage at Downstairs at the Upstairs that night. "I went to her dressing room after her show and said, 'Listen, I'm Ahmet Ertegun from Atlantic Records, and I would like to sign you.' She said, 'That's it! That's what I've been waiting for.' I signed her the next day" (40). It wasn't long afterward that she went into the studio to begin to record the album that would let the whole world know about the outrageous redhead who began in the Baths.

The gig at Downstairs at the Upstairs was truly the one that was the charm. In the October 3, 1971, issue of the *New York Times,* Bette received her first major review. Written by John S. Wilson, it really captured her strengths and her weak points at that time. Wilson admitted, "She has presence, she has a fine voice, she has wit and total mobility, including an unusually expressive face." However, with all of her divergent musical styles, he felt "she never clarifies what she is trying to do." In spite of that, he pointed out that, his opinion notwithstanding, "The night I saw her, the audience had no doubts; they thought she was absolutely wonderful" (41).

Ahmet Ertegun couldn't wait to get her into the recording studio, but what was he going to do with her when he got her there? Ballads? Boogie-woogie? Rock & roll? Early sixties girl-group pop? "She posed a great problem," he admitted, "because she didn't fit into any categories; it's very hard to make a record that doesn't fit into any categories, it's *very* hard to make a record that doesn't fit into any category and then find an audience. Also, it was obvious that a lot of her appeal was her onstage magic. So there were lots of different theories as to what to do with her, and her first album was a compromise between people tearing her in different directions" (4).

Atlantic Records was not only the label that Bette's idol Aretha Franklin currently recorded for; it was also the home of one of the music industry's newest success stories: Roberta Flack. Roberta had been singing in a Washington, D.C., jazz club and had become a local sensation. She was signed to Atlantic and put into the recording studio with a producer who was working for the label: Joel Dorn. Dorn's success with Roberta's first albums, and his ability to recapture the intimate magic that existed between Flack and her audience at the Bohemian Caverns in D.C., made him seem the ideal person to turn the diva of the Continental Baths into a recording star.

Joel Dorn was the perfect producer for Roberta Flack. The song "The First Time Ever I Saw Your Face" brilliantly illustrates this fact. At the time Roberta was projecting the image of a very focused jazz and ballad singer who accompanied herself on the piano. Dorn was great at showing off Flack and her music and its delicate and intricate sound. While several songs in Bette's repertoire were heartfelt ballads, there was nothing intricate or delicate about her sound, her music, or her appeal.

Barry Manilow felt that since it was he who had polished Bette's stage act and done all of her arrangements, he should also be given a chance at producing her in the studio. He was quite disappointed when he learned that Dorn had been selected as Bette's producer.

"Bette's first album was the most painful experience of my life," remembers Manilow. "They never wanted me to produce it. They got Joel Dorn, a fantastic producer who unfortunately did not know her well enough. I was called in at the very beginning, to lay down the basic arrangements, and they said, 'Thank you very much. Good-bye.' So I left. I was very mad, but I left. It was Bette's first time out, so she didn't know what to do. I said, 'Bette, how could you let me leave?' But she was scared" (38).

After that, Barry was always looking out for his opportunity to make his own mark in the music business. He wanted to write and to produce his own material, and he was going to find a way to market himself. "It was a case of two strong egos clashing," he recalls (38). And so, in the fall of 1971, Bette began recording her debut album with Joel Dorn at the helm.

In February of 1972 Bette returned to the Continental Baths for what she thought would be her final engagement there. Rex Reed joked in the *Sunday New York Daily News* that Bette at the Baths had given "more farewell appearances . . . than soprano Kirsten Flagstad ever made at the old Metropolitan Opera House" (33).

"Gawd, I don't know how long I've been there. It seems like forever," commented Bette during that run at the Continental. "But they are loyal. Loy-a-al! I played more glamorous places than a steam bath. I had a two-week booking at the Downstairs at the Upstairs, and the guy who owned the joint was in love with me. What he really loved was my fans. They came in droves and practically stood on tables cheering. My two-week gig turned into ten weeks. Listen, you think the Baths is the pits? Next week I'm playing Raleigh, North Carolina, in a place called the Frog and the Nightgown. Who do you think lives there?" (33).

After having her as a guest on *The Tonight Show* on several different occasions, Johnny Carson asked Bette to be his opening act during his upcoming engagement at the Sahara Hotel in Las Vegas. The Divine Miss M, in the town where even the sunshine is artificial? Naturally, she accepted.

As she explained it, "He asked me to open his show in Vegas for him and I was pleased to do it for him because he had been very good to me. Really good. The more consistent I became, the more he warmed up to me. I like working for him. He's a professional with an astonishing kind of professionalism. He's 'up' every night. He gives the same-caliber performance every night" (25).

So, in April of 1972, Bette opened for Johnny at the Sahara Hotel in the Congo Room, which she kept referring to as the "Congoleum" Room. According to her, "Vegas was amazing. You have to see it once before you die. It's culture shock. Not my style. Everyone wears wigs. It's a heavy wig town. I got real good reviews, but I had lots of trouble dealing with the audience. I have to have love from an audience. When I feel warmth, then I'm warm. They just didn't know what to make of me. They didn't understand why they had left the gambling tables. Las Vegas—puh-leeze! Honey, I hated it, but it was an experience, you know" (25). In her put-downs, she snidely referred to Las Vegas as "Lost Wages."

In May of 1972 she played the Bitter End on Bleecker Street in Greenwich Village, and she returned to Chicago for a third engagement at Mr. Kelly's. Her next gig in New York City was the big enchilada: Carnegie Hall. "Another first," she said in anticipation of the date. "The first time anyone has ever played the revered Halls of Carnegie without having made it big on records. From the steam baths, straight to Carnegie Hall. Can you dig it?" (33).

This really had to be special. Miss M had to pull out all the stops this time. At this point she was commanding $1,500 a night in clubs across the country, but she had to pay the band as well. Nevertheless, she felt that she needed to scrape together enough money for her own background singers. She had once announced on *The Tonight Show* that she always dreamed of having backup girls, and she wanted to call her act "Bette & the Bang-Bangs." Instead, she hired three girls and dubbed them the Harlettes.

As she explained the selection process: "I called up my friends who sing and I had them all down and we sang together. I wanted to pick up people who I could really get along with" (25).

The first girl Bette asked about possibly singing backup in her Carnegie Hall debut was a singer she knew from the showcase club scene: Melissa Manchester. Melissa was interested in discussing the opportunity and suggested a friend of hers named Gail Kantor. Bette, Melissa, and Gail finalized the deal over lunch at Wolf's Delicatessen on Sixth Avenue and Fifty-Seventh Street, on the block north of Carnegie Hall. A third girl, Merle Miller, was suggested by Barry Manilow. Although they all had aspirations of becoming lead singers on their own, a Carnegie Hall gig was a Carnegie Hall gig and quite prestigious. Naturally, they accepted, and so were born the first in what is now a long series of Harlettes.

Carnegie Hall is the type of place that can be booked without the aid of a booking agent, and that's exactly what Bette and Barry did. Never in their wildest dreams did they think that they could sell it out, but they did. Bette's devoted fans from the Continental Baths came out in droves, and the evening was a smash, even though Bette later admitted that she was "terrified" of failure. The concert date was June 23, 1972.

Because of stipulations with the musicians' union contracts at Carnegie Hall, the use of personal tape recorders was strictly forbidden. However, since Barry was Bette's musical director, he figured that he would simply make his own cassette tape from the stage. He was very surprised to be told that he was forbidden to tape any part of it. Later that day the hall's soundman—who had a little sideline going for himself—offered to run a "bootleg" tape off the master soundboard, on the sly. Manilow agreed and paid the man $275 for a reel-to-reel copy of the show.

Among the songs that Bette performed in Carnegie Hall were her at-this-point traditional opening number, "Friends"; Bessie Smith's raunchy "Empty Bed Blues"; Helen Morgan's "Something to Remember

You By"; and Dorothy Lamour's "Moon of Manakoora." The Dixie Cups' hit "Chapel of Love" closed the show, and as the encore she sang Bob Dylan's "I Shall Be Released." The concert was a roaring success, and everyone who saw it knew that Bette Midler was something more than a flash in the pan—or rather . . . a flash in the tubs.

In the 1970s, Schaffer Beer Company sponsored an annual summer music festival in Central Park in the Wollman Skating Rink. And the opening act that night was her friend Moogy Klingman. As he explains it, "She did the Carson show, and she became really big really fast. It was like mostly a gay following in New York City. The thing that happened was that I had my first album come out, I guess around the same time as hers. It was called *Mark "Moogy" Klingman*, I was on Capitol Records, she was on Atlantic. Anyway, somehow I got to open for her, at the Schaffer Music Festival. No one really knew that I was the guy that wrote songs. I was playing with my band, and we were playing some heavy instrumental stuff, some jazz, some blues, some rock. It was like almost like a cross between Chick Corea and the Meters. I was singing like bluesy songs, and everyone was there to hear the biggest phenomenon in America—Bette Midler. They couldn't have cared less: we were totally bombing with this audience! This was like the climax of our tour to play with Bette Midler at the Schaffer Music Festival. People wouldn't even applaud after the end of our songs. Then during one of our climactic songs, a guy in like a jockstrap with clothespins on his nipples, and stuff in his hair—ran down the aisles. He started at the front row, and he ran down the aisle to the back and it was still light out. So he was really weird looking, and everybody in the audience got up and turned around to look at the guy. So we're doing the climax to our song, and the whole audience stands up and turns their backs to us" (36).

"We went backstage, and it was the end of the tour, and the album hadn't sold and Bette Midler went on stage and it was like the biggest celebration of a superstar. People were just going insane. That was the end of my band right there. I couldn't hold it together. I said, 'Look at how great she is doing, and how lousy we went over, let's break this thing up.' It was a bad circumstance. Like, my manager shouldn't have booked us with her. We had nothing to do with her music, even though I co-wrote her theme song. I mean, she went out and she opened with 'Friends,' and they went insane. Now here I was, the co-writer of 'Friends,' and they didn't even know who the fuck I was, and didn't even applaud for me" (36). With that, Klingman decided to disband his group and go back to the drawing board.

However, for Midler, it was a night of total triumph. According to Bette, the Schaffer Music Festival outdoor concert that night—August 16, 1972—was one of her finest hours. "I thought I was in a newsreel. It was like the Marilyn Monroe newsreel, you know, when she was in Korea; it was just exactly what I thought I was. It was the happiest I've ever been in my whole life. I was wonderful!" she added modestly (11).

With her first set of Harlettes, Bette began her tradition of making them the butt of her bitingly sarcastic onstage humor. "I guess you're wondering, 'Who are those cocktail waitresses up there with Miss M anyway?'" she would ask. "They're my girl singing group, the Harlettes . . . they're real sluts!" (25).

In September, Bette played at Mr. Kelly's in Chicago for the fourth time. This was a two-week engagement. For the first week it was her and the band, but for the second week she brought in Melissa, Gail, and Merle—who were also fondly referred to as "MGM."

At this point in her career, Bette was being "managed" and booked by a company called Artists Entertainment Complex (AEC). She had signed with AEC after her one-year contract with Bud Friedman lapsed and Friedman had exhausted all of his big contacts to assist her career. However, by the summer of 1972 AEC was trying to talk her into signing a deal as a lounge act at one of the big Las Vegas hotels for a large amount of money. With that plan afoot, Bette realized that AEC had no concept of what she was all about. Unbeknownst to her—at first—one of her biggest followers over the past years was a very aggressive promoter/manager named Aaron Russo. Russo was madly infatuated with Bette, and he approached her and told her that he could turn her into a hot property. Bette toyed with the idea, but informed him that she didn't want to be just another singing star. She looked him squarely in the eyes and told him that he could manage her if he accomplished the task she most desired: "Make me a legend!" (42).

Not only was Russo a man who loved a challenge, many felt he was also one of the most universally disliked people in the business. Ahmet Ertegun was among the most vocal in his opposition to the installment of Russo as Bette's manager. But she was determined to become "a legend," and she believed in Russo's devotion to her. She dumped AEC and hired Aaron.

According to her during this era, "We met, and it was instant love and devotion. Ours is a long and interesting tale . . . ah, Aaron and Bette. There's a great deal of love and terrible rows. He's a lot like my father. He's a bellower and in that way he intimidates people, but he's a real softie underneath. But that's what my mother says about my father, and I don't believe it" (14).

One of the most discussed myths about their relationship during their six and a half years together as manager and client was that they were lovers throughout this time period. Aaron repeatedly spoke of their intense personal relationship. In 1979, when she had fired him, Bette reported bitterly in *Rolling Stone* magazine: "What do you think he's going to say? That I *schtupped* him once and threw him out because he wasn't good enough? That wasn't the way it was, of course, but he has his pride" (13).

With regard to the "Make me a legend" statement, Bette admits, "I said exactly that. I was half joking and half desperate. And what I meant was that I didn't want to be just another chick singer. I don't want to go to Vegas and wind up singing other people's stuff. That was like throwing down the gauntlet, dearie. His eyes just lit up!" (13).

In a very real sense, Russo did make Bette a legend in the business. He also alienated just about all of her friends. Insiders allege that when Aaron Russo came onto the scene, he systematically got rid of everyone who had been with Bette before, because he wanted exclusive control of her career.

Meanwhile, during all of this activity, and between various other club dates across the country (including two weeks at the Princess Hotel in Bermuda), Bette was recording her first album. By June of 1972 it was clear to several people that the recording sessions with Joel Dorn weren't going as excitingly as expected. Bette had recorded well over a dozen songs with Dorn, and several of them were totally rejected for release by Atlantic Records. Everyone was beginning to panic.

Manilow recalls that the songs that Dorn cut with Bette were stiff and lifeless. Speaking of Dorn's recordings with Roberta Flack, Barry claimed, "Roberta Flack's records were sooo tasteful, they really were. Delicate as crystal, cool as a cucumber, controlled, serious—everything Bette wasn't. It made no sense to me that she'd picked him" (43).

Manilow was secretly hurt and disappointed that—other than surrendering a couple of musical arrangements to Dorn—he hadn't been asked to contribute his talents to Bette's recording career. However, he was about to seize the opportunity to change that. According to Barry,

"Just at that time, we did a concert at Carnegie Hall. I managed to get a bootleg tape of it and played it for Bette" (38).

As Barry later explained, he talked to Bette on the phone, and she was depressed. When he asked what was wrong, she informed him that she was upset over the way her recordings were going. Ahmet Ertegun was especially unhappy with everything that Joel Dorn had recorded with her. And she had to confess that she didn't like what she heard either. Barry invited her over to his apartment, because he had something that he wanted her to hear. When she arrived, he sat her down in a comfortable recliner chair and handed her a marijuana joint and a glass of wine. Then he put a pair of headphones on her, and let her experience what the audience had heard that magical evening at Carnegie Hall. She had the same reaction: This was the kind of energy that was missing from the tracks that Joel Dorn had recorded with her.

"She just freaked out," Manilow claims. Bette instructed Barry to phone Ahmet and to set up a meeting for him to listen to the concert tape. Barry went over to Ertegun's office in Columbus Circle and played him the tape. According to him, "Then Ahmet Ertegun heard it and said, 'Yes. That's what's missing from the album. Can you fix it?' And I said I'd try. We went back to the recording studio and ended up redoing nine songs. The album came out: half produced by me and half by Joel Dorn" (38).

One of Bette's close business associates tells of the confusion: "The first album, which she had labored on for over a year—she made them go back and redo it. And she forced Atlantic to let Barry produce a few of the cuts, and Ahmet went with it. The stuff that she left on that [album] from him [Joel Dorn] is superb, but the rest of it she wasn't ready to release, and most of it she never did. She did subsequently release 'Old Cape Cod,' on the *Songs for the New Depression* album, and 'Marahuana.' After they remixed it with [male singing trio], Gotham doing the backups—which was much better in the original Joel Dorn version, because the way he had it, it sounded like an old seventy-eight being played with all that scratchiness and everything. It was fabulous. Those tapes are amazing. She also did Joni Mitchell's 'For Free,' which she has never released, and a few other songs. But she wanted other stuff on the album. She had an idea, and Aaron did help her to convince them that she shouldn't be able to do this and run over budget and over schedule" (35).

At this point in his career, Barry Manilow had never produced an album cut before in his life. His work on TV jingles and a couple of failed singles with a group calling itself Featherbed were his two main forays into the complicated world of the recording studio. However, he told Ahmet Ertegun that he could produce a record, and he insisted that he knew how to record Bette the way she needed to be recorded. Figuring he had nothing to lose, Ertegun gave Manilow his lucky break. With Ertegun in the control booth, Manilow was about to get the best on-the-job training available. Barry figured that if he could produce the sound that everyone was looking for onstage, why couldn't he simply reproduce it in a recording studio? He knew that Bette's real energy came from performing in front of a live audience, as opposed to standing in a glass booth recording her vocals to an engineer and a producer.

In order to get the magical sound that Bette had during the Carnegie Hall concerts, Barry's first order of business was to change the mood of the session—from a cold glass-encased sound booth—and to have her record live with musicians and background singers in the studio with her. Manilow later recalled, "I would create an atmosphere as close to a live performance as I possibly could. I hired Bette's band instead of the veteran studio musicians Joel had hired. Bette's band was fresh, enthusiastic, and excited to be there. Then I rented some theatrical lighting and had it hung in the recording studio. I invited an audience of about twenty close friends of Bette's and the band's. I set up the Harlettes and the band as if we were doing a live performance. I had some drinks and food brought in for the audience and kept Bette busy outside in the hallway while Ahmet and the engineer got the levels set on the band" (43).

The first song they tackled was "Superstar," which is about a woman deeply in love with a guitar player. According to Manilow, "From the outset, we knew it was going to work. As soon as Bette could feel and react and play to a live audience, the previously missing energy was there. Ahmet, who was in the control booth, kept giving me the thumbs-up sign. Even Bette was having a good time" (43).

Over the thirty years since its original release, Bette Midler's *The Divine Miss M* still holds up as one of the best, most varied, most exciting, and most perfect debut albums ever released. Cut for cut, it still represents one of the highwater marks of her entire recording career. The other Midler albums that are up to this same dramatic mood-swinging peak are *Bette Midler* (1973), *Thighs and Whispers* (1979), and *Bathhouse Betty* (1998).

The secret to the success of *The Divine Miss M* album is that it is so incredibly diverse in mood, song selection, and style—there is pop, rock, blues, ballads, and swing, and somehow it all holds together as a unified album. On one song Bette is the forsaken lover ("Am I Blue?"), then she is the trashy biker chick ("Leader of the Pack"), then she's brought to tearful sentimentality ("Hello in There"), then she is all three of the Andrews Sisters ("Boogie Woogie Bugle Boy"). There isn't a mood or a mode that she misses. This album was perfect in 1972, and it remains timelessly perfect over three decades later.

Part of the reason for this is that half (actually, five) of the songs were finely crafted and very tastefully produced by Joel Dorn, and half (actually, six) of the songs were produced and arranged in an exciting and lively fashion by Barry Manilow. The juxtapositioning of these two production styles made this album breathtakingly successful. (Although those six cuts are credited on the album's liner notes to Manilow, recording engineer Geoffrey Haslam, and Atlantic Records president Ahmet Ertegun, clearly 90 percent of the credit belongs to Barry, who understood Bette's voice, appeal, and energy better than anyone else).

Dorn's production on the opening cut, "Do You Want to Dance?," is stripped down, slowed down, and made into an achingly pleading invitation to dance. The original 1958 Bobby Freeman single had been a catchy, sock-hop-worthy, medium-tempo pop/rocker. Bette's slower, more sensual rendition transformed the song into a dramatic, sexual come-on. It still holds up as one of her best and most emotionally electrifying recorded performances.

Then, in complete contrast, it is directly followed by Barry's production of Midler's speeded-up, trashier, and flashier take on the Dixie Cups' 1964 classic "Chapel of Love." It is frantic and rocking, and nearly out of control with energy. Ending with Bette's cackling laugh and the comment, "This is the 'pits' ending for a really terrific song," it shows off just enough of the bawdy Miss M persona to poke fun at the whole affair—making it suitably campy and very tongue-in-cheek.

Next is the song "Superstar," which was originally written by Bonnie Bramlett, Leon Russell, and (uncredited) Rita Coolidge. Most people don't realize that it was actually written about Bonnie's and Rita's separate backstage crushes on guitar superstar Eric Clapton. The original studio version of the song was recorded by Bramlett, and the original "live" version of it was sung by Rita on the famed 1970 Joe Cocker all-star concert album *Mad Dogs & Englishmen*. Ironically, it was Bette's nemesis, the ever-tasteful Karen—and Richard—Carpenter who had turned it into a million-selling Top 10 chart hit in 1971. However, it was Midler who here really milked this song for all of its bittersweet passion and pain.

Then the mood swings again—this time into the totally slutty "Daytime Hustler," which is overtly sexual in content—then back again to touching emotion on "Am I Blue?" Back and forth the pendulum swings until every base is covered, song after song.

On John Prine's touching "Hello in There," Bette's performance takes the listener into the eyes of a sad old woman who is wearily looking back at her life. With "Delta Dawn," Miss M dramatically tells the story of a disillusioned girl in love—in a song extravaganza that perpetually builds like a five-minute-and-sixteen-second mini-drama. And on the anthem "Friends"—penned by her friends Buzzy Linhart and Moogy Klingman—Midler received the true signature song of her career. It is on that song—which is presented twice on this album—that the contrast between the Joel Dorn recording approach and the Barry Manilow approach is best illustrated. The Dorn-produced version is centered and evenly plotted, while the Manilow version is wild and festive and sounds more like a raucous party in the studio than a formal recording session. Both styles are valid and satisfying, for different reasons. Between the two approaches, different shadings of Midler's personality are highlighted to maximum effect.

It is also interesting to note that in the background was a fascinating "who's who" of top-notch singers and musicians. The voice of Melissa Manchester can clearly be heard in the background of "Chapel of Love." And it is Whitney Houston's mother, Cissy, who leads the choir on "Do You Want to Dance?" Fittingly, Manilow handles the piano parts on all of the songs he produced, which also featured Midler's touring band—Dickie Frank on guitar, Michael Federal on bass, and Kevin Ellman on drums. Also, percussion wizard Ralph MacDonald (*Saturday Night Fever*) is heard on several of the cuts, as is noted jazz bass player Ron Carter. Yet, amid it all, the star here is clearly Miss M herself.

The end result was a brilliant fusion of style, substance, nostalgia, sleaze, heartbreak, joy, and celebration. Regardless of the production credits and the behind-the-scenes story, the finished product, Bette Midler's *The Divine Miss M* album, is brilliant, and she sounds great in every song. Somehow, every side of her multipersonality musicality comes through. In theory, an album consisting of so many divergent styles shouldn't have worked and should have failed to find an audience. But the LP was an instant smash, and over 100,000 copies were sold in the first month of its release, when it hit the stores in November of 1972. From the poignant "Hello in There," to the trashy "Leader of the Pack," to the rocking "Daytime Hustler," every cut stands out. Like a jigsaw puzzle, each song represents another equally valid piece of Midler's singing talent. Each song is like a vignette or a one-act play. She convinces you that she *IS* that dejected senior citizen in "Hello in There," that she *IS* that gum-chewing motorcycle slut in "Leader of the Pack," and that she *IS* all three of the Andrews Sisters—Patty, Maxine, and LaVerne—on "Boogie Woogie Bugle Boy." Talk about an incredible album!

After a year in the making, finally, this album was the ideal debut album for Bette. She showed off her ability to really connect with a sensitive and heartfelt ballad. Joel Dorn was the perfect producer to bring out this side of her vocal talent on songs like "Do You Want to Dance?" and "Hello in There," while Barry Manilow was perfect for showing off her bawdy, trashy, retro-loving side on "Chapel of Love," "Leader of the Pack," and "Daytime Hustler," which were fittingly ragged and wild. This became the mass public's introduction to the rock & roll side of Bette Midler's career.

At the time of the release of *The Divine Miss M,* Mike Jan of *Cue* magazine wrote, "Considering the spectacularly funny nature of her career thus far, she would have been forgiven for seizing the opportunity to goof off on the record, to present ten or twelve puffy parodies of old rock songs and popular songs from the thirties and forties, and that would be it. Few probably expected more. Yet Miss Midler has provided much more. Half the album's ten songs are ballads. Nobody opens her recording career with five ballads without shooting for vocal respectability. Miss Midler clearly is and for it she richly deserves praise" (44).

"Do You Want to Dance?" became a smash hit when it was released as a single in December of 1972. The song made it to Number 17 on the *Billboard* charts. When it came time to release a second single, Barry Manilow and Bette went back into the recording studio and completely rerecorded "Boogie Woogie Bugle Boy," with a punchier and much more modern arrangement. For this one single song, it was Manilow—alone—producing Miss M. Like the original Dorn-produced LP version, it featured Bette singing all three of the vocal parts. On the

Manilow-produced version there is a brief section without instruments, where three different Midler voices—in slightly different keys—can distinctly be heard harmonizing together. The Manilow-produced single version of "Boogie Woogie Bugle Boy" became Bette's first Top 10 hit, peaking in *Billboard* magazine at Number 8.

To further illustrate the contrast between Dorn's approach and Manilow's style, one need only listen to the two versions of "Boogie Woogie Bugle Boy" back-to-back. Joel's version is on *The Divine Miss M*, while Barry's is featured on Midler's 1993 greatest hits album, *Experience the Divine*. The Dorn one is more faithfully 1940s-sounding, while the Manilow version is snappier and has more sassy bounce to it.

Originally released in 1972, *The Divine Miss M* album made it to Number 9 on the LP chart in America, and it was quickly certified Gold, signifying sales of over half a million copies in America. A single version of "Friends," with "Chapel of Love" on the "B" side, was released in 1973 and made it to Number 40. Very quickly, because of the unprecedented success of *The Divine Miss M* LP, Bette Midler wasn't just a New York City cult performer anymore; she was suddenly an overnight national sensation.

HIGHER AND HIGHER

With the release of Bette's *The Divine Miss M* album, the obvious
course of action was to go out on the road and promote the hell out of
it. That's when Aaron Russo really swung into action.

Russo had come from a New York City garment-district family. The
family business was women's undergarments—and Aaron had no interest in that line of work whatsoever. Instead he opted to get involved in
the rock & roll scene. He worked for a nightclub called the Electric
Circus in New York City, and in the late 1960s he moved to Chicago,
where he managed a group that never made it big, called the Flock. His
biggest claim to fame in the Windy City was as manager of a multimedia
entertainment club known as the Kinetic Playground. He was also involved in the East Town Theater in Detroit.

In the early 1970s, Russo had been following Midler's career from
afar, having seen her on *The Tonight Show* and having been in the
audience with his wife, Andrea, when Bette performed at the Bitter
End in New York City. His growing infatuation with Bette was said to
be the reason for the demise of his marriage. When Bette had become
something of a local legend in Chicago at Mr. Kelly's, he plotted his
course of action and won her allegiance.

His timing was perfect. Things were beginning to happen so fast for
her that she was frightened of fouling it all up before she really hit the
big time. How could she break away from the Continental Baths and
the gay scene and into the mainstream without alienating anyone in the

transition? And how was she going to break into the big time without having to become some sort of "cheese bomb" Las Vegas creation? She knew that she needed help, and all of a sudden . . . there was Aaron Russo.

With her debut album busy disappearing from record-store shelves, the time was ripe for Aaron to make good his promises. In November of 1972, Bette performed again at the Continental Baths. This engagement, at long last, was her final farewell night at the steam bath that had made her a star. She joked onstage that Steve Ostrow was having a difficult time filling her spot—and her bra—at the Baths, now that she was playing there for the very last time. She announced that Josephine the Plumber (actress Jane Withers's fictional character in 1970s kitchen-scouring cleanser TV advertisements) had been approached, but not even SHE could remove the stains from the drains at the Continental! But beneath the jokes, Bette was not at all happy about that last gig.

Steve Ostrow had obviously sensed that this was to be his last shot at exploiting his gay bathhouse with Miss Midler, and he was going to take full advantage of the situation. So many people were jammed into the place that last night that it was a true fire hazard.

Bette later recounted, "When I looked out and saw how many people that bastard Ostrow had packed into that place, I was sick!" (45). Although Ostrow was made out to be the villain, one of Midler's intimate friends confided that Russo "was the one who made her go back to the Baths, because he thought he could milk them for a buck. And she was furious with him ever after for that. He packed the place. She didn't want to do it. Ostrow has been asking her to come back, but the place was small and everything, and she at that point was very dedicated to growing. But Aaron knew that there was a buck to be made, and he packed the house. It was like sardines in there" (35).

Looking back on her experiences at the Continental Baths, Bette later stated in her book *A View from a Broad,* "For some reason, which will forever remain a mystery to me, the idea of a woman entertaining an audience dressed only in towels—an all-male audience, and homosexual, yet—is to every reporter I have ever met at once repulsive yet endlessly fascinating. . . . I always performed *en costume.* It's true that occasionally I did wear a towel. But on my head, with some bananas and cashews hanging from it, as part of my tribute to Carmen Miranda and all the fruits and nuts of the world. . . . And by the way, just for the record, I never laid my eyes on a single penis, even though I was looking real hard" (46).

In any case, Midler's days at the tubs were officially over, and it was on to bigger and better gigs. Although she was a legend in New York City at this point, there was a whole country out there that didn't know what she was all about. Right after the Baths she headlined several small rock clubs that were famous launching pads for recording artists: the Troubadour in Los Angeles, the Boarding House in San Francisco, and the Club Bijou in Philadelphia.

The real triumph came when she returned to New York City in December of 1972 to headline two sold-out concerts at Philharmonic Hall on New Year's Eve: one early show at 8:00 P.M. and one late show at 11:00 P.M. Those two shows at Lincoln Center were the hottest tickets in all of Manhattan that New Year's Eve!

Bette dazzled the crowd from her very first seconds on stage. She was carried in from the wings in a sedan chair swagged in red velvet drapes, so that only a dangling leg protruded. When the curtain was drawn, there was Bette sheathed in white satin, with a big "shit-eating grin" on her face. The crowd went wild that night, especially at the late show when she made an exit before the stroke of midnight and reappeared in a diaper and a sash with the numerals "1973" emblazoned across her chest. The audience was aglow in silver and sequins, and she made it clear for them that the new year was going to become known as "the year of Bette Midler."

The press had a field day, lavishing her with praise for her appearances during the last two months of 1972. *The New York Times* called her "a bona fide original . . . an enormously theatrical young woman who possesses an uncanny singing talent. . . . the first white show woman of the current pop era!" (47). *Billboard* magazine exclaimed, "Bette Midler showed how spellbinding a true entertainer can be in this era of mediocrity hiding behind the banner of laid-back naturalness!" (2). And the *New York Daily News'* rock critic, Lillian Roxon, who was blown away by Bette on New Year's Eve, declared, "It was heaven. . . . I can't remember when I last saw a performer work so hard and give off and get so much love. . . . she does all the things no one does anymore, and I wish the rock & roll brigade would learn from her. . . . [She was] stalking and stomping around the stage like a hyena on speed!" (49).

That particular night was another turning point in Bette's career, and she herself knew it. She was going to become the major music-industry sensation that she had hoped to become, but she knew that it was time for some changes. She looked out into the audience that evening and announced to her cheering fans who had fallen in love with her when she was the wild woman of the Baths, "I hope you stay with me, even when I don't always do what you want me to. Next year you won't even recognize me" (26).

Was she going to abandon the gay crowd who discovered her first? This was the big question that particular statement posed to many members of the audience that night.

"Me and those boys, we just went somewhere else. It was so much fun. I had the best time. It was something I just had to do, and I did it for them, and I did it all. And I must say, they probably saw the most inspired of it. It was really abandon. I did some crap, I did some good stuff, and I learned a lot," she explained of her emergence from the Continental Baths (8). "Essentially, they gave me a big push and we had some good times, but they are all there, and I'm constantly moving" (11). Indeed she was.

The year 1973 saw changes in her act as well. Melissa Manchester left the troupe right after New Year's, and she was replaced by Charlotte Crossley. Charlotte recalled having seen Bette's act at Mr. Kelly's in Chicago: "I checked them out, you know, and they were real cool. They were like very bland white girls, in a way, but kind of great. Bette kept screamin' at them to get an attitude. I thought they were really slick, but bland. I mean, blander than the Ronettes. It was nice, because they all had dark hair, and they all looked alike, and they were real cute, but they were real quiet. They sounded great, of course—they had all been studio singers, and they sounded great" (48).

According to Charlotte, Melissa was her favorite Harlette, "I noticed her because she had the most personality." When Crossley was asked to become her replacement, Melissa got together with her to teach her the singing and the choreography. "We just got right down and started singing songs together. Melissa left me with great feelings and really taught me a lot about the music. I got to know her pretty well. It's funny, because a lot of people say that she's a lot like Bette. Vocally, they go to the same voice teacher, and they do have little things in their voices that are similar, I think. But they're not at all alike. Personality-wise, Melissa is a very cooled-out calm person" (48).

In Bette's personal life, her affair with Michael Federal had cooled down, but he remained her bass player. According to Midler at the time,

"I'm good when I'm in love. I'm hot on stage, too. I just enjoy it. I try to be in love all the time, I keep my eyes open" (8).

According to Buzzy Linhart, Bette was still in love with drummer Luther Rix at the time, and she resumed her affair with him. Buzzy explains that around this time, "Bette got so sick of being separated all of the time, 'cuz she was touring by this time, and I was touring with Luther, that we actually, like a baseball team, traded Luther Rix to Bette Midler, and I got this young genius named Kevin Ellman—twenty-two years old at the time—who became the first drummer in the great band Utopia, that Moogy, my co-author of 'Friends,' was also a co-founder of. We traded Luther and Kevin straight-away so that they could finally be in love and on the road together" (37).

Now that her dreams of stardom were coming true, Bette was becoming more realistic about show business. "I used to want to be Bette Davis in one of those great thirties movies where everyone's wearing furs and drinking martinis. I used to believe that," she explained. "I don't think I'm rabid to be a star. Now that I've met a few, I realize it's all the same, we're all the same. There's no difference. I met Bob Dylan, after looking for him for seven years, and I was in shock. I had worshiped him. But he lives, he has flesh, has these shirts, sometimes he plays good, sometimes he plays bad, sometimes he sings good, he writes a good song, he writes a bad song, he's a human being" (4).

"I'm all my fantasies!" she was quick to admit. No matter how realistic she attempted to become, she was addicted to performing: "Every time I get up there, it's 'magic time.' I have a little event. It's getting more and more theatrical, too; when we work on a stage that actually has a proscenium, it's fabulous, it takes on a whole other dimension, it really is like a little show. What I have is the ability to make people look at me. It just comes on like a light bulb. And it feels like a light bulb. It feels warm inside" (8). Bette Midler was in the perfect position to become a major superstar as 1973 began, and she was about ready to really turn the wattage on—full blast.

Bette Midler's first mammoth cross-country 1973 tour began in Rochester, New York, in February. The press that she had received up until this point had greatly accentuated that she had really gotten her start singing in a gay bathhouse, so the audiences that she drew, even in the remotest places, were very gay. Much of her comedy patter on stage would be culled from references to whatever gay bar, gay street, gay area, or gay figures existed in any given city. Members of her entourage sought out such information, and Bill Hennessey wrote up special material to tailor Bette's jokes to the vicinity.

After several months of playing places like Troy, New York, and Passaic, New Jersey, the spring tour concluded in San Francisco—the gay Mecca of them all. After that, both Merle and Gail followed Melissa Manchester's lead and resigned as Harlettes to pursue their own musical careers.

During this period, Bette continued to make appearances on television as well. One of the TV shows during this era was a guest spot on a special called *Burt Bacharach—Opus No. 3*, on which she performed "Boogie Woogie Bugle Boy." Thanks to a "split screen," on the show Bette portrayed all three of the Andrews Sisters in 1940s outfits.

According to her, "It was great fun. I don't remember any of the parts 'cause I've sung the melody all these months. So Barry and I re-did all the parts, each part one on top of the other, and it was great. It was a great experience, 'cause I never thought I could do that. I never thought my ears were that good, 'cause it's really tricky. Those harmonies are very hard. I don't know how those girls did it—I don't know how the Andrews Sisters did it!" (6). It was this version of the song that was ultimately released as the single version of "Boogie Woogie Bugle Boy," because it was so much livelier than the original album version of the same song.

Due to the fantastic job that Bette did on the Burt Bacharach special, which was produced and aired by ABC-TV, the network struck a deal with Bette to have her own special the next season. On June 19, 1973, ABC-TV issued a press release with the headline "First Starring Television Special for Singer Bette Midler Will Be ABC Television Network Attraction during 1973–1974." Although this show was optioned, it never materialized. ABC was very reserved about the show's potential content, and Bette and Aaron wanted to make the show as outrageous as possible. They never saw eye to eye.

Bette explained at that time, "I really wanted to do a shabby show, a really sleazy, tacky, shabby show. But the agency and the network are a bit conservative. They wanted Johnny Mann, they want the Ding-a-Lings. I want sleaze, I want sequins" (6). It would be several years before she finally had her own TV special . . . on another network.

At this time, Bette was still stinging from an ugly television experience she had had a couple of seasons before when she appeared on the very staid *Mike Douglas Show*. Also on the bill for that particular show was Lawrence Welk, the old-guard king of polka/swing.

"He thought I was a dirty little girl," recalled Bette of the Welk nightmare. "Welk was supposed to dance with me and he wouldn't. . . . Maybe I wasn't his type. We were supposed to do this little polka and he immediately went for someone who looked a lot different from the way I looked even though I certainly polka as well as Lawrence Welk, God knows! And I remember I used to talk about it in my act, because I was quite hurt by it. . . . That was the last time I did *Mike Douglas*, and I vowed I would never, never appear with them again" (8).

The joke that she used to tell in her act had to do with the fact that Lawrence Welk was afraid that she was going to give him a case of body crabs. And according to her, "He should be so lucky!" Although she poked fun at the incident, in a way it did upset her, because Lawrence Welk was one of her father's favorite performers, and it was like making a fool of yourself in front of one of your parents' friends.

Although Bette was becoming quite a big star in America, her parents never came to the mainland to see their daughter perform. This was a two-edged sword. On one hand, she was relieved that her mom and dad had yet to witness their little girl telling dirty jokes and gyrating in front of thousands of totally off-the-wall people, while dressed in outfits that were suitable for any of the Frederick's of Hollywood catalogs. Yet she was also hurt that her parents would be ashamed by her behavior in public.

She admitted to the *New York Times* in early 1973 that "They've seen me on TV, but I would never work live in front of my parents. My father would kill himself, he would jump off the roof, he would die. My father is very, very conservative, and I wouldn't do that to him, because he's okay, you know, he's a good man. He always tried real hard" (3).

Since *The Divine Miss M* album had sold almost three million copies at this point, it was time to go back into the recording studio to work on her second album. After Barry Manilow had proved his talents to Atlantic Records by supervising the rerecording of several of the cuts on Bette's first album, he was enlisted the produce the entirety of the *Bette Midler* album—along with Arif Mardin.

By now, Barry Manilow was justifiably self-confident about his talents. While Bette was doing other things, Barry had busily put together his own demo tape and had negotiated his own recording contract with Bell Records. He wasn't about to spend the rest of his days playing second fiddle to Midler. (Oddly enough, Clive Davis, the president of Columbia Records, who had not been impressed with Bette's act at Downstairs at the Upstairs the year before, had bought Bell Records, changed the company's name to Arista Records, and signed Manilow—*and* Melissa Manchester—and turned them into two of the label's biggest stars.)

When Midler's self-titled second album was released, it was a matter of: If you liked *The Divine Miss M,* you LOVED the *Bette Midler* LP. It took the schizophrenic formula that made its predecessor a smash and kicked it up several notches.

Again, it owed much of its success to the production talents of Barry Manilow. Although it is accredited as being produced by Arif Mardin and Manilow, Barry's influence in the studio was again paramount to the finished product. This statement is in no way meant to discredit or lessen the vast talent of Atlantic Records' house producer, Mardin—who is responsible for so many wonderful albums (by Aretha Franklin, Carly Simon, Chaka Khan, *and* later Midler albums). However, on the *Bette Midler* album, Manilow's influence fully permeates every single cut. He is not only the coproducer, but all of the songs were completely "arranged and conducted" by him. Furthermore, he plays all of the piano parts, plays percussion, and even sings in the background. Knowing this, it is easy to understand why Bette later felt lost without Manilow, when he left her camp to pursue his own massively successful singing career. This album's liner notes feature the prominent line "Barry Manilow appears through the courtesy of Bell Records," so the die was clearly already cast for his own exit.

Several of New York City's top studio musicians were used on the Bette Midler album. Ralph Mac Donald, Will Lee, Steve Gadd, and Don Grolnick are among the professionals on the tracks. In addition, Bette's boyfriend, Luther Rix, was utilized on the drums and on percussion.

The original 1973 vinyl album was divided into two distinct sides—the first side was the torch and blues side, and side two was the camp and rock side. The album opens with two of the songs that Bette had heard on Aretha Franklin's 1964 tribute LP to Dinah Washington—*Unforgettable*—which she had fallen in love with years before. They were Hoagy Carmichael and Johnny Mercer's optimistically longing "Skylark" and the desolate "Drinking Again," by Mercer and Doris Tauber. Midler had played the *Unforgettable* album over and over again, and she had sung those songs so many times that when it came time to record them here, she was able to milk every emotion-filled lyric for all its worth. The desperation in her voice on "Drinking Again" makes one want to just open a bottle of booze and drown one's sorrows along with her.

Next came her gutsy and soulful rendition of the ultra-trampy Denise LaSalle hit "Breaking Up Somebody's Home." On this wailing recording, there is no question that Miss M doesn't give a damn whose marriage she ruins in her hot pursuit of love. She then exposes her theatrical roots on her interpretation of Kurt Weill's "Surabaya Johnny." In this song Bette switches roles—from the homewrecker in "Breaking Up" to the heartbroken lover in "Surabaya," professing love with a lying and deceitful man. The album side then concludes with her impassioned rendition of Bob Dylan's "I Shall Be Released," which she turns into a woman's liberation anthem. Her singing is so conviction-filled, and Manilow's arrangement is so sweeping, that she sings the hell out of it and makes it all her own.

Although modern compact discs run these ten album cuts back-to-back, originally you had to get up and walk over to the turntable to flip over the disc to switch to the campy and comically side of Miss M. The second half of the album kicks off with a couple of lines of the Munchkin-sung *Wizard of Oz* song "Optimistic Voices," which is used as a lead-in to the Busby Berkeley camp of "Lullaby of Broadway."

Milking her 1940s nostalgia trip for maximum joy, next comes Bette's jubilantly swinging rebirth of Glenn Miller's "In the Mood." It is followed by the ultimate trashy girl group medley: "Uptown" (The Crystals), "Don't Say Nothing Bad (about My Baby)" (The Cookies), and "Da Doo Ron Ron" (The Crystals). Then on "Twisted," Bette takes the silly Annie Ross (of Lambert, Hendricks, & Ross) mental therapy classic and transforms it into a wacky two-faced conversation with herself—making it truly twisted with self-mocking humor. Finally, she interprets the Jackie Wilson classic "Higher and Higher," which she sings faster and faster, turning it into an exhaustive smash. The *Bette Midler* album is a worthy successor to *The Divine Miss M*—in many ways, surpassing it in style and excitement. With it, she had recorded and released a pair of successive hit albums—which created a hard act for even her to follow.

On this disc, Manilow distilled the two sides of Bette's musical personality and devoted one half of the album to each distinctly different persona. The *Bette Midler* LP, which was released in late 1973, was to become a huge success. It peaked at Number 6 on the *Billboard* magazine album charts, surpassing *The Divine Miss M*'s peak position of Number 9.

There was only one single released off the *Bette Midler* album. It was the nostalgic Glenn Miller song "In the Mood," which made it to Number 51 in America on the pop chart.

During the recording of the album, Aaron Russo had been busily planning a grand tour of large auditoriums across America for the fall of 1973. The tour was to provide the final push toward Bette's dramatically growing stardom. Her mainstream popularity had begun in the spring of 1973 with a small college-town tour. With the *Bette Midler* album in the can, it was time to hit the road and catapult Midler to solid superstardom. The four-month-long road show was to end up back in New York City, with Bette starring in her own Broadway revue version of the same show at the Palace Theater. The planning was brilliant, and the strategy was going to work to a tee. By the end of the tour, Bette *would* a legend.

But real conflicts were about to occur along the way. When Bette came to Barry with the final details for the upcoming tour and handed him the itinerary, he announced that he had just recorded his own album and his contract called for him to perform live in concert to promote his record. If Bette wanted him as her musical director and piano player on this tour, she would have to give him his own spot in her show. She was mad, pissed, frightened, scared, furious, and shocked . . . all at once. What was she going to do? No one could do what Barry could with her music. She didn't have time to train a new musical director, and she knew that she couldn't be confident with anyone else behind her on this crucial tour.

This was professional blackmail, and she had only one choice. Bette's show was to be divided into two acts, with an intermission in-between. She would do the first act, the curtains would come down, and an intermission would begin. Then Barry would be introduced at the end of the intermission, he would play three of his own songs, and Bette would make her own second-act entrance. While he was onstage, Barry would continue as her piano player. And that is exactly what happened.

It was perfect for Manilow, because he was scared to death of performing alone onstage at this point in his career. He could overcome his stage fright with his first-act piano playing, and even if no one paid any attention to his three second-act numbers, Bette would soon make her entrance and save him. By the end of the show the crowd would be on its feet in thunderous applause for the evening's entertainment, and Barry would share in the glory.

Stage-frightened Manilow knew that he had played his cards just perfectly, and this tour was going to get his own solo singing career off to a brilliant start. As he explained it several months afterward, "I was thrown from behind the piano! Because at that time [Arista] was Bell Records, and they wouldn't give me an album deal unless I promised I would go out and perform. I didn't really want to go out and perform, but I did want to make records, because I really loved being in the studio. So I put an act together, you know, I think I know how to do that: I've been doing that for about ten years and coaching people. So it was easy enough to put that together. I made sure that part was solid, because I had never performed, and I figured if I fainted on the stage, nobody should know it. The act would be so good, so strong, that nobody would realize that I was just dying up there. So we put it together, and it came out real strong, and it gave me a foundation to be able to make mistakes as a performer" (50).

Bette and Barry auditioned over seventy potential Harlettes for this tour and finally hired a petite black girl named Sharon Redd and a tall white girl named Robin Grean, to join statuesque black diva Charlotte Crossley. By this point, a comedy writer named Bruce Vilanch had also joined Midler's inner circle. So much of Bette's stage act was howlingly funny because of her snide and witty comments delivered mid-act. Vilanch established his comedy writing career based largely on the bitchy one-liners he penned for Bette.

According to Bruce Vilanch, he had met Bette in Chicago, during one of her engagements at Mr. Kelly's. He was writing a column for one of the local newspapers at the time. Openly gay, Vilanch brought his own bitchy/witty sense of humor to Miss M's act. They have been working together ever since.

The 1973 tour began in August and encompassed thirty-five cities over a period of four months. It was a roaring success. During the tour, both Bette's and Barry's albums were released: *Bette Midler* and *Barry Manilow I*. All six of the Harlettes—to date—contributed background vocals to either or both albums.

One of the first stops on the tour was Honolulu, Hawaii—Bette's hometown. She was a nervous wreck during her whole stay there. On one hand, she was fulfilling a lifelong dream of showing off as an un-precedented success in front of her former classmates, who never thought she'd amount to anything.. And on the other hand, her mom and dad still lived there, and she had to deal with her decidedly risqué act and her onstage antics falling under the scrutiny of her parents.

Both nights that she played Honolulu, there in Row C was her mother, Ruth Midler; her sister Susan; and her brother Danny. Her father out-and-out refused to attend. Bette said that she was relieved, but in actuality she couldn't help but be a bit upset and hurt that he wasn't there to share in her glory.

"One parent was there," she explained of that night. "My mother came, but my father, oh, he just said, 'Oh, I just can't.' He's read some things about me, you know, and he's very conservative. He likes Law-rence Welk! He doesn't like too much cleavage. In fact, every time I went over there for dinner, he made me safety-pin my dress together. I was glad my father didn't come to see me perform. I would have been afraid to be dirty or gross, afraid that he would walk out or start yelling at me. He's a good, old-fashioned man. He doesn't want anyone to think that anyone from his family is cheap. I don't know why I love to parody all that cheap music stuff. It's so dumb. But I have so much fun doing it" (4).

Ruth Midler loved seeing her daughter blossom on stage. Said Bette, "Oh God, my mother got a charge, though. She kept screaming, 'Faaaa-bulous! Faaaabulous!'" A thrilled Ruth explained after the concert, "We always knew she was witty, but we didn't know she was THAT witty. I'm so proud of her because she makes so many people happy!" (4).

The second night in Honolulu, Radford High's class of 1963 held a reunion. That night on stage Bette announced, "Well, I'm going to a reunion of all the people who couldn't stand me!" Naturally, by the end of the class reunion that evening her face was wet with nostalgic tears: "I don't want to leave so early. I didn't get a chance to say 'good-bye' to Judy and Jane and . . . Oh, I just wish I could stay" (4).

The tour continued on to Los Angeles where she played at the Uni-versal Amphitheater. At that engagement, there were several Holly-wood stars in the audience, including the two surviving Andrews Sisters, Patty and Maxine. Patty Andrews was heard to exclaim, "She's certainly different!" after meeting Bette (6). Oddly enough, Bette's ver-sion of "Boogie Woogie Bugle Boy" was such a smash that it revived interest in the Andrews Sisters, and the following spring Patty and Maxine opened on Broadway in their own hit show, *Over Here.*

Wherever she went on this tour, audiences and critics were astounded by the amount of energy that she expended on stage, pacing from one side of it to the other in her chunky platform shoes and sequined gowns slit up to her crotch. Explained Bette, "When I'm out here I work. If people are paying money, they're entitled to see an artist work his buns off. I want to do something beautiful that will last forever. Maybe I'll never do it, and maybe everyone will laugh at me and say, 'She's just a fool,' but I don't think I am" (4). Neither did her growing legion of fans. In mid-October, when the tickets went on sale for her dates at Broadway's Palace Theater, Bette set a record for one-day box-office ticket sales of $148,000!

"Well, are you ready for low-rent retro rock & roll?" she would shout on stage from San Francisco, California, to Austin, Texas. And the answer was always a resounding "Yes!" Shaking her breasts and her rear end, she would announce, "I want you aaaall to know from the outset that we really busted our buns on this next one."

Although she was a singing superwoman on stage, every once in a while she had self-doubts. Was the world really in love with homely little Bette Midler from Honolulu, or was it the fictitious Miss M who was the real star? "I had a real trauma on this tour in Denver," she later admitted. "We were playing out in the middle of God-made country in the Red Rocks Amphitheater, and I felt so helpless against the elements that I thought I had to do this big show-biz thing, you know, where I was giving the people only what they expected of the Divine Miss M—but nothing of myself. During the break I sat there and figured it out, and for the next set I took off my makeup, put on my pants and shirt and tried to harmonize with Red Rocks just by being little old me. Miss M is a show—much larger than life. Bette Midler is just a person with a few things to say and a few songs to sing. From now on, I'm going to be Bette Midler" (4).

From October 18 to 20, Bette played in Detroit at Masonic Auditorium. It was the hottest ticket in town since the Motown Revue had disbanded and the original Supremes went their separate ways. By the time Bette took the stage, the regally decorated hall reeked of marijuana smoke. After her opening number Midler glanced overhead to the two huge crystal chandeliers that hung down from the ceiling and announced, "If this place ever goes bankrupt, they could sell those two chandeliers to Diana Ross for earrings!"

The tour was a roaring smash, but there was a lot of pressure on the road as well. Barry and Bette loved to fight with each other. Manilow is a perfectionist, and he wanted things to go exactly the way he had planned them. Bette was forever changing the order of the songs midshow. "Oh, Mr. Music," she would say, looking across the stage to him. "Let's not do 'Surabaya Johnny' tonight, let's do 'Superstar' instead" (38). Barry would give her a look that could kill, grit his teeth, and comply with her request. Backstage after the show, he threatened to strangle her with his bare hands if she ever did that again. They threw tantrums, and sometimes ashtrays, at each other backstage in anger.

"I like fighting," explains Bette. "I always thought that a woman fighting was very sexy. My sister and I would always fight night and day. I think I have a strange sense of humor" (38).

But her fights with Barry were great for releasing tension. "Barry and I worked so fast. It was two ambitious Jews in one room, such bitchiness!" she remembers. "We would bitch at each other all the time. He very rarely did an arrangement I didn't like. He's a much better musician than I. We would mostly bicker about which song should go where and how the show should be paced . . . and whether he was going to wear white tails or not. . . . and would he pleeeeeeeeeeeeeas stop waving his head . . . and would he not sit on phone books, if he didn't mind . . . and could he get the bass player to stop tossing his blond locks around. He would always want to know how come I was always half a note under and why I didn't come in on time. And it's true that sometimes he would insist on something that I would take to heart and get real spiteful about" (38).

By the time Bette rolled back into New York City, she was ready to take the world by storm, and the fights with Aaron Russo reached a peak. She had commanded him to make her a legend, and he was doing it. For her engagement at the Palace Theater, the portrait of Judy Garland was removed from the lobby and one of Bette hung in its place.

To most of the people in Bette's entourage, Russo represented a very driven and talented person who was able to get things done. He was also someone who was used to getting his own way.

At the time that Bette was about to open at the Palace Theater, Russo was already looking ahead to bigger and better gigs for her. His attitude alienated several people, however. "We're open to all offers, but we're in no hurry," he proclaimed, prior to the Broadway opening. "I believe in taking things one at a time, and right now it's just the Palace and probably another album after she gets some rest. She has no financial worries—I've invested all of her earnings in gold—and I'm trying to keep her from getting too grand. At heart, you know, Bette Midler's just a 'schlepper'—a good Jewish girl who happens to have a lot of ability" (4).

Typical Aaron Russo. Building up Bette Midler, while putting her down at the same time. One night during the Palace engagement, which ran for three weeks, Bette and Aaron had a knock-down drag-out fight backstage before the curtain for Act One went up, and just to infuriate her, Aaron dumped a full glass of Coca-Cola on top of her head. Bette was so humiliated and mad at him for having done that to her that the incident was later repeated in the film *The Rose.*

For Bette Midler, 1973 had been one hell of a year, and she was really turning into the legend she had hoped to become. However, with the prize within her grasp, superstardom began to seem as terrifying as it was exciting. "Now that it's beginning to happen," she explained at the time, "I really don't think a lot about the theater or movie offers or about the money. I have a small four-room apartment in the Village in New York with a little garden, and I still ride the subway all the time. Marriage? I'm not going to get married. Who's going to marry me?" (8).

7

INSTANT STARDOM / INSTANT BREAKDOWN

By the end of the year, the whole country was talking about the divine Bette Midler. When *Newsweek* magazine put her on the cover of its December 17, 1973, issue, not even conservative Middle America could miss the arrival of the outrageous Miss M.

In the *Newsweek* piece, writer Charles Michener raved about Midler's appeal. "In this age of pseudo-phenomena, Bette Midler is the genuine article—and a surprising one at that," he proclaimed. "Few performers since the Beatles have been so heralded as the harbinger of a 'new era'—or analyzed so seriously by the media. In March [1973], the normally sober *National Observer* called her, in a feature that top-headlined the front page, 'Probably the brightest, hottest superstar to rise above the pop music horizon in the '70s" (4).

In a decade remembered for its hedonistic excesses, Bette Midler was the wise-cracking new multimedia goddess of the 1970s. Her blend of old and new fashion and musical styles, her onstage excitement, and her bawdy persona made Miss M a breath of outrageously fresh air. In a world that craved the "next big thing," Bette had suddenly become "it."

When her fall 1973 tour came to an end on Broadway, the box-office grosses for the thirty-five-city extravaganza came to a dramatic $3 million. *Variety,* the weekly show-business Bible of a newspaper, described the Palace debut: "Klieg lights (despite the energy crisis), celebs, drag queens, and the Broadway opening night establishment were out in force for the event." Although her fans were going berserk with sheer delight, several critics took pause. The same piece in *Variety* noted that she was "less than fresh from an exhausting national tour" and that her "voice was strained, unable to sustain higher registers and sometimes breaking mid-note. She still lacks the sustained confidence and/or guidance to just stand there and sing, but when she manages it, as she did briefly on opening, she is a knockout. . . . Developing a wider range and protecting that tough vulnerability that is her own should ensure Midler the kind of lasting career her raw talent deserves" (51).

The *New York Daily News* proclaimed that she was "not divine . . . but Miss M is very special. . . . when the current is on and that oh-so-clever patter is off, she is very special, for her voice goes deep and her voice gets throaty, her voice goes folksy, and her voice goes bluesy and just about every which way you might choose a lyric to be caressed." The same review also noted, "Her showstoppers came after she descended a stairway molded like a glass slipper silhouetted against a New York skyline backdrop . . . when she walked out on the Palace stage . . . the boys who worshiped Judy Garland, Bette Davis, and Tallulah Bankhead started cheering" (52). If the newly established 1970s "gay liberation" movement needed a prom queen diva to call its own, Bette Midler was assuredly this—hands down.

This tour de force of a tour had indeed left Bette Midler exhausted and exhilarated. But according to several insiders, her behind-the-scenes battles with Aaron Russo left her wanting to chuck the whole thing, to run away and hide. For the most part, that is exactly what she did in 1974. After working her butt off for the entirety of 1973, the next year she made only two or three major public appearances and then disappeared from sight.

Bette Midler's collection of accolades, honors, and awards had begun in April of 1973 when gay-slanted *After Dark* magazine had awarded her its Entertainer of the Year prize, the Ruby Award. But it was in 1974 that she was to garner two of the biggest awards in the business: the Grammy and the Tony.

The Grammy Awards show was telecast in the beginning of March 1974. In her act Bette always poked fun at performers she didn't like or whose public personas were diametrically opposed to her own flamboyantly liberal self-image. And conservative Karen Carpenter was one of the ones she had the most fun ridiculing. Bette used to say onstage: "Karen Carpenter is so clean, you could run your finger down her and she would squeak!" When Bette Midler won the "Best New Artist" Grammy Award, who should present her with the statuette on national television but Karen and Richard Carpenter! Smiling for the cameras that night, Bette stood between the brother-and-sister singing team and announced, "Isn't that a kick? Me getting the award from Karen Carpenter. It's a wonder she didn't hit me over the head with it!" (25).

That spring, Bette was given a special Tony Award for her one-woman show at the Palace Theater. This time around, the award was presented to her by someone who had been very instrumental in creating the legend of Bette Midler: Johnny Carson. That evening was one of the happiest events of her career.

Whenever people suddenly hit it big, their past seems to come back to haunt them. This also happened to Bette Midler, in the form of a low-budget film she had participated in at a time when she was broke and desperately needed the cash. Filmed in 16mm in 1971, the project, a religious satire about the birth of Christ, was originally entitled *The Greatest Story Overtold.* Bette was paid $250 to appear for twelve minutes of screen time as . . . are you ready for this? . . . the Virgin Mary! Talk about casting against type!

When Bette suddenly hit it big, the film's director and producer, Peter Alexander (McWilliams), sensed a quick cash-in. After Alexander invested an additional $40,000 to transfer the film to projection-standard 35mm film stock, it was announced that Bette Midler's film debut was going to open at the Festival Theater in New York City under the advertised title "Bette Midler in *The Divine Mr. J.*" Aaron Russo did what he could to stop the film from opening, but failed. Since the advertising announced that the film starred Bette, Russo had people outside the theater handing out leaflets that carried a statement from Midler disavowing the project. The leaflets read: "In my opinion the movie is dreadful. However, I did it and there's nothing I can do about it except advise you of the true facts. If you still wish to see me in the film, *c'est la vie.*"

Although its critics felt that the film was a cheaply produced experiment, it was not without a sense of humor. Just before the Immaculate Conception, Bette is seen singing "I've Got a Date with an Angel." In another scene, looking obviously pregnant with the Christ child, Bette swings into "It's Beginning to Look a Lot Like Christmas." Although Russo was unable to stop the screening of the film, he succeeded in having the theater marquee title simply changed to *The Divine Mr. J.*, to further distance the project from Bette.

During 1974, two of Bette's former associates were busily attempting to launch their own careers, apart from Midler. Their association with her was so strong that both Melissa Manchester and Barry Manilow had to work twice as hard to establish their own identities.

According to Melissa, "When I first went solo, there was a tremendous amount of comparison, and interviews were mainly about Bette, which was very difficult to handle on any level. I don't like that. But that was just in the beginning, and it was understandable. It's always easier for people to compare you to someone else than to try to find something authentic or original. I am quite sure that there were lots of traits left over—it's difficult not to have them—but then, hopefully, after the years you come into your own" (53).

Manilow, however, took the momentum from his work with Bette in 1973 and used it to launch his own very successful career. In fact, when he began his first solo tour in 1974, he brought the Harlettes along with him as his backup singers. "I had them for my first tour," he explained. "They were out of work, and I knew them and they still knew my material. So I took them along with me. But when I came back from my first six months on the road, I decided I would get my own girls, because it was Bette's Harlettes. It's Bette's girls, it's not my girls. You know, even though I had them doing different things, it was still Bette's Harlettes. So I figured as long as I had decided on that type of group for Bette, I decided on the same type of group for me. So I hired three different girls" (50).

"I'm really not working with her anymore," he emphatically announced in 1975. "I'm her friend, you know, we hang out together, but I'm really not involved in that part of her life anymore. Eventually, I'm sure we'll get back together again. I mean, there's just no time. Frankly, I'd love to go back and get it out for her, to go back on the road with her would be a lot of laughs, but there's just no time. I don't know, in a couple of years we'll wind up with 'Bette and Barry'—in a tasteful BOXING RING!" he snidely quipped (50).

Meanwhile, in the Midler camp, the headlines could have read: "Diva goes into Seclusion . . . Nervous Breakdown Suspected." The negotiations with ABC-TV turned into one big mess, and her previously announced special was "on hold." Everything was happening too fast. Her fights with Aaron, whose jealousy of everyone around her was becoming unbearable, left her worn out and in desperate need of a rest. And so Bette Midler literally fled the country in a fit of soul-searching depression.

"I was so battered emotionally and physically that I thought I WOULD break down!" she explained. "I'd been in four or five cities a week with the same people who would always come to me with their problems. I had no one to talk to. Aaron and I had one of our famous battles." And so it was off to France to seclude herself in a hotel for several months. "I went to Paris, I swam, I read, I wrote, and watched TV. I had a mad, torrid love affair with a Frenchman. I really liked him for about two days, and then he held me captive" (8).

"Where was I? I was sitting around getting very chubby for a year!" she later disclosed, laughing. "I was so bruised and battered and I needed to rest. So I went to Paris, France, to become very elegant and I failed *mi-ser-a-bly!* You know, I thought I spoke French. Then I got there and I realized I didn't. But I ate my brains out!" (38).

In between croissants and other high-calorie French delicacies, Bette pondered the past few years. "I was on the way up, young and innocent," she illuminated philosophically, "and I didn't know that when you're on top, people took it upon themselves to shove you down. I thought I would be beloved. I thought they would love it for me. But they throw you out like yesterday's news. I didn't know that, really. I couldn't understand it either. I feel I'm generally generous, especially in terms of my performing. I would love it for someone else. [It] scared the hell out of me. I think in a roundabout way, that's why I took the time off. I needed a respite from the drive. After a while you get worn out. I'm not going to compare [myself with Greta] Garbo, but I think she made the right decision" (54). Like the equally divine Greta Garbo, did Bette really "*vant* to be alone"? Well, in reality—only long enough to reflect on what she had just accomplished and where she wanted to go with it.

Her view of the whole fame game had truly changed now that she had attained it. Originally, she had taken the stance that "I just try to have a good time and let the audience in on a secret. It's like giving a party and I am the *Grande Hostesse*. I always wanted to be Gertrude Stein and have a salon" (26). Suddenly, that innocent version of "everything is lovely" disappeared, and she was able to see show business for what it was.

Barry Manilow had quit working for her to concentrate on his own career, and several critics who originally loved her were now disparaging her. When her first album came out, *Rolling Stone* magazine gave her a glowing review. When her second album was released and her Palace engagement was over, the same magazine chewed her up alive. The reviewer, Jon Laudau, claimed the album "contains the artifacts of style without nuance, content, or intelligence" and further denounced it by saying that "Bette Midler's recorded performance of 'I Shall Be Released' is the worst performance of a Bob Dylan song I have ever heard" (55). That particular review was quite upsetting to her, according to several of her close friends.

When Bette returned from Paris at the end of the summer, she had had time to think and was beginning to adjust her perspective. "I don't really pay too much attention to the signs of success," she explained, "the people screaming. I don't want to be caught up in it. It's very dangerous to believe all the things they say about you. You can't be swept off your feet by it because it's not the truth, it's not everyday life. It doesn't have anything to do with being a human being. It has to do with being above the ordinary mortal. Real life is not like that" (8).

She was beginning to accept stardom without getting caught up in it. "I did it all for my own satisfaction," she continued, "to see if I could do it. To see if anyone could understand it if I put it in front of them, to see if there was anyone else out there who was dreaming the same dreams I was dreaming. I'm very lucky to have found my thing. I cannot fathom people doing for years what they hate. I think if you look hard enough, you're going to find something you like to do. I work like a dog, but I'm lucky to be able to. My first tour was so-o-o tiring, but it was fascinating. I could do anything I feel like doing if I put my mind to it. So now I'm trying to figure out what is the whole thing about? What is life about? And why is it people do certain things to each other and treat each other in certain ways?" (8).

By the end of 1974 it was time to quit asking questions and to discover some of the answers. The one question that everyone was asking as the year came to an end was: "Whatever happened to Bette Midler?"

CLAMS ON THE HALF SHELL

The reemergence of Bette Midler began in February of 1975 with an appearance on a highly rated television special, a gala press conference in Grand Central Station, and the announcement of a return to Broadway that spring. She was about to end her self-imposed exile on Barrow Street in the only way that she knew how to do anything: dramatically.

The television show that brought Bette back into living rooms across America was Cher's extravaganza, entitled simply *Cher*. It was something of a comeback for Cher, as well as for Bette. The two ladies had become friends when Cher showed up at the Universal Amphitheater in Los Angeles during Midler's 1973 tour. Cher had split up with her husband, Sonny Bono, the year before filming this special. The two of them had starred in their own highly successful variety series, *The Sonny & Cher Comedy Hour,* from 1970 to 1974, but their headline-grabbing divorce had split up the decade-long act the previous spring. Sonny's own fall 1974 TV series on ABC-TV was a huge bomb—critically, as well as in the ratings—and it had already been canceled. Now it was Cher's turn at starring in her own solo series.

The *Cher* show, the pop diva's own weekly Sunday night series, was due to debut on February 16, 1975. To kick off her return to TV-land, CBS broadcast an hour-long special the previous Wednesday evening. Cher wanted to make a big splash, so her high-profile guests were Elton John, Flip Wilson, and Bette Midler. Although Wilson was famous for his own early 1970s TV series, Elton and Bette were rarely seen on network television, and the show was a highly rated, delicious treat.

According to Cher at the time, "Everybody I'm having on the show are people I like to see. I'm tired of seeing the same old guest stars who show up on every show. I think it's important on a variety show to see people you don't ordinarily see" (56).

Bette's rationale for appearing on the special was a bit different from Cher's. Said Midler, "I wanted to do Cher's show because we're good friends. I thought I'd go out there and learn how to get my nails done and we'd call it a night. But then I looked so hot on the show! Ah, but that was later. Ya see, when I first arrived and went into rehearsal, I had just had a permanent. I looked like death. For the whole two weeks of rehearsals my hair was frizzed out and I wore no make-up. Well, they all looked at me like, 'Oh holy shit, what did Cher drag in from the East Coast?' Then when I showed up on the set for the taping looking like a human being, I swear there was an audible gasp from the control room. They were so relieved!" (38).

Most amusing at that time were Bette's views on California. "Hollywood! It's a very strange atmosphere," she commented after taping the Cher special that winter. "I find it very amusing. It doesn't have the soul New York has. I couldn't live out there. I couldn't deal with the fierce competition of the lifestyle—not just the work, but who you're seen with and what you're seen wearing. That environment depresses me. Also, it seems that every asshole in the U.S. lives in Los Angeles. . . . They have these little antennae that draw them to the West Coast" (38).

In retrospect, these comments are very ironic indeed, since Bette was destined to move to Los Angeles years later, when she became a movie star. However, for the time-being, she considered herself a dyed-in-the-wool New Yorker, through and through. Yet a career in the movies was already clearly fixed in her sights.

While in Los Angeles, Bette and Aaron met with several film producers to discuss her inevitable movie debut. According to Bette, "The one we really wanted was the film version of *Little Me*. Now we lost that one under very unusual circumstances. It all goes back to when [producer] Ross Hunter's *Lost Her Reason* [*Lost Horizon*] came out. Well, my dear, they threw us out of the theater, we were laughing so hard. . . . I never miss a Liv Ullmann musical! Well, anyway, Ross Hunter was very insulted. Aaron is not one to mince words, and when he met with Ross Hunter about another project, Aaron said something to him about questioning his judgment because he thought *Lost Horizon* was abominable. Well, word got out that we were after *Little Me,* and wouldn't ya know it, Hunter went out and bought it for Goldie Hawn!" (38).

Another bungled movie opportunity came when Bette was under consideration for the female lead in Mike Nichols's production of *The Fortune,* which would have found her opposite Jack Nicholson. Bette ended up provoking Nichols by asking him who he was and what his credentials were.

"I would have loved to work with Nicholson," she later explained, "but when I met Mike Nichols, I ended up insulting him because I had just been molested in the steam room [at] the Beverly Wilshire [Hotel]. I was staying there, and that the time, the masseur was the kind of guy who, if you wanted, would jump on your bones. I did not want, but I guess he thought I needed to have my bones jumped on, because this guy came on to me and wouldn't let go. He threw me into the shower and started soaping me up. I was very frightened because I'd never had that happen to me before. I was terrified he was going to whip 'it' on me any minute. And I couldn't get away. The guy kept me there past my hour, making me twenty minutes late for my meeting with Nichols" (30).

"By the time I got back to the suite, I was a nervous wreck. I sat down and didn't know where I was or who this guy was. I looked at Nichols, and all I thought was, 'Who is he?' I wanted to talk about his work, but I couldn't remember any of it. I couldn't even remember his name. . . . He ended up storming out of our meeting, absolutely furious. He told everybody what a *cooz* I was and how I had no business in the [movie] business" (30).

"Don't worry, we'll get around to doing a film," Aaron explained to the press. "For right now, though, I want Bette to come back to Broadway. She was offered *Mack and Mabel* and lots of other shows this year. That's not the kind of thing I want for her. I want to bring theatricality to rock and I want to make Bette the Queen of Broadway" (38).

Bette's career got a real shot in the arm when she was asked to appear on the TV special that kicked off Cher's post-Sonny TV series. The TV special made a huge splash, with a small fortune spent on costumes alone. The elaborate wardrobe for *The Cher Show* was as much a key element of the show as its star was. According to designer Bob Mackie at the time, "Depending on the number of costumes, Cher's clothes bill for her weekly show runs between $3,000 and $10,000. And for the special she did with Elton John and Bette Midler, the bill hit $30,000. I understand Cher's wardrobe is the biggest ever for a weekly TV show. But then, of course, her gowns are very much a part of the show—and since she owns the production company, she also owns all the clothes" (57).

Cher was very excited about her new special and weekly television show . . . at first. "The look is really hot!" she exclaimed before either of her shows aired. "It's not quiet. It doesn't lay back. It's just hot. It comes out and punches your brains out" (56). And that was just the set and costumes she was talking about.

During the 1970s, Bette Midler and Cher were best buddies. Later in the decade it was known that Cher also had a close friendship with Diana Ross. Cher liked these diva buddies so much that in the late '70s she included drag performers in her own act to impersonate Midler and Ross. Also from this era, Cher presented Bette with one of Midler's most prized possessions—a pair of multicolored rhinestone platform shoes. The shoes were later immortalized on the cover of the 1999 disco remix single of Bette's "I'm Beautiful." In 1999 *Ladies Home Journal* magazine ran a photo of the shoes, with Midler proudly explaining, "Those are my favorite platform shoes from 1972—Cher gave them to me" (17).

By 1975 Bette had elevated to a new level of media fame, and she began hanging with the superstar crowd. According to her at that time, "I don't think of myself as a star, I wish I could. I had fantasies about getting there, but I never had any about what I would do when I got there. I'm sort of in the lurch about how to behave. Actually, after expenses I made some good money. I ain't no Elton John, though. I'm not in that league. Elton showed me a check he'd just gotten for eight million bucks. But he did that just to be spiteful" (38).

In an interview that Bette had given Andy Warhol's *Interview* magazine before her year-long creative exile, she was asked what was next on her schedule. At a loss for an answer, she jokingly replied that she was going to star in *Dolores Jalapeno's Clams on the Half-Shell Revue*. Much to her surprise, when she returned from France in the autumn of 1974, Aaron informed her that the Minskoff Theater was booked and gave her a list of rehearsal and opening dates for her return to Broadway.

Exactly one week after the highly successful *Cher* special was broadcast, Bette hopped into a limousine in front of her Barrow Street apartment building and schlepped her way up to Grand Central Station to the underground restaurant the Oyster Bar, to discuss mollusks and music—and what one had to do with the other.

Over lunch with the press, she announced that she was to star in *Bette Midler's Clams on the Half-Shell Revue,* which would open on Broadway in April. She posed with the chef at the Oyster Bar, while munching on the raw seafood delicacies. The following Sunday, there was a full-page ad in the *New York Times* for the show, announcing that tickets would be going on sale the following day at the theater box-office. That was the only announcement that was made.

The very next day was a freezing cold rainy Monday in February, and people waited in line all day to get to the Minskoff ticket window. With a total gross of $200,000 that one day, Bette again broke the existing Broadway record—the one that she had set at the Palace a year and a half before.

Bette Midler's Clams on the Half-Shell Revue was to be the extravaganza to end them all, the one-woman show that even Cecil B. DeMille would be proud to have produced. It was to be Bette, her new musical director Don York, the Harlettes, Lionel Hampton, and the Michael Powell Ensemble, with sets by Tony Walton, directed by Joe Layton, and comedy material written by Bill Hennessey, Bruce Vilanch, and Jerry Blatt.

As Bette herself described it, "I never imagined it would turn into this epic of death. . . . the most mind-boggling, stupendous production ever conceived and built around one poor small five-foot-one-and-a-half-inch Jewish girl from Honolulu. All of a sudden I'm a whole industry. People run, they fetch, they carry, they nail, they paint, they sew. I had always dressed my girls from stock, and now there they are in real costumes. . . . they're pinning here and tucking here and pushing tits up to the neck and showing calves. Do you know what this is? It's a celebration of the sexual rites of a New Yorker!" (38).

The first and most important part of the production was to find a director who was used to variety revues. That was where Joe Layton came in. He had won an Emmy for his direction of Barbra Streisand and in fact had directed four of her TV specials.

The idea behind this extravaganza was to show off as many sides of Bette's talent as possible, while leaving enough room for Midler to be the semispontaneous Miss M persona she had created and nurtured. "She basically sings and talks a lot, but she is guided," is how Layton described the show's concept. "She's framed and cushioned so that she doesn't have to do two hours of killing herself. What I like about working with Bette is that she wears her whole presence on the outside. If she's mad at you, she comes at you with a knife. If she loves you, she gives you a smile. You never have to worry what she's thinking. It makes it much easier to deal with and gets the work done with great efficiency" (38).

The show was to have one of the jazz and swing greats from the 1940s open the second act and usher Bette into her "Boogie Woogie Bugle Boy"—and "Chattanooga Choo Choo"—era tunes. The producers originally tried to hire Benny Goodman for the slot, but he wasn't interested in a long Broadway run. Instead, they hired the vibraphonist who first found fame in 1936 playing with Goodman's trio and changed the act into a quartet. After leaving Goodman in 1940, Lionel Hampton formed his own big band. He had been a star in his own right ever since.

"Look at Lionel out there," said Bette during rehearsals. "He says doing this show is a learning experience for him. I say it is for me. Now I'll tell you something. I have never dared to sing Hoagy Carmichael's 'Stardust.' Really, it's a dream of mine. But now with Lionel playing 'Stardust' behind me, I'm doing it. We sound real good together. Wherever I go, he goes right along. You're really singing and it's a big challenge for me to keep up with him, because he knows a helluva lot more about music than I do. My ears are opening up!" (58).

Joe Layton admitted that the teaming of Bette and Lionel was a way of stretching Miss M into some new areas, especially since in that second act she would be sharing the stage with someone of whom she was in awe. "Take Hampton," said Layton. "Now that's a nice meeting of the minds. Bette does nostalgic stuff, music of the thirties and forties as well as the sixties and seventies. We're extending her, putting her with an all-time great who lived those years before she was born. They both love jazz, and he's reaching forward, and she's reaching back. They're stretching." Said Bette of Lionel, "We wanted someone of his strength to work with me. He was willing, and he was available. He wants to open a new door, and here he is seventy years old, opening new doors. He has more chops, more interest, more enthusiasm than most guys I know half his age. He just loves to work, and so do I. This is a revue, a salute to Lionel and a salute to me. It's not just me anymore standing out there busting my butt. My girls are working: The Harlettes. And we have the Powell gospel group. We have a new dimension" (58).

Hampton had just recently come out of the hospital, where he had been suffering from an intestinal infection. "After my illness, I wanted to come back with a big bang," he said prior to the opening. He was also enjoying working with Midler. "Bette does everything from the blues to rock. It's always the beat, has been since we were making it with 'Beat Me Daddy, Eight to the Bar.' There's nothing wrong with rock, nothing. So together we'll do it all. And I'm likely to teach her some authentic jive talk!" (58).

Bette promised to give her all for her audience this time around. "Suffice it to say there will be lots of tits and ass. The sets are beautiful. The costumes are gorgeous. Tony Walton, who did [the film] *Murder on the Orient Express*, created them. The sets are extremely gaudy and real expensive-looking in a sleazy sort of way. People want color. They want explosion. It's pretty gray out there, so I gave them an evening of color. The show is staged within an inch. There isn't a moment that's not choreographed!" (59).

The show wasn't without anxieties for Bette, who proclaimed of her production company, "We are now taste-free." In fact, she admitted right before the opening, "It's extremely frightening. I was relatively calm until last week and then I think I psyched myself into a fit. I had two or three days that I literally hit people and called them horrendous names. I also started dreaming. Strange dreams. I had a nightmare that David Bowie opened up across the street from me and he had the same sets and he was wearing my costumes!" (38).

Bette was also nervous about working onstage for the first time in years without Barry Manilow to play piano and fight with her on and off stage. "Yeah, I'd have to admit that Barry's unavailability delayed my getting back to work," she said. "My new accompanist, Don York, is brilliant. He's not as volatile as Barry, but he's wonderful" (38). She was at least reassured by the fact that York had been broken in by Manilow personally.

Prior to her opening on Broadway, Bette made a highly memorable appearance on the 1975 Grammy Awards telecast, live from New York City. She presented an award to Stevie Wonder. What she wore was a riot. She was dressed in a tasteful low-cut gown, and atop her head was a 45 r.p.m. single. The record was angled slightly to one side and bobby-pinned to her hair. "It's 'Come Go with Me' by the Del Vikings." She explained in typical Miss M fashion. "A great record, but a better hat!" She was the highlight of the entire show.

Her *Clams on the Half-Shell Revue* opened on April 14, 1975, and it was such a huge success that its original four-week run was extended to ten weeks to meet the demand for tickets. Bette was back, and Broadway had her.

The show was totally outrageous from start to finish. The opening number was a showstopper to end them all. Meant as a parody of every great Broadway musical of the past thirty years, Bette's *Clams on the Half Shell Revue* began with the title song from *Oklahoma!* and segued directly into a number from *Showboat*. The *Showboat* routine had all of the supporting players and extras "down by the levee," supposedly pulling on ropes that might have been the bow lines to the docking riverboat, the *Robert E. Lee*. What they were hoisting in from the wings, however, was a giant scalloped clamshell from the deep blue sea. As the shell was brought center-stage, the music shifted to a melody from *South Pacific,* and who else should appear within the shell as its halves opened up, but everyone's favorite pearl of the Pacific—Bette Midler— looking dazzling! The cheering and screaming from the astonished audience seemed to go on for several minutes.

Here was the unpredictable Miss M, emerging from a seashell like the goddess of Botticelli's masterpiece of a painting *The Birth of Venus*. Bette had shed several pounds and revealed a sleek new figure with plenty of curves.

The show was the revue to end them all, combining the best of Bette's recorded signature songs, plus several new numbers that she was never to capture on record: David Bowie's "Young Americans," Elton John's "The Bitch Is Back," and several songs that Billie Holiday made famous, including "We'll Be Together Again," "If Love Were All," and "Sentimental Journey." Bette also sang Paul Simon's new composition "Gone at Last," announcing that she had just recorded the song as a duet with him for his upcoming new album.

Act One concluded with one of the most ingenious and hilariously insane pieces ever staged in a Broadway theater. While Bette made a grand exit, the Harlettes were left onstage singing "Optimistic Voices" from *The Wizard of Oz* and the opening lines of "Lullaby of Broadway." As the upstage curtains parted, a downward-rolling backdrop gave the audience the illusion that they were ascending the most famous of Manhattan skyscrapers, the Empire State Building. Who else should be atop the famed building but a huge, fuzzy, purple King Kong! Through a clever use of stage mechanics, Kong's huge left arm swung outward toward the audience—with Bette Midler passed out in his outstretched hand. Here was a supine Miss M in a nightgown, with her feet dangling stageward in a pair of marabou-feather-covered high-heeled slippers, awakening from what she thought was a dream. Opening her eyes and sitting upright, she looked at King Kong, looked out at the audience, and dead-panned ala Streisand, "Nicky Arnstein, Nicky Arnstein!" The audience members all but wet their pants. Slam, bang, and Bette and her tart-like Harlettes swung into a rousing rendition of "Lullaby of Broadway."

Act Two opened with a backdrop of a jukebox and stacks of classic swing-era 78 r.p.m. records, and there atop the stack was the classy Lionel Hampton in a cream-colored suit with his famous vibraphone (a melodic variety of xylophone). After a couple of solo jazz numbers, out popped Bette, to join the swing legend in some of the tunes that had become the hottest hits of the 1940s: "In the Mood," "How High the Moon," "Boogie Woogie Bugle Boy," and Hampton's own composition, "Flying Home." Bette took over from that point and followed Hampton's exit with more of her famed song stylings and trashy pop-camp excursions.

In her *Clams on the Half-Shell Revue,* Bette Midler hit every mood, era, and sound that had made her the toast of the rock, pop, and nostalgia worlds. The show ended with Bette and the choral-singing Michael Powell Ensemble launching into the gospel-tinged "Gone at Last."

Critics went crazy, and her fans went berserk. Bette even ended up gracing the cover of *People* magazine, the publication that she had once referred to in her act as "*Peep Hole* magazine."

"It's raunchy, it's riveting, it's regally welcome!" raved Rex Reed in the *New York Daily News* (60). Even though tough-to-please Clive Barnes in the *New York Times* found her buried in gimmicks, he had to admit that she was a unique talent and that the audience loved her.

Barnes, in his review, pointed out that "Bette Midler, the tackiest girl in town, has come home to roost. . . . She is a modern phenomenon, the low priestess of her own juke-box subculture, an explosion of energy and minutely calculated bad taste, a drizzle of dazzle, a lady both brash and vulnerable, a grinning waif singing with a strident plaintiveness of friendship and love. . . . She uses the theater as if it were a nightclub, and plays with the audience as if it were a shoal of fish. Her rapport is extraordinary, and she can laugh and insult, and laugh again. But what has happened to Miss Midler in this show! Oh, of course enough of her comes through to keep the fans whirring, but something has happened. The vulgarity has become glossy rather than tatty. . . . For all this, when everything is said and done, by heck, New York is still her town, and she is still its best Bette!" (61).

Portland Opera magazine glowed, "The revue is indeed a devastating delight: a play without a plot, a concert without the gaps. Director Joe Layton has taken each of the elements that makes Midler magnanimous, and has structured a lush, non-stop show around her, equipped with sets, costumes and best of all, has left plenty of leeway for spontaneously unabashed Bette to spread her wings. . . . Clad in what looks like a combination of Liberace leftovers and a basement sale at Frederick's of Hollywood, Bette Midler and her *Clams* are cracking Broadway wide open with Ziegfeldian zest in THE stage extravaganza of the year" (62).

Richard Goldstein in the *Village Voice* glowed of the juxtapositioning of the styles found in the show, "[Director Joe] Layton's touch is barely visible in the staging and the choreography, which are spare enough to allow Bette the dominance she needs to work effectively. Still, it is strange at first to see the good ol' Harlettes backed by Tony Walton's lavish deco sets, just as it is strange to hear Lionel Hampton on a swing version of 'A Day in the Life.'. . . A samba rendition of 'Strangers in the Night' is backed by a mock-rumba about the clap. An exquisite sequence of harmonies blends the Andrews Sisters and the Dixiecups. And the aforementioned Hampton medley segues 'Day in the Life' with [David] Bowie's '(I Want a) Young American.'. . . But it is precisely these jarring moments which make Bette's revue the intelligent and provocative entertainment which it is" (63).

According to several sources, there was always a backstage rivalry between Bette's three main comedy writers, Vilanch, Hennessey, and Blatt, over who wrote what and to whom credits for the laughs belonged. One of the *Clams'* production assistants remembers Bill Hennessey presenting everyone with opening-night gag gifts. Said the assistant, "Bruce Vilanch is one of those people who takes credit for everything. And the present [Hennessey] gave Bruce was a T-shirt with the Virgin Mary and the Christ child in her arms on the front of it. And on the back of the T-shirt it read: 'I Wrote Their Act!' " (35).

Bill Hennessey wasn't the only person to give out presents on opening night. Aaron Russo presented Bette with an expensive ring that was meant to be an engagement ring. Bette, however, said, "No!" to his proposal. And she and Aaron proceeded to have one of their famous fights. Bette's mother, Ruth, had come to town for the opening, so she and her mom left a hurt and steaming Russo in the backstage area of the Minskoff Theater and zoomed across Forty-Fourth Street to Sardi's restaurant to await her glowing reviews in the next morning's newspapers.

Bette had no intention of marrying Aaron. At that moment she was already happily married—to her legion of cheering fans.

THE NEW DEPRESSION

One of the biggest questions raised by the success of the *Clams on the Half Shell Revue* was why there was no new album to promote while Bette was setting box-office records at the Minskoff? She had certainly learned enough new songs for the show—couldn't she have selected some of those tunes?

The fact of the matter was that Bette was recording during this period—song after unreleased song—and still she wasn't satisfied with the finished product. Originally, her third album was going to be a "Miss M Goes Motown"–type of soul extravaganza. She went into the studio with one of the key Motown producers, Hal Davis, who was responsible for many Jackson Five and solo Michael Jackson hits. These four or five songs that Hal Davis and Bette did record are, to this day, on the shelf somewhere, unreleased. Davis went on during the next year to produce the Number 1 hits "Love Hangover" for Diana Ross and "Don't Leave Me This Way" for Thelma Houston, but Bette didn't like the songs that she and Hal did together. People from Atlantic Records who did get a chance to listen to the Hal Davis/Bette Midler recordings still rave about them as being among her best.

Midler also went into the recording studio with another pair of Motown hitmakers, Nicholas Ashford and Valerie Simpson. She recorded a composition of theirs written especially for her, entitled, "Bang, You're Dead." While Bette was in Nick and Valerie's own personal recording studio, working on the song, a disc jockey friend of Ashford and Simpson's dropped in to say "hello."

"She threw a fit!" recalls the DJ of that afternoon. "'Who is he?' she demanded when she saw me looking in from the control room. She insisted that I be thrown out before she would sing one more word. Nick and Valerie just looked at each other, and I knew that I had to leave that second" (35). A studio version of "Bang, You're Dead" was eventually released as the B side of Bette's "Married Men" single in 1979.

After the Broadway run of *Clams,* several more people left the Midler camp. One of the Harlettes, Robin Grean, announced her departure, and Bette's longtime press agent Candy Leigh also quit. Bette had gotten to the point of hating to grant interviews because she was sick of being asked about the Continental Baths, Barry Manilow, and Melissa Manchester. Candy found it an impossible situation. When Aaron Russo asked Candy what he was going to do for a press agent for Midler, Candy suggested that he place a want-ad in one of the local newspapers—under the heading "Masochist Wanted!"

Bette was beginning to get a reputation for being difficult to work with. "I am a bitch," Bette explained in a *Playgirl* magazine interview. "I am a bitch in the sense that I like the wonderful things about being a bitch, but not the negative things. When I say 'bitch,' I mean being on top of it, being aware and knowing the answers. I like that part. But I don't like doing it at the expense of other women. I don't like to sit around and dish the dirt with the girls. . . . I think of it in terms of, 'Do I know what I'm talking about?' or 'Do I not know what I'm talking about?' If I do know, then it doesn't matter if I'm a man or a woman. I have to know what I'm doing. If I don't, I'm going to get shit upon, no matter what!" (21).

During the late summer and the fall of 1975, people were bugging Bette to death. Aaron was begging her to start rehearsals for her upcoming cross-country concert tour, and Atlantic Records was bugging her for her third album. There were several scraps of things that Bette thought she would allow to be released on her third album, but on some of them she didn't have the time to complete her vocal tracks.

One of Bette's biggest thrills during the recording of her third album came when she met and worked with Bob Dylan, who was one of her idols. They had recorded a song together called "Buckets of Rain," which was one of his compositions. "He absolutely charmed the pants off of me," she claimed, but not literally. "But close! I tried. Actually, I tried to charm the pants off him. And everyone will be disappointed to learn I was unsuccessful. But I got close. Oh, you know . . . a couple of fast feels in the front seat of his Cadillac. He used to drive this hysterically long, red Cadillac convertible, and he couldn't drive worth a pea. He's not a big guy, and he always drove with the seat all the way back, refusing to pull it up to the steering wheel. He was just fabulous" (30).

Bette decided that she was going to have to concentrate on the tour and on finding a third Harlette. For the moment, the album would have to be Atlantic Records' problem. The result was ultimately going to end up to be something of a patchwork quilt of an album.

Bette was to find her third Harlette for the tour in Ula Hedwig, a tall Polish girl with a flair for Bette's kind of comedy. And so, Bette and her new troupe began to prepare for what was to be billed as "The Depression Tour." The only other concert appearance that Bette had made earlier that year had been on the fundraising telethon for the United Jewish Appeal. While on the show, Bette announced that she was willing to give more than her singing for the charity. She promised that if someone would pledge the sum of $5,000 dollars, she would throw in something extra. According to her, "You know, this cause means so much to me that I am prepared to drop my dress for Israel! Out there in television land, I know there is someone who wants to see it. Someone who wants to be responsible for allowing all of New York to see the end of my reputation, the end of my career—and my legs, which are the most beautiful in the business. Thank you, thank you, and kiss my tuchas!" Well, to make a long story short, after she sang "Hello in There," someone pledged the five grand, and she promptly stripped down to her lace slip.

It was later that year that things started to go awry. When Paul Simon's album *Still Crazy after All These Years* did finally come out, the song "Gone at Last" was included, but Bette Midler's vocals had been stripped off the track. Apparently, following an artistic dispute with the Midler camp, Simon rerecorded the song with Phoebe Snow. Bette never forgave him.

Paul explained at the time, "The version with Bette had more of a Latin street feel. I changed the concept with Phoebe and tried a gospel approach because she was perfect for it" (64). However, it always seemed like there was more to the story.

Finally, over three decades later, a close friend of hers—who refused to be identified—shed some light on the incident. Apparently, the rumors were true about Midler having a romantic flirtation with Simon. It was when this went sour that he removed her from his album. "I can't be quoted about her sex life," says the source, "because I know what she did to Geraldo Rivera. I am going to stay away from her sex life. But, yes, she was unhappy that he took her voice off and put on Phoebe's. It was *more personal* than that—if you know what I mean. I think things started with the duet, and it progressed from there. She never actually came out and told me that. . . . she kinda hinted that it was sexual. She never came out and said it, but she sure intimated it, and hinted that their falling out was 'highly personal,' and that 'Paul Simon is a total prick'" (65).

Bette and the Harlettes were still in rehearsals for the upcoming tour when Midler became ill. She was stricken with appendicitis on her thirtieth birthday—December 1, 1975—and she was rushed into Beverly Hills Medical Center. Bette quickly recovered, and the tour opened as scheduled on December 21, in Berkeley, California.

The emergency appendix operation served as inspiration for a brand-new opening for the show. Originally, the curtain was going to open to reveal a pile of laundry and junk on the stage, and Bette was going to emerge from its depths, singing the old Patti LaBelle & the Bluebelles hit "I Sold My Heart to the Junkman." Instead, she devised a whole hospital-bed scene, with the Harlettes carrying enema bags and tubes, bed pans, and IV bottles while she sang a medley of "Friends" and the Ringo Starr hit "Oh My My." The Starr song starts out with the line, "I called up my doctor, to see what's the matter," so it all worked perfectly around the newly devised medical motif.

While still in the surgery setting, Bette quipped, "Many of you may have heard that I was stricken with appendicitis. But I'm here to tell you the truth . . . and that is: that in a spasm of sisterly generosity, I donated my tits to Cher! And she was so glad to get them—I can't even tell you!"

According to Ula Hedwig, that was a night she will never forget: "I'd only seen Bette once, back at Mr. Kelly's in Chicago years ago. I'd never experienced working with her in front of an audience until we opened in Berkeley. When she came out in that bed and started singing her song, the audience went wild. I got such a rush, you know, and she did such a great show—she got my adrenaline going, too, and it was such an 'up.' Rehearsals had been nothing, but once we got on that stage, it was magic. As a performer, I suddenly understood the whole Bette thing" (48).

Most of the material on this tour consisted of slightly altered versions of the *Clams on the Half-Shell Revue,* complete with the King Kong set to close Act One, and without Lionel Hampton. There was one major addition to the act, however, a segment called "The Vicki Eydie Show," and it was Bette's interpretation of a tacky lounge singer who is accompanied by her once-famous back-up group, the Dazzling Eat-ettes. The character of Vicki Eydie was borrowed from the group Gotham, a campy New York–based male singing trio that was being managed by Bill Hennessey.

Gary Herb of Gotham explains the origin of Vicki Eydie: "We were all working in Washington, and we were working with a girlfriend named Toby Stone, who is a singer. We were just being real crazy one night, and coming up with names for her, and we came up with Vicki Eydie as a lounge-act singer. It was basically a little backstage name that we used with Toby" (66).

"We went out to lunch with Bette, about a month or so after that," Gary continues, "and we were talking, and we explained to her Vicki Eydie, and our girlfriend Toby. Well, Midler thought it was hysterical, and she said, 'I'm going to work on this. I want to use this. Is that okay?' And we said, 'Oh sure!' But Toby was PISSED OFF when she heard that Miss Midler decided to do it. Miss Stone—I don't think I've spoken to her since! So that's the story of Vicki Eydie, and from there it went" (66).

The next stop on the four-month twenty-city tour was Los Angeles, and the closing night of this particular engagement was New Year's Eve. The California state legislature had passed a bill that would go into effect at 12:01 a.m., January 1, 1976, which reduced the charge for possession of marijuana from a felony to a misdemeanor. Hence the penalty for possession of a single joint would become all but inconsequential. Bette had an outrageous idea that would turn her New Year's Eve concert into one of the most memorable nights of the entire tour. Under each of the venue's seats she was going to have one marijuana joint taped for everyone in the audience, as a little gift from the incorrigible Miss M.

The day of December 31, Bette and her entire troupe of band members, background singers, and crew members were busy—rolling joints. They had rolled their little fingers off and were all the way up to joint number 1,800 when they were informed that word had leaked out to the press and the local police had been tipped off to the planned party favors. Everyone was crushed. It was such an excellent idea, and try as they might, no one could come up with any idea as outrageous to replace it with.

Bette was so looking forward to midnight and the look on the audience members' faces when they all reached under their seats to find that "the marijuana fairy" had left them all a little treat under their seats. She realized, while perched in King Kong's hairy purple hand and the first second of 1976 tolled, that she had to give the crowd something extra to remember the evening by. And so she pulled her top down and exposed her famous breasts to the audience. The crowd, most members of whose consciousness—to say the least—was already considerably altered, went crazy with screaming and cheering at this sight.

Bette later explained, "At the New Year's Eve show, you have to do something. You have to have balloons or confetti—you have to have a surprise. And we had one. We were going to have joints. The marijuana laws had just been changed, and as our New Year's Eve surprise were going to have a joint taped under each seat, so that at midnight we could yell 'Happy New Year' and tell everybody to look under his seat. Well somebody leaked the plan to the press, and the cops said, 'No, that's not going to be your surprise.' So at the last minute, we couldn't do it. Oh, I was desperate" (30).

According to her, "I kept hoping until the last minute that someone would come up with another idea as marvelous as that. But when push came to shove, I realized it was up to me, and what did this poor woman have to barter but her own body, the flesh of herself? So at the stroke of midnight, I dah-ropped my dress to thirty-six hundred people. I don't think they even saw it, you know. It was just my little chest: nipples to the wind!" (67).

"When in doubt, go for the jugs!" she contended. However, when the curtain came down, and Russo got hold of her, all hell broke loose: "Aaron FREAKED out, called me every name in the book." They proceeded to have a huge fight, and he accused her of being totally reckless and self-destructive. Security guards had to break up their argument, and Act Two went on as scheduled. Bette recalls, "I went through the rest of the show under this rotten cloud of ghastly doom" (67).

During this time period, Bette was dating one of the members of the Average White Band, who also recorded for Atlantic Records: Hamish

Stuart. Following the concert, she and Hamish went to a big party that was being thrown by Atlantic, and several music-industry heavyweights were also present. The company, which was getting ready to ship Bette's new album in January, had pressed several copies of her first single from the LP and sent preview copies of it to some of the key radio promoters. The single was her disco/samba version of the Frank Sinatra song "Stranger in the Night," and one of the people invited to the party was a man named Paul Drew. It was Drew who was responsible for deciding which new records would—or would not—be played on over three hundred RKO-owned radio stations across the country.

When Drew waltzed over to Bette—in the middle of the party—and announced that he did *NOT* like her new single, she was a bit miffed. This was not the night for someone to pick a fight with Bette, but she decided to let it ride. She simply went to another part of the party to cool out, but the anger proceeded to build up in her, and she really became enraged over the fact that this man would have nerve enough to ruin her New Year's celebration by insulting her. She marched back over to him and, according to her, "My heart was pounding and I was so livid! The whole evening was just so: uggggh! So I grabbed the record from his hand, broke it across my knee, and smacked him across the face." She stormed off in a huff after telling him that if he didn't like the song, "Don't play it!" Bette Midler's records were promptly banned from all of the RKO radio stations that Drew programmed. "What can I say? I'm sorry it happened, but that's show biz," she commented later, but the damage was already done (68).

Alas, the evening was far from over. More surprises were in store. When Bette returned to her hotel, she decided to knock on Russo's hotel room door, only to find that he had staged a suicide attempt. Said Midler, "Aaron was back at the hotel, on the floor. He'd taken a bunch of pills, trying to pass out and scare me, because I had a date with someone else that night. He was in love with me and didn't want me to be with anyone else" (30).

"When I got back to the hotel, I rang up to his room and banged on the door. 'Aaron, Aaron, open up!' I said. And from the inside, from this cavern, I heard, 'Aaaahhhhhhh . . . aaaaahhhhhhhh.' He wouldn't let me in, so I had to run downstairs and get the concierge. I mean, my dear, this was drama. When we opened the door, there Aaron was, all two hundred pounds of him, in his bathrobe, flat on the floor, with just

me and this pissant concierge to drag him onto the bed. Lord, what a
night that was!" (30).

For Bette, the year 1976 wasn't exactly off to a roaring start. Things
proceeded to get even worse when her long-awaited third album, *Songs
for the New Depression,* was released later that month, and the critics
across the country unanimously hated it. Worse yet, almost no one
bought it.

The albums *The Divine Miss M* and *Bette Midler* had been such
delightful hits and had come out in such rapid succession in 1972 and
1973. Yet it seemed like it took "forever" for her third one to be released
in January of 1976. And by the time it appeared in record stores, the
momentum created by its predecessors was all but lost. Although it did
have a brief moment in the sun—making it to Number 27 on the album
chart in *Billboard*—it was perceived as a "dud." What went wrong?

Instead of *Songs for the New Depression* emerging as a bigger and
better Bette, she seemed to be all over the place, stylistically. While her
first albums had been widely varied—and hung together through it—
this album is somehow uneven and disjointed.

Part of the problem was clearly the fact that Barry Manilow was gone
from the proceedings, and so were his snappy musical arrangements.
Instead, three separate producers contributed to it: Moogy Klingman,
Arif Mardin, and—via a pair of unreleased cuts from the *Divine Miss
M* album—Joel Dorn. It was like an audible patchwork quilt of styles
from beginning to end. Furthermore, Bette took the two Dorn productions and added her own touches; she is credited as coproducer of those
cuts.

The album opens with a disco version of the Frank Sinatra hit
"Strangers in the Night." Although technically good, the song—
produced by Mardin—can't seem to decide whether it is trying to be
serious or a tongue-in-cheek parody. And it doesn't succeed on either
level. If she had only given it some of that wise-cracking Miss M fire
and campiness, it might have much more fun. Not even Luther Vandross, singing his heart out in the background chorus, seemed to help
this song.

When Bette sang her version of Phoebe Snow's touching "I Don't
Want the Night to End" in her *Clams on the Half-Shell Revue,* it was
a wonderful and bittersweet performance. However, here, her studio-
recorded version of the song comes across as hollow and stiff. The original song and Bette's live performance of it both had several effective

lines of opening lyrics about standing under the gaslights and crying over the fact that jazz legend Charlie Parker had died. For some reason, on this album the beginning of the song is chopped off, and here it seems to lose all its meaning and its poignancy in the truncation. Todd Rundgren is featured on guitar on this song.

The satirical song "Mr. Rockefeller," which was comical as a stage piece in *Clams,* is neither tuneful nor amusing here. Meant to come across as a mock-the-rich political statement—and written by Bette and Jerry Blatt—this studio version of the song is more annoying than fun. It was better as a stage piece.

The biggest highlight on the first half of the album is the leftover Joel Dorn production of "Old Cape Cod." This faithful version of the old Patti Page classic achieves the same campy time-warp effect that Midler had created with the Andrews Sisters' "Boogie Woogie Bugle Boy."

Next came Midler's odd duet with Bob Dylan, on his quirky composition "Buckets of Rain." Unfortunately, their voices simply don't work at all well together on this song. This uninspiring cut ends with a garbled bit of in-studio chat between Bette and Bob. In it, Midler takes a jab at Paul Simon—for having stripped her off "Gone at Last" on his 1975 Number 1 album, *Still Crazy after All These Years.* Furthermore, the Simon and Snow duet became a Top 40 hit on the singles chart. Bette's muttered jab at Simon on "Buckets of Rain" comes across as more mean spirited than funny. The next song is the one-minute-and-37-second ballad called "Love Says It's Waiting." While it is beautiful sounding, it is so brief that it seems like a snippet of undeveloped musical filler.

The second half of the album contains much more lunacy and passion and is far superior to the first half. Bette sings a touching and beautiful version of Tom Waits's song of the sea "Shiver Me Timbers," which finally finds her much more emotionally connected to the lyrics she is singing. This melancholy song segues right into a bit of inspired insanity composed by Midler and Moogy Klingman, entitled "Samedi et Vendredi." The song's chorus, sung in French—"*Bievenus a mes cauchemars*"—literally interprets as "Welcome to my nightmare." It is a loopy phone book of celebrity names—from the Jackson Five to Mamie Eisenhower—all of whom dance through the mind of slumbering Midler, set to a samba beat.

For a bit of drama, the songs "No Jestering," with its bouncy reggae rhythms, and "Tragedy," effectively shift the album's gears to more of a serious love song mode. "No Jestering" has a nice relaxed sound to it,

with guitar work by Todd Rundgren. However, the album's most satisfying *high* point comes on "Marahuana." With the vocal chorus sung by
the all-male trio of Gotham, Bette is—at long last—heard on this album
at her outrageous best. On the song, Midler lyrically begs for a joint of
"grass" so that she can forget the lover who has broken her heart. This
reworking of the original 1972 production by Joel Dorn is the most fun
cut on the whole album. It was a song that she used in her act back in
her Continental Baths days and was originally featured in the 1934 film
Murder of the Vanities.

Finally, the album ends on a touching note, with Bette singing Klingman's beautiful composition "Let Me Just Follow Behind." On that cut
she had Rick Derringer on pedal steel guitar, Todd Rundgren singing
background voices, and Moogy Klingman on piano and harmonium.

The problem with *Songs for the New Depression* seems to be that
Midler can't decide where she is going with any of the songs. With the
exception of "Marahauna," "Cape Cod," and "Shiver Me Timbers," little of it contains either the joy or the passion found on her first two
albums.

After she performed David Bowie's "Young American" in her *Clams
on the Half-Shell Revue*, why was it skipped over here, since it was such
a hip show-stopper on Broadway? And what happened to the beginning
of "I Don't Want the Night to End"? Why was that deleted, since the
missing section contained the whole meaning of the song?

There also seems to be an underlying theme on this album, of trying
to vocally homogenize Bette's vocals into something more melodic and
less frantic. With the exception of her bitching about Paul Simon, there
were no ragged and passionate rough edges to be found on *Depression.*
While her singing is technically good on this album, much of it unfortunately comes across as lifeless. What this album seems to beg for is a bit
of trashiness—an old '60s girl group song—or a dash of lusty craziness.
Unfortunately, none is to be found here.

David Tipmore's review of the album in the *Village Voice* was typical
of the criticism she received. According to him, "Her formerly charac-
teristic voice sounds like a blended quartet of Barbra Streisand, Janis
Ian, Phoebe Sow, and Melissa Manchester. . . . On *New Depression* we
discover that this quartet can sing jazz, folk, pop, rock, reggae. We see
an industrious show of 'versatility': Campy Low-Rent Gal ('Marahuana'), Mistress of Song ('Love Says It's Waiting'), Real Hip Chick
("Buckets of Rain'), Sensitive Interpreter of the Ballad ('I Don't Want

the Night to End,' 'Shiver Me Timbers,' 'Let Me Just Follow Behind'),
Female Impersonator ('Old Cape Cod'), Ironic Social Commentator
('Rockefeller'), New Songwriter in Her Own Right ('Samedi et Vendredi'), and Experimenter with Foreign Rhythms ('No Jestering'). This
extensive posturing makes Midler sound absolutely unavailable: distant,
electronic, hoarse, and scared. She does not sound at home, as she did
in *Clams on the Half Shell.* . . . *[Songs for] the New Depression* is the
first record I have ever heard which aims for an Academy Award. And
as such, the record is a big mistake" (69).

As she later explained, "I want to sing things that I really like to sing
and express this very particular point of view I have about life and the
confusion of it. My whole style is based on chaos, which is what I think
life is: a constant process of dementia, and learning to laugh at it. All
right: *Songs for the New Depression* was a funny little record, but I
liked it. It's certainly not like a recording anyone else would make" (8).

Gary Herb explained how Gotham ended up singing the backgrounds on "Marahuana." "There was a benefit show for AMDA (American Musical & Dramatic Academy) that they do every year, this was a
few years ago, and this was done at Avery Fisher Hall, and it was for Ira
Gershwin. The Harlettes were scattered around town—I don't know.
And Bette called us up and said, 'Can you sing with me for this one-
night thing at Avery Fisher Hall?' So, anyway, to make a long story
short, since we sang with her that day, she was in the middle of recording that album, and called us and asked us if we would do the backup
singing on that one song. And that's how that came about" (66).

ᴗᴗ

With Bette in a position to have worked on *Songs for the New Depression* with any number of record producers, how did she end up in the
recording studio with Moogy Klingman? In the year 2002, he explains,
"At some point I gave Bette tapes of my songs, and she had recorded
another one of my songs. For her first album she also recorded one of
my songs called 'Mr. Freedom and I.' She recorded it for her first album
or her second album. But it was in that period she never put it on a
record, but I went over [to her apartment] with her, and she gave me a
copy of it. It sounded pretty good. Barry did the arrangement. So one
day I was out walking and I bumped into her on the street, and she was
with S. J. Perelman who was a famous writer—a humorist like from the

'30s and the '40s, and he was wearing his funny glasses. And he had a funny mustache. He just looked like a guy from that era, too. He had to go, and I walked her home, and she lived down in the Village. I walked her home to her place on Barrow Street, and then we talked, and she told me she was having trouble on the third album. She had been like trying to work with different producers, she was off the road. She was having a block trying to record. Nick and Valerie produced a cut with her . . . Hal Davis. . . . She did like all these big producers. Now I had produced my two albums—I coproduced with Todd Rundgren, and I produced a James Cotton album, and I had a recording studio in my loft that I co-owned with Todd at the time, too. So I was in a good position to say, 'Bette, if you want to come over sometime, we'll work on some songs, and record them. And, we'll just do it, and I won't charge you anything, unless you decide to use them, and we'll just see how it goes.' So she came over one day, and we started writing a couple of songs together" (36).

Being with Moogy in his studio, Bette found her "recording block" to be subsiding. Recalls Moogy, "In 1974 we started working together, and she had *Clams on the Half-Shell* on Broadway, so we were working on and off while she was doing *Clams.* The first song that we did was called 'Mr. Rockefeller.' And she had the words and melody and I put chords to it. Jerry Blatt helped her with the lyrics. I actually kinda wrote the music. I didn't take a writing credit on it. I mean, I didn't 'write' the music, maybe I just put the chords to her melodies, which is what I do a lot with people. But in retrospect, I probably wrote that music. She had words, and we worked together—with her and Blatt and we came up with 'Mr. Rockefeller,' which I recorded in my studio. Then she liked a song that was off of my second album, which was unreleased here, it came out in Europe on EMI, but wasn't released here—called 'Let Me Just Follow Behind.' So, we recorded a track of that. And, then we did a third song" (36).

Since she had temporarily broken off contact with Aaron Russo, Bette was free to experiment musically and to create the kind of music she wanted. According to Klingman, "When I was hanging out with her, she would come over every day without any makeup on, and she'd wear a bandanna on her head, like a cleaning lady bandanna. She'd be in a plain shirt and dungarees, and little shoes, no heels, and no make-up. And this cleaning lady bandanna on her head, so you could never see her hair, and she was unrecognizable. We could go anywhere, and nobody recognized her. She was completely invisible. Unless she did her 'Bette Midler' drag, she was an invisible person. She could go anywhere and do anything. She was just working on her record, she wasn't partying hard. . . . We were very close for a while, because we were working night and day on this record, and we would hang out and we would go see shows. We were close. I thought that I was 'in,' that she was gonna let me finish the album I started" (36).

One of the most entertaining stories from the *Songs for the New Depression* sessions involved Bette's duet with Bob Dylan. At face value, one might assume that they had met at some celebrity event, and she had asked him to record a track with her. In actuality, it grew out of a chance meeting between Moogy and Bob, at a folk music hang-out in the Village. "We had a night off from recording," says Klingman, "and I was at a bar, and Bob Dylan walked in, which was pretty funny. [It was] The Tin Angel on Bleecker Street, it was right next to the Bitter End—and it became the Other End. So, he walks in, and he's with a bunch of people. I got this idea, because I knew Bette really admired Bob Dylan: 'Why don't I set up this duet?' So, I walked up to David Blue, who was with him, who I knew, because he was a folk singer and friend of Bob's. So I told this to David Blue, and I went back to where I was sitting, and then David Blue said, 'OK, Bob said he'll do it.' I said, 'He'll do it?' And he said, 'Yeah.' I said, 'Great, when does he want to do it?' He said, 'I don't know.' So, I walked over to Bob, and he was really drunk. And said, 'So Bob, you gonna really do it?' He said, 'Yes.' I said, 'Well, when do *you* want to do it?' And he said, 'When do you want it? Just tell me where to be and when.' 'Well,' I said, 'we'll do it tomorrow night at my studio, I have a recording studio.' And he said, 'Great man, all right—I'll do it! Great!' So, I gave the address to David Blue, and Bob was kinda drunk, and he sounded sarcastic—like he was goofing on me—like he didn't believe I was working with Bette Midler and he was goofing on me" (36).

Moogy wasn't at all positive that this planned session wasn't a big joke or an idle promise made by Bob in a drunken haze. "So, I went home and I didn't tell anybody,' says Klingman. 'I didn't set up a recording session, the next day was a day off. So, I was sitting at home alone at 9:00 [at night], and Bob Dylan rings the doorbell. So, he comes upstairs to my studio, with Roger McGuinn from the Byrds, and we're just hanging out. And I said, 'Everyone's on their way over.' So, I go and I hit the phones, and I call Bette, and she's home. And I said, 'Bob Dylan's here. Come on over, let's do this duet.' And she said, 'Great.' I made like 500 calls, and I got a band to come over, and an engineer to come over, and everyone was there like in an hour. I had to entertain Dylan for an hour in my living room, playing my songs, or me imitating him—whatever we did" (36).

How they hit upon performing Dylan's composition "Buckets of Rain" was a decision made on the spot. Reveals Moogy, "Well, it was funny, because Dylan originally wanted to record '(You Got to Have) Friends.' And we rehearsed it. And again, I thought he was goofing. He said, 'No man, "You gotta have friends. . . ." ' " And, Bette didn't really want to do it, and I didn't really want to do it. With him doing it, it kinda sounded like a joke: Bob Dylan singing '(You Got to Have) Friends' with Bette Midler? And, worse than sounding like a joke, I figured it could really be detrimental for his career—like him doing 'Friends' would turn him into a MOR [middle of the road] act, and his fans would go nuts. So I stopped, and I said, 'Let's do one of yours, instead of one of mine.' Here's one for the history books: I stopped Bob Dylan from recording one of my songs! So, he said, 'OK,' so we recorded 'Buckets of Rain,' which was off of his most recent album, *Blood on the Tracks.* So he rewrote it, rewrote some of the words, he was just a wild guy: very Dylan-esque. And we recorded that one. Bette really liked him a lot, and he was supposed to do more songs. So, the next few nights we were waiting for Dylan to come back, or he would tell us to meet him somewhere, and we'd go meet him at rehearsal for his band, and he would ignore us. And after four or five nights, we realized he was never coming back to the studio. So, instead, we had this one song, 'Buckets of Rain.' And, when Ahmet Ertegun found out about it, he called me the next day to his office, and he said, 'Wow, this is the greatest thing. You got Bob Dylan on my label, at Atlantic Records!' And he was insanely happy. But he wanted to rerecord the rhythm section, so he came in with different bass players and drummers to give the rhythm section different beats that didn't really fit with the vocals. But this is what he wanted to do, and he ran the company. So we did the sessions, with him coproducing with me, but he didn't put his name on it for credit. So, he really took that out of my hands—my Dylan song—and kinda made it something less than what it was or what it could have been. He had the guy from Average White Band playing on it, and he had him do a double time country feel to a half time rock feel, and it didn't really fit—in my opinion" (36). According to Klingman, there is still a tape floating around somewhere, of Midler and Dylan rehearsing "Friends" as a duet.

Originally, the *Songs for the New Depression* album was supposed to have a new direction to it. This was going to be the album that really showed off her creativity. "There was this whole idea that she was going to become more of an artist like Joni Mitchell—more of a singer/song-writer type, which she could have done," Klingman reveals. "There was a whole concept of turning her career around . . . into something different, and doing something really big. Like we had—one side of the album was going to be [exotic] songs—we had a song that was from Rio, we had a samba song, just all these different genres, but either written or co-written by her basically. We wrote this one song—Dave Brubeck's 'Blue Rondo ala Turk.' Me and Jerry Blatt, we wrote the words. I still get royalties, and to my knowledge it was not released anywhere. We recorded it for months, because she sang all the parts. She sang all the chords. It's Dave Brubeck's [jazz instrumental classic] 'Blue Rondo ala Turk,' with lyrics for the whole song: 'He was a fool, a perfectly unimportant person, nobody liked him, he dibba dabba doo . . .' It all had words and they were really funny words. We wrote the whole thing. And, she recorded it and it took just a long time, because she wanted to do all the different vocal parts. And then it just came out amazingly good. You know—unbelievable" (36).

Moogy estimates that there are at least eleven finished and unreleased tracks in the Atlantic Records vaults from these sessions: "Well, about eleven songs. I wrote them down once. 'Young Americans' was one. A song I wrote with her called 'Oh Jerusalem,' which was done with just two pianos and her singing it—which was a really good ballad. A song I wrote with her called 'Hey Bobby,' that was like a love song to Bobby DiNiro that we worked on for months and really had potential to be a hit single. Another one we co-wrote together was a song that she wrote called 'Vacation in Rio,' that I kinda put music to—but she had the writer's credit on that one. Right there were two songs that we had co-written, and one song that she was taking the full credit on. Then there was a song called 'I Had to Resort to Beauty,' that she wrote, which we recorded with an old-time orchestra at a hotel, just for authentic sound—like a 1930s ditty—really funny. 'I Had to Resort to Beauty,' she wrote it with Jerry Blatt" (36).

The tracks that did get released on *Songs for the New Depression* vocally sounded overly perfected. There were no rough corners, and some the edginess of her previous albums was missing. Why was this? Klingman claims, "She was a workaholic, she would do her vocals, and then she would redo them, and then she would redo them again. It was just endless recording sessions. . . . it was just endlessly worked over, and worked over, and worked over. She insisted on redoing all of her vocals over and over again, and you'd have to choose, you'd have five tracks of vocals, you'd have to pick the best of each track and assemble a vocal track, and have four more open tracks, and she would go back and do four more lead vocals that would take a long time to punch them in. It was a lot of hard work. . . . She had me record a bunch of versions of 'Strangers in the Night' disco-style. Like the last thing I ever wanted to do in my life is record 'Strangers in the Night' as a disco song. And she had me record three different versions of it, some of them came out pretty well, before just taking the whole thing to Arif Mardin and having him record a version of it" (36).

According to Moogy, after months and months of work, Aaron Russo returned on the scene, and suddenly Moogy was out: "She worked really hard in the studio, and what happened was, her manager, Aaron was away. They had a big blow-out fight and she hadn't seen him for a year or a year and a half. When I was working with her, he wasn't around for a year. And then he came in, and the only way he felt secure around me, was to get me out of it. He had to push me out of the whole thing, because he figured that I could become his ultimate threat. I was producing her album, I was writing songs for her, I was going to be her new musical director" (36).

With regard to the song "I Don't Want the Night to End," Klingman laments, "It had this great intro, and they cut the intro. . . . They did a lot of stuff. They remixed stuff, they redid stuff, and then they gave me the album credit, 'cuz they knew it was such a messed-up record. 'Marihuana' was a song she had done years ago, and she turned it into a grab bag, instead of being a concept album that would have blown people's minds. She would have written so many of the songs on it, and done so many accomplished things on it vocally. . . . Of the stuff that I did with her, that was put out, some of it was pretty good. Some of it wasn't so good. My version of 'Strangers in the Night' was replaced by Arif Mardin's version, which wasn't so good. My version of Dylan and her doing the duet, with the original band at the session, was good, and ultimately the version where they replaced the rhythm section wasn't so good" (36).

To this day, Klingman laments, "The stuff that was left off of the album was better than the stuff that was put on the album. It has never seen the light of day. I'm still thinking of calling up Atlantic, and saying, 'Let me go through your tapes man, I know you got another album here.' The real album never came out. It is the missing album. They should read your book and demand that these other ten or eleven cuts come out. There is no reason why Atlantic shouldn't put them out either. I am sure they have them in the vaults, and she is not on Atlantic anymore. This stuff was really good, and this is the missing Bette Midler album" (36).

According to him, Midler later regretted what happened with her third album. "She did one interview years and years later where she said, '*Songs for the New Depression* when we started recording it, I had the feeling that this was the best recording of my life, and that we were doing something really great. Then outside forces came in and made me doubt that, and we kinda ruined that record.' She kinda laid it out there, and that she was really insecure about it, and in retrospect, how good all that material was" (36).

What they were left with was an album that no one who was involved with it liked or was 100 percent happy with. "Then they threw out ten or twelve of the songs that we had recorded, and put on some older Joel Dorn stuff. So, the thing had a very disjointed feel, and a very confused feel. There was one reviewer that wrote, how he suspects that her insecurities drove her to rerecord and pull things from all sources. And, obviously, she was very nervous," recalls Moogy Klingman (36).

⌐⌐

February 1976 wasn't a much better month for Bette than January had been. When the "Depression Tour" rolled into Buffalo, New York, three members of her band and four of her technicians were busted for drug possession. Aaron Russo's comments to the *New York Post* under the headline "Bette: Shuffle Off in Buffalo" only made matters worse. "Most towns are liberal in this day and age, and really don't care if they see a musician who seems to be a little high," he bellowed at the conservative city. "But Buffalo is in the midst of this silly anti-vice crusade. They're against pinball machines here. The other day they busted three people at a bus stop for reading pornographic magazines. So you can see what's happening!" (70). Midler was fortunately not available for comment. Although she was not busted, the incident reflected poorly upon her.

Bette made more headlines later that week when she went to Boston to accept the 1976 Hasty Pudding Award from Harvard University as its "Woman of the Year." She decided to give them a little more of herself. When she strutted up to the stage to accept her award, she swung open the back of her slit dress to "moon" the audience with her bare derriere. The audience and the press flipped out over the audacious Miss M. Over the next week, several publications carried a shot of Bette—turning the other cheek, so to speak—for all of Harvard to see. Oh, the joys of higher education!

On the Chicago leg of the "Depression Tour," Bette received some bad press through a misunderstanding. The item that appeared in print quoted Bette as saying, "I have no gay friends. I wouldn't know a homosexual if I saw one" (8). This did not sit too well with the gay community, which comprised the largest segment of her most devoted fans.

The incident was later explained by a member of her entourage. According to the source, "There was a journalist who was not friendly, and she managed to get through to Bette at her hotel at eleven in the morning. In those days, Bette slept until two or three in the afternoon, and she gets Bette on the phone and says 'I'm so-and-so from the *Chicago Tribune.*' And Bette says, 'Yes?' 'Tell me about your gay audience.' At that point Bette was tired of being hounded about that all of the time, because she had already gone on to a big crossover audience, but everyone was refusing to acknowledge her. That was when she said this, just like, 'Ugggh, leave me alone,' and she hung up on the journalist. The journalist immediately rushed into print with that statement" (35).

The tour was fraught with pressure for Bette. Although she was playing every night to cheering crowds, she knew that Aaron, Atlantic Records, and now even she herself was disappointed by the less-than-warm reception her latest album was receiving. It failed to even enter the Top 40 on the American album charts and sold less than 500,000 copies. When the tour reached Detroit, Bette called an important meeting of her entire troupe after one of the shows. For this particular meeting she had several dozen cream pies delivered to one of the hotel conference rooms. What ensued was one of the biggest and silliest food fights that the Motor City had ever seen. They left the poor room a virtual snowbank of whipped cream and pie remnants.

By this point in the trip, Bette had to let off some steam . . . and this seemed like quite an effective way to bring some of the joy back to the tour.

One of the most important stops on "The Depression Tour" was Cleveland, Ohio. It was in Cleveland that the entire show was video-taped for an upcoming Home Box Office (HBO) television special. After years of negotiating back and forth with ABC-TV for a cleaned-up and watered-down version of Bette, Aaron had struck a deal with HBO to tape and broadcast her act totally uncensored, as only cable television could do. Also, Atlantic Records made a complete audiotape recording of several of the Cleveland shows for an upcoming "live" album. Atlantic was convinced that the producers of her studio albums were failing to capture her essence and her humor on record. The exec-utives at Atlantic were determined to capture the excitement of an eve-ning with Bette on vinyl.

After four months, in the spring of 1976, "The Depression Tour" came to its final destination: Caesar's Palace, in Las Vegas, Nevada. The gig was great for earning quick cash, but it seemed that no one in the Vegas audience had any idea who on earth Midler was or what her unique sense of humor was all about. In a town where moderately tal-ented TV stars were big draws, Bette's witty humor was lost on the crowds. According to Bruce Vilanch, the only segment of the show that went over well was "The Vicki Eydie Show," which was assumed to be presented in total seriousness.

One night backstage during the Vegas engagement, word circulated among the troupe that *The Fabulous Bette Midler Show* was going to debut on June 19 on HBO as a television show, and that a "live" album had also been recorded, and that no one but Bette and Aaron were going to receive one cent of extra pay for either project. Well, it was like *Mutiny on the Bounty* in Vegas that particular evening. The Harlettes and the entire band threatened to walk out on the next show if the situation wasn't resolved. Somehow a settlement was reached, but the episode did nothing to improve Bette's relationship with her band, with her singers, or with Aaron.

Fortunately, when the Cleveland concert was broadcast on HBO as *The Fabulous Bette Midler Show,* it was a roaring success. Whatever disenchantment the *Songs for the New Depression* album had created with her fans and her critics, the TV special quickly eclipsed.

Since the beginning of "The Depression Tour," Bette had lost her appendix, flashed two audiences, been banned from three hundred RKO radio stations, seen her band arrested, released a "bomb" album, lost her confidence, and regained her composure. Was she upset? To sum it all up in her own words: "Fuck 'em if they can't take a joke!"

10

THE BUMPY ROAD BACK TO THE TOP

The next two years for Bette Midler were highlighted with several peaks and marred by several disappointing valleys. On the positive side of things, she fell in love with an actor, starred in an Emmy Award–winning TV special, released a critically successful live album, and embarked on a sold-out global concert tour. On the negative side, the Harlettes left her for their own career as a trio, she released her poorest-selling studio album to date, her rented house in Los Angeles was robbed, and Aaron drove her crazier than ever before.

It was that same year that Bette admitted publicly that what she wanted most in the world was to become a movie star. Many of her most famous songs, especially "Hello in There," "Delta Dawn," "Boogie Woogie Bugle Boy," and "Superstar," were essentially acting pieces set to music. According to her, "I have definite feelings about the songs I sing and I try to convey that to my audiences. Like 'Do You Want to Dance?'—most singers wouldn't have sung it the way I did, making people think of Saturday night dances" (8). Since her stage show was filled with characters like Vicki Eydie and Nanette, the bag lady, why not go all the way with acting?

"I'd like to become a great actress—there, it's out!" she declared during "The Depression Tour." "I started that way, you know. I studied with [Lee] Strasberg—I didn't understand a blinking thing! They had no sense of humor—and I've learned a lot since. I'd like to do a comedy full of whimsy. I'd like to make a perfect comedy, the perfect musical, the perfect melodrama. Anything less than that will be dissatisfying. I'd like to do a classic, sure, I can take direction: that's not the hard part. The hard part is figuring out yourself, being able to churn up all those instincts and make it yourself" (54).

In an effort to move her career into more artistically challenging areas, Bette held a press conference to announce that her next project would show off more than just her self-proclaimed "brains, talent, and gorgeous tits." It was going to show off her taste and refinement as well. Bette heralded the fact that she was going to sing and dance with the New York City Ballet in its upcoming production of Kurt Weill and Bertolt Brecht's light opera *The Seven Deadly Sins.*

The production got under way on schedule in early 1977. Bette was already involved in rehearsals. The ballet's famed director, George Balanchine, had posed for several promotional portraits with Bette, which were photographed by Richard Avedon. Unfortunately, a strike by the Ballet Musicians' Union put the whole event on ice. The strike dragged on, and Bette became entrenched in two new projects that took precedence. Recording her next album and taping her years-in-the-planning network TV special caused scheduling conflicts, and, unfortunately, Bette's ballet debut was never rescheduled.

For more than three years ABC-TV had tried to come to satisfactory creative terms for a Midler special, and still no plan had been agreed upon. Finally, Aaron worked out a mutually agreeable plan of action with NBC, and Bette began rehearsals for *Ol' Red Hair Is Back*, which was to begin taping in California in May of 1977.

Meanwhile, Bette had fallen madly in love with a young actor named Peter Riegert. She had gone out one night in New York City to see the Off-Broadway show *Sexual Perversity in Chicago,* and Peter was in it. (The play was later made into the 1986 film *About Last Night.*) Bette visited Riegert backstage after the performance, and, according to her, she was immediately attracted to him. "There was this guy with this beautiful face and this great body and these gorgeous eyes and this wonderful manner," she recalls (71).

"'Well, let's just go out for a little drinkie, what do you say?'" Bette asked Peter. "So we got drunk and I asked him if he was listed, 'cause I'd like to call him up. Sometimes I think I'm turning into a man, and it scares me!" she exclaimed (71).

They hit it off immediately. They both loved to go out and see old movies and act silly with each other. The relationship was just what she needed. It took away a lot of the pressure of being an unapproachable "star." With Peter, she could just act like an eccentric girl in love.

Peter genuinely cared about Bette, and even the Harlettes commented that whenever he was around Midler, she seemed calmer and more centered. On top of that, he understood the insanity of life in show business. He was later to find fame of his own in the cult comedy film *Animal House*, as Boon, the fraternity social chairman. Although their love affair didn't last forever, their friendship has, and in the 1990s, when Bette starred in a new filmed version of *Gypsy*, she cast Peter in the role of Herbie, Mama Rose's lover.

As their relationship was just beginning, Bette did her best not to show up at public functions with Peter, in an effort to keep her affair with him private. However, since they both lived in New York City, it wasn't long before members of the fifth estate took note. Gossip columnist Liz Smith meant no harm when she casually mentioned to her daily newspaper column that Bette and Peter were dating. It was just another gossip item to Liz, but Bette saw it as an invasion of privacy and none of the public's business.

Bette was so worked up about it that she picked up the phone, dialed Liz Smith's number, and let the journalist have a piece of her mind. Said Midler, "I think my WORK is important! The cult of personality has exploded and it keeps people from knowing the real artist through the one reality—their work or their art. People should be interested in ideas rather than in a performer's private life. So I think people have their priorities all screwed up. I want to be known, evaluated, judged from my work alone. What I do otherwise is nobody's business!" (72).

"Let's be realistic," she continued on the subject, "I don't think the public is craving to know who I sleep with or what I ate for breakfast. My God, look at Cher. She can't even break a nail without having to give an interview about it. That stuff takes all the mystery away. I mean, it whittles your heroes down to nothing, doesn't it?" (72).

Said Liz Smith in retaliation, "When a performer goes up to accept an award at Harvard and flashes a bare backside at the boys, or says vulgar things on [her] Home Box Office concert, it naturally gets them and their giant talents talked about. And then people want to know more about their inside story and the way they live off stage" (72).

Since the cat was already out of the bag, it wasn't long before Bette began to discuss the details of her affair with Riegert openly. According to her at that time, "Peter is the first man I've really felt this way about—been able to be myself with. I've got all these crazy characters living inside of me, and I always have to act them out. Most people think I'm nuts. Not Peter. He has his own set of characters. We give each other a show every night till we collapse about four in the morning. It's great!" (17).

That February, after years of putting down Los Angeles, Bette decided to give the West Coast a try. In May of 1977 she appeared on a Bing Crosby TV special, and she sang a standout version of "Glow Worm," on which she was joined by the Mills Brothers. Reportedly, even her father tuned in to see her in that particular show. It was one of the only occasions Fred Midler saw his daughter perform. After all, he figured, how obscene could she be on the same stage with Bing Crosby?

In its April 1977 *Album Reviews* bulletin, sent out to the press, Atlantic Records announced the release of Bette's fourth album, the two-record set *Live at Last,* which was taped in concert the year before at the Cleveland Music Hall. According to the press release, "The new double live set is the necessary step in her recorded career—bridging the gap between studio and stage" (73). However, several sources confirm that many of Bette's vocal performances on this album were rerecorded in the studio to make them sound closer to the studio-quality performances of her previous albums. Hence, on the back of the album jacket appear the words "produced by Lew Hahn" and "remote recording produced by Arif Mardin." Atlantic Records was taking no chances with this album. It was, as Atlantic had hoped, a critical hit, and it did enter the Top 40 album charts, at Number 49, but it wasn't the million-selling smash Atlantic had aimed for.

The album contained a newly recorded nonconcert song called "You're Moving Out Today," written by Bette and Carol Bayer Sager. The song is about Midler asking her boyfriend to pack his things up and leave her life. She sings it in an odd little Betty Boop–like voice, which doesn't sound like her at all. It was ironic that Bette was now writing songs with Carol, since Carol had co-written most of the songs with Melissa Manchester on Melissa's 1973 debut album *Home to Myself.* It was also a strange twist of fate that by 1977, both Barry Manilow and Melissa Manchester each had scored huge hits on the record charts ("I Write the Songs" and "Midnight Blue," respectively), yet Bette, who was considered a bigger star, was still trying unsuccessfully to produce a hit record.

According to one inside source, the only reason that "Bang, You're Dead" appears on Bette's *Live at Last* album was because Nick Ashford and Valerie Simpson had threatened to give the song to someone else if Midler didn't hurry up and release it. It was a last-minute addition to the album, and it replaced "I Sold My Heart to the Junkman" on the LP. "Junkman" appears on the videotape of the HBO special; "Bang" does not.

What the *Live at Last* album did accomplish was to reestablish Bette's image as a live concert performer par excellence. It was a testament to her enormous dexterity as an onstage singer, actress, and stand-up comedian. Even the usually snide *Village Voice* admitted, "This double album catches Bette at the best—when she is working a crowd, milking it for laughter, delight, and applause. . . . her singing here has a limpid, liquid quality that never made it onto her previous recordings. She sounds spontaneous—eager and breathless" (74).

Live at Last contains most of the songs that made Midler famous— like "Friends," "Boogie Woogie Bugle Boy," and "Delta Dawn," Bette also sang several songs that were unique to this album. They include her version of the Supremes' "Up the Ladder to the Roof," the sexual entendre–filled "Long John Blues," and Neil Young's "Birds." "Long John Blues" is actually an overtly lewd and wickedly amusing song about a dentist with a very large "tool" made for filling a "cavity" in need of attention, which Bette successfully milked for laughs. In addition to the songs and intermittent patter, the album also features some of Midler's comedy bits, including her raunchy Sophie Tucker jokes and her own trademark stand-up routine, labeled here as "Comic Relief." The inclusion of "Up the Ladder to the Roof" was obviously an outgrowth of her attempts at recording several songs for her aborted *Bette Does Motown* album.

Also captured on this record are two of her acting vignettes, in which she portrays different characters to embody some of her songs. "The Vicki Eydie Show" gave her the platform to perform a global cavalcade of "cheese"—including "Around the World," "Hawaiian War Chant," and "Istanbul." For her sad and downtrodden tunes, Midler portrayed a character she called "Nanette," a bag lady whose life somehow eclipsed her sense of reality. As Nanette—the crazy lady with a fried egg on her head—Bette brought to life her songs "Mr. Rockefeller," "Ready to Begin Again," and a bittersweet version of "Do You Want to Dance?"

Live at Last is part concert, part mini-Broadway musical, part stand-up comedy, and 100 percent Midler. The one totally studio-recorded cut on the album, the quirky "You're Moving Out Today," is presented at the end of the first disc as a musical "Intermission" between acts. So much more than just a musical concert performer, the album clearly captures Miss M in transition to becoming an actress who sings—as opposed to being a singer who acts.

It was clear by this point that Bette Midler was one of the most critically lauded and original performers of the 1970s. *The Los Angeles Times* proclaimed that "Midler shows more range and vision on stage than either Barbra Streisand or Liza Minnelli," and *People* magazine glowed: "She is a showplace of exhausting versatility, singing, dancing: she brings S.R.O. houses to their feet night after night" (8). However, the biggest problem facing her career was the inconsistent quality of the projects, songs, and showcases she chose to show off her talents.

The one single that was released off *Live at Last* was the studio-recorded cut "You're Moving Out Today." It was the song that Bette wrote with Carole Bayer Sager—together with Bruce Roberts. Sager's record company decided that the song would also be a great single for her. For whatever reason, both singles were released at the exact same time. Bette had the biggest hit—at Number 42 in America—while Sager had the bigger hit in England, at Number 6, as well as in Australia. Sager's version of the song peaked at Number 69 in the United States. Carole's version of the song was produced by Brooks Arthur, and Bette had Tom Dowd producing her version of the song. Bette was friends with Carole and not only co-wrote "You're Moving Out Today" with her, but can also be heard on the 1977 *Carole Bayer Sager* album. Midler sings a featured solo on the song "Shy As a Violet" and provides background "harmony" vocals, which were written by Sager and Peter Allen.

On September 18, 1977, Bette found herself in the uncomfortable position of headlining a gay rights rally gone awry. The so-called "Star Spangled Night for Rights" turned into one of Aaron Russo's biggest fumbles.

In an effort to smooth over any bad blood between Bette and the gay audiences who had given her initial start on the road to stardom, Aaron used Bette's name to enlist the services of several other big-name stars. Proceeds were to be donated to the San Francisco–based pro-gay rights organization Save Our Human Rights Foundation (SOHR). Unfortunately, the event cost over $200,000 to produce and barely cleared $100,000 for the cause. That $100,000 was to be held in escrow by another holding company called Star Spangled Night, Inc. In the confusion, several hundred tickets to the event went unsold by show time. Some Los Angeles–based gay organizations even boycotted the event. Such backstage intrigue notwithstanding, the real battle was waged onstage when the show began.

The event boasted a star-studded line-up that included comedians Lily Tomlin, David Steinberg, and Richard Pryor; singer Tom Waits; rock groups War and Aalon; actor Christopher Lee; ballet dancers Johanna Kirkland and John Clifford; the Hollywood Festival Orchestra, and, finally, Bette as the closing attraction. The evening was long and slow moving, and by the time Richard Pryor took the stage, the audience was restless. Pryor began his directionless monologue by complaining that none of the other performers had admitted to personal homosexual experiences. After discussing his own experimentation in the early 1950s, his remarks became increasingly hostile.

"We've got a lot of faggots in the ghetto, but not a single homosexual. Niggers don't want nothing to do with homosexuality," he contended. After several minutes of antigay comments, Pryor shouted at the hecklers he was inciting, "Kiss my happy rich black ass!" (75). With that, he stormed off the stage to a sea of "boos" from the crowd.

An apologetic Russo took the microphone and was promptly booed off the stage. Likewise, whiskey-voiced blues singer Tom Waits was jeered and booed while the stage was hastily prepared for Bette's entrance. She had no idea what she was about to walk into the middle of: a hostile crowd with no sense of humor.

According to Bette: "I was in my dressing room, running lines with the PA system turned off. I had no idea that anything unusual was happening until one of the Harlettes came back and told me that Richard Pryor had walked off the stage and told the audience to kiss his 'rich black ass.' 'Hmmmmm,' I thought, 'that's interesting. I've said worse than that to a lot of folks.' And so, not grasping the context in which he's said it, I went on stage and said, 'Who'd like to kiss my rich white ass?' I sensed right away that something else was going on out there besides me . . . something scary. Still I really didn't have any idea of how deeply Pryor had offended the audience until after the show when somebody described to me what had happened, and then I went into shock, too" (67).

To make her entrance even more dramatic, Bette had staged a whole bit of business that found her dressed as the Statue of Liberty, swathed in chains and shackles, and dragged on stage by the Harlettes, who were dressed in Ku Klux Klan robes. After Pryor's racist remarks, Bette's humor was seriously out of line. Not even her Anita Bryant jokes were coming out funny. After a quick medley of her hits and two additional songs, she realized she had gotten in over her head. "I think I really need a few friends," she announced and was joined by Tomlin, Steinberg, Waits, Kirkland, and Clifford for a finale of the song "Friends." Unfortunately, the "Star Spangled Night for Rights" left a sour taste in several people's mouths.

"That sorry business brought me so far down," Bette later admitted. "I've thought and thought about it, and I'm still not sure what happened that night." Her harshest comments were reserved for Pryor's hypocrisy" (67).

"Well, Christ . . . what was Richard trying to do?" she wondered. "I couldn't tell you because I haven't talked to him since. Some said that he showed up without enough material, and when he ran out of stuff to say, he simply went on the attack. Others claimed he was right in introducing a serious political issue into the program. Whatever it was, was very dangerous. I mean, ranting and raving about 'where were the faggots during the burning of Watts?' That's serious? That's political? I don't know Pryor very well—he's always kept his distance from me—but I've always thought of him as much more Jewish than black, and as I recall, the first few years of his career he was exceedingly like a cop— VERY much like a cop. And as to where all the heavies were during Watts: Pryor's manager was backstage that night and he said, 'I can tell you where Richard Pryor was during the Watts riots. He was at my house watching them on television!'" (67).

One of the performers on the bill was someone who was becoming one of Bette's best friends: Tom Waits. "I first ran into him at the Bottom Line in New York," she explained. "He was singing 'The Heart of Saturday Night,' and I just fell in love with him on the spot. We got passingly acquainted that first night, and then I ran into him out here [L.A.] someplace, and I suggested we get together for a visit. Tom lives . . . well, sort of knee-deep in grunge, so he was reluctant for me to see his apartment. I grew up in lots of clutter myself, and delicate I ain't so I kept after him till he finally invited me over. He acted ultra-shy at first, but he finally ushered me around, and he's got his piano in the kitchen, and he only uses the kitchen range to light his cigarettes, and then there's this refrigerator where he keeps his hammers and wrenches and nuts and bolts and stuff like that. He opened the fridge door, and with an absolute poker face he said, 'I got some cool tools in here.' I howled for an hour, and we've been buddies ever since. Tom can always get me tickled, and he really helped jack up my spirits after the disaster of that gay rights benefit in Hollywood" (67).

During this same period, Bette was preoccupied with the recording of her fifth album, which was to be titled *Broken Blossom*. It was being produced by Brooks Arthur, and she used several singers on the background vocals, but she did not employ the Harlettes. Ula, Sharon, and Charlotte performed with Bette in the Hollywood Bowl gay rights show and on the TV special *Rolling Stone: The Tenth Anniversary*, but for most of the year, the Harlettes were unemployed. Between Bette Midler tours, there was no source of income for them. It was in the spring of 1977 that the trio began to pursue projects away from Bette.

According to Charlotte Crossley, "After Bette recorded her albums, when we sang background, she would go on promotional tours, and when they ended, Bette would say that she was going to take a couple of months off to prepare the next album. We each went off into our own thing—studio singing, straight acting, things like that. A club owner, who knew us with Bette, called Sharon and asked if we ever appeared as a group when Bette was not working. She told him that we had not worked up a solo act. He suggested that we do this and appear at his club, since he felt we were strong enough to draw an audience" (76).

"We got together and began to play with songs and material to see whether it might work," explains Ula Hedwig. "My neighbor, Marc Shaiman, a professional musical coach, agreed to work out the musical harmonies. Sharon's friend, Andre De Shield, who played the role of the Wizard in the Broadway musical *The Wiz*, gave the act some direction" (76).

This is the year of Marc Shaiman's introduction to the whole Midler camp. Bette liked Shaiman, and in time he became Midler's piano player, musical collaborator, and sometime producer. (On Midler's ill-fated 2000–2001 TV sitcom, the character of "Oscar" was based on Marc Shaiman.)

Andre De Shield had worked with Bette as a choreographer on *Clams on the Half-Shell*, and in addition, the Harlettes found that several former Midler employees were thrilled to lend a hand. Bette's former publicist, Candy Leigh, became the trio's manager, and it wasn't long before they landed a record deal. The producer was David Rubinson, who had produced the first Pointer Sisters' albums, and he got the girls a deal with Columbia Records. Sharon, Ula, and Charlotte billed themselves as "Formerly of the Harlettes," and away they went on their own career—sans Midler.

Naturally, it wasn't long before the trouble started. The name of Bette's background group, "The Harlettes," was never copyrighted, and although Aaron Russo attempted to sue the trio, he didn't have a legal leg to stand on. As a sort of compromise, the album and the group were billed as "Sharon Redd, Ula Hedwig, Charlotte Crossley: Formerly of the Harlettes." Long, but to the point. The cover of the album, which was released in early 1978, was done by artist Richard Amsel, who had painted the covers of Bette's first two albums.

November 1977 to January 1978 were three months of high visibility for Bette Midler. First came the release of her *Broken Blossom* album, followed by her first "network" television special, which overlapped with her first tour of small nightclubs since 1973. The album got great reviews but sold poorly, the TV show was a hit, and the tour was a sellout. Two out of three wasn't bad.

In an effort to come up with an album that was fresh, sparking, contemporary, and harmonic, Bette teamed up with producer Brooks Arthur. Brooks is known in the music business as a vocalist's producer. A singer himself, he knows how to get the best out of a vocal artist. This was just the kind of producer Midler wanted at this time. Among Arthur's biggest hits as a producer are Janis Ian's 1975 Top 3 hit "At Seventeen" and the studio version of "I Go to Rio" by Peter Allen.

"I have many thoughts on *Broken Blossom,* the album," says Brooks. "First of all, it was Carole Bayer Sager who introduced me, or reintroduced me to Bette, and recommended that I produce Bette's album. I loved working with her" (77).

Broken Blossom is known as something of a "lost" Bette Midler album. It was one that drew great reviews, and in fact some reviewers praised it as being the best singing of her career. However, it didn't succeed in producing a huge hit for her. According to Brooks Arthur, *"Broken Blossom* has sort of like peaks and valleys for me, it was kinda like an electrocardiographic kind of an experience for me. The highs were songs like 'Yellow Beach Umbrella,' which to this day, I thought should have been a hit record. And then Ahmet Ertegun loved the song and wanted to recut it, thinking there's maybe a more commercial way we could go. And we tried another version, and even with the great Ahmet Ertegun by my side, it didn't pan out quite as well as the record we released. We were trying for something, but we just couldn't catch it. But we thought we caught it with the record that did come out. I thought it should have been at least—not a Top 10 record—but a Top 15, Top 20 kind of a record" (77).

Brooks reconfirms Bette's strong work ethic by stating, "She's a great artist. In terms of dedication, she needs to put in a minimum of an eight- or nine-hour day. And if, somehow, you got through in three or four hours, she would still want to try things and keep on working, just to know that she put in—what she calls—a 'full day.' She'll want to do some vocal work, or trying things, or background work" (77).

He has several fond memories of working with Bette on *Broken Blossom:* "I do remember cutting 'You Don't Know Me.' And, I remember Cher standing by the door at the Record Plant, just glued, watching her do the vocal. And I looked to the door, and there was Cher, with her ear pressed up against the door, and I said, 'You can come in.' She came and hung out for a while. and then I said, 'Cher, you must sign a photo to me.' About an hour later, a photo comes in, signed to me, and it says, 'I hope we can work together some day.' Of course we never did, but I love the photo" (77).

However, the recording sessions had their frustrating downside as well, when Bette and Aaron gave the "thumbs down" to a song Brooks was convinced should have been a hit for her. As Arthur explains, "The heartbreak of the album for me was: when we were making the album, I said, 'Bette, I think we need one more song to really make sure this album is, bare minimum: a *Gold* album—one more song. Out of the blue, Gerry Goffin, of Goffin & [Carole] King fame, called me with his partner at that time, Michael Masser, comes to the studio—the old Record Plant studios in L.A., on Third Street and Fifth: 'I gotta play you this song!' He plays me this song, and I fucking died: 'Oh God, this is a Top 5 song if I ever heard one in my life!' And I called Bette, and she comes running to the studio, and she hears the song, and she loves it, and I call my very good friend Artie Butler to come in and do an arrangement on it. And, in a matter of 72 hours, the record was done. We had to rush it, because Masser said if we don't commit to it right away, he's going to show it to other people. He didn't want us to dick around with him and his song, for more than a short amount of time—

otherwise he was gonna bail, and get someone else to cover it. We cut the song, and I swear to God, I am sitting in the control room saying to myself, 'Wow, I think I got myself a smash here!' And I was feeling very, very good because the way I was connecting the dots, was I was still thinking: 'At Seventeen' by Janis Ian, and I am still searching for a follow-up to that kind of success. I had had some modest success between that, it wasn't a lot of time, but I was in creatively desperate need for a Top 5" (77).

However, that is not how the story ends. Continues Arthur, "So, I fucking cut the tune, and I get a call a couple of days later, from Bette . . . maybe two, three, four in the morning, and she says, 'I don't want to release the song.' I said, 'Why?' She said, 'Because, my manager, Aaron Russo, felt that the album didn't need another gushy ballad, it needed more energy.' So, we wrestled, we wrestled—we talked until four, five, six, seven in the morning, we did this for about two days straight. And, finally, Aaron just says . . . he got Ahmet Ertegun to agree with him on this . . . in this sort of conference call, that 'we definitely don't want to release this record, we want Bette to have another 'Friends' or 'Boogie Woogie Bugle Boy.' So, I called the writers and I said, 'Man, I can't believe this. I'm dead in the water here.' This song would have completed my album and put me over the top, and now I'm still one song shy of a hit here. And, I have to give the song back, and lo and behold, Natalie Cole cuts the song, and the song is called 'Someone That I Used to Love.' And then Barbara Streisand cuts the tune, and the next thing I know there are two hits on it. Natalie's record was a huge success, but it was not nearly as important a record as the record I made with Bette. It's lying 'in the can' somewhere at Atlantic Records. I never even kept a cassette of it" (77). Arthur's instincts proved correct when Natalie Cole's version of "Someone That I Used to Love" went to Number 21 in *Billboard*.

With that song suddenly missing from the album, Brooks knew that it needed another big song to replace it. "So, I said to Bette, 'What do you want to do now?' She said, 'I don't know. What do you want to do?' So, I said to her, 'I've always loved the idea of cutting the old [Carla Thomas] song "Gee Whiz," and do it like "Do You Want to Dance?"' She said, 'How would you cut it?' I said, 'Slow and sexy.' And she said, 'Brooks, you wouldn't know sex if it fell on you!' So, that song goes by the wayside. So, I said, 'What do you want to do?' She said, 'I want to do "Make Yourself Comfortable," the old Sarah Vaughn record.' I said,

'That's a great idea. I love that idea, except, I've got to tell you, it has to be campy and fun. But I don't know if it's gonna be the song of doom— the smash that we want it to be.' She said, 'No, let's give it a shot.' I said, 'OK.' So, we cut the song, and it turned out great, not nearly as sexy as I had hoped it would be. For some reason, I didn't think that it was going to be a hit. [The album] was still missing some ingredient, but time had moved on. Our budget was exhausted. Atlantic was growing impatient for the record. Bette had other commitments, and other crisis in her life—nothing major, but I had to cut her loose. Had it been these days, she wouldn't have left that studio till I had one more monster hit" (77).

However, that is not the end of the story. Continues Brooks Arthur, "During the time between Bette and whatever [1980], I get a call from Bernadette Peters, who I knew as a child. And Bernadette says, 'Hey, I'm getting a deal with MCA, would you produce my album for old time's sake?' I said, "I would love to.' Bernadette said to me, 'What was that tune you and your sister used to sing to me in the subway all the time?'—my sister Donna. I said, 'Oh, it's called "Gee Whiz," let's cut it!' She said, 'Really?' I said, 'Yeah, I've been thinking about that song.' So, we cut the song, and it goes about Top 12 or Top 15—with Bernadette singing it [Number 31 in *Billboard* in 1980]. It was a big success for her on MCA. Here's how the story continues: you know I can't make this story up. Here it comes. . . . I'm sitting at the sushi bar on LaCienega Boulevard in Los Angeles. I ran into—coincidentally, a couple friends of mine who were with Manhattan Transfer—specifically, Tim Hauser and one of the other guys, and I'm sitting there having sushi. And, the place had tile floors. And, I hear these heels going across the tile, and I said to Tim Hauser, 'It sounds to me like Bette is in the room.' And, he picks his head up and says, 'My God—you're right, it's Bette!'

"She comes walking over and she says to me, 'Eat shit, you son-of-a-bitch, you stole my song!' And I said, 'What the hell are you talking about? I stole *your* song? What do you mean?' She said, 'I wanted to cut "Gee Whiz," and Bernadette Peters has a hit with it!' I said, 'You know what? Do me a favor, Bette: get off my back, because I just got the news from *Billboard,* the record has lost its bullet, and it's now sliding down the charts, and in two weeks it's not going to be a big record anymore. But, you didn't want to cut that song.' She said, 'I did, too.' I said, 'No, no, you didn't. When I told you I wanted to cut it "slow and sexy," you told me, "I wouldn't know sex if it fell on me." I said, 'But you've got "The Rose," and you are at the top of the charts and the top of your game, so get off my back.' She said, 'Really, it's dead?' I said, 'Yes, it is.' She said, 'Move over, I'm having sushi with you'" (77).

Meanwhile, the 1977 *Broken Blossom* album that Brooks Arthur did produce for Bette Midler nonetheless had several strong highlights. Without a doubt, the most bawdy cut on the album was the very sexual old Bessie Smith song "Empty Bed Blues." In the 1920s, Bessie was known for her very blue double entendre songs, like "Need a Little Sugar in My Bowl (Need a Little Hot Dog in My Roll)." "Empty Bed Blues" was a song that Bette used to sing in her act back at the Continental Baths. At one point in this song, Midler sings in kitchen metaphors—"when he slipped the bacon in, he over-flowed the pot." In another part of the song she sings of oral sex, referring to her lover as a "deep sea diver" who really knew how to hold his breath while going down.

After doing so many New York City songs on her first two albums, here Midler sings her first song about the West Coast: her pumping and snappy upbeat version of Billy Joel's "Say Goodbye to Hollywood." She got seductive on her version of "Make Yourself Comfortable," and even went a little bit country on Eddie Arnold's "You Don't Know Me."

She attempted to stretch out by recording a duet with her new singing/songwriting buddy Tom Waits. Her melodic voice and his gruff and raspy tones didn't necessarily mix very well together on the song "I Never Talk to Strangers." However, the song is a fun little vignette set to music, which features the two singers as people who meet at a smoky bar—and try to pick each other up.

Midler sings of her own favorite color on Sammy Hagar's raucous rocker "Red." But Bette's best rock & roll performance on the album is her rendition of Harry Nilsson's "Paradise," a dramatic and sweeping ballad with an ethereal chorus behind her—including famed Brill Building songwriter Ellie Greenwich. The song is very Phil Spector "Wall of Sound"–sounding, with a dramatic instrumental accompaniment and a huge chorus behind her.

The optimistic pop song "Yellow Beach Umbrella" is a lighthearted summer-on-the-beach type of tune. Bette also sings a beautiful version of David Pomerantz's "Storybook Children (Daybreak)," which is a nice love ballad with—of all things—the sounds of a banjo. Yet, somehow, it works here. Pomerantz wrote several notable songs in the 1970s and had previously written "Tryin' to Get the Feeling Again" for Barry Manilow.

One of the most effective performances on the album was Bette's slow and serious English-language version of Edith Piaf's "La Vie en Rose." That same year, Grace Jones recorded a disco-ized version of the song, which had been a huge hit in the gay dance clubs the previous year. So this was a song that had suddenly resurfaced. Miss M's version was more faithful to Piaf's original—which naturally had been in French. It is also worth noting that this was the first "rose" song that Midler recorded. Roses became Midler's signature blossom, and in reality, it all started here.

One of the most memorable things about the *Broken Blossom* album was the George Hurrell photograph of Bette on the cover. In 1930s Hollywood, Hurrell established himself as *the* hottest portrait photographer in the business. He had a reputation for turning attractive-looking actors into virtual gods and goddesses. His portraits of stars like Bette Davis, Joan Crawford, Greta Garbo, Gloria Swanson, and Jean Harlow are among the most glamorous photographs of the screen divas' lives. How fitting that he should give the glam treatment to la diva Midler. It remains the most spellbinding and dazzling portrait of her career.

However, the cover concept and the title of the album might have ended up a little different if Miss M had gone with her original idea. On the back of the album is another Hurrell photo of Midler—a body shot, with her bust prominently displayed. Explains Brooks Arthur, "You know the photo on the back of the album of her in a bra? She wanted to call the album *So Many Mammaries!*" (77).

The playful girl-group campiness and poignant emotion of Bette's first two albums were nowhere to be found on this disc. In an attempt to turn Midler into an accomplished 1970s chanteuse, it was too contained, homogenized, and restrained to ever find an audience—with the exception of her most die-hard fans. Although the Bessie Smith number and a rocking version of Sammy Hagar's appropriate song "Red" showed off a rougher side of Midler, the disc missed its mark on all counts. The one single that was released off the album was the ballad "Storybook Children," which made it to Number 57 on the *Billboard* magazine Pop Singles chart. The *Broken Blossom* album made it only to Number 51 in *Billboard*, signifying her slipping popularity with her once-strong record-buying audience. This was her third album in a row *not* to be certified Gold in the United States.

Arthur Bell, in the *Village Voice,* had the opposite opinion. According to him, *"Broken Blossom,* her latest album, is her best, with hardly any camping, and yet it's selling worst of all. But to ask that she stretch, expand, play it straight, is tantamount to suggesting that Muhammad Ali go on a parsley diet. As it stands, Bette is neither middle-of-the-road nor far left. She's stuck in a soft shoulder" (78).

According to Brooks Arthur, "'Yellow Beach Umbrella' could have been a hit. 'Paradise' could have been a hit. 'La Vie En Rose' could have been a great record overseas, but unfortunately, it was just one of those records. Everyone who I meet—and I'm baffled by this because it doesn't have a lot of popularity—says, 'Oh, *Broken Blossom* is my favorite Bette album!' And I say, 'Wow!' But I dug in for those vocals, 'cuz she gave them to me, and I was able to coax ever better ones out of her. And me being a singer, and having a sixth sense about singers, I was able to burn some great vocals together with Bette" (77). Unfortunately, *Broken Blossom* was not the hit album that everyone had hoped for. Had Aaron and Bette listened to Arthur's advice with regard to "Someone That I Used to Love" and "Gee Whiz," things might have turned out differently.

While Bette was recording *Broken Blossom* with Brooks Arthur, they had a lot of fun together. Remembers Brooks, "I took her to a baseball game one time at Dodger Stadium, and I was telling Ahmet Ertegun that I am taking her to the Dodgers' game, and I had box seats—the dugout box, and the security is great. I talked to the public relations office and had her name on the scoreboard: 'Dodger Stadium Welcomes Bette Midler.' Ahmet Ertegun warned me, you've got to be very careful with Bette. She's precious cargo. She's my talent: don't let her get lost, and be very security conscious.' I said, 'Ahmet, I will guard her with my life.' And I went with her and my wife, Marilyn, and her friend at the time was Peter Riegert. Before we got to the Dodgers game, we were passing Echo Park, right near Dodger Stadium. And, there's a big fair, called 'Pan-Pacific Day.' All the Pacific countries are having some kind of a fest and a feast. Bette says, 'Stop the car, I've got to participate in this. After all, I am from Hawaii, you know.' She runs out, and—Oh my God! She's lost in the crowd!—I fucking lost her! I am having visions of Ahmet Ertegun looking for me with a hangman's noose. Finally, after about 35 minutes, I found her eating some food, talking Samoan, or some kind of Hawaiian talk with some beautiful Asian women. We got her to the stadium, and of course they put her name on the scoreboard, and she got a big round of applause, and we had a great time. It was a wonderful, wonderful time!" (77).

According to Brooks, "I met new friends through her: Bruce Vilanch, and a few other folks along the way. Bette and Carole Bayer Sager and Peter Allen used to come to my home for dinner all the time. It was one of the best times of our lives. I had 'I Go to Rio' with Peter Allen, which was a smash across the boards. Around that same time, Carole Bayer Sager had 'You're Moving Out Today'" (77).

On Wednesday, December 7, 1977, NBC-TV broadcast Bette's special *Ol' Red Hair Is Back*. Her co-stars were Dustin Hoffman and famed circus clown Emmett Kelly, Jr. The show opened with Bette emerging from her seashell, resurrected from *Clams on the Half-Shell*, complete with the overture from *Oklahoma!* She performed "Hello in There" emotionally to sad-faced clown Kelly and even undressed Hoffman while he played piano. Nick Yanni in the *Soho Weekly News* announced of the special, "Bette is terrific—absolutely spectacular, most engaging and endearing not only to her legions of loyal fans, but probably, after this show, to many new converts" (79).

Oddly enough, for the special, Bette used a new group of Harlettes: Sharon Redd teamed with former Harlettes Robin Grean and Merle Miller. Although much of Midler's material was lifted and restaged from her concert act, considerable expurgation of her in-concert material was required for TV. Example: "We washed, we showered, we FDS'd [feminine deodorant sprayed] ourselves into a stupor" was changed to "We washed, we showered, we gargled ourselves into a stupor." However, she did manage to get enough zingers into the script, just under the noses of the network censors. Giving an "aside" to the Harlettes, Bette commanded, "Try to remain vertical, girls—at least until the first commercial" (80).

According to Gerrit Henry in the *New York Times*, "The 31-year-old Miss Midler has made it to the small screen largely intact. Those who know her stage show or albums are aware that Miss Midler's act is anything but standard television fare. Her onstage persona, 'The Divine Miss M,' is a feverishly schizoid creation—a sex crazed, foul-mouthed hussy with a heart, and eyes of a lost child. . . . Add to this non-stop patter full of acid-tongued put-downs, salty language and sexual innuendo, and you have a performer who generates love-or-hate-her reactions almost of the kind elicited by the late Judy Garland" (80).

TV Guide found Bette a bit restrained yet fully appealing: "There are some racy moments in the special—costumes—gestures, lyrics, and double entendres—but Bette is actually rather restrained by her own stage standards. No profanity. No nudity. No bumps and grinds. Even her dad ought to be able to watch her perform this time" (81). The trashy diva was a TV star now!

When writer Gerrit Henry of the *New York Times* inquired of her future in television, Midler snapped back at him, "A future in TV? Who'd want a future on TV? Television is a medium that eats you alive. You can't keep turning out good material week after week! Another special maybe" (80). If she had only listened to her own advice in the year 2000!

The following year, Bette's *Ol' Red Hair Is Back* won an Emmy Award as the Outstanding Variety Special of the season. When the awards were handed out, Bette was on her first European concert tour, so Aaron accepted for her at the awards ceremony. However, he never once thanked Bette in his speech, and she never let him forget it.

The TV special's broadcast date was in the middle of Bette's highly publicized nightclub tour, entitled "An Intimate Evening with Bette." The tour encompassed dates at the Cave in Vancouver, Bimbo's in San Francisco, the Roxy in Los Angeles, the Park West in Chicago, the Paradise Theater in Boston, and New York City's famed Copacabana. A truce was finally worked out between the Harlettes, Bette, and Aaron Russo; and Sharon, Ula, and Charlotte were featured as Bette's opening act. Then Bette would make her entrance, and the Harlettes would remain on stage as her background singers.

According to Aaron at that time, Bette "has turned down offers in excess of $3 million to perform large concerts across the country. She sincerely believes that while stadiums would produce higher income, an intimate atmosphere is more vital in generating electricity between people and the performer" (82). Although the tickets to the engagement varied from city to city from $15 to $25 a head, scalpers were reportedly getting up to $100 each for them. (One has to keep in mind that this was 1978, when it was unthinkable that twenty-two years later a face-value ticket to see Midler on New Year's Eve was $500 a head.)

In New York City, the January 20, 1978, show was nearly canceled due to a huge blizzard that dumped thirteen inches of snow on the city streets. That night when Bette hit the stage, she quipped, "They promised us five inches and gave us thirteen. If life were only like that!" Bette was indeed in fine form. Discussing the fact that she had attended an EST seminar, she deadpanned, "EST! Oh, please . . . I wouldn't recommend it. I should have gone to Bloomingdale's instead!" (83).

The unfortunate thing about Bette's Copacabana engagement was that the club's owners jammed far too many seats into the once-glamorous basement nightspot. Rex Reed wrote in the *New York Daily News* that "it wasn't just crowded, it is miserable. . . . The act isn't just sold out, it's been oversold. . . . mobs pushed, shoved and groped their way along the narrow stairs in a reckless disregard of the fire regulations" (84). In the *Village Voice,* Arthur Bell wrote, "Ron Delsner, Aaron Russo, and whoever else is responsible for overcrowding the Copa during the Bette Midler run should have their asses kicked. They've done a disservice to their talent and to the establishment. The Second Coming couldn't get me inside the Copa again" (78).

In addition to the admission charge, the Copacabana also imposed a two-drink minimum. Laughing, Midler said to her audience, "You fools, they bought Manhattan for less money than it cost you to see me!" (83). Nevertheless, it was worth every cent, and the reviews were glowing.

According to Rex Reed, "Finally, the star herself emerged. Her hair, blonder than its usual maraschino color, looked like 40 rats had spent the winter in it. Her spangled shirt looked like a sofa cover from Sister Ione's tarot card parlor and mung bean salad bar. Beneath, she wore black toreador pants with a lace garter around the knee and yelled fearlessly to the roaring mob: 'I stand before you, nipples to the wind!' She was pure dynamite" (84).

As 1978 began, Bette Midler had already conquered the record charts, the Broadway stage, the television screen, nightclubs, and concert halls. There was just one more obstacle in her push to become a total superstar: movies. That was the final medium that Bette had to master before Aaron Russo would have made good on his promise to make Midler into a "legend."

After the last shows at the Copacabana in January of 1978, Harlettes Redd, Hedwig, and Crossley officially struck out on their own, never again to work as a trio behind Bette. They had all made it clear that they *very strongly* disliked Russo. during this era, Ula publicly proclaimed, "Aaron's not one of my favorite people. I wish Bette would break up with him. I think he's making her untouchable. Whenever he wasn't around, we actually had a good time together. We hung out together—we bowled and we'd stay at the same hotel. But whenever he was there, she'd be whisked away to some—you know—the best hotel in town and we'd never see her. He'd never let anybody get close to her. He just sort of scares away her friends" (48).

According to Charlotte Crossley, Russo did things just to anger Midler. One of his famous stunts involved not bathing for several days at a time. An article that was printed in *New West* magazine in 1978 described Aaron as "so insignificant and classless and altogether slob-like. The moon-pie Jewish face framed by greasy ringlets, the Cookie Monster belly, the grungy gray sweatshirt that hikes up the rear to show suet and hair decorating his backbone" (67).

While Bette was in San Francisco on her nightclub tour, Aaron had a huge run-in with concert promoter Bill Graham. The next week in Los Angeles, Russo showed up for the dates at the Roxy packing a pistol and surrounded by several burly and intimidating bodyguards.

Although disliked by the people around Bette, Russo made an important move at exactly the right time. Bette Midler was going to make her long-awaited movie debut, and the cameras were about to roll that spring. So begins the final episode of "Bette and Aaron" and the start of Midler's career as a movie star.

11

EVERYTHING COMES UP ROSES

Bette Midler was destined to become a film actress. It was predicted for her early in her career, but it took several years to finally get her to the screen. Aaron Russo's decision not to allow Bette to appear in several film projects that came her way was a strategic move to his credit.

It was reported that Bette's major film debut could have been in any one of a dozen different films. Among the roles that Midler and Russo passed on were Stockard Channing's role in *The Fortune* (1975); Barbara Harris's in Robert Altman's *Nashville* (1975); Talia Shire's in *Rocky;* Madeline Kahn's in *Won Ton Ton, the Dog Who Saved Hollywood* (1976); Jessica Lange's in *King Kong;* and Goldie Hawn's role in *Foul Play* (1978). Film versions of the lives of vaudeville star Sophie Tucker, scandalous author Dorothy Parker, Broadway legend Ethel Merman, and the bawdy Texas Guinan were also discussed as screen vehicles for Midler. There was, however, a biography that kept surfacing, entitled *The Pearl,* based on the life of tragic rocker Janis Joplin. It was this script that eventually evolved into *The Rose* (1979).

The script for *The Pearl* was written by Bill Kerby, and it was commissioned by one of the producers at 20th Century-Fox, Marvin Worth. It was one of the initial projects that was offered to Bette when she first became the toast of the entertainment business in 1973. Worth wanted Bette to play Janis Joplin.

"It was first sent to me," recalls Midler, "not long after Janis passed away. I thought it was in very bad taste to send the script to anyone. It was like dancing on someone's grave before the body was cold. To be blunt, I didn't like it very much. By '75 or '76 we [Bette and Aaron] were at Columbia, trying to tailor-make a screenplay and having very little luck, mostly because the writers were unfamiliar with my work, or I didn't communicate with them. This script kept coming back like clockwork. Eventually, I sat down and reread it, and it wasn't bad. It's not exactly the strongest plot in the whole world, but for a performer like me, it had a big emotional range, and I was interested in range" (85).

"We eventually left Columbia. Maybe we were even thrown off the lot—I don't remember. When it came down to the wire, *The Rose,* as it was called by then, was the one script we'd been offered in all those years that was a real big part and a real big good part," says Bette (85).

"By this time I was worn out, but I wanted to do films, I felt I had a contribution to make. Aaron called me up and said, 'Why don't you look at this again?' I read it. I said, 'These are the elements I'd like to keep: I'd like to keep this person a rock & roll singer, and I would like to keep the sorrow and a certain amount of self-hate, this constant seeking of hers for approbation. Everything else has to go.' And that's what they did. It's a fine framework to hang the songs on, something to hang the character on. We did a lot of improvising" (85).

Director Mark Rydell has said that he was also offered the script of *The Pearl* in 1973. "I wanted to use Bette Midler, but at that time the studio didn't appreciate my suggestion. So I passed. The script went to many directors, including Ken Russell, and finally back to me five years later with a test of Midler, which to my mind made it possible," says Rydell (85).

Mark Rydell and screenplay writer Bo Goldman began revising Kerby's original script. "At first it was more directly about Joplin," explains Rydell. "Bo and I fictionalized it and made it into a much more personal story instead of a documentary. We wanted to reveal some of the heroism of virtuosity. There's a price that people who are that gifted pay—a kind of deep hunger that's hard to satisfy" (85).

On April 24, 1978, filming of *The Rose* began. Bette Midler, Alan Bates, and Frederic Forrest starred; Mark Rydell directed; Bo Goldman, Michael Cimino, and William Kerby wrote the screenplay, based on the story by Marvin Worth and Michael Cimino; Marvin Worth and Aaron Russo were the producers and Vilmos Zsigmond, the photographer. Music for the film was produced by Paul A. Rothchild, who had produced Janis Joplin's last and most famous album, *Pearl*. The film had a twelve-week shooting schedule and a $9 million budget. Filming took place in New York City and Los Angeles. The concert footage was shot at the Wiltern Theater in L.A., and the Long Beach Veteran's Memorial Stadium was the site of *The Rose*'s final concert sequence.

According to Bette, that segment was one of the most disorienting ones to shoot. "It was really bizarre," she explained. "It was like playing a double part or even four parts. There was me knowing that some audience were fans of mine, pretending that I was this girl, pretending that they liked the girl, and then pretending back to me. All of this pretending really showed who was who. Then, of course, the kids—even though they were fans of mine—were all dressed up in those '60s togs. Some of them had short hair, some of them had long hair, some of them had taken acid, and some of them smoked grass. It was the strangest experience to be doing this in 1978 and all of them acting like they were in the '60s. By the end of the day I was convinced I was in 1969!" (8).

One of the prime pressures on Bette was to create this singer called the Rose, bearing in mind the self-destructive nature of someone like Janis Joplin without pretending to be Joplin. The drugs, sex, and rock & roll credo and the emotional hollowness of life in the fast lane had to come through, while an underpinning of emotional vulnerability had to show.

"I didn't want to concentrate on Janis," said Bette. "I avoided Janis because I didn't feel I could do justice to her. I adore her and I had seen her work live and she really changed my life. Changed a lot of people's lives. I think women were particularly moved by her because she was aggressive and yet she seemed vulnerable. I really adored her and I didn't want to use her to further my own particular aims. I have a certain ethical code that I try to work by. The character in the film has a little bit of everybody in it. Physically, there is a lot more of men than there is of women in it. The men tend to strut and they tend to get into the gymnastics of rock & roll" (86).

Mark Rydell agreed with Bette's feelings. "Though it was never intended to be about Joplin," he explained, "the film does embrace the spirit of those people who, like Joplin, like Hendrix, like James Dean, like Marilyn Monroe or Monty Clift, were tormented and driven to grave ends in their desperate attempts to reveal creative truth. Judy Garland is a perfect example of someone on the edge" (85).

According to Bette, the film required a lot of preparation. "I did a lot

of dieting and I worked in the gym a lot," she stated. "I listened to Sam
Cooke till my ears were bleeding, did a lot of reading about the '60s,
watched a few video tapes, and talked to some people. I did it all. I
actually spent a good six months at it" (86).

One of the most important aspects of the film was the selection of
music. Using Paul A. Rothchild was an inspired move. Paul listened to
over 3,000 songs, chose 30 of them, and played them for Bette for her
reactions. The final version of the film contains 7 of those 30 songs, and
Bette brought in 3 of her own choices: "When a Man Loves a Woman,"
"Stay with Me," and "Let Me Call You Sweetheart."

Among the songs that Paul submitted to Bette was a ballad written
by an aspiring actress-turned-songwriter named Amanda McBroom.
The song was called "The Rose." According to McBroom, "My manager
told me it was time to write some Bob Seger–type tunes so we could
get a record deal. I sat down and forty-five minutes later there was 'The
Rose.' It was the fastest song I've ever written and I never changed a
word. 'The Rose' is most unusual in that it's just one verse repeated
three times. When I finished it, I realized it doesn't have a bridge or a
hook, but I couldn't think of anything to put in there!" (87). The song
was to become the signature song of the film and, for that matter, of
Bette Midler's career.

The filming of *The Rose* was completed on July 18, 1978, two days
under schedule. Bette had scarcely recovered from the experience
when Aaron announced the dates of her upcoming world concert tour.
It opened on September 11 in Seattle, Washington—a three-day domestic "dry run"—then on to London, Brighton, Gothenburg, Stock-
holm, Copenhagen, Lund, Hamburg, Frankfurt, Munich, Paris, The
Hague, Antwerp, Amsterdam, Sydney, Melbourne, Perth, Adelaide,
Brisbane, and finishing up in Sydney again on November 14, 1978.

Bette invited the girls who now called themselves Formerly of the
Harlettes to accompany her on the tour, but Redd, Hedwig, and Crossley declined her offer. Then she placed a want ad in the *Hollywood
Reporter* and held open auditions for a new set of Harlettes. The girls
she ultimately hired for the world tour were Linda Hart, Katie Sagal,
and Frannie Eisenberg.

Bette felt that she had to come up with some new gimmicks for this
tour to enhance the show. It was on this tour that "Dolores DeLago—
The Toast of Chicago" was born, along with her mermaid outfit and her
electric wheelchair. For her entrance in her foreign concert dates, Bette

admitted that she wanted a costume that was completely unique and totally American. One day she hit upon the perfect outfit: She would enter the stage dressed as a hotdog—complete with mustard! Unfortunately, the costume was a colossal pain in the ass to put on and take off, and she stopped wearing it after the second night in Seattle. The wheelchair, the character of Dolores, and the mermaid costume, however, became staples of Miss M's stage shows from that point forward.

Conquering England was one of the Bette's goals. She had already had hit records in the United Kingdom—like "You're Moving Out Today"—but the Brits had yet to experience her insanity live. On September 3, 1978 her *Ol' Red Hair Is Back* TV special was broadcast on England's ITV network, and from September 21 to 23 she headlined the London Palladium, as part of her first European tour. With her mermaid costume in tow, she was determined to make a splash in the British Isles, and splash she did!

London loved Bette. The critics couldn't say enough glowing things about their first taste of Midler live and in person. The *London Evening News* raved, "With this one, dazzling, magic spellbinding show, Bette Midler conquered Britain." The *London Times* marveled that "she received the kind of tumultuously genuine reception which only a star who is many stars in one can evoke." And the *London Daily Telegraph* exclaimed, "Miss Bette Midler has hit London, and London will never be the same again. In a series of dazzling solo performances she has rediscovered and updated for all the essentials of great music-hall" (8).

During one of her London Palladium shows, Bette glanced up to the balcony to spot a huge banner that some of her fans had made that read, "We Love Your Tits." That was all the encouragement she needed: down went her corset. There she stood in tasteful London, "nipples to the wind." In Copenhagen, the locals loved Bette's mermaid costume and took it as a tribute to their own famed Little Mermaid statue in the harbor. The whole tour was a roaring success, especially London and all of the dates in Australia.

As a publicity ploy, Aaron announced that during the tour, Bette would be paid in gold. An item in the business section of the July 3, 1978, *New York Times* stated that half of her $600,000 fee was to be paid upon contract signing in South African gold Krugerrands. It made a great press release, especially since the last person to make such a demand was Sarah Bernhardt, around the turn of the last century. Unfortunately, the deal did not work out, and Miss M had to settle for standard currency this time around. "I was supposed to be paid in gold, but things got mixed-up," she later explained (88).

As 1978 drew to a close, everything seemed perfect for Bette. Her first movie had been made and was in the editing and postproduction phase. She had conquered the rest of the globe on her latest tour, and her business and personal lives seemed quite happy. In fact, her confidence level was at an all-time high. According to Aaron Russo, "She's got the best of both worlds now. She's got Peter [Riegert] at home, who cares for her and is dedicated to her, and me at the office, who cares for her and is dedicated to her" (81).

Bette was indeed very much in love with Peter. According to her at the time, "Since I met Pete, my life has been kind of quiet—not too many orgies, and we've been staying out of the hot tub. I've been working on my craft. I would like to have children before my uterus falls out!" (8).

In January of 1979, tragedy struck when Bette's mother, Ruth, died of cancer. "She had leukemia for a long time, cancer of the liver—and of the breast, incidentally, when I was a kid. She suffered most of her life. She just thought I was 'it!' She thought I was so funny and so adorable; she just loved all the excitement. She used to say I was the only thing that brought her joy," said Bette (8).

The year 1979 was obviously going to usher in several changes in her life, some of them good, some of them not so good. With the sudden death of her mother, Bette decided that it was time to take control of her life. She was so determined to find happiness that in February she decided she could do without several large complications in her life: namely, Aaron Russo. There was never a contract between the two of them, and as far as she could see, he had served his purpose. He had made her a "legend" in her own time, and he had to go.

"I couldn't take it anymore," she explained. "I felt that what he was doing for me professionally wasn't worth what he was doing for me personally. I couldn't sleep. I was in a state of anxiety all the time because I never knew what he was going to pull on me next. It was either, 'I'm dying of leukemia' or 'I'm carrying guns because they're out to get me. You're all that's left!' It was a lot of mind control. I was going to say 'mind fucking,' but I don't think it's an attractive term for a lovely lady to use. And always, of course, there was drama—much, much drama. Eventually, I outgrew my need for drama. At a certain point, when you're 32 or so, you just no longer require the raving. You start enjoying pleasant days where there is no drama, where instead you have a little food and some pleasant conversation about wine and books" (30).

When *The Rose* was released in November of 1979, audiences saw several scenes where Rose fights with her manager, Rudge (Alan Bates). There are those who felt that those scenes bore a startling similarity to Midler's real-life experiences with Russo. According to one of her business associates, "They were fighting constantly, and [in 1974] she wanted to give up the business completely. That's where the whole thing in *The Rose* came from: 'I want to take a year off!' There is a lot drawn from her story. The firing scene, where the manager fires her—that happened. The psychological subtext of that *IS* the Bette and Aaron story" (35).

Midler was later to underscore those comments by stating, "Our relationship was so much sicker than anything in that film. Aaron was very protective of me—in his way. He made a lot of enemies on my behalf. You see, we had a personal relationship at the beginning of everything, and when our personal relationship floundered, it tainted our professional relationship. I was so dumb; I didn't think that'd happen. He was so overbearing, and he kept me very isolated, kept the bad stuff away from me and a lot of the good stuff, too. For a long time I never saw people backstage, never read anything about myself, never had fun. He would have a magazine article about me in his hand as I was going on stage, and I'd say, 'Oh boy, lemme see that!' But he'd say, 'I don't want you to read it now or later. It'll only upset you.' Long, long afterward, I would find out it said bad things about HIM, not me!" (8).

While *The Rose* was in production, Aaron took credit in the press for steering Bette into the film. He told the *New York Times,* "I wanted her first film to be a role that only Bette Midler could play. I mean, who else could play 'The Rose?' Liza Minnelli? You know what I'm saying?" (89).

According to Bette, her lowest point came during the 1978 world tour, on which Aaron accompanied her. "I used to do shows," she explained, "and no matter how good they were, it didn't matter until HE told me it was okay. And he used to withhold this approbation from me all the time. THAT game. And that's a real horrible mind-fuck to get into. I was pretty messed up there for a long time. I don't know why—emotional retardation, I guess. He was the only one I trusted. I started out with a lot of people around me and eventually they all left, and I was alone with Aaron. I knew that if I didn't get out at that point, I would never be happy again" (8).

In May 1979, Bette appeared as the musical guest on the TV show *Saturday Night Live.* She sang her latest song, the Top 40 hit "Married Men," and a song by Tom Waits about lost love, called "Martha," which was never released on record. By the time she finished singing the Waits ballad, tears were running down her cheeks. She later explained, "That song calls up a lot of deep things for me. That night of the show, I was thinking about my mom" (8).

In September, Bette released her first album since breaking loose from Aaron Russo. At long last she had recorded an album that matched the fun, the emotion, the excitement, and the total listenability of her first two LPs. The album, which was produced by Arif Mardin, was entitled *Thighs and Whispers,* and it drew immediate critical acclaim. *Stereo Review* proclaimed that "her wonderful new Atlantic album . . . certainly shows that she hasn't forgotten any of her old tricks." And *Billboard* announced that "Midler covers a lot of ground. . . . [she] has been searching for her niche on record since her big initial success with *The Divine Miss M* in 1973, and she may have found it in the sheer diversity of this package" (8).

However, Steven Holden, in the *Village Voice,* hated the album—a lot. According to his review, "Midler's latest studio album teams her with Arif Mardin, whose elegant pop-soul arrangements obviously scared her to pieces. Though for a change she stays on pitch most of the time, this hard-won precision requires a near-total sacrifice of personality. The best cut, 'Big Noise from Winnetka,' is an arranger's showpiece. The worst, Johnny Bristol's 'Hang On in There, Baby,' has Midler sounding like a luded-out Donna Summer, her voice a frightened mew in a swamp of production" (90). Oh well, you can't please everyone.

However, if you loved this album, you really loved it. The highlights on *Thighs and Whispers* include the rousing '40s swing number "Big Noise from Winnetka," which was borrowed from Bob Crosby & the Bobcats. This was the perfect song to rekindle Midler's association with the songs of the 1940s swing era. Her background vocals were fittingly provided by three of her Harlettes: Ula Hedwig, Robin Grean, and Merle Miller.

James Taylor's "Millwork," from the Broadway show *Working,* was a real treat. Bette took this song and gave it the same kind of slow and pensive treatment that she gave to "Hello in There." On this song she brings to life a character who is singing of her sad and dismal life, working at a mill, day after monotonous day. With just a simple piano and cello behind her, this is one of Midler's most touching vocal performances.

"Cradle Days," which was written by Aaron Neville, gave Miss M a great, torchy rhythm & blues song, singing about the love of her life. After recording so many pristine and smoothly produced songs in recent years, on this one she delivers a nice, occasionally ragged torch performance. The backgrounds here are provided by Luther Vandross, disco singer Ullanda McCullough, and Diva Gray—on her way to becoming a Harlette.

The outrageously tongue-in-cheek "My Knight in Black Leather" was just the kind of silliness that Bette's last two studio albums lacked. It is the Divine Miss M here, singing to a disco beat, of falling in love with a hunk in black leather who "smelled just like a new car." This totally crazy disco number was understandably a huge hit in discotheques in 1979, which was the absolute height of disco mania. With a chorus of background singers, including Luther and Ula, Midler unleashes her strong belting voice. This song was a smash at Studio 54.

Bette's seductive "Hang On in There, Baby" is the Bette's disco homage to Johnny Bristol's 1974 hit. She gives the song the same sexy come-on that "Do You Want to Dance?" possessed.

Again trying her hand at songwriting, this time with Randy Kerber, Midler penned the song "Hurricane." A song about love, "Hurricane" features the diva singing, "you blow me away," with an ethereal choir, to a sweeping disco beat. Her version of the Dr. John (Mac Rebenack) composition "Rain" emerged as an arty jazz blues ballad.

Finally, the album ends with Bette's comic version of the song "Married Men," which is another disco-ized spree. On the comic dance song, Midler sings of her advice about the pitfalls of dating philandering married men who are never going to divorce their wives.

Thighs and Whispers was a lively and excellently recorded album, and Bette was finally on the right track musically. It peaked at Number 65 on the *Billboard* chart, as compared with *Broken Blossom* having made it to Number 51. Although it wasn't a huge seller, *Thighs and Whispers* did win a German Record Award as 1979's best international album, and it won an avalanche of critical acclaim that *Broken Blossom* and *Songs for the New Depression* had failed to draw.

Bette herself was quite pleased with *Thighs and Whispers*. According to her, "People say it's the best thing I've done in a long time and that's gratifying. I really do love the ballads. For someone like me, they keep you alive. I think 'Cradle Days' is one is one of the best things I ever did. I love old tunes and disco and rock, but ballads really are the key to my soul" (85).

In the summer of 1979, Bette went back to Europe for a brief tour and then a one-shot American concert tour that took her into autumn. Billed as *Bette! Divine Madness,* the show was a preparation for a Broadway opening on December 5 at the Majestic Theater. Her engagements in San Francisco, Seattle, Portland, Los Angeles, Phoenix, and Detroit were all successful, especially teamed with the advance word on *The Rose* as a tour de force for Miss M. Her Harlettes for this tour were Linda Hart, Frannie Eisenberg, and Paulette McWilliams (who had replaced Katie Sagal).

One night onstage in Detroit, the ever-unpredictable Bette spontaneously showed more of herself than usual. She had done the encore number, and the crowd was still clamoring for more. Midler was already in her dressing room, wrapped in a towel, when Jerry Blatt came and knocked on her door to tell her to come out onstage again. Jerry half jokingly said to Bette as she walked into the wings, "Please, whatever you do, don't flash them" (16). That was all the encouragement that she needed!

〜〜

The date was November 6, 1979. The place was the Ziegfeld Theater in New York City. The event was the world premiere of *The Rose.* And the opening night party was—where else?—the Roseland Ballroom. Said the newly blond Miss M, "It was the most exciting opening I've ever been to, and I've been to a few. Thank God, this one was mine!" (91).

The film tracks the last year in the life of a flamboyant rock & roll star. Through a haze of booze and drugs, the Rose (Bette Midler) fights with her tyrannical manager Rudge (Alan Bates), desperately clings to a male lover (Frederic Forrest), confronts a former female lover, tries in vain to reconcile with her parents, and comes up emotionally empty-handed on all fronts. In the final scene she ODs on stage, drowning in a sea of misery.

The opening-night premiere and party in New York City was used to raise funds for the famed drug-rehabilitation organization Phoenix

House. "It's such a good cause," remarked Midler that night. "I only wish the opening-night party in Los Angeles was for Alcoholics Anonymous. That would be PERFECT!" (92).

The benefit raised $60,000 for Phoenix House. According to the president of the organization, Dr. Mitchell S. Rosenthal, "We're happy to be connected with *The Rose* because I think the film shows how people who get caught up in drugs are in as much pain as they are. Drugs have been glorified in show business and in rock, and this film punctuates that." (92).

A couple of ironies punctuated the night, however. At the party, several darkened corners of Roseland reeked of marijuana smoke, and the antidrug fundraising was hosted by none other than automotive industry czar John DeLorean, whose own cocaine troubles were later to become headline news.

The ballroom of Roseland was decorated that night with three thousand real roses, imported from Michigan. But the starring flower that evening was Bette herself. She was resplendent in a strapless black lace dress, a $2,500,000 diamond necklace, her golden locks—which she referred to as being "Venetian blond"—and her nouveau svelte figure. She had lost twenty pounds for her transition to movie star. According to her, she accomplished the weight loss by living on liquid protein. "It came in these plastic bottles that looked just like Janitor-in-a-Drum [liquid cleaning soap]. It tasted like it, too!" she laughed (89).

Her date for the premiere and the party afterward was her current boyfriend, Peter Riegert. Speaking to the press about her love life, she stated at the time, "I've been lucky in love lately. I think I've been lucky in that I've experienced all kinds of men, and I've learned a lot about the way human beings are with one another. So that in part, I've been lucky. But there has been a certain amount of pain, too" (86).

The following night the West Coast Premiere was held in Los Angeles at the Plitt Century Plaza Theater, and a party was given at the Century Plaza Hotel. The benefit premiere raised $130,000 for the Los Angeles International Film Exposition. The star-studded crowd that gathered that evening included Raquel Welch, Nick Nolte, Jacqueline Bisset, Milton Berle, Hugh Hefner, and Bette's former musical mates Melissa Manchester and Barry Manilow.

The reviews and—even better—the crowds that *The Rose* drew were phenomenal. Bette was an instant hit in the film role. The reception to her acting was so overwhelmingly good that everyone wondered what took so long to get her up on the big screen! She truly threw herself into the demanding role of the Rose and obviously released gallons of pent-up emotional venom on the characterization. She was able to act out her resentment toward Aaron Russo in the scenes where Rose battles her fictional manager, Rudge. She also, very poignantly and painfully, brought to life her frustration with her parents and her lifelong unsuccessful struggle to create a rapport with her father.

One of the most emotionally devastating scenes in the film shows Bette in a phone booth before the final concert. Forlorn, pathetic, and frantic for the helping hand that she needs so desperately, Rose telephones her parents in a last attempt at communication, only to find that they have nothing much to say to each other. It is one of the most depressing and draining scenes ever captured on film. The emotions were obviously real—as they were drawn from Bette's own life. The scene ends up with the drugged-out Rose collapsing on stage and dying, without ever finding the kind of love and acceptance that she so desperately sought.

"It was very moving, the whole evening that we shot it was very moving . . . and then there was the memory that I used when I was doing. . . . whenever I see that clip it brings it all back. . . . To be honest, it was real," Bette later admitted. "They took something very lovely out of that scene that really burned my ass, because I thought it was the most telling thing in the whole film. She [Rose] says, 'What are you watching [on television]? . . . Oh, she's good, I like her.' Those two or three sentences told the whole story of the relationship between the mother and father and daughter. They'd prefer to watch somebody else, some other girl on the show. It's so mystical, it makes me all misty-eyed" (16).

The telephone scene is very close to me," she claimed (86). "I used to phone my parents every time something came up. Of course, being so far away from each other, everything always has a distance to it—you know, death, sickness. They used to not tell me a lot of stuff about sickness, and I never told them the bad parts. Until real desolation set in, like when my sister died. What happens when you leave home is you turn around to watch and see how your folks are doing, and they're the same. I tried to say everything to my folks, but they never listened, they never asked for any daughterly advice. I told them to try to have a little more fun, but they couldn't get themselves into that frame of mind. It used to drive me mad, because I could see them wasting away before my eyes" (8).

When Fred Midler was reached in Hawaii for his comments on his daughter's first starring movie role, it was clear that something wider than the Pacific Ocean separated Bette and her father. "I'm just not interested in that kind of entertainment," he said. "Now I hear she's in the movies, though. Something about Janet Joplin? I think she was some sort of rock singer. I don't like to spend money and I think charging four or five dollars to see a movie is outrageous. But to see my own daughter . . . well, I guess I'll splurge" (15). Reportedly, he never did go to the theater to see *The Rose*.

One of the strangest things about being in a movie is seeing yourself up on the screen for the very first time. You have a mental picture of what you think you looked like doing it, what you were supposed to be doing while the cameras were rolling, but it is rarely the same as what appears in the final cut of the film. Bette had a very negative reaction to her first look at herself as the Rose.

"There was a cast and crew screening of *The Rose* at a huge theater at Fox," she explained, "and I was so upset that I was gasping for air in the last row. People were turning around and looking at me, and they couldn't watch the picture because I was so frantic" (18).

According to her, "I had a strong mental picture of myself. You know, someone sort of very glamorous and exquisite, I mean, in this body is a thin white duchess. And imagine my surprise when I saw a sort of ratty, broken-down, exhausted, split-ended, bleached blond creature on the screen. I mean, I know I made her up and I did my hair myself, but when I finally saw the rough cut, the mental picture I had been carrying all these years crumbled. It was a big shock. The second time I saw it, though, I really enjoyed it" (86).

The critics all agreed that the Rose was a character that only Bette Midler could successfully portray. No other singers-turned-actresses could or would tackle such a part and let themselves be seen as so self-debased. There was also a scene that depicted explicit lesbianism. According to Bette, the scene was more graphic before editing. "That was a nightmare," she said. "I'm real straight, but we were really trying to be sympathetic. I jumped into it, hugging and kissing this girl. When my [former] manager Aaron Russo saw the dailies, he about jumped out of his drawers. He said, 'How could you do that? I told you, "No

tongue!'" I thought it was nice, though they cut it all out in the film"
(71).

This film gave Bette the chance to be totally over-the-top with frank-
ness, whether she was dealing with sex, foul language, or the excesses
of rock & roll. The very first scene with Midler in *The Rose*, she is
shown descending an airplane staircase, obviously stoned out of her
mind. Halfway down the staircase toward the tarmac, she stumbles and
falls. Once she gets up on her feet, she accidentally drops a fifth of
booze she had been clutching among her possessions. This scene sets
the tone for the downward slide of the singer who calls herself the Rose.

In one of the first concert sequences, her manager, Rudge (Alan
Bates), warns her that several VIPs and camera crews are in the audience, and he implores her, "Please don't say 'motherfucker.'" Naturally,
the first words out of her mouth once she hits the stage are "Hiya,
motherfuckers!"

Mid-movie, after a night of lovemaking, the Rose confesses to her
new boyfriend Houston (Frederic Forrest) that she once took on the
whole high school football team—sexually—and woke up on the fifty-
yard line. When this revelation fails to shock him, she feels that she has
met her match—a man who can accept her on her own terms. Another
sexually charged scene is the one where the Rose introduces Houston—
her current male lover—to Sarah (Sandra McCabe), her female ex-
lover.

Bette was able to weave so many aspects of her own life into *The
Rose*. After a wild ride together in a limousine, the Rose takes Dallas to
a drag bar in Greenwich Village. As they walk in, the performer on stage
is impersonating her real-life namesake—Bette Davis. When another
drag queen impersonates "The Rose," it as a sequence that pokes fun
at, and simultaneously spotlights, who she was, who she is, and who she
wanted to be—a legendary movie star.

In another tongue-in-cheek self-parodying scene, she chases Hous-
ton into the all-male Luxor Baths, where they have a heated discussion.
The sequence emerges as a strange sort of tribute to her past at the
Continental Baths.

There is also a fascinating postconcert sequence, in which Rose and
Rudge are seen having a dialogue before getting aboard a waiting helicopter. They are standing on top of what was then the Pan Am building,
on East 42nd Street. Directly behind the actors are the lights of the
World Trade Center, looming in the background. Now, with the World

Trade Center a tragic piece of American history, it is haunting to see Bette as the Rose, standing in front of it.

It seems that every scene between the Rose and her manager directly echoed Bette's real-life relationship with Aaron Russo. In the film, the Rose escapes him by dying; in reality, Midler escaped Russo's clutches by firing him right before the film opened.

In *The Rose,* the concert footage—especially on "When a Man Loves a Woman," is very intense and lovingly filmed. Bette's portrayal of the Rose is complex, emotionally multilayered, raw, frank, and quite tragically magical. She charges every one of her scenes with drama and crackle.

Rose's final conversation with her parents—from a phone booth—is a devastating reflection of her awkward relationship with her own father. It mirrored the fact that her dad refused to see her in concert—even when she was a star, headlining a stadium full of screaming fans in her own hometown.

There are also some interesting cameo appearances in the film. Doris Roberts, who in the 2000s is known as one of the stars of the hit TV series *Everybody Loves Raymond,* appears briefly as the mother of the Rose. And late disco star Sylvester is seen in the drag bar sequence as a male Diana Ross impersonator.

In the Rose's final self-destructive hour, cranked up on a fatal dose of heroin, she is led to the stage like a fragile rag doll. However, she is able to come alive long enough to sing an impassioned version of "Stay with Me, Baby." Over twenty years later, *The Rose* is still one of the best movies about the excesses of rock & roll ever made.

When the film came out, Bette was very verbal about pointing out that drugs were the crutch of the Rose, and not with Bette. With regard to the drugs, she proclaimed at the time, "I don't do drugs. I have a devil. I don't like to get stoned because then it comes out and I can't control it and it's very sick. In the early days, I used to smoke dope and drink stingers before I worked. I had a lot of fun, but I used to lose my voice all the time. At least I think I lost my voice. I was so stoned, I was never sure" (30).

According to Frank Rich in *Time* magazine, "Midler is not a great singer or a subtle actress or an exquisite beauty; yet she just may be a movie star. . . . For Bette Midler, self-styled queen of 'trash with flash,' *The Rose* is an ideal throne!" (93). David Denby, in *New York* magazine, raved, "What a storm of acting!" Jack Kroll, in *Newsweek,* said, "Bette

Midler's performance is an event to be experienced—a fevered, fearless portrait of a tormented, gifted, sexy child-woman who sang her heart out until it exploded," while in the *New York Daily News,* Rex Reed exclaimed, "Remember this day. It's the same one that will go down in history as the day Bette Midler made her movie debut" (16).

Even more gratifying were the phenomenal figures at the box offices across America. Twentieth Century-Fox reported that in its first three-day weekend, *The Rose* grossed a spectacular $793,063. In its first five days of release at the Ziegfeld Theater in New York City alone, $91,111 was taken in; and in four days at the Egyptian Theater in Los Angeles, the total came to $60,189. *The Rose* was a huge hit in less than a week, and Bette Midler became the year's hottest new film star.

The soundtrack album from *The Rose* was unlike any of Bette's previous albums, as it is recorded in the character of the Rose, a woman who—like Joplin—holds back nothing to pump emotion into every song, no matter how raspy or dragged out her voice sounds. This was in complete contrast to the controlled, heavily orchestrated sound on Bette's *Broken Blossom* album. The tone is set by the opening cut, the rocking guitar and horn-driven "Whose Side Are You On?" The Southern rocker "Midnight in Memphis" and the rock anthems "Sold My Soul to Rock 'n' Roll" and "Keep on Rockin'" showed her off in a hard-rocking light that she had never dredged up before in her concerts. Tracing the physical downfall of the character of the Rose, by the time Bette gets to the song "Stay with Me," her voice is low down, raspy, and filled with gutsy emotion. Finally, the album ends with the bittersweet ballad of "The Rose," which is more clearly sung by a recognizable Bette Midler, as opposed to the Southern Comfort–laced character of the Rose. For the most part, Bette clearly poured out her heart and soul on the recording of these songs, like never before.

The first single that was released from *The Rose* album was Bette's raw and conviction-filled version of the soulful "When a Man Loves a Woman." Originally, it was a Number 1 hit for Percy Sledge in 1966. Midler's hard-edged version, sung from a female perspective, became the album's first Top 40 hit, peaking at Number 35 on the *Billboard* singles chart.

But that was just the beginning. For such a heavily rock & roll–themed movie, it would have seemed that the rock numbers would have been the best single choices. However, when the sentimental ballad of a theme song, "The Rose," was released as the second single from the film, it went on to became Bette's biggest single hit (Number 1 on the Adult Contemporary chart, Number 3 on the *Billboard* Pop chart). The song spent eight weeks in the American Top 10, and it was all over the radio airwaves in the summer of 1980. Catapulted by the success of its title song, the album hit Number 13 in *Billboard,* and it was her first Platinum certification for an LP, signifying a million copies sold. Suddenly, she was the toast of the record world all over again. Whatever momentum she had lost on her last four albums was quickly dispelled by the success of the song "The Rose." Ultimately, the soundtrack to *The Rose* and the theme song of the same name went on to become the biggest-selling records of her career—up to that point in time. She had set a new high-water mark for herself.

Regarding the song "The Rose," Bette claimed, "It's the kind of song singers wait for all their lives. My real fans know me as a ballad singer anyway. They don't pay attention to the nutsy stuff. But for me to finally get some kind of mass recognition as a straight-ahead balladeer is probably the greatest thrill of my career" (87).

Commenting on the film, music producer Paul A. Rothchild noted that it "shows all the negative aspects of a performer's life, and then closes with a song that's a total positive statement. And Bette's vocal is very melancholy and beaten, which I like as a counterpoint to the optimism of the lyric. The film opens with 'Let Me Call You Sweetheart,' an a cappella ballad, and closes with 'The Rose,' which starts with single voice and piano. So it opens with her singing a girl's plaint and closes with a grown woman's affirmation" (87).

The rest of the music in the film is out-and-out screaming rock & roll, with Bette hitting some the harshest notes of her career. "I've always loved that kind of music," she stated, "but I never really had the nerve to sing it. I wasn't sure about my own credentials and people in rock & roll can get real uppity about that. I always sort of skirted the issue: I'd throw in one of those songs every now and again, but I never came out and said that's really all I want to do" (87).

Rothchild decided that the soundtrack version of "The Rose" was a bit too sparse for radio airplay, so he sweetened it a bit for release as a single. "I had fought scoring all along. There's not one note of scoring in the film: it's all live music except for the diner scene where there's music coming out of the juke box. I told them, 'We haven't used one violin in this entire movie and I want to keep it that way!' But when it came time for the single, I didn't dare release it to AM radio with just piano and voice. So for the single I added strings, French horns, and some woodwinds" (87).

The Rose added the frosting to a career that was already an outrageous piece of cake for Bette Midler. When it came time for industry accolades to be handed out, her name was prominently displayed. For acting, she won not one but two Golden Globe Awards, for Best Actress in a Musical or Comedy and for New Female Star of the Year. *The Rose* also won a Golden Globe for Best Song from a Feature Film. The cherry on top of the icing came when Bette was nominated for an Academy Award for Best Actress in a film. Although she ultimately lost the award to Sally Field's performance in *Norma Rae*, Bette was now considered a bona fide "A list" movie star.

The song "The Rose" was not nominated for an Academy Award. Explained its writer, Amanda McBroom, "The Academy requires a song be written specifically for the film. They send you a form to fill out and I told them the truth. So now I have a reputation for being stupid, but honest" (87).

However, for Bette, the awards and accolades were just beginning. In 1981, her recording of "The Rose" was nominated for a Grammy Award as the Record of the Year and for Best Pop Performance—Female. She ended up winning the award in the latter category.

The Rose was such a smash that the big question now was how to follow it up. Among the film possibilities discussed was a 1930s-style comedy called *The Polish Nightingale*, a bizarre domestic comedy called *Strike and Hyde,* and even the first mention of a big-screen remake of the Gypsy Rose Lee musical *Gypsy*, with Bette starring as Mama Rose. According to her at the time, she liked the idea of staying with the "rose" theme. "I'd like to spend the rest of my life doing only characters named Rose: *The Rose Kennedy Story . . . The Life of Rose Marie*," she laughingly claimed. "I was really sorry that the Rose died. I could have gone on forever: I loved her with all my heart, she had everything, and people loved her, too. I could have done *Rose II, Rose Goes to Vietnam, Rose Shops at Dior . . .*" (94). For Midler, suddenly everything seemed to be coming up roses.

TOTALLY JINXED

Every rose has its thorns—and Bette's life and career have had quite a few. Between 1980 and 1982, several things went wrong. She was sued by the Harlettes. She made a financially disastrous concert film called *Divine Madness*. She starred in one of the most tragic comedy films ever made, entitled *Jinxed*. And she had a nervous breakdown. The real problem with achieving great heights of success is the distance one has to fall when things turn sour.

The one question on everyone's mind was whether Bette Midler could effectively manage her own career? She had one enormous hit under her belt, and she had fired Aaron. Now the ball was in her court and she was calling all the shots.

Since she now had a smash film and a soon-to-be hit album in the stores, it seemed like an obvious move to do what she did best—go out on tour. From December 1979 to January 1980, her latest stage incarnation—*Bette! Divine Madness*—ran as a huge success on Broadway. It gave her the platform not only to utilize the material that made her famous, but to incorporate some of the hard-edged rock & roll that she had put in her film portrayal of the Rose—notably, the songs "Stay with Me" and "The Rose."

On the closing night of the show's run, Aaron showed up backstage to tell Bette what a mess she was making of her career without him. "I was, of course, at my worst, my lowest ebb. Aaron always had a real nose for knowing when I was feeling terrible about myself and my life," she remembered (8).

Bette had made the decision that her next movie would be a time-capsule film of her present stage act. She decided that she wanted to capture on film her wild stage persona and improve on her 1976 HBO special, with better camera angles, more elaborate costumes—showing off her newly svelte figure—and better acoustics. The film was to be called *Divine Madness,* and she was paid $850,000 for starring in it.

It was later alleged that for the run of the Broadway show, Bette had promised the present set of Harlettes—Frannie Eisenberg, Paulette McWilliams, and Linda Hart—that if they completed the run in New York City, they would be taken to Los Angeles to appear in *Divine Madness* and would be paid $14,500 apiece per week for their perform-ances. The day after *Bette! Divine Madness* closed on Broadway, each of the three girls was informed—by telegram—that she was fired and that her services would not be needed for the film. That same week, Bette ended her relationship with Peter Riegert.

Harlettes Eisenberg, McWilliams, and Hart were not amused and they entered into a joint breach-of-contract suit against Bette Midler and the film's producer, the Ladd Company. The suit asked for $3 million and was filed in Los Angeles Superior Court in Santa Monica on January 31, 1980. The suit was ultimately dismissed, and filming began with three different Harlettes: Jocelyn Brown, Diva Gray, and Ula Hed-wig. Hedwig was available, as Formerly of the Harlettes had disbanded.

Although the movie was shot in only four days, in four separate con-certs at the Civic Auditorium in Pasadena, California, it was fraught with problems. To begin with, Bette was battling pneumonia, and, with the exception of Ula, she was working with all new people. She had even fired her band and hired new musicians, so the production had the distinct feeling of a dress rehearsal.

For four nights, from February 13 to 16, 1980, ten separate camera crews shot more than a million and a half feet of film. According to the movie's cinematographer, William Franker, "The normal time to reload a camera is ten minutes. We kept practicing until we got it down to two minutes flat. I felt as if I was heading a pit crew at the Indianapolis 500!" (8).

In a very real sense, the whole project was one mad race with time. Much of the music had to be rerecorded, but the film was edited, printed, and playing in theaters by September 1980. It premiered in Los Angeles on the 17th of that month.

As a movie, *Divine Madness* is a highly entertaining concert film and brilliant historical look at Bette's onstage bombastic display of kinetic musical energy. For the opening, "Big Noise from Winnetka," the Harlettes are dressed in high white chefs' hats, and Bette is carried on stage atop a plate with giant carrots and an ear of corn—as the main course of "fowl." Standing upright on a blanket of faux-edible greenery, Midler reveals that she is the Thanksgiving turkey, complete with tail-feathers. She carries a purse made of a plucked rubber chicken, as she announces, "Welcome to another fowl evening with the Divine Miss M, in another feeble-minded attempt to turn chicken shit into chicken salad. . . . Make no mistake—eggs will be laid tonight."

The cinematography is consistently good, with most of the screen time devoted to Midler close-ups—but with enough wide shots and widescreen views of the Harlettes. Bette is newly blonde and beautifully svelte.

As it was meant to be, *Divine Madness* is a fitting time capsule of what Bette was like here onstage during the most fascinating decade of her career—the one in which she truly blossomed as a star in full rose-like bloom.

It is still the wild and off-color Bette, with a slick production number–filled theatrical revue of a show. However, unlike most musical revues, this show isn't composed of several performers; instead, it's one singular sensation of a star—but she is many performers rolled into one body. She is the rock diva, the pantomime artist, the bawdy stand-up comedian, the Broadway-style star, and—thanks to *The Rose*—she is now also a movie star come to life.

When an audience member shouts out something about her now-famous breasts, Bette rips open the front of her Velcro-affixed dress to reveal her elaborate brassiere underneath.

As mermaid tail–clad Dolores DeLago, she sings a dainty ditty called, "All He Wanted Was to Eat Me." And, mid-number, she fondles two large coconuts on the phallic palm tree that is attached to her wheelchair.

Still in the electronic wheelchair and the fish fin, Bette continues to mine the Frank Sinatra song catalog, by singing "My Way," her way. It is done with goofy tongue-in-cheek flair.

But, ultimately, it is her sincere singing and her inexhaustible energy that make her act, and this film, artistically successful. One of the most touching sequences features Bette singing a poignant version of her newly recorded hit ballad "The Rose." Her rendition of "The Rose" is mesmerizing.

"Chapel of Love" comes to life with an elaborate costume that Bette wears, with a groom on one side and the bride—Midler—on the reverse. The Harlettes are dressed as bouquet-bearing bridesmaids. When the number comes to an end, the girls strip away their wedding drag to reveal slips, while Bette peels her costume off to show her in a 1940s-style one-piece bathing suit. Across her chest is a beauty contestant's sash, which in this case reads: "Miss Community Chest."

She does it all in *Divine Madness*: from vaudeville (her Sophie Tucker jokes) to mime (on "Ready to Begin Again.") As the character she once called "Nanette," Bette's forlorn bag woman is used to give "Do You Want to Dance?" a bittersweet setting, making the question in the song the request of a desperately lonely woman.

Bette does her tough-girl rock & roll set against a Manhattan backdrop. She covers Bruce Springsteen's "E Street Shuffle" and her own now-famous "Leader of the Pack," which ends up with Midler flat on her back on the stage floor, having sex with an imagined lover.

As the concert's grand finale, Midler continues rocking, using Bob Dylan's "I Shall Be Released" to end the proceedings on a feverish high pitch. Bette ends up on the stage floor in exhaustion, while the crowd cheers for the divine dose of madness they have just witnessed.

From a marketing standpoint, it would seem that everyone who flocked to the concert series would love to go out and see the filmed version. However, this was not what happened. Perhaps it was a case of "been there, done that." Whatever the reason, this film was "in" and "out" of movie theaters in rapid succession.

The critical response was positive. The *New York Daily News* proclaimed, "*Divine Madness* is a Grade A achievement . . . captures the essential Midler." *The New York Times* said, "*Divine Madness* presents Miss Midler's act in all its gaudy, irrepressible glory." And the *Los Angeles Times* called it "a winner" (8). Unfortunately, it was a big disappointment at the box office, and it seemed to come and go very quickly in theaters. The song "My Mother's Eyes" was released as a single, and the soundtrack album of *Divine Madness* made it up to Number 34 on the *Billboard* charts.

In many ways the *Divine Madness* album was much more of a strong live rock concert album than *Live at Last* had been. The comedy bits and all of the monologues that took up much of *Live at Last* were left off this single disc. That is not to say that, musically, one is better than the other; it's just that *Live at Last* plays more like a Broadway show soundtrack, while *Divine Madness* is a much more fast-paced and entertaining rock & roll concert disc. Some of the songs unique to this LP are Bette's rocking versions of Bruce Springsteen's "E Street Shuffle," Bob Seger's "Fire Down Below," and the Rolling Stones' "You Can't Always Get What You Want." It is fascinating to note that although the Harlettes are seen and heard cavorting on stage with Bette and singing background vocals, they are joined by an off-stage voice. Luther Vandross, who was still just a background singer and a songwriter at this point, is heard singing on this album—in the background. He had sung background on most of the songs on her *Thighs and Whispers* album. He was brought in to give the Harlettes—and Bette—a fuller sound. In this way, Luther—who became a recording star on his own in the 1980s—was Bette's first and only male Harlette.

As a concert film and in creative terms, *Divine Madness* is great. Bette worked her ass off—as she always does in concert. She looks great. She sounds great. The camera work is wonderfully varied, zooming in closely at the appropriate times, yet there are enough wide shots to give the viewer the scope of the onstage action. However, in its theatrical release, it was a box-office "bust."

One of the most striking omissions was the song "Friends." The reason for its exclusion from the album and the film was that Bette got into an argument with Moogy Klingman over the publishing rights to the song. According to him, "She was going to use 'Friends' in a film, in her concert film, *Divine Madness*. And, we were negotiating for a week on the fee she was going to pay for the publishing on the song at that time, and she didn't put it in her film" (36).

Divine Madness is also subject to some of the oddest editing and marketing decisions for an album, a movie, and now, in the twenty-first century—a DVD. The film contains songs that are not on the album. The album contains a song—and a hit single—that is not in the movie. And the 1999 DVD release dropped two of the songs that appeared in the original film. "Shiver Me Timbers" appears on the soundtrack album and the film, but was edited from the DVD. "The Rose," "My Way," and "Ready to Begin Again" appear in the film and on the DVD, but are not on the soundtrack album. And "My Mother's Eyes" is on the album, but is not in the film—or the DVD. Why would a single be released from a soundtrack album if it doesn't appear in the film? And why would a DVD—in an era of "extra features"—drop not only "Shiver Me Timbers" but a piece called "Rainbow Sleeve" and the obviously filmed "My Mother's Eyes"? Who knows? Perhaps one of these days the complete and unedited version of *Divine Madness* will be restored and released. The film was intended as the ultimate Midler-in-concert time capsule, but the full version has yet to be seen.

Miss M obviously had other things on her mind when some of these decisions were being made. She was whirling like a dervish with activities—especially since she was now making all of her own business decisions. The next thing on her plate was her emergence into still another arena of the entertainment world—as now she was an author.

In April 1980, Bette Midler's first book, the semiautobiographical *A View from a Broad,* was published, Bette wrote the first draft during her first global concert tour in 1978. In it, she refers to Aaron Russo only as "my manager." In fact, his name does not appear anywhere. The book is a compilation of tour adventures like being Krazy-Glued into the hotdog outfit and making fun of Hitler in Germany. There are also segments about Dolores DeLago and the Magic Lady—who was an outgrowth of her Nanette character. Color photos and scrapbook-like layouts added to the whimsy of the book, and it became a best-seller.

"It's jaunty. Some of it is absolutely real, and some of it is totally off-the-wall, but that's the way my life is, you know? It's up to the reader to tread this sodden, marshy fen and come up with some kind of conclusion, if he's interested, about my life," Bette joked (8).

On May 1, in New York City, Bette autographed 750 copies of *A View from a Broad* for fans who lined up around the block to get a look at, and get a personal signature from, the literary Miss M. In Los Angeles three weeks later, Bette set a new record for the most autographed books in one session. From 7:30 P.M. to 1:30 A.M. she signed 1,500 books. For that little feat she was entered into *The Guinness Book of World Records.*

One of the most riotous aspects of her autograph sessions were her millinery works of art. In New York City, Bette wore a hat with a veil and a typewriter on top of it. In Los Angeles she wore a hat that featured a globe of the world and a jet plane.

Soon afterward, a lawsuit regarding Bette's outrageous costuming was filed. Dorothy Baca of Baca Designs Unlimited, the designer of

Midler's famous mermaid costume, as well as certain "pineapple head-pieces," sued the diva for $425,000, claiming that the mermaid outfit appeared on the cover of the *Divine Madness* album and *A View from a Broad* and that Baca didn't receive proper credit. It was beginning to seem as if each of Bette's accomplishments was directly followed by some new dilemma.

During this same year, Carly Simon's sister Lucy, together with David Levine, produced an LP for *Sesame Street*, a children's album entitled *In Harmony*. Lucy Simon assembled songs and used several well-known artists. Linda Ronstadt and Wendy Waldman sang a song called "I Want a Horse." The Doobie Brothers harmonized the story of "Wynken, Blynken and Nod." James Taylor wrote and sang a song called "Jelly Man Kelly." Also on the album was a song sung by Bette Midler called "Blueberry Pie." It's a cute little ditty about a "flaky" blueberry pie who is shy and won't come out of his "shell." It was written by Bette, Bruce Roberts, and Carole Bayer Sager.

The album was given a notable advertising campaign and sold quite well for a children's record. The next year it was nominated for and won a Grammy Award as the Best Recording for Children. Grammys went to Bette, the Doobie Brothers, James Taylor, Carly Simon, the Muppets, Al Jarreau, Linda Ronstadt, Wendy Waldman, Libby Titus, Dr. John, Livingston Taylor, George Benson, Pauline Wilson, Lucy Simon, and David Levine. This brought Bette's Grammy Award total to three.

By this point in her life, Bette had truly become bicoastal. She had moved out of her small apartment on Barrow Street in Greenwich Village and had purchased a spacious loft in the southern area of Manhattan known as Tribeca. The building itself is a landmark, erected in 1891. Bette passed her Village apartment on to her sister Susan, and she was kept busy jetting from coast to coast.

Bette had always said that she wanted to do a perfect screwball comedy. Now that it was time to select her next film project, she settled for a humorous black comedy that was originally called *Hot Streak*. It ultimately went through several rewrites, was called *It's All in the Game*, then *Three of a Kind*, and then *Jackpot*. By the time the film was released, it was given its final and most apt title: *Jinxed*. The title changes alone should have been a clue that this project was desperately in need of a direction.

Divine Madness was simply written off as a fluke or a failure, but again on *Jinxed*, Bette was given almost total creative control. Ever since

she had fired Aaron Russo, she had begun to realize what being a manager was all about. Still, she insisted that she could do it better than
anyone else, especially when it came to making decisions about her
career.

"I'm doing fine without a manager," she proclaimed of her freedom
from Russo. "I have a lawyer and lots of help. If I ever get a new one,
I'm going to get one that's oh, blind to my sexual charms. [A manager]
has very little to do with creativity. A good one makes sure that the
artist survives, is compensated properly for his services, and the moves
he makes in a career—build it rather than lay it to waste" (85). Bette
had full script, co-star, and director approval, and she was determined
to make up for the disappointment of *Divine Madness*. Unfortunately,
this was not to be.

After Bette chose the script, she next picked the director. Her selection was Don Siegel, whose forté was adventure films. His credentials
included *Invasion of the Body Snatchers* (1956), *Dirty Harry* (1972),
The Shootist (1976), and *Escape from Alcatraz* (1976). He had been in
the movie business since 1934, and he seemed like the kind of seasoned
professional that Bette longed to work with.

"I liked *Jinxed* [the script] because of its dialogue—nice and slangy,"
Bette said. "It didn't know whether it was a comedy or a thriller, but I
thought a good director could find the proper tone for it. Siegel had
directed *The Killers* [1964] and all those Clint Eastwood movies, which
were kind of somber, so I thought, with Siegel being good at that, and
me being good at comedy, we'd have a nice marriage. Many, many,
many people told me I was crazy, and this is one time in my career I
should have listened. I just had never encountered Mr. Siegel's school
of directing—the adversary school of directing—where everybody
chooses up sides and it's a fight to the death!" (30).

Her next decision involved her male co-star and love interest. She
ended up with Ken Wahl, whose previous films were *The Warriors*
(1979) and *Fort Apache, the Bronx* (1981). Oddly enough, Wahl was
Bette's first choice, but once she met him she realized that working with
him was going to prove difficult.

"To tell you the truth, I suggested him," she later admitted. "but
after I read with him, I felt it wouldn't work. Mr. Siegel felt the same
way, but Steven Bach [the former heard of United Artists Pictures]
wanted him, so we were gracious about it. However, Mr. Siegel immediately told Ken that he had not been our choice, which right away set

the guy's teeth on edge. He never recovered from that particular blow to his pride" (30).

Filming began in Lake Tahoe on May 5, 1981. It started out bad and only got worse. "I never knew it got so ugly," Bette later said in amazement. "I never knew it got down to such mudslinging. It was an enormously painful experience" (30).

The script was reportedly changed almost daily. The final plot revolved around the murder of a slimy gambler by his wife and the blackjack dealer he keeps stacking the deck against. Rip Torn played the gambler who has a formula for winning. He has his lucky cigars and his own lucky dealer (Wahl), whom he keeps breaking the bank with. Aside from gambling, his other favorite pastime involves slapping around his wife [Midler], who is an aspiring gambling-casino lounge singer. Wahl keeps getting fired from job after job because the casino owners think that he is in cahoots with Torn.

Wahl seduces Midler, and the two of them conspire to kill Torn and split his insurance money. However, Torn commits suicide after losing a bundle one night, and it is up to Midler and Wahl to make his death look like an accident. After Torn's death, Midler discovers that she is endowed with her ex-husband's gambling prowess, and after a falling-out with Wahl, she gets him fired from his job by setting him up at the blackjack table. At the end of the film Midler surprises Wahl by splitting her winnings with him, and off they ride into the Vegas neon sunset to live happily ever after. It was a bit off-the-wall, but as a black comedy it *could* have worked. Unfortunately, it didn't. One of the most gigantic problems was the chemistry between Bette, Ken, and director Siegel.

Bette and Ken Wahl loathed each other upon sight. "Ken was unbelievably hateful to me. All during the shooting he was sending over these 'mal' vibes and wanted everybody to know it. That's the kind of guy he is. The first time I met him, the first thing he said was, 'I want you to know that I hate niggers and faggots.' That was the first thing out of his mouth after 'hello.' I had no idea why he said that, because we had neither of those in our picture. It wasn't as if I said to him, 'We're going to introduce you to a lot of gay black people who are going to do your hair and dress you every morning!'" (30).

"After that comment, he turned to an Aubrey Beardsley that was hanging on the wall and said, 'What the fuck is that?' Now, I had not decorated these rooms. But I felt compelled to tell him, 'That's an Aubrey Beardsley.' And I told him about Beardsley and Oscar Wilde. To which he replied, 'Well, I don't know nothin' about that fuckin' shit, and I don't want to know nothin' about it. I'm a baseball player.' By that time, of course, I knew what particular terrain I had stumbled onto" (30).

"Originally, I felt Ken Wahl had what we used to call 'animal magnetism,' even though he's a little on the chubby side. And I still feel he photographs beautifully, and that there is a place for him in show business, somewhere—although hopefully not in my pictures!" she stressed (30).

Changes in the script and reported demands for retakes caused Siegel and Midler to clash. According to one source in the Midler camp, Bette would get her comedy writer Jerry Blatt on the phone every night before the shooting, and they would rewrite the scene and the dialogue. Each morning, Bette would show up on the set with new pages of rewrites to be shot instead of the current script.

The name "Brian Blessed," which appears in the film's credits as screenplay writer, was actually a name that was made up by the original writer, Frank D. Gilroy, so that his name wouldn't be associated with the film. Jerry Blatt's name was never on the film because there was a writer's strike, and no one was supposed to know that he was working on the film. At different points in the production, Don Siegel, Bette Midler, and Jerry Blatt each separately rewrote scenes. "At times," according to Siegel, "the three of us worked together" (8).

Siegel claimed that he tried to enter the project objectively. "She was the one who picked me to direct the picture. So it became, I guess, rather strange and awkward. I can't say that I enjoyed making the picture. I'm very glad that she took the responsibility, because the picture's terrible!" (8).

It is unclear exactly at what point in the making of *Jinxed* the production became an out-and-out battlefield, but the rumblings were heard early on. Not only did Siegel dislike working with Bette, but he also had very little power over what happened on the set each day. United Artists vice president Anthea Sylbert sided with Bette time and time again in disputes and overrode Siegel's decisions. Somehow it became a matter of squaring off into opposing sides and taking aim. It was, oddly enough, the men against the women. Bette and Anthea were on one side, and Siegel and Wahl were on the other.

"I'd never realized how men can gang up on women," said Bette. "I mean, in the back of my head somewhere, no doubt, I had plenty of leftover vestiges from my childhood about guys beating up on me emotionally, but I don't dwell on that kind of thing. I don't like to be mired in mud. And I had never really realized how men don't like a woman to be in charge, or to have power" (88).

Siegel said Bette was one of the most problematic people he had ever worked with. "It was very difficult working with her. She comes on as an expert in every facet of the business. I've worked with many stars who are difficult, but she's really a rough customer. . . . It shouldn't have been anywhere near $15 million," he said about the cost of the production. "It's not up there on the screen, but she was constantly rewriting, rewriting, rewriting. All this from a girl who made two pictures, one a bomb" (95).

"In every major disagreement I had with Bette Midler, and there were hundreds, UA [United Artists] backed her. They always gave in to her and that made my life an unhappy one. If I could have my name taken off it, I would. I wish to God I hadn't made it. There were many things I expressly wanted to do, but they were all blocked by those two women who work there [Sylbert and UA studio president Paula Weinstein]" (95).

At the same time, there were Bette's battles with Ken Wahl. During the shooting of the film, Ken told the press that every time he was required to kiss Bette on camera, he had to think of kissing his dog in order to bear embracing Midler. "I just don't get along with Bette very well," said Wahl. "We come from two different worlds. It's been miserable with her and took all my concentration to get up and go to work in the morning. If I knew before how this was going to be, I wouldn't have done the movie. She doesn't talk, she yells. I think the main problem is that she's so insecure about everything. I enjoy being happy: Bette's the kind of person who thrives on being miserable" (96).

In her own defense, Bette claimed that the rest of the production company was being sloppy and lazy about the film. "I was trying to make the best movie I could make, and I was resented for it. Listen, when people make films, their work lives forever. I'm not modest about this: it happens to be a fact. And when somebody gives you that much money to make a picture, you can't short-change them. But these people—there wasn't a single one of them who wasn't out to stiff the studio. When I'm paid that much money, I feel that I have to do what they're paying me for and not slough off. So I did it and I got kicked for it. And that's hard, because when you are raised with that ethic, and you believe it, it's debilitating to find that you're surrounded by people who are actually just petty thieves. They're lazy and they're not committed, and they resent you for being so square. It was like pulling a caravan up Mt. Everest all by myself. I had a horrible time. I thought it was the worst experience of my life" (88).

Someone else who didn't have his name on the production was director Sam Peckinpah. Explained Bette, "Sam Peckinpah came in and did one scene, which was a second-unit scene, a trailer-goes-over-a-cliff scene. I guess it was too much work for Mr. Siegel" (88).

The atmosphere on the set had deteriorated to the point where Bette dreaded going to work every morning. "It was an enormously painful experience, but it was pain about something as trivial as a movie. A movie is basically a piece of fluff and entertainment."

She began to break down. "Every day, every morning toward the end, I felt I was holding on for dear life. I would wake up with heart palpitations. And sometimes, in the middle of the night, I would wake up, not screaming but not being able to breathe. I would just wake up with a shudder and have to pound my back or chest to catch my breath. On the set, it was as though a wall had come between them and me. I kept thinking, 'If I can just get through one more day, one more day of having to face them and their awful hatred—or if it wasn't hatred, indifference.' Every day I walked between those walls feeling complete alienated and alone and worthless" (30).

After the filming was completed, Bette continued in a downward spiral. "I had a terrible nervous breakdown," she later admitted. "I was sick for a good three months. I was very, very ill. And I started to see a doctor because it was just too much for me to deal with by myself. . . . I couldn't walk, I couldn't get out of bed. I just cried for weeks on end. And anything would set me off. I couldn't control myself. I had just been so attacked, and so humiliated. It was as though they wanted to destroy me, and I couldn't understand what I had done" (88).

In the September 15, 1981, issue of *Variety*, in Army Archerd's column, Siegel stated that Bette demanded "twenty to twenty-five takes and print four or five." However, a United Artists interoffice memo dated September 18, 1981, addressed to Anthea Sylbert from Dennis A. Brown, tells a very different story. It stated that the "average number of takes" was 2.7, with 1.3 printed takes. The memo also went on to conclude, "All of which means that over a third of all the scenes with Bette were done in only one or two takes and over half were done in three or less takes, while only five percent took more than nine takes. Only one take with Bette (or with anyone, for that matter) took more than fifteen takes and that was scene 99, which took twenty-one takes and involved the cat" (96).

While Bette spent the rest of the year recovering from her nervous breakdown, United Artists was sorting through the footage of *Jinxed* and trying to figure out what to do with it. According to Siegel, he turned in three different versions of the picture, each with a completely different ending. United Artists also went on to edit the film even further. According to Siegel, "There was a marvelous scene in which Rip Torn breaks down and says he's sorry for how he treated her. He was just marvelous. I was told to take it out. I refused. They felt it worked against Miss Midler. She's wrong. The better he is, the better she is. She had another marvelous scene. They're living in a trailer; she's threatening to leave, they took that out, to my astonishment. It's the first time I've ever had to go through things like that. I know Midler wasn't pleased with the way she looked. I think [cinematographer Vilmos] Zsigmond did a very good job with her. Considering all we went through, it's miraculous the movie turned out as well as it did" (95).

She later sympathetically said of *Jinxed,* "I don't think it was that bad a picture. He [Siegel] actually cut it quite sensitively. Even though he didn't like me, he didn't make me look bad" (97).

Recalled Siegel, he turned in three different versions of *Jinxed,* each with a slightly different ending: "The one I liked was the longest. She leaves her boyfriend, sings a song and goes out in a blaze of glory in a remarkable sunrise-sunset shot by Vilmos Zsigmond" (95).

On a upbeat note, Bette Midler got to sing a bit of country music in *Jinxed,* which never appeared on record. As she explained, "We sing 'Cowgirl's Dream' which is out of Snuff Garrett's office. It was written by Cliff Crawford and John Durrell; that's the opening song. And then there's a whole little medley in the middle, which is just, you know, *en passant,* because the plot comes during this number. But it's cute, and it's very Vegas-ey, with lots of fringe and rhinestones and balloons and stuff" (88.)

Critics were mixed on the results. It seemed that the best the *New York Times* could say about it was to call it "an entertaining jumble of a movie" (98). Yet the *Video Movie Guide 2001* found "Bette Midler in peak form as a would-be cabaret singer . . . (in) this often funny black comedy. . . . If it weren't for Midler, you'd notice how silly and unbeliev-able it all is" (99).

In the year between the completion of *Jinxed* and its release in Octo-ber 1982, Bette recovered from her breakdown, got a new boyfriend, and began work on a new album. She was feeling well enough by early spring to virtually steal the entire Academy Awards telecast with just five minutes of time on screen.

Entering the stage in a low-cut and shiny gold gown and red-and-blue silk spangled scarves billowing from the sleeves, Bette beamed at the television cameras. "I guess you didn't think it was possible to over-dress for this affair," she said. The audience roared with laughter. "So this is what it feels like to be up here. This is fantastic. I've been waiting for two years for the Academy to call me up and say they made a mis-take! Don't you hate it when presenters come out and use this moment for their own personal aggrandizement? This is the Oscars. We have to be as dignified as possible. That is why I have decided to rise to the occasion," she said with her hands tugging her breasts upward with her hands. She then proceeded to present the award for the Best Original Song, complete with her own snide comments about each of the tunes. She was a sheer riot to watch, and all of the articles about the show made clamorous mention of her spontaneous and humorous perform-ance. She was the hit of the show.

"That sure was fun," she said later of her appearance on the Academy Awards. "And the feedback on it was extraordinary! I couldn't have had more people call or wire or write or send flowers if I had actually won the damn thing!" (88).

Jinxed landed on the movie marketplace the following fall with a resounding thud. The posters for the film carried the headline, "This tootsie's on a roll!" Well, she gambled, and she certainly rolled anything but "sevens." The majority of the critics hated it and were unable to tell whether the film was a comedy, a tragedy, a spoof, a love story, or none of the above. The review Bette received in the *Hollywood Reporter* was among the most sympathetic: "*Jinxed* actually isn't cursed as much as it is wildly uneven. . . . Midler's screen Opus No. Three falls far short of its two predecessors in coherency, importance and impact, but still imparts enough breezy entertainment value to doubtless gather partisans to its cause" (8).

What it did fail to find was an audience. Less than three weeks into its release, the ticket sales were already dwindling. The film reportedly lost United Artists $20 million.

This was the beginning of one of Bette's bluest periods. In the movie business you are only as big as your latest hit or as small as your latest bomb. "Nobody wanted to hire me," recalls Midler (100). Suddenly, word spread that Bette's temperamental displays on the set of *Jinxed* had ruined United Artists and left it broke. In 1980 she was an Academy Award–nominated superstar. In 1982 she was labeled "production poison" in the film industry.

READY TO BEGIN AGAIN

In 1982 Bette had strengthened her ties to the West Coast by purchasing a large Hollywood home in Coldwater Canyon. The Midler mansion was designed in a Mexican style, with high ceilings, windows with cut glass, and a huge fireplace. Over the fireplace hung a portrait of silent film star Mary Pickford.

According to Bette, she liked to gaze up at that particular sad-eyed portrait and ponder. "She had all that money and she was miserable! That's why I schlepped up to the auction at Pickfair and bought that picture. It slayed me to think that this woman would have had the world by the short hairs and still would have been so unhappy. Every time I look at it, I think, 'There but for the grace of God' . . . And in fact, I'm sure I may end up that way yet" (88).

Since her disastrous *Jinxed* experience, Bette had been dating and living with a man by the name of Benoit Gautier. It was Gautier with whom she had an affair in Paris in 1974.

Speaking about him, Bette explained in the summer of 1982, "Benoit I've been with, on and off, for about a year. We went to Europe together last fall. He's a personal manager. He's in *zee show biz-i-ness*. He manages Jon Anderson, who used to be the lead singer in Yes, who's now on his own and is making those wonderful records with Vangelis. Beautiful symphonic pieces, long tone-poem things. But Benoit has a public relations firm in Paris. We see each other evenings, we have dinner together. It's very traditional: nothing *'kinqué.'* Calm, always calm, because there's so much of people screaming during the day, you really do need a chance to catch your breath" (88).

At that same point, Bette definitely nixed the idea of marriage. "Oh *nevair, NEV-AIR!* There's community property in this state. I'm not giving away one nickel," she stressed (88).

Now it was time to piece her career back together. This started in the summer of 1982 when she began working on her ninth album, to be entitled *No Frills*. Since she had documented her 1970s stage act in the HBO special and in *Divine Madness*, Bette felt that it was time to move on to something new musically, something between the cabaret campiness of her early albums and the screaming rock & roll belting of the Rose.

It was time to bid the past a fond farewell and move on. Bette decided to concentrate on rock and ballads with synthesizers and no embellishments. "Because that's exactly what it is," she explained of the title of the album *No Frills*. "It's music with no strings and no horns. It's bare-bones music, as unpretentious as it can be. Just stark. But I'm enjoying this album more than any other I've ever made. I haven't stopped laughing since I started making this record, because the people I'm working with are fabulous, funny, silly, silly people. Danny Goldberg is executive producer. Chuck Plotkin is producing, Toby Scott is the engineer, and Brock Walsh is the musical director. I've never been silly about my records" (30).

Bette was very optimistic about her *No Frills* album. She hoped that the ballad "All I Need to Know" would turn out to be a hit on the order of "The Rose." She recorded the Rolling Stones' "Beast of Burden," Marshall Crenshaw's melodic "Favorite Waste of Time," and the electronic techno-pop song "Is It Love?" She also composed a song with Jerry Blatt and Brock Walsh called "Come Back, Jimmy Dean." Although she and Cher were no longer close buddies—for some unexplained reason—it seemed odd that Bette would write a song with this title and subject matter, as Cher was concurrently starring on Broadway in the show *Come Back to the Five and Dime, Jimmy Dean, Jimmy Dean.*

Several of the songs on this album she found by listening to an endless stack of "demo" tapes submitted for her consideration. Of the '80s music scene, she explained, "I know what's going on—I listen to the 'greats' and the 'near-greats.' I do. I know what synthesizers are! You know, I'm an up-to-date kinda of gal. I like that song 'Is It Love?'" I couldn't resist it when I heard it. Actually, that was one of the two thousand tapes that I got that someone had sent me—it's a Nick Gilder song. I chose it out of that great big pile" (94).

"I found some great songs. I found a little group from Wichita, Kansas. . . . what was the name of that band? It was an all-girls band and they had the strangest songs. But I couldn't get ahold of them, so I couldn't cut the songs. They didn't have a phone, they didn't have a manager. I had this tape in this pile of two thousand. They had songs like 'Alien Love.' I mean, those songs are really out-to-lunch. They were fourteen years old—these little girls had written these songs. They were very young. I did flirt with the idea of cranking out a teeny bopper album. But I'm really not that. You have a face up to that" (94).

She spent a year gathering and recording new material for the album. She went to the Greek Theater in Los Angeles one night to see Marshall Crenshaw, who was the opening act for Joe Jackson. From her meeting with Crenshaw, she came away with the song "My Favorite Waste of Time."

Three singles were pulled from the *No Frills* album: "All I Need to Know," "My Favorite Waste of Time," and "Beast of Burden." Unfortunately, none of the singles became big hits, nor did the album itself go far on the record charts. Bette's version of "All I Need to Know" made it to Number 77 on the *Billboard* singles chart. Ironically, when it was rerecorded in 1989 by Linda Ronstadt and Aaron Neville—under the title "Don't Know Much"—it went to Number 2 and revived both Ronstadt's and Neville's recording careers. Bette's recording of "My Favorite Waste of Time" made it to Number 78 on the charts in 1983, and "Beast of Burden" peaked at Number 71. The *No Frills* album itself only made it as far as Number 60 in America.

It was a big disappointment for Bette. She did everything possible to promote the album. She did a half-hour TV special for HBO entitled *No Frills*, and in early 1984 she even released her first video for MTV. It was her version of the Rolling Stones' "Beast of Burden," and it co-starred Mick Jagger, who was seen in the video getting up and dancing with Miss M. The video, which was taped at the now-defunct New York City nightclub the Peppermint Lounge, was hysterical fun. Unfortunately, it did not save the album or the single from disappointing sales.

On her 1985 comedy album *Mud Will Be Flung Tonight*, Bette mentioned her video with Mick. "We were fabulous!" she exclaimed, adding, "I know what you're all thinking: 'Did she fuck him?'" But,

according to Midler, they were just friends. "A lovely man. Great sense
of humor. Hard worker," she said, describing Jagger. "He's very funny.
And he really knows how to live. He's very sharp, and I like him. [But]
he's a man's man. He likes to be with the guys. He doesn't want to sit
around and talk to some girl who thinks she knows the blues" (18).

In retrospect, Bette lamented, "The last record I made [*No Frills*]—I
was in the studio for over a year, and I don't like that process. There's
so much technology, whatever humanity I had was slowly being eroded.
And I spent a year making that record and nobody bought it. Nobody
cared except me. I considered not singing anymore. I thought I wasn't
taking my singing seriously. I wasn't paying attention to it. It wasn't just
because I wasn't selling records anymore. It had just fallen by the wayside" (101).

Coinciding with the release of *No Frills* had come the announcement
of a 1982–1983 concert tour to be entitled *De Tour.* The tour opened
on December 6, 1982, and it played at the Universal Amphitheater in
Los Angeles on New Year's Eve. Just as she had done in New York's
Philharmonic Hall ten years before, at the stroke of midnight, Bette
bounded onstage dressed in a diaper—this time as "baby 1983." However, this time around she was accompanied by "old man 1982," who
was none other than Barry Manilow! It had been almost a decade since
they had been onstage together. Although they had never done a duet
of any sort, that night they sang "Auld Lang Syne" together, much to
the delight of her audience. It was of her best New Year's Eve surprises
since she had flashed a crowd from King Kong's hand.

When *De Tour* was announced for its Radio City Music Hall run in
New York City, the response was overwhelming. Fans stood for up to
twelve hours in freezing-cold January temperatures to purchase tickets.
With a gross of $1,327,000, Bette's latest tour broke all the existing box-
office records at Radio City.

The *De Tour* shows represented the first time in a decade that Bette
performed almost all new material. She basically left the character of
the Divine Miss M at home and decided to attempt something completely different. The only old Midler songs that she performed in the
show were "In the Mood," "Stay with Me," and "The Rose."

There were some hysterical new bits of staging and conceptual comedy. There were several minutes of stage time devoted entirely to her
breasts. "I've been wearing my bra for years and years," she explained.
"That is my field of expertise, you know: brassieres. I know all about

them. Well, I've just been wearing mine for years and years, and I got my first one when I was eleven years old—I was a 'D' cup" (94). In the show she did a tribute to her "tits" called "Pretty Legs and Great Big Knockers." While the Harlettes (Ula Hedwig, Katie Sagal, and Linda Hart) held pairs of large puppet breasts with talking mouths, Bette ran backstage to put on enormous inflated balloon *bazooms.*

In a comedy bit she explained to the audience that one day, out of curiosity, she wanted to find out exactly how much her breasts weighed, so she got hold of a postage scale and positioned herself strategically upon it. "I won't tell you how much they weighed," she announced, "but it costs $87.50 to send them to Brazil" (94).

Since she was famous for poking fun at herself, Bette pulled down a huge movie screen to introduce a segment from *Jinxed.* However, this segment was dubbed—badly—in Italian, with comic new English subtitles. She also joked about popular singers—including Olivia Newton-John: "I love Olivia's new song, don't you? 'Let me hear your body talk. . . .' Mine said, 'Fuck you!' "

One of the most successful songs of the evening was her version of Jonathan King's 1965 pop hit "Everyone's Gone to the Moon." Bette performed the song in a starry-eyed techno-pop version, which was dazzling to hear.

She also hauled out one of her most popular characters, the famed mermaid in the electric wheelchair, but this time all three of the Harlettes were in identical get-ups. Their entrance was heralded by an off-stage MC who announced, "The internationally acclaimed Dolores De Lago, the Toast of Chicago, and the semi-somnambulant De Lago Sisters in their spanking new review, Disco Memories." They came out doing Busby Berkeley–inspired dance routines (complete with an overhead mirror for aerial views) in their wheelchairs. Their medley included "We Are Family," "In the Mood," and "I Will Survive."

Bette's *De Tour* was a huge success, and the critics loved it. The show was conceived and written by Bette herself and Jerry Blatt, and Blatt directed it. It ultimately grossed $8 million, and even though it didn't help to sell many *No Frills* albums along the was, it was itself a triumph.

During the summer on 1983, Bette took a trimmed-down version of the show on still another cross-country tour. For this journey, she had a new set of Harlettes: Jenifer Lewis, Siobhan O'Carroll, and Helena Springs. Bette has jokingly suggested that since she had gone through so many Harlettes, "I'd love to have a reunion and get all of them in one room!"

By September, Bette was beginning to burn out emotionally and physically. It was only days after videotaping the show in Minneapolis for the HBO Special *Art or Bust* that Bette collapsed midshow at Pine Knob in Detroit and had to be hospitalized to recuperate from exhaustion. Although she was heading for another nervous breakdown, she recovered enough to finish the tour and then took a well-deserved rest.

The fall of 1983 found Bette back on the charts and in the Top 10. It wasn't on the record charts, though: it was on the *New York Times* bestseller list. *A View from a Broad* had been such a success that Midler was encouraged to pick up her pen again. This time around, it was a children's book. Beautifully illustrated in lush color by artist Todd Schorr, the book is all about a little girl whose first spoken word was "More!"

The Saga of Baby Divine was a huge success during the Christmas season of 1983. On December 1, its author celebrated her thirty-eighth birthday at a big bash thrown in her honor by Benoit. Among the guests were Johnny Carson, Barry Manilow, Rosemary Clooney, Martha Raye, Neil Diamond, Toni Basil, Burt Bacharach, and his new wife, Carole Bayer Sager. It was really a big Bette Midler reunion. Barry was her former musical director, Carole was her former writing partner ("You're Moving Out Today,"), and Toni (who had gone on to record her own hit record, "Micky") was Bette's often-utilized choreographer (*Bette! Divine Madness*). Also on hand were several of her former Harlettes: Charlotte Crossley, Ula Hedwig, Katie Sagal, and Linda Hart.

In 1984, Bette was busy doing some heavy-duty regrouping. In January, her "Beast of Burden" video was released. Later that year she broke up with Benoit and tried to figure out what her next career move would be. To top it all off, by the end of the year she was going to meet and marry the man of her dreams.

In 1984 the Paper Moon Graphics company in Los Angeles, California, debuted a line of greeting cards with the image of Miss M on the front. The specialty cards were entitled the "Greetings from Bette Midler" line. One of the all-occasion cards features a photo of Midler on a beach in a two-piece bathing suit bottom and a flower lei/feather boa on the front. On the inside the message reads: "To make your life a tropical blast you don't need a snort or a toke. Just heed this fine Divine Advice: *!@# 'em if they can't take a joke! Aloha!" Another one featured Midler in a beehive hairdo atop a red Corvette convertible. On the inside it read: "You got gas or what?" The birthday card in the series depicted Bette in her Delores DeLago mermaid outfit. On the inside was inscribed, "Kiss My Bass! Best Fishes for a Happy Birthday!"

August 20, 1984, marked the HBO debut of Midler's latest TV special, which was called *Art or Bust*. Most of the footage was culled from Bette's *De Tour* shows—taped in 1983 at the University of Minnesota. The footage was then enhanced and bridged by animation and special effects. Among the animation segments were stills of famous paintings—from Matisse to Warhol—all with Bette as the subject of the masterpieces. The TV special opens with Bette singing her version of Bruce Springsteen's "Pink Cadillac." It was a song she had hoped to put on her *No Frills* album, but Bruce wouldn't grant her permission. He claimed at the time that it was a song for a man to sing, and he refused to let her release it on record. This special has the only version of Midler singing that song. She also managed to work a plug for her *Saga of Baby Divine* book into the special.

The wheelchair disco medley of Dolores and the famed DeLago Sisters gets a prominent display here, with Jenifer Lewis getting to do an accordion solo of "Hold That Tiger." The songs from her *No Frills* album were given an ample spotlight here, including "My Favorite Waste of Time" and "My Eye on You." There is even a closing number that finds Midler wrapped in a stretchy Martha Graham–inspired garment, which she pulls over her ahead in a dancer-augmented segment. Her chilling version of "Everyone's Gone to the Moon" is the centerpiece of this clever segment.

According to John Corry of the *New York Times*, "Bette Midler takes risks that other performers do not. She attempts to be touching, bawdy, and funny, often simultaneously. When she succeeds she is brilliant, and when she fails she is done in by her own excess. On *Bette Midler: Art or Bust!* she succeeds more often than she fails; she is, in fact, close to being an absolute winner, and if she were an Olympic gymnast, going for a perfect 10, she would get a 9.9" (102).

Art or Bust was later released on video with two "extra features." There was a vintage clip of Bette at the Continental Baths in 1971. She is seen in grainy-looking black and white, dressed as Carmen Miranda and singing her famed hemp song "Marahuana." She is also seen in a risqué halter top, singing the Glenn Miller classic "Chattanooga Choo-Choo." The second bonus feature is a clip of Midler at the United Jew-

"The Divine Miss M" is what Bette Midler became known as in the early 1970s when she began her singing career in a Manhattan gay club, the Continental Baths. *(Courtesy of Kenn Duncan / Atlantic Records / MJB Photo Archives)*

Baby Divine! Bette Midler as a baby in Honolulu, Hawaii. She was named after actress Bette Davis. *(Courtesy of Photofest)*

Adrienne Barbeau, Bette Midler, and Tanya Everett in the Broadway cast of *Fiddler on Roof* in the 1960s. *(Courtesy of Photofest)*

With her clunky 1940s-styled platform shoes and her retro repertoire of songs—like The Andrews Sisters' "Boogie Woogie Bugle Boy"—Midler had the ability to make everything old seem suddenly new again. *(Courtesy of Atlantic Records / MJB Photo Archives)*

Bette Midler trucked her way across America in the early 1970s, and became known as one of the hardest-working live performers in the pop and rock music realm. Here, the diva is seen clowning around outside the Atlanta Civic Center. *(Courtesy of Tom Hill)*

Midler carved out a unique niche for herself in the music world in the 1970s. She was part chanteuse, part comedienne. *(Courtesy of* The Rochester Democrat & Chronicle */ MJB Photo Archives)*

Bette's 1975 stage show, *Clams on the Half-Shell Revue*, was a roaring hit on Broadway and on tour. In the act she awoke in King Kong's hand and sang the 1930s hit song "Lullaby of Broadway." *(Courtesy of Atlantic Records / MJB Photo Archives)*

In her *Clams on the Half-Shell Revue*, Midler's repertoire covered a wide array of music, from David Bowie's "Young Americans," to her own classics like "Hello in There" and "Chapel of Love." *(Courtesy of Playbill / MJB Photo Archives)*

In addition to her retro 1940s fashions, Bette in the 1970s also had a flair for off-the-wall funkier clothes like this eclectic rock & roll creation. *(Courtesy of Atlantic Records / MJB Photo Archives)*

Elton John, Cher, Flip Wilson, and Bette were the stars of the visually spectacular *Cher* TV special in 1976. Dressed by Bob Mackie, Bette got her first taste of Hollywood glamour on this show. *(Courtesy of CBS-TV / MJB Photo Archives)*

ish Appeal telethon in 1973, stripping off her dress to reveal her slip when someone pledges $5,000, as promised on camera.

In September 1984, Bette and Dan Aykroyd hosted the First Annual MTV Awards show, broadcast live from Radio City Music Hall. Bette was in rare form that night, and as she said, "It's been great exposure for me." At the end of the show she wore a black-and-white striped gown with a floral brassiere on top of it. For the second half of the show she wore what looked like an orange prom gown that billowed out at the waist and had huge shoulder pads. Instead of several costume changes, she simply changed her hats. Her *chapeaus* included a 1940s mesh hair net, a bow of black gauze, a sequined black mantilla covered with glittering rose blossoms, a metallic-orange turban, and even an electronic contraption in black and white that spun around like the blades of a feathered helicopter. Describing this last hat, she announced, "This is what is called a special effect. I have named it 'Turd Curls from Outer Space!'"

At the beginning of the show Bette referred to the telecast as "This Night of at Least Half-a-Dozen Stars." She then proceeded to add her own commentary on the guest stars whom she introduced to present awards. After announcing ZZ Top, she added, "Nobody knows what lives beneath those beards or lurks behind those sunglasses."

The funniest moment came after Madonna had just finished gyrating on stage, while singing "Like a Virgin." Said Bette, "Now that the burning question of Madonna's virginity has been answered, we are free to go on to even more GAPING questions, such as: How a video is made. We KNOW Madonna's story!"

Bette's "Beast of Burden" video was nominated for awards in several categories, including "Best Female Video," "Best Choreography," and "Best Stage Performance." Unfortunately, she failed to take a prize home with her that night. "I thought this was the 'Miss MTV Awards!'" she quipped.

⌒

Although she had sworn up and down that she would "NEVER, EVER" get married, in October of 1984 Bette ran into someone she had met a few years earlier, and she immediately fell in love. According to her, they met "years ago. We went out with a party of people to a show—

King Crimson or something. We didn't get a chance to talk very much" (18).

"Harry Kipper, that's his stage name," continued Bette. "Most of his friends call him Kipper. He actually sells commodities under the name of Harry Kipper as well. And he performs with Brian Kipper, which is not his real name either. I had met some performance artists, and I wanted to meet others. And a girlfriend of mine, Toni Basil, introduced me to him as one of the Kipper Kids. I always remembered him as that. I thought it was his real name. I ran into him a couple of years later, and he reminded me we had met and I put his name in my book. Two years later, he called me out of the clear blue. After two months of INTENSIVE dating, we were married" (18).

Much to the surprise of everyone, including Bette herself, on December 16, 1984, she became Mrs. Martin von Haselberg (a.k.a. Harry Kipper). In true Miss M tradition, Bette and her betrothed were wed in ever-tasteful Las Vegas . . . by an Elvis Presley impersonator!

"The Elvis impersonator was an accident. We wanted to get married quickly, and Vegas sounded like a good place to do it. We didn't know he was an Elvis impersonator till the end of the ceremony, when he handed us his single. It was the Chapel of the Twilight or something. We had fun. We got all dressed up. I had my dress that I wore to the premiere of *The River.* And Harry had two used-car-salesman suits. The first one was a hounds-tooth check suit that he'd made a couple of years ago. He looked like something out of *The Music Man.* I said, 'no, Harry, I really can't marry you in that suit.' So he changed into a nice black suit. The long drive to Vegas had been a lot of laughs. But the long drive back from Vegas was kind of quiet. We were fairly shaken. We went there on a lark, but it now was going to be real" (18).

Kipper, who had been married and divorced once before, is three years younger than Bette. "For the first couple of weeks after we got married, it was, 'Uh-oh, what did we do?' There were some rough spots, but we did our talking, we did our compromising. Fortunately, we liked what we got to know," she remembers (100).

Harry, who was educated in England, had actually been born of German parents in Buenos Aries, Argentina. Bette said that she was a little surprised that she ended up married to a German. "I married a Kraut. Every night I get dressed up as Poland and he invades me," she quips (100).

On January 28, 1985, Bette Midler was one of the many record industry superstars to come together at A&M Recording Studios in Los Angeles to record the Number 1 mega-hit song "We Are the World." The funds that the song raised were to assist relief efforts in famine-plagued Africa, and especially the people in Ethiopia. "We Are the World" was written by Michael Jackson and Lionel Richie, and produced by Quincy Jones. They were able to get the participation of a virtual "Who's Who" of the current recording world, primarily because it was recorded the night of the annual American Music Awards telecast. It was kind of like those old Judy Garland and Mickey Rooney movies, where someone would announce, "I've got a barn—let's put on a show." Somehow, it seemed, everyone—including Bette—wanted to be involved. In alphabetical order, the cast of singers included Dan Aykroyd, Harry Belafonte, Lindsey Buckingham, Kim Carnes, Ray Charles, Bob Dylan, Sheila E., Bob Geldof, Daryl Hall, James Ingram, Jackie Jackson, La-Toya Jackson, Marlon Jackson, Michael Jackson, Randy Jackson, Tito Jackson, Al Jarreau, Billy Joel, Cyndi Lauper, Huey Lewis & the News, Kenny Loggins, Bette Midler, Willie Nelson, John Oates, Jeffrey Osborne, Steve Perry, the Pointer Sisters, Lionel Richie, Smokey Robinson, Kenny Rogers, Diana Ross, Paul Simon, Bruce Springsteen, Tina Turner, Dionne Warwick, and Stevie Wonder. The record received much airplay and raised millions of dollars. However, so much was made about the song, and what a wonderful humanitarian effort it represented, that "We Are the World" soon became the butt of several jokes.

The funniest jokes came from none other than Bette Midler herself. Although most of the people sang a solo vocal on the record, she was among the vocalists who were heard only in the chorus. She referred to the song as "We Are the Rich, We Are the Famous." She recalls with sarcasm, "It was a fantastic night. I stood next LaToya. She was wearing a headband. I felt naked. Bruce Springsteen was there. He was chatting with the soloists. I ran up to him. I said, 'Bruce, you look fabulous! What happened?'" (7).

On April 30 and May 1, 1985, Bette recorded her tenth album, before a live audience at Bud Friedman's Improvisation comedy club in Los Angeles. It was something entirely new for Midler, a comedy album called *Mud Will Be Flung Tonight!* A completely different concept for Bette: an evening without mermaid outfits, without wheelchairs, without Harlettes, and without costume changes. The result, which was released late in the year, presented two sides of Bette Midler: the stand-up comedian and the singing satirist.

The album is very funny and contains several of her zanier bits of comedy and a couple of ribald songs. The highlights include a song about her weight, entitled "Fat As I Am"; the tale of Otto Titsling—inventor of the bra; her Sophie Tucker jokes; and a running commentary on life called "Why Bother?" A sticker on the original vinyl LP warned record buyers, "Contains material that may be deemed offensive by Bruce Springsteen, Madonna, and Prince."

"I haven't had much luck with music," Bette gave as her reason for recording a comedy album. "I wasn't camp for a long time, and I really miss it. Life is a drag and people need to be ticked by someone as twitty as my own self." She was especially pleased with the idea of poking fun at herself. "What I've got a really good take on is tits. Because I've had mine for so long, and they're such a big part of me. I weigh more now than I've ever weighed, more than I could ever conceived of someone my size weighing. But you know what? I was zooming toward forty [years old], and I suddenly realized I didn't care anymore how I looked. It's a great weight off my mind" (103).

Mud Will Be Flung Tonight received favorable reviews. Unfortunately, it failed to find an audience, and it sold fewer copies than any Bette Midler album before it. In less than a year, it was already in the discount bins at record stores.

As 1985 ended, Bette Midler found herself a happily married forty-year-old woman, whose career was desperately floundering and who was in need of a hit. She was about to get the reward that she had been waiting for, and she could sense her forthcoming glory. "I really feel like what's coming up," she said prophetically, "is going to be better than anything I've ever done" (103).

14

HER OUTRAGEOUS FORTUNE

It was just two months after she married Harry that something surprising and wonderful happened to Bette. Just when she thought that she might never make another movie again in her career, and that she had been totally blackballed in the industry by *Jinxed,* she was offered a role in a film that would revitalize her career completely. *Down and Out in Beverly Hills* was the life raft that rescued the drowning diva.

The film was the brainchild of director Paul Mazursky, whose illustrious track record includes *Bob & Carol & Ted & Alice* (1969) and *Moscow on the Hudson* (1984). Paul had long recalled a French film that he saw in the 1950s at the Museum of Modern Art in New York City called *Boudu Saved from Drowning (Boudu Sauvé des Eaus).* The 1932 film by Jean Renoir was based on an original play by Rene Rauchois and was about a well-to-do Parisian gentleman who saved a homeless bum from suicide and then ended up being responsible for him and his well-being.

"I'd seen *Boudu Saved from Drowning* in the early fifties," recalls Mazursky. "I had a vague memory of a vagabond who jumps into the Seine and of a bourgeois bookseller who saves him and brings him into his house. That's when the trouble begins. Years later, in the late seventies, I started thinking about the film again. I mentioned to [screenplay writer] Leon [Caperanos]—who like me is a great fan of Jean Renoir's, that it might be interesting to switch *Boudu* to the United States. We decided to poke fun at Beverly Hills—to make fun of my own life, so to speak. Of course, we had to invent a new family and update the notion of the romantic vagabond, which in today's society just doesn't ring true. As we wrote, we aimed for something completely new and contemporary" (8).

The script that Paul and Leon came up with transferred the original story concept to 1980s Beverly Hills. Their characters are a homeless street person, Jerry Baskin, who tries to drown himself in the swimming pool of a nouveau-riche couple, Dave and Barbara Whiteman. Dave made his fortune in the wire coat-hanger business, and his wife is a spoiled Rodeo Drive matron who lives a world of gurus, psychoanalysts, aerobics, flawless manicures, and hours and hours of nonstop shopping.

When it came time for casting, Mazursky had Richard Dreyfuss in mind for the role of Dave Whiteman. "I met with Richard, " he explains, "and definitely wanted him as Dave, but I didn't want to commit until I knew who would play his wife and vice versa. The same is true of the actor who would play Jerry. These things are very tricky" (8).

Mazursky's first choice for the part of Jerry was Jack Nicholson. "He read the script," says Paul, "but it became quite evident within a few weeks that there was to be no clear starting date for another project of his, *The Two Jakes* [which ended up being postponed]. By then I had already cast Richard Dreyfuss, and when Richard read the script, he suggested Nick Nolte [to play Jerry]. I'd already had that idea, so it was good to have the confirmation" (104).

Next came the casting of the role of Barbara Whiteman. "For the wife," explains Mazursky, "I thought about Dyan Cannon, or Cher, but decided on Bette Midler, because the casting would be funnier. It would be a surprise. When I told the studio executives, they were ecstatic" (104).

Bette had never met Mazursky, and when he contacted her and set up a meeting to discuss the possibility of doing the film, she didn't know what to expect. "I thought I was going to meet some silver-haired Hollywood type," says Midler, "but Paul turned out to be an ex-stand-up comic, a guy with whom I had an instant rapport" (97).

Paul recalls their meeting. It was not the wild and crazy Divine Miss M who showed up that day, but a very modest Bette. When Mazursky described the film role, it was Bette who had misgivings. "Do you think I'd be real?" she asked shyly. Says Mazursky, "Pretty soon she lit a cigarette and was relaxed. I knew she'd be funny" (104).

Although she didn't think that the part of Barbara Whiteman had anything to do with herself, something about the role and the opportunity appealed to her. "I don't consider myself even remotely a Beverly Hills matron," she explains, "although I certainly know what they're like. And I sort of appreciate them, too, in a way that a lot of people don't. I find them amusing and colorful. They try to be exotic flowers—daisies trying to be orchids. And I like people who try to get better, even if it's only in a physical sense" (18).

The film was originally called *Jerry Saved from Drowning*, but a month before filming began, the title was changed. According to Mazursky, he changed his mind one night with his card-playing buddies. "At the poker game I play once a week with people not in the movie business, I mentioned the title and everybody thought it was some rescue movie, like *The Poseidon Adventure*" (104). And so the film became *Down and Out in Beverly Hills.*

Both Bette Midler and Nick Nolte did extensive research for their roles in the film. Nolte spent several hours at the Union Rescue Mission in downtown Los Angeles dressed as a bum, to try and understand the part. According to him, "Three months prior to the start of production, I started to get into character by letting my personal appearance go. I stopped bathing, and I no longer brushed my teeth or combed my hair" (8).

Bette's role preparation was quite the opposite experience. "I walked all around Beverly Hills, and I shopped until I was blue," she laughs. "I decorated, I went to lunch at the Rodeo Collection and met all kinds of people. I met landscapers, pest-control people, and dry cleaners. You'd be amazed at how much the people who work in the backstage of the rich and famous know about the people who are actually on the stage. I also spent some time with ladies who actually live the guru life. You know, rather wealthy women who are in search of fulfillment. Barbara Whiteman is an amalgam of all those ladies. They're fabulous people in their own way. I mean, I wouldn't want to be in a world where they don't exist" (8).

Before the cameras rolled, Mazursky insisted upon rehearsing every scene thoroughly. Recalled Midler, "We rehearsed for three weeks. If you're doing a stage production, that's not a lot, but it's a lot for pictures. It was a big help—a tremendous help. We knew each other, and we knew what the relationships were. We had explored all that, even to the point of knowing what our blocking would be" (8).

"I have no real empathy for matrons who don't have a lot to do with themselves," she continued. "You know the type—so much time on their hands and no real imagination. However, Paul showed me what was wonderful about Barbara and how to make her amusing. Barbara Whiteman is a soul in torment. The reason it's funny is that she really doesn't have anything to be in torment about. She has a lovely family, lots of money, and the freedom to do whatever she wants to do, and yet she feels unfulfilled. She's a character who's searching blindly for the way to live her life. She's nothing if not an explorer of the psyche and—trends, she loves a trend" (8).

"I was able to bring my own saltiness to the role," she went on to say. "Barbara is quite cynical and more than a little angry. I have those elements in my own personality, but the rest is totally new to me. I've never worn clothes like this, or nails like this. The whole visual thing is completely different from my own life, and I can't tell you how bizarre it is to be playing a woman with grown kids" (8).

One of the most unique aspects of the casting of *Down and Out in Beverly Hills* was that Midler, Dreyfuss, and Nolte all had reputations in Hollywood for having personal problems that spilled over into their movie careers. Principal photography began on May 20, 1985, and on the set, Mazursky fondly referred to his stars as "the Betty Ford Kids"—after the famed rehabilitation clinic (100).

"That hurt our feelings," said Bette, who had to admit, "We all had these strange reputations. I was supposed to be impossible to work with, Richard had certain drug or alcohol-related problems, and God only knows what they said about Nick" (100). Nolte had a reputation as a heavy drinker.

One of the most amusing ironies about the production was that it was produced by Touchstone Films, which at the time was the new adult division of Disney Films. Imagine the raunchy Miss M's surprise to awaken one day and find herself a Disney employee. The outrageous singer who exposed her breasts was suddenly working shoulder-to-shoulder with Mickey and Minnie Mouse! This was the film that marked the beginning of a long and very creatively productive phase of her film career.

"I never tell people I'm working for Disney," exclaimed Bette at the time. "Walt would roll over in his grave! If I hadn't made my name practically taking my clothes off and being bawdy, I'd be delighted to work for the straight Disney guys. I grew up watching Dumbo and those movies. And Hayley Mills—I was crazy about her" (101).

Recalls Mazursky, the entire cast really projected themselves into their roles. While Midler was in Beverly Hills studying the lives of rich matrons, Nolte was wearing bum's clothes and wandering the streets. "He started wearing those clothes for two or three weeks. All during the rehearsal he didn't shower. He sort of . . . became Jerry. In rehearsals he didn't immediately snap out of it. He'd walk off by himself and sit in a corner. I remember Bette looking at him as if to say, 'Is he all right?' But this was really what I wanted. I tried to create an atmosphere in rehearsal that would really make them believe that what was going on was actually happening. That's good. I think comedy has to be [more real] than drama" (105).

The result of the pleasurable working relationship between Midler, Nolte, Dreyfuss, and Mazursky was an instant hit when it was released in January 1986. According to Bette, being a member of an ensemble rather than being the lead character was a welcome change of pace. "That's why *Down and Out in Beverly Hills* was such a relief for me," she said. "Paul wants everyone to get in the spirit of the silliness. I can generate that kind of silliness myself, in my shows, but at home I don't because I'm too beat. So it's nice when somebody else is the clown and the host for a change" (97).

Although he was gregarious and charming, Mazursky ran a tight ship. "With Bette's problems and Richard Dreyfuss's problems, perhaps we should have filmed at the Betty Ford Center. Instead I made it clear that if either stepped out of line, they would be replaced," he later admitted. In fact, said Paul of Bette, "She managed to pull Richard Dreyfuss and Nick Nolte out of their shells" (8).

David Whiteman (Dreyfus) became wealthy in the wire coat hanger business. So wealthy is he that he lives the lush life in Beverly Hills, drives a Rolls Royce, and even his dog—Matisse—has its own psychiatrist. His wife, Barbara (Midler), employs both a nutritionist and a personal guru. She hasn't had an orgasm in ages. And David and Barbara's two teenage children are already having their own separate identity crises.

David saves Jerry (Nolte) from drowning himself in David's immaculate backyard swimming pool. Much to the shock of Barbara, David decides to move the rescued bum into their house until Jerry gets his act together. In the ensuing action, Jerry, the bum, ends up improving the lives of each member of the Whiteman family. They come to find out that, although financially broke, Jerry is rich in wisdom, and much more so than any of the members of the Whiteman household.

Down and Out in Beverly Hills has a lot in common with the classic William Powell and Carole Lombard comedy *My Man Godfrey* (1936). As Godfrey, Powell goes from living under the 59th Street Bridge to owning a ritzy bar under the 59th Street Bridge. In many ways, this is the 1980s West Coast version of that tale.

Jerry plants charm and wisdom everywhere he goes. And before he is finished, he has slept with every female under the Whitemans' roof—including their maid. And, yes—thanks to Jerry—by the end of the film, Bette's Barbara comically achieves her elusive orgasm.

In another delightful twist of casting, rock star Little Richard co-starred as one of the Whitemans' neighbors. His appearance further upped the ante for zaniness.

Midler fans and critics alike were surprised and delighted with the amusingly restrained Miss M on the screen in the hilarious comedy role. "I was holding back as much as I knew how," she explained. "When I saw the picture, I thought I was in a Jerry Lewis movie—I looked like I walked in from another set" (18).

The critics and moviegoers alike loved this film. Even fussy Roger Ebert in the *Chicago Sun Times* gave the film four stars (out of four) and proclaimed, *"Down and Out in Beverly Hills* made me laugh longer and louder than any film I've seen in a long time" (106).

Time magazine's Richard Schickel claimed, "The old film that *Down and Out* most consistently evokes is Mazursky's own *Bob & Carol & Ted & Alice,* also a nervously ambiguous but hilariously etched carica-ture of the bourgeois at self-improving play. . . . on a basically farcical level where it chooses to stay, it is a funny and likable movie" (107).

One of the most complimentary reviews that Bette received for *Down and Out* came in the *News and Observer* in Raleigh, North Caro-lina—a town she once performed in while she was still a fledgling singer wishing for fame and fortune. "[The film] gives Miss Midler a chance to catch up with her image, proving that she's an actress as well as a star. That's what she dreamed about when she was playing clubs like the old Frog and Nightgown in Raleigh. She's achieved what she set out to achieve" (108).

Down and Out in Beverly Hills represented a rebirth in Bette Midl-er's career. After years of playing the role of a star who had to shock, stun, and amaze her audiences time and time again, she suddenly found she was a bigger star than ever in a role that required her to tone herself down.

In January of 1985, Bette went on *The Tonight Show* as Johnny Carson's guest and sang a song from her *Mud Will Be Flung Tonight* album. The song was the self-parodying "Fat As I Am." In the song Bette sang that "they could park a DC-10 on my rear." It just so happened that three of the millions of people watching the show that night were brothers David and Jerry Zucker and their business partner Jim Abrahams. They were busy developing a film property that they were going to direct for Touchstone Films, called *Ruthless People*. Zucker, Zucker, and Abrahams had become famous for their first hit comedy, *Airplane!* (1980), which starred Robert Hayes and Julie Haggarty. According to Abrahams, "We knew she would be perfect" for the role of out-of-shape Barbara Stone in *Ruthless People* (109).

When *Desperately Seeking Susan* became a huge box-office hit in the spring of 1985, however, Disney decided that it wanted to sign that film's big star—Madonna—to play Barbara Stone. Disney/Touchstone had already signed Danny DeVito for the part of Sam Stone, and it was going to be a bit of a stretch for Madonna to play his wife of fifteen years, but the role was the only one the studio had available. Happily for Bette, Madonna instead went on to film the huge box-office disappointment *Shanghai Surprise* (1986).

By October, Zucker, Zucker, and Abrahams still did not have a female star. According to a November 1, 1985, item in *Variety* headlined, "Disney's People Still Searching for Femme Lead," "Both Madonna and Bette Midler's names have been bandied about, but Madonna is rumored to be pregnant and Midler reportedly is not interested" (8). Well, Madonna was not pregnant, and Bette was interested. She was signed for the role, and in January 1986, before *Down and Out in Beverly Hills* even opened, she was in front of the cameras, doing her second Disney/Touchstone film.

The film was originally called *Would Anyone Please Kill My Wife?* and is about a man who plots to murder his obnoxious spouse. *Ruthless People* ended up being one of the funniest movies of the past ten years. It is filled with plot twists involving mistaken identities, sharp dialogue, and snappy performances by the entire cast. As in *Down and Out in Beverly Hills*, Bette accepted a role that was not the lead. Instead she is part of an ensemble effort that includes Danny DeVito, Anita Morris, Judge Reinhold, and Helen Slater.

In this film, Bette not only had to portray an obnoxious moneyed matron, but she was padded to show off the character's weight problem.

The film is something of a twist on the classic O. Henry short story "The Ransom of Red Chief." In that story, a little boy is kidnapped, and he is such a spoiled little beast that the kidnappers offer to pay the parents to take him back. In the film *Ruthless People*, on the day that Sam Stone (DeVito) plans to kill his wife, he returns to their overdecorated home to discover that she has been kidnapped. Not only has he no intention of paying the kidnappers what they demand, he actually encourages them to make good their threats to murder her.

As Barbara Stone, the kidnap victim, Bette Midler is at her zany, fire-breathing best. She ends up locked in a basement with nothing to do all day but watch exercise tapes and make dietary demands of her kidnappers. In the course of the film she ends up losing weight and conspires with her captors to get even with her husband. One of the funniest moments in the movie comes when Midler discovers that her husband has not paid for her freedom, even though the kidnappers have continually reduced their demands. "I've been kidnapped by K-Mart!" she wails in disgust (110).

Barbara Stone's mid-film self-improvement was one of the things that appealed most to Midler. "Once again, I had my nails done," she says with reference to her *Down and Out* role. "This time I got long, but very wide acrylic nails painted dark purple. They make me feel like a caged animal, which is how I believe my character felt" (8).

In her first scenes, Bette does look like a demonically possessed creature from hell. She was even startled when she first saw herself on the screen in *Ruthless People* and explained, "I was pretty shaken when I saw the movie. I didn't realize just how terrible I was going to look. I wouldn't have done the role five years ago. I would have thought it was too small a part, that it was beneath me, because this was when I was going to be a great dramatic actress. And yes, I cared too much to look like that" (111).

Speaking of the fact that her character has an onscreen metamorphosis, Midler claimed, "I love the fact that she changes from horrible to wonderful in the course of the picture. And, the screenplay was as funny as anything I've read" (112).

To make the transformation of Barbara Stone even more dramatic, Bette lost additional weight and worked out with trainers Jake Steinfeld and Bob Carrricro. She had put on twenty pounds in recent years. "Oh, I've gained a lot of weight since I've been married," she admitted. "My husband loves restaurants, and I've never gone about eating with the gusto he's taught me. I've been eating food from countries you didn't even know had food!" (101).

"Ten pounds is like blimp city for me, so I made a resolution to lose the weight. I went on a juice fast, and I started working out. Jake worked me over. That was good, because I have a whole exercise scene where I have to do push-ups and sit ups," Bette explained (18).

During the filming of *Ruthless People*, on February 6, 1986, Bette became the 1,821st celebrity to have her name emblazoned on a star on Hollywood's Walk of Fame. "I hope you'll come and walk all over it!" she told the crowd that gathered on Hollywood Boulevard. She gushed with astonishment at the ceremony, "It really does have my name on it, but I really feel this star is the work of the fans. I am really overwhelmed and I am flabbergasted, and I think this is probably the greatest thrill of my whole life" (8).

In March 1986, it was announced that Bette was expecting her first child in the fall. She was still working on *Ruthless People* at the time. The press had a field day heralding the arrival of Bette's own "Baby Divine." Midler had her own ideas about bringing up baby. "Well, I'm going to put my baby in boarding school as soon as possible, in a far corner of England—no, Scotland, near the heather and the high-lands—so my baby will never hear any of this!" she laughed (10). On a more serious note, she added, "I'm going to have to keep doing some-thing, because that's my livelihood. Joan River's child [Melissa] seems to be developing okay, hasn't turned into a serial killer or anything. And Joan's much more abrasive that I" (97).

Things were suddenly going beautifully for Bette. She had one hit movie in the theaters, one in the can, and another one in production. She had a husband who was wild over her, and she was expecting a baby. She had even come to an understanding with her father. "My dad was very ill last year," she said, "he had two bypasses. I thought I was too much of a wimp to look after him and pull him through, but I wasn't. He didn't want to go on, he really wanted to lie down and die. And I said, 'No, what's the point of doing that?' And I got him through it. I rose to an occasion I didn't think I could rise to—and I feel that a lot of that was because I had Harry in back of me saying, 'Yes, you can do it'" (8).

"My father needed me, and I think he was very, very happy that I came through. I think he felt that he didn't deserve any support be-cause, when he was raising me, he didn't really pay much attention. But

I just went ahead and gave him all the help I could. I guess he thought I wasn't so bad after all, even thought I do stand up and tell dirty jokes" (8).

Bette had just discovered that she was pregnant when Fred Midler suddenly died. "He was very happy. I kept saying, 'Pop, you gotta stick around to see the baby.' And he said, 'Oh I will, I will. . . . ' But he didn't. He was seventy-eight. I thought he'd live longer," she remembered (18).

Her strained relationship with her father was a lifelong source of pain and disappointment for Bette. "He wanted me to be a professional person and to have a stable job and not get into trouble, not make any noise, not have people look at me," she said. One of Bette's perpetual sources of regret was that no matter what she accomplished in life, Fred Midler would not acknowledge her achievement, or as she puts it, "He wouldn't give me any reward" (18).

When *Ruthless People* opened in theaters in June 1986, it became the summer's hit comedy film, gleaning excellent reviews. Eleanor Ringel in the *Atlanta Journal* called it "A riotous comedy that's not only full of funny people but is also exceedingly well-written. The funniest of the funny people are Bette Midler and Danny DeVito. They play Barbara and Sam Stone, a wealthy Bel Air couple who are a kind of Bizarro World version of the prosperous pair played by Midler and Richard Dreyfus in *Down and Out in Beverly Hills*" (113). And, Rich Beebe, in the *Torrington, Connecticut, Register Citizen*, wrote, "*Ruthless People* is a blaring boom box of a movie comedy. It's rude, obnoxious and crass; it's about as subtle as a dirty joke. It's also funny, extremely funny. . . . Bette Midler's brutal comic portrait . . . makes her transformation in the second half of the film into a vengeful, but likable Harpy all the more amazing and fun" (114).

Bette Midler had wanted for years to have a hot winning streak like this, and she wasn't about to let go of the momentum. Almost immediately, she began work on her next Touchstone comedy, *Outrageous Fortune.*

Cameras began rolling in New York, with Arthur Hiller directing. One of the first scenes was filmed at the Newark International Airport in New Jersey. The company then moved to Santa Fe, New Mexico, for six weeks of location filming. Bette's co-stars this time around were Shelley Long, George Carlin, Peter Coyote, and John Schuck. Bette referred to the plot of the film as *"Abbot & Costello Go to Santa Fe"* (110).

On the set of *Outrageous Fortune,* reports of Bette Midler and Shelley Long feuding with each other began to leak out. The disagreement occurred over which actress was going to receive top billing in the movie. To quell any arguments, the Disney company struck upon a settlement. Half of all of the film prints, press releases, television advertisements, and film posters used Bette's name first, and the other half used Shelley's first.

In the film, Bette plays the part of slobby Sandy Brozinsky. For her role in *Outrageous Fortune,* her fingernails are stubby and polished in alternate colors: yellow and green, and glittered. Bette's fingernails were indeed becoming an important part of her characterizations. Says Bette, "Laurence Olivier changes his nose, I do it with my nails" (111).

Shelley Long and Bette Midler play two very different women who unwittingly have their lives entwined. Lauren (Long) is a classically trained actress, who has yet to land a paying gig. Sandy is a brash, streetwise New Yorker, whose main acting credit is for her role in *Ninja Vixens.* Not only do they end up in the same acting class, much to their horror, they also discover that they are both sleeping with the same man: Michael (Peter Coyote).

Bette's first line on camera consists of a loud entrance into the lobby of an acting school office and the utterance, "Holy Mary, isn't there one fucking phone in this whole town that works?"

After Michael fakes his death, Lauren and Shelley run into each other at the morgue, where they go—separately—to identify the body. They know it's not Michael, after a look at the corpse—below the belt. "It's a fucking pencil!" exclaims Bette as Shelley, in typical Divine Miss M fashion. Complaining of a body mix-up, she asks a guard, "Does the phrase 'needle dick, the bug fucker' mean anything to you?"

Both wanting to track Michael down, to find out which one of them he truly loves, the pair ends up in a series of harrowing misadventures together. While surviving together on their wits, they eventually discover that their bond as friends is stronger than they could have imagined.

What the two battling women don't realize is that Michael is a crook, and one who would kill to succeed. It seems that he possesses a serum that could defoliate the planet, and he is holding it for ransom. As a pair of sleuths, Shelley and Lauren each get to show off their best "method"

acting, by throwing themselves into situations that require new identities.

Chasing Michael out to Santa Fe, New Mexico, the girls end up chasing their prey into the mountains. One of their funniest sequences together comes when they are disguised as fourteen-year-old boys visiting
a whorehouse. As a comic foil, they enlist the help of Frank (George
Carlin), who is their "Indian" guide through town. However, Frank is
not sober and not an Indian. Carlin proves a great comic "banana" for
both women to play off. Showing that New Yorkers can handle themselves in any situation, the duo refuses to give up the chase until they
get their man.

"Nuts," says Bette, as she takes a pause from dodging bullets and
running for her life; it seems she has broken one of her fingernails.
However, in the end, the two women finally see Michael for what he
is—a foreign espionage agent and a colossal rat.

Outrageous Fortune is a laugh riot from start to finish. As unlikely as
it seemed, this pairing of Bette Midler and Shelley Long brilliantly
works on camera. They play off their diverse, contrasting characters,
and it looks like they are both having fun while being funny.

When *Outrageous Fortune* opened in January 1987, it became an
instant box-office smash. Bette and Shelley, as rival actresses in love
with the same deceitful man, showed off the best of each other's comic
strengths. Midler's bitchy bawdiness provided the perfect counterpoint
for Long's deadpan prissiness, and vice versa. In *Outrageous Fortune*
it became obvious that Bette was the silver screen's hottest comedy
chameleon.

This time around, the critics unanimously loved it. Peter Travers, in
People magazine, claimed, "Bette Midler and Shelley Long bring out
the bitchy, bawdy best in each other in this breakneck farce. . . . A
particular howl comes in watching Long's slow descent into shock as
Midler, in return for information, offers oral sex to a tobacconist. . . .
Midler and Long's low-comic high jinks make *Outrageous Fortune* the
perfect laugh cure for the blues" (115). David Ansen, in *Newsweek,*
wrote, "*Outrageous Fortune* has the obvious, but long overdue comic
concept: It's a buddy movie with two *women* in the leads. . . . The plot
is madcap nonsense, and the comic aim is sometimes very broad and
very low, but the belly-laugh quotient . . . is the highest since the last
Midler movie, *Ruthless People*. . . . The libidinous Bette, of course, gets
the best of the down and dirty zingers, but Long isn't just a straight

woman. . . . They could become the Hope and Crosby of female raunch!" (116). And, in *Time* magazine, Richard Corliss called Shelley and Bette, "The lady and the tramp," announcing that "in this witty, rambunctious caper movie, the lady is Lauren (Shelley Long). . . . when she does meet a dashing, sympathetic hetero (Peter Coyote), he turns out to be sharing his favors with a tramp in Lauren's acting class. This would be Sandy (Bette Midler), who has a bulldozer mouth and the sensitivity of a whelk. . . . Midler breezes through her role, looking fine and giving the punch lines pop. . . . Cheers all around!" (117).

Having just left the popular TV series *Cheers* to pursue a film career, Shelley Long had a lot on the line in this pivotal film. The landscape is littered with ambitious careers dashed by small screen stars aiming for big screen success. And Midler was still undergoing her own film career resuscitation. *Outrageous Fortune* was a home run for both of them.

To accommodate the sudden demand for Bette Midler movies and to reward her explosion of creativity on the screen, Disney gave Miss M her own production deal, to plan, develop, and execute her own films. To fulfill the order, Bette established her own production company, which she named "All Girls Productions." Her business partners were her longtime assistant Bonnie Bruckheimer and Margaret Jennings. The company's motto, according to Bette, was "We hold a grudge" (8).

"I've decided to be as realistic about what I do as I possibly can be. And what I can be is very, very funny, which not a lot of ladies are doing. And very few of them sing and are funny in the same picture. So I've been inching my way toward that. I'd like to have a niche, a little piece of the pie, where I can do what it is that I do and I don't step on anyone's toes and I'm not disappointed if I don't get their part" (18).

The people who have worked with Bette on *Down and Out in Beverly Hills*, *Ruthless People*, and *Outrageous Fortune* had nothing but great things to say about her. Jeffrey Katzenberg, who was the head of Disney's TV and movie division, claimed, "This lady is as smart and nailed down as anyone I deal with" (111). Actor John Schuck claimed, "She creates such extraordinary characters. She has the same type of scathing good humor" (118). According to Paul Mazursky, "If Bette could tap everything she has as an actress, she could play Lady Macbeth!" (100).

Said Bette at the time of her newfound screen success, "You know, these kind of comedies, I'm happy that people like them and I'm happy that they make them. But you always want to do something more, something better. I guess I feel like I have to pay some dues and then I'll be okay. I can do my Lady Macbeth. Actually, what we're going to do is call her 'Lady Macbecky!'" (110).

Throughout 1986, several different projects were discussed as films for Bette. For a while it looked like a Mae West biography might be her next role, but this didn't pan out. A comedy called *Stand Up Detective* was under consideration. All Girls Productions was developing a musical comedy about 1940s female big-band leader Ina Ray Hutton. "Of course, there'll be a romance with a saxophone player," promised Bette (8).

In addition to her Disney films, NBC-TV optioned a book for Bette called *Winnie: My Life in the Institution,* a dramatization of the life of a girl who enters a mental institution and grows up trying to prove that she is capable of living in the outside world. Six months after being released from the institution, however, the woman opts to move back into it. The character was based on the life of Gwina (Winnie) Sprockett, who died at the age of forty-four after writing her life story.

Said Bette at the time, "NBC has optioned the book for me. I've never done a piece for television before. I thought it would be interesting. It doesn't necessarily mean that I have to play the part. I might like to direct. I've never directed before" (18).

In August 1986, Touchstone/Disney announced that Bette's next movie would be called *Palm Beached.* Midler was to have portrayed Mollie Wilmot, the Palm Beach, Florida, socialite who awakened one day in 1984 to find that a severe storm had beached a Venezuelan freighter, the 190-foot *Mercedes I,* in her backyard. Ironically, that very day was the date that Wilmot's backyard and pool were to be photographed by *Town & Country* magazine. Said Wilmot of the announcement that Midler was to portray her, "She's a wonderful actress, but she's terrible for the part" (119). The script that was written would have had Bette as the startled Mollie, serving the Venezuelan crew caviar and paté off her best china in the backyard.

As fate would have it, Bette was never to appear in any of these proposed projects that were being bantered around. Instead, she was about to portray a brand new character in her life—the suddenly maternal Miss M was about to become a divine mom.

A DIVINE NEW PLATEAU

Bette acknowledged that she had undergone amniocentesis during her pregnancy, but she didn't want to know in advance whether her baby was going to be a boy or a girl. "I want a surprise. And that's what I'm going to get. I'm sure my baby will be divine. If it's a boy, I hope they don't saddle him with 'Baby Divine.' Oh my, I'd have to send him away!" (8).

Bette was never alarmed by the audible ticking of her biological clock—she was too busy with her career and her life. "I was caught up in my superwoman thing. Now it's sort of like waking up from a dream and seeing that everyone wishes to be in our shoes. It's so surprising because I never had that hankering to marry and have children. Well, I got married at thirty-nine. I'm having my first baby. And anybody can do it. It's true!" (110).

After all the horror stories that Bette had heard about first pregnancies after the age of forty, she was pleasantly surprised by how uncomplicated it was for her. "Talk about being struck by lightning—I haven't had any morning sickness or any of the stuff they keep talking about. I have shortness of breath and I tend to waddle and I can't sleep on my stomach anymore, but that's it" (110). She did suddenly develop cravings for certain things to eat, though. "I hardly ever eat sweets," she explained in her fifth month. "But since I've been pregnant, I crave them. I thought it was a joke, but I really crave ice cream—vanilla. I'm very plain" (18).

Although it was originally predicted that she would give birth on October 27, it wasn't until Friday night, November 14, 1986, that the divine moment occurred. She had an eight-pound, eleven-ounce baby girl. It was several days before Bette and Harry settled on a name.

While she was contemplating baby names, she had commented, "I like Bob Geldof's baby's name: Fifi Trixibelle. But my husband says when she's forty and she's a librarian and a spinster, she's not going to be so happy with Fifi Trixibelle!" (18).

Seemingly, just as Bette's mother had named her for her favorite movie star—Bette Davis—she named her daughter Sophie the name of one of her favorite stars: Sophie Tucker. However, Bette begs to differ.

"Her name is Sophie, and there's a reason. *Sophie* means wisdom" (120). Her daughter's full name is Sophie Frederica Alohilani von Haselberg. How is that for a mouthful? With regard to how she chose the name, Bette says, Sophie ("not for Sophie Tucker") Frederica ("for my father, Fred") Alohilani ("Hawaiian for 'bright sky,' which is what I always wish for her") von Haselberg. After Sophie's birth, Bette gushed to the press, "I adore her. Her face swims before me when she's not there, and I think about her before I go to sleep at night and I dream about her, and I wake up and I can't wait to see her" (20).

Prior to her pregnancy, Bette had been talking seriously about raising a family. She had thought about how she wanted to raise her children. "I think I would raise them in a very Victorian way," she admitted, months prior to her pregnancy. "I sort of like the idea that I'm very tough and very hard-nosed. But I guess underneath it all I'm quite sentimental. I would give them an 'everyone-around-the-piano' kind of life. I wouldn't let my kids watch television eight hours a day, and I would be careful about what they watched. I'd teach them to paint and be creative. You can be lonely, you can be all on your own, but if you can make something out of nothing, you can be happy. I've learned that" (8).

Circa 1987, Bette Midler was at a new plateau, both in her career and in her personal life. From that vantage point, she looked around and surveyed the situation. She had been a huge singing star in the early 1970s. She had been an Academy Award–nominated actress in 1980, when everything was coming up roses for her. She had fallen flat on her face in the early 1980s, when the films *Jinxed* and *Divine Madness* nearly derailed her film career. She felt like a wounded bird when both *No Frills* and *Mud Will Be Flung Tonight* both came up with disappointing sales on the record charts. However, thanks to her marriage and the films *Down and Out in Beverly Hills, Ruthless People,* and *Outrageous Fortune*; her motion picture career was back on track, while her marriage and the arrival of baby Sophie grounded her. Childbirth, and the temporary break that she took from working, proved the perfect time for Miss M to reflect on the past, appreciate the present, and plan the future.

Her natural instincts made her think about her own childhood. She said at the time, "I had a fairly dull upbringing; I spent a lot of time in the library. We didn't get a TV until I was twelve or thirteen, and I think that was better for me. I read a lot of fairy tales—I overdosed on them. Eventually, I started reading grown-up books—the Frank O'Haras and the Henry Millers—but I'm glad I had that basis in happily ever-after, because that's what gives you hope," she said, with the optimism that has enabled her to create all of the things that have become the milestones of her career (8.) She chose to raise her daughter in much the same way.

Marriage and motherhood were always two subjects that Bette Midler had thought were not in the cards for her. Did these two new modes in her once unpredictably outrageous life tame her? She didn't think so. "I'm still a wild and crazy gal," she proclaimed at the time, "even if I pretend I'm completely domestic. I have my periods where I'm nuts. This doesn't happen to be one of them. The baby will be a big, big change. I don't know what that means in terms of how much work I can do, whether I can bring the baby around with me. I'd like to have someone to help out, but I don't want to leave my baby in the hands of someone other than myself or Harry" (18).

According to Bette, marriage to Harry didn't curtail her zaniness. Actually, it allowed her to be more confident about being herself. "We laugh a good deal," she explained (110). "He backs me up and feeds me back a sense of my own identity, and I try to do the same for him. I feel a responsibility to give back as much as I'm given, and that's the best part. Who knew?" (24).

"Harry is quite charming and just what I was looking for. And he's incredibly interested in domesticity; he loves having a home, he loves to cook, and he's nuts about me, which is so shocking. You think, well, I'm a good gal, I'm okay. But when somebody likes you this much, you think, 'Gee, maybe I'm better than I think I am.' And that's terrific!" (24).

"Harry says that I make him younger, and you know, it's really true. In public he presents a very stern image, and yet when he's with me we rough-house a lot; he's like a kid." Bette claimed that she never wants to grow up. In fact, she views herself as a perpetual teenager. "I think that everyone feels thirteen; everyone is surprised when the skin starts to get weird and the hair starts to fall out. I never feel like a grown-up. When I met my husband, I thought he was a grown-up; that was one of the things that attracted me to him. And then I discovered that we're both pretty much the same. I think most human beings are. The outside is grown up, but the inside is still looking for Mom. It's nothing to be ashamed of; it's just the human condition. I used to think you were grown up when you had a rug in the bathroom!" (24).

Two of the things that Bette has always appreciated the most in life have been food and creativity. "I love food!" Bette explained during this era. "I eat my own cooking, I eat my husband's cooking; what I really like to make—and this shows my peasant roots—are big pots you cook twenty-four hours: casseroles, stews, red beans and rice, which we eat for a week, and we're always happy at first and then we're really sorry" (24).

The song "Friends" had been a trademark of Bette's since she first sang it at the Continental Baths in the early seventies. By the late 1980s, who were Bette Midler's friends? At that point, there were several disgruntled people who claimed that they were dumped by the wayside as she made her way to the top. Aaron Russo would certainly fall in this category. She—however—disputed that: "My closest friends ARE people I've worked with for years," she says. "They've seen me at my best and at my worst. Toni Basil is one of my dearest friends. She's choreographed my shows since 1976. Jerry Blatt has been with me for over twelve years. Bob DeMora, who makes clothes for me, has been with me since about 1971. Frannie Vanzella has been a good friend since she was wardrobe lady when I was in *Fiddler on the Roof* almost twenty years ago. My Harlettes—Linda Hart is a good friend of mine—all my girls I still consider good friends" (18).

Still an ever-present friend, too, was Bette's brash and trashy alter ego, the Divine Miss M. "She chats in my head, you know," Bette proclaimed. "She's like a little demon. She has a very loud voice and she panics me sometimes, because she's the one who keeps saying, 'We're going to do this, we're going to do that.' And the other voice is saying, 'Aw, shut up, let's just sit. We'll read a book, we'll have a bite to eat.'

But she says, 'No, no, we have to go out, we have to be seen!'" (24).
And so the saga of the Divine Miss M was destined to continue to
grow—in new recordings and in new stage shows.

Ensconced in her glamorous Hollywood area Coldwater Canyon
home, she began to plot new directions that she wanted to take her film
career. "I've always been grateful for my drive," she proclaimed. "I want
to work with Dustin [Hoffman] and Warren [Beatty] and Meryl
[Streep] and Sylvester [Stallone]—everyone. You know in the old days
you used to go from picture to picture and make eighty of them over a
lifetime. Now it's like twelve" (101).

She explained, "In the old days, people used to do a lot of pictures—
eighty in a career. I got a late start, and I'd like to have a body of work
to show at the end. I'm doing as many as I can. I like the process. I want
to make eighty, so I have seventy-five left to go. That's four a year for
the next twenty years" (121).

"From now on, I'm just going to take chances and not treat everything like it was a career move. And that way, I'll make eighty pictures,
all right!?" she promised, after completing *Outrageous Fortune* (101).

In the mid-1980s, Midler literally put Touchstone Pictures on the
map, with three back-to-back box-office hits: *Down and Out in Beverly
Hills, Outrageous Fortune,* and *Ruthless People.* She really was the acknowledged darling of Disney.

Jeffrey Katzenberg, who was at the time the chairman of Walt Disney
Studios, signed Midler to a three-picture deal. According to him in
1987, "Bette Midler is the single greatest asset as a performer we have"
(20).

Without losing a bit of momentum from her hot comedy streak, Disney quickly paired Bette with another comedy actress of her own Oscar-
nominated stature. By teaming her with Lily Tomlin, they upped the
ante on the antics with a bit of onscreen silliness known as *Big Business,*
which hit the theaters in 1988.

In the middle of nowhere—Jupiter Hollow, West Virginia, to be specific—two pregnant women suddenly go into labor. One married couple
is the Sheltons of Manhattan, and the other is the rural Ratliffs. Both
women are pregnant—and each is about to give birth to twin girls.
When the only medical facility is a local manufacturer's company doctor, Mr. Shelton simply buys the company on the spot, so his wife can
get instant medical attention. The elderly nurse on duty is so dizzy, she
mistakes a urine sample for apple cider on a lunch tray. When the nurse

mixes up the sets of twins, the film's premise is born. To top off the confusion, at a loss for baby names, Mr. Ratliff overhears Mr. Shelton naming his daughters "Sadie" and "Rose," and he does so as well. Before the opening credits have run and the story unfolds, the babies have grown up to be a set of mismatched Bette and Lily twins in Manhattan and another in West Virginia.

The premise—and the comical contrast between the two sets of twins—is amusing in itself. Here we have bitchy city Sadie (Midler); aspiring sophisticate, country Sadie (Midler); feisty country Rose (Tomlin); and modestly big-hearted city Rose (Tomlin).

In New York City, Sadie Shelton has grown up to be a terse and cold business woman, and her sister Rose Shelton is a hapless klutz. Since their parents have died and left them the family company, Moramax—whose greedy motto is "More for America"—they know very little of the town in which they were born. Making a corporate decision, Sadie wants to sell Hollowmade Furniture and sell the town of Jupiter Hollow for strip mining. When asked her reason for dumping the company, Bette shouts in disgust: "They still make porch rockers!" Aside from accidentally affixing a blueberry from a muffin to her front teeth mid-meeting, Rose is unable to do anything to deter her business-aggressive sister.

Meanwhile, we have their Jupiter Hollow country counterparts: aspiring social climber Sadie Ratliff and her rabble-rousing sister Rose. It seems that Rose Ratliff is leading the movement to defeat the big business swindle that Moramax is about to hand out. When it comes time to head to New York City to fight Moramax, while Rose is set on defeating the New Yorkers, Sadie is determined never to return to West Virginia.

The first time we see Bette onscreen in *Big Business,* she is onstage, performing at a Hollowmade company picnic. While Bette sings the yodeling country song "Little Ole Lady," she is actually milking a cow and wearing a gingham dress. This scene alone is worth the price of admission—or video rental. In her time, Bette has certainly milked several things for laughs, but *never* before has she publicly milked a cow! And midsong no less.

It seems that the big Moramax showdown is to take place at the annual stockholder's meeting at the Plaza Hotel on Central Park South. As they prepare for their trip, Bette, as Sadie Ratliff, says to her sister Rose, "I gotta get me some of those Press-On nails. Do those things stay on?" Several minutes later in the film, as she arrives in New York, she looks at her semi-nailless hands and bemoans, "Gee—these Press-On nails. I guess I shoulda pressed harder, huh?"

When the Ratliffs come to Manhattan, there is an establishment shot of the lower island and the glittering World Trade Center towers. This pair of comic country mice has officially arrived in the Big Apple. When a limousine meant for city Rose and Sadie Shelton accidentally picks up country Rose and Sadie and takes them to the Plaza, where the Shelton sisters are staying, the mistaken identity gags swing into full gear. Both sets of sisters end up in suites next door to each other. When all of the suitors, boyfriends, and ex-husbands get into the mix, the men all fall for the opposite twin, in good Shakespearean style—ala "Twelfth Night."

One of Lily's funniest bits comes as she plays Rose Ratliff. Whenever she is up against one of her corporate enemies, she goes into her rattle-snake impersonation and puts a country curse on them. Bette likewise is at her goofiest as her country incarnation.

Disney producers Michael Peyser and Steve Tisch populated this film with a cracker jack cast of supporting players. They include Fred Ward as Rune, Rose Ratliff's hunky back-home miniature golf pro boyfriend; Michael Gross as Sadie Shelton's suitor; Mary Gross as the ditzy recep-tionist at Moramax headquarters; Seth Green (Scott in *Austin Powers*) as Sadie Shelton's rambunctious son; and Edward Harrmann and Dan-iel Gerroll as bumbling gay corporate henchmen Graham and Chuck.

Right before the big stockholder's meeting, Bette as country Sadie and city Sadie both purchase an identical polka dot dress from the same ladies shop in the Plaza lobby, heightening the confusion and the possi-bilities for sight gags. When the two Midlers end up in a mirror-lined ladies room, it is a classic sight gag waiting to happen. Via split screen, Bette has one of her most hysterical moments on film, mimicking the Marx Brothers' famous two-Grouchos mirror routine from *Duck Soup* (1933).

It turns out that Sadie Ratliff's idol is Joan Collins on the 1980s prime-time TV soap opera *Dynasty*. When she is called upon to imper-sonate her Manhattan twin, Sadie summons the essence of Alexis Car-rington to personify terror at a shareholder's meeting.

The plot of the movie begins to lose momentum somewhere in the middle, but the comic outcome is well worth the journey. Bette and Lily are great fun to watch, no matter which sister act they're portraying in this clever comedy.

Some critics loved it. *People* magazine glowed, "Midler and Tomlin . . . make a red-hot roaringly funny comedy team." And TV's *Good Morning America* proclaimed that *Big Business* had "Guaranteed big laughs" (122). The film did respectably well at the box-office and further cemented Midler's reputation as one of the hottest comedy actresses in Hollywood in the mid-1980s.

On the other hand, the reviews for the film were decidedly mixed. Roger Ebert, in the *Chicago Sun-Times,* gave *Big Business* the old "thumbs down," affixing two and a half stars (out of four) to it. According to him, "The life all seems to have escaped from this movie. Midler and Tomlin can be funny actors, but here they both seem muted and toned down in all of the characters they play. The most promising character probably is Sadie Shelton, Midler's New York company executive, who has the potential to be a bitch on wheels but never realizes it. The Jupiter Hollow Midler seems unfocused, and both Tomlins seem to be the same rather vague woman who has trouble with her shoulderpads" (123).

Bette's second movie of 1988 was a project that gave her the quintessential Disney role of her career—it made her into a cartoon character in a full-length animated film. In *Oliver & Company,* Bette provided the voice of Georgette, a diva-like pampered poodle. She was even given her own musical number in the middle of the film.

This kid-oriented full-length cartoon feature is a tale of a gang of dogs, which is very loosely based on Charles Dickens's *Oliver Twist.* However, this time around, the evil Bill Sikes is a rich man in a limousine, and Fagin is a scruffy bum living in lower Manhattan. The voices to the cartoon characters include many luminaries from the rock, film, and television realms. In addition to Midler, the film also stars the voices of Billy Joel, Cheech Marin, Ruth Pointer, Sheryl Lee Ralph, Richard Mulligan, and Joey Lawrence. On the soundtrack, Billy Joel, Huey Lewis, and Ruben Blades all contribute songs. Another pop diva, Ruth of the Pointer Sisters, performs the song "Streets of Gold."

The film opens up with an accurate animated establishment shot of lower Manhattan, with the World Trade Center prominently intact. As the action starts, a kitten named Oliver (Joey Lawrence) is abandoned on a New York City street and is taken under wing—so to speak—by a street-wise dog named Dodger (Billy Joel).

When Oliver is adopted by a little girl in an upper Fifth Avenue townhouse, stuck-up Georgette cannot stand the competition the kitten poses. Convinced that Oliver has been snatched against his will, the doggie gang decides to spring the kitten loose from the tortures of his new aristocratic life on Central Park East.

In the voice of Georgette, Bette has fun playing the pampered poodle with an attitude. It seems that Georgette is a six-time national champion dog show winner and is used to getting a lot of attention lavished upon her. This spoiled doggie is such a diva, in fact, that she even wears hats and billowing scarves for an outdoor walk. In one sequence, Georgette is seen watching human exercise shows on TV and doing canine leg lifts to them.

In the film Georgette is romanced by tiny Tito the Chihuahua (Cheech Marin). When it was inquired of her whether or not she wanted to play with him, she sarcastically snipes, "I'd like to play with him all right—the little furball!"

One of the best aspects of the project was that it rekindled her working relationship with Barry Manilow. As Georgette, Bette sings a brassy song called "Perfect Ain't Easy," as she surveys her own reflection in the mirror. In the song, Midler immodestly sings to her canine self, "I'm beauty unleashed." The song was written by Barry Manilow, Jack Feldman, and Bruce Sussman and was produced by Barry Manilow. It was fun—even if only for one song—to hear Bette with Barry reunited, in this doggie diva routine.

After Dodger and the gang "rescue" the kitten, Oliver isn't so sure whether they saved him or just out-and-out kidnapped him. However, when Fagin gets a look at the new tag on Oliver—with a Fifth Avenue address—he greedily decides to hold him for ransom. As the criminal scheme rolls along, they end up kidnapping the little girl of the household and Georgette as well.

Following is a car chase, that leads to a subway chase, and then evolves into a chase across the Brooklyn Bridge. Naturally, in the end, Oliver the cat is rescued, to be returned to his Fifth Avenue address, and everyone lives happily ever after in good Disney fairytale-style. Even Bette's stuck-up canine alter ego, Georgette, bonds with Tito, and the two of them dance together at the film's finale. Running a fast-paced seventy-three minutes, *Oliver & Company* is a cute and clever cartoon adaptation of the original classic. And besides, it gave Midler a chance to do a film for the fun of it, without making it a career move.

On March 19, 1988, the diva and her husband, Martin von Haselberg, were seen in her latest HBO TV special: *Bette Midler's Mondo*

Beyondo. Based on a character that Bette invented with Jerry Blatt, the hour-long program is presented as a spoof on late-night cable TV shows—with poor lighting and tacky sets. On the program, Bette has taken on the character of an Italian "Euro-Trash" female who calls herself "Mondo Beyondo," and she introduces a host of bizarre performance artists. Dressed as Beyondo in a mound of mercurochrome-red hair and a loud bosom-revealing low-cut white and black dress, Bette hosts film clips of performance artists Bill Irwin, Paul Zaloom, and, last but not least, the Kipper Kids (Martin von Hasselberg and Brian Routh). She also introduces us to Eudora P. Quickly, who is actually Midler singing a Jeanette MacDonald song. Unsurprisingly, the special was executive produced by Martin von Haselberg. Although they don't appear on camera together, we do get to see Midler introduce her husband in a bizarre act of physical comedy, under his stage persona: Harry Kipper.

A low-budget television romp, it was an unpretentious little spoof for the chameleon-like diva—who just happens to look fabulous here. According to Marvin Kitman in *Newsday,* "Bette Midler is hilarious. The show is the best spoof of the TV variety format. . . . Midler is making fun of the public access show, one of those wonderfully tacky vanity cable programs. Midler as Mondo Beyondo—a character created by Jerry Blatt and Midler—continues demonstrating she is one of the most outrageous funny people on TV, a maximalist comedienne in a minimalist age" (124).

In the final sequence of *Mondo Beyondo,* Bette at long last introduces the public to the man she married. Beginning with several jokes on flatulence, Midler and her camera crew venture into the men's room of the cheesy TV studio to investigate who is making all of the "fart" noises. What she—and the audience—finds there are two men in Speedo bathing suits, barely visible through the automobile-tire inner tubes they wear around their waists. With clown-white makeup on their faces and white bathing caps on their heads, the self-christened Kipper Kids proceed to wage a battle of sorts. First they break raw eggs on each other's heads, then douse each other in baking flour, canned Spaghetti-O's, and various gooey concoctions. At the end, they apply whipped cream to each other's heads, insert firecrackers in the foam crowns, and ignite them. Not exactly high-brow humor, but humor nonetheless.

According to Midler, as Italian-accented chat show hostess Beyondo, "Those-a boys, they are-a sooo bizarre and yet, so wonderful."

In good Midlerian fashion, *Mondo Beyondo* ends with her singing the "Mondo Beyondo" theme song and shaking her prominently displayed breasts. Obviously, the product of the "I've got a video camera and a studio" kind of brainstorming, no matter what Midler put her hands on, it drew a crowd. This TV special was decidedly silly, but a frothy, no-risk bit of nonsensical fun.

Meanwhile, as Bette was filming *Big Business*, she was also busy with her own film production company. She had earned so much money for Disney that she was thrilled to have her own chance at selecting, developing, producing, and starring in her own movies, with her own production office on the Touchstone lot. The two women whom Bette brought in to work with her—Bonnie Bruckheimer-Martell and Margaret Jennings South—had been working hard to launch their first full-scale production. Bette felt very confident teaming up with both women. Bonnie once had been employed by Aaron Russo, and Bette recalled that she was very detail-conscious. Bonnie excelled in overseeing contracts and planning logistics. Margaret had previously worked for 20th Century-Fox, where she was a story editor. She excelled at finding strong scripts and coming up with story ideas.

By naming their company All Girls Productions, Bette felt she was making a strong statement. "We wanted to be liberated, but we wanted to be girls," she explained at the time. "We didn't want the business to perceive us as aggressive, domineering females. We thought if we had, like, this twitty title they'd give us some room" (125).

One of the things that frustrated Bette the most about the movie business was that everything took so long. From making major artistic choices, to putting them into action, everything seemed to move so slowly. Now that she had her own production company, she could make decisions much quicker. According to Bette, "Everyone likes to pussyfoot in this business. And we don't want to pussyfoot. We just say, 'Oh, that stinks. What are you thinking about?' Then the ice is broken and it's a relief and people can speak their minds. We'd rather have that comfort" (125).

She was, however, quick to add, "I have the last word because my name is above the title. But I try to be good and not abandon any idea out-of-hand and say, 'Oh, that's garbage!' I try to let it develop and give it a chance to blossom—and then step on it!" (125).

Several of the projects that All Girls was initially considering were musicals—specifically, dramas with music. At the time there was a projected biographical film about famed Austrian actress Lotte Lenya, a film about a group of USO singers, and their proposed movie about the leader of an all-girl band: Ina Ray Hutton. Since the days of late '70s blockbusters *Grease* (1978), *Fame* (1980), and *Saturday Night Fever* (1977), musical films had pretty much been a bust. After the Village People's *Can't Stop the Music* (1980) and Olivia Newton-John's *Xanadu* (1980) proved to be expensive box-office miscalculations, it seemed that musicals were rarely ever mounted.

According to Midler at the time, she was determined to somehow make the formula of blending music and dramatic acting viable for her again, the way it was with *The Rose*. "I think people really do like them. I like the musical formula a lot. The only people who hate musicals are the studios, because they don't know how to make them and they're too expensive and time-consuming. My feeling is they can be made. They just have to be well-planned" (125).

She was also very dismayed that she was never considered by other producers for dramatic roles. After the bawdy reputation she had acquired for herself—via her stage act and her campy musical sense—she was basically looked at as a comedian. Not even her Oscar nomination for *The Rose* made people perceive her as a gifted dramatic actress. She was determined to change that. With all of these ideas in mind, Bette and her partners at All Girls set about to find the perfect picture to kick off their production company. They didn't have to look for long.

Among the first film ideas that came to Bette and her new business associates came from a writer by the name of Iris Rainer Dart. When Iris wrote the story about the friendship of two women and called it *Beaches*, she claimed that she had done so with a clear vision of who should star in the movie. She told Midler point-blank, "I'm writing a book with a part you'd be perfect for" (125). She was right.

Beaches was a project that was several years in the making. In the May 16, 1985, issue of the *Hollywood Reporter*, under a headline that read, "*Beaches* to Disney as Midler Picture," the publication announced that the film would be directed by Lynne Litman (*Testament*). Fascinatingly, the debut hardcover edition of *Beaches* wasn't due in bookstores until July 1 of 1985, so it was published with its film rights already optioned by Disney and earmarked for Midler. During the three years of its development, it underwent several changes along the way, including the replacement of Litman with Garry Marshall as director.

From the very beginning, Midler was really intrigued with the story. However, she was a bit apprehensive about playing the role of C. C. Bloom as claw-her-way-to-the-top ambitious as the character in the book was written. "This character was much bigger in her personal life than I ever was," Bette claimed. "So domineering and so pushy and so aggressive, and I'm not really like that" (125). Yet the story seemed like the kind of film that would appeal to her.

With that, the production rights to *Beaches* were passed on to All Girls Productions, with Disney marketing and distributing. Bette was thrilled with the idea of being very "hands on" with this project. According to her, "I wanted to be responsible for the color of the movie, what the clothes looked like and the style. But I was so anxious and nervous about picking who should play the other part. I was so afraid I would make a mistake. I don't like being responsible for people getting or not getting jobs. It's really creepy" (125).

However, "creepy" or not, if she was going to be a movie producer, and if she was truly going to be in the driver's seat, she did have to have a hand in casting who would play opposite her onscreen in *Beaches*. Since the film is about two very different women, Midler also had to be believable on camera with the other woman. Bette was fixated on the fact that she wanted to act opposite Anne Archer. When Bette finally settled on starring in *Beaches,* one of the first people she had audition for the part was Archer. "Whenever I read the script, I had her in mind," Bette claimed. "Anne was really, really good. And Donna Mills turned in a surprising performance. But when Barbara Hershey came in to test, you couldn't ignore her. Her test had such a fragile quality to it. . . . But I really didn't want to have to say, 'I want so and so.' It really took a toll on me" (125). Regardless of the emotional toll it took, finally Bette and her two partners decided to hire Barbara Hershey for the role of Hillary in *Beaches*.

The plot to *Beaches* is a perfect "women's picture"—or, as they are now known, a "chick flick." Two eleven-year-old girls meet on the boardwalk at Atlantic City's beach in the 1950s. C. C. Bloom is a precocious redhead from the Bronx, with a pushy stage mother (Lanie Kazan). Hillary Whitney is an Ivy League school–bound girl from a blueblood family from outside San Francisco. The two girls remain pen pals during their growing-up years. In the early '70s, Hillary shows up in New York City for their first face-to-face reunion since Atlantic City. They hadn't seen each other since childhood; C.C. (Bette) has now become a struggling actress, and Whitney (Barbara Hershey) has fled the West Coast and the clutches of her controlling and restrictive father.

Beaches follows their very different but parallel lives through the next several years. An unlikely duo of friends—the film offered them two of the most fascinating and multilayered roles in their individual film careers. In addition, *Beaches* gave Bette a platform to sing several great songs. The mechanical-sounding techno-pop "Oh Industry" is presented as a stage piece, personifying the dehumanization of the American Worker. She also sings "Otto Titsling" (resurrected from her *Mud Will Be Flung!* album), which is used as a showcasing sample of her character's Broadway career, and "I Think It's Gonna Rain Today" is presented in a recording studio scene. She also sang three jazzy standards from the 1930s and 1940s: "The Glory of Love," "Baby Mine," and Cole Porter's "I've Still Got My Health."

C.C. and Hillary become adult roommates, vie for the same boyfriend—John (John Heard)—and forge ahead with their career goals. While C.C. is intent on launching a show business career, Hillary becomes a socially conscious lawyer.

One of the funniest scenes takes place in C.C.'s over-the-top Manhattan apartment, when Hillary comes to visit her friend who is now the star of *Sizzle '76* on Broadway. After running on and on about herself, Bette takes a breath and says to Barbara, "But enough about me. Let's talk about you. What do *you* think about me?"

It became known as the movie's most memorable line—quoted by everyone who saw the film, and several times by Bette herself—onstage and off. If one were to select the most famous line from a Bette Midler movie, that is undoubtedly it.

One of the most wonderful scenes is that between adult C.C. and her mother, Leona, on a beach in Miami. When Midler whines about the demise of her marriage and the fact that people are constantly disappearing from her life, her mother informs her that it's because she is so demanding, that she simply wears people out. As Kazan delivers this piece of information, the look on Midler's face is priceless.

Hillary's marriage falls apart, and C.C.'s career falls apart, and the two estranged friends revive their friendship. When Hillary becomes pregnant, and her husband leaves her, the two friends have a new bond of comradeship. Together they face childbirth—and finally illness. As

Hillary's illness progresses, the two old friends find themselves again on a beach.

Bette has a very funny sequence when she suddenly announces that her career is through. C. C. Bloom decides to give it all up and settle down as the wife of a successful man, Dr. Richard Milstein (Spalding Gray). Modeling her successful-doctor's-wife outfit, Midler parades in front of her childhood friend, looking completely ridiculous in a Chanel-styled suit and an insane-looking hat. There she stood: the Suburban Miss M.

The film *Beaches* also features some very strong supporting characters. Lanie Kazan is perfect as C.C.'s pushy stage mother. And the child actor who played young C.C., Mayim Bialik, is astonishing. She looks and acts exactly like Bette herself must have appeared at the age of eleven. Also, former Harlette Charlotte Crossley and then-current Harlette Jenifer Lewis can both be seen very prominently in the "Otto Titsling" number. In addition, Bette's longtime pianist and musical director Marc Shaiman is seen in the Hollywood Bowl rehearsal scene at the beginning of the film.

Beaches became the showpiece of Bette's All Girls Productions. She was listed as producer/coproducer, Bonnie Bruckheimer-Martell as the producer, and their partner Margaret Jennings South as producer/coproducer. The director they hired was Garry Marshall, who is best known for directing such hits as *Pretty Woman, The Runaway Bride,* and *The Princess Diaries.* He is also known as an actor in such films as *Soapdish* and *Jumpin' Jack Flash.*

With Midler and her production company in creative control, *Beaches* became the ultimate showcase for her acting and singing. The entire soundtrack of *Beaches* is one Midler number after another. Although she sings a number of different tunes throughout the film, the song that really epitomizes the film is the powerful anthem of devotion that Bette performs, "The Wind beneath My Wings." The song, which was used at a pivotal climax in the plot, went on to become the most successful song of her career. The song and the soundtrack album were both such huge hits that they literally revived Bette's long-sagging recording career.

Produced by Arif Mardin, the *Beaches* soundtrack album is a complete Bette Midler album from start to finish. The only cut that she isn't on is an under-two-minutes instrumental number, "The Friendship Theme." Bette sounds great on this album. Obviously, the push to come up with a hit single took a backseat to just coming up with a strong soundtrack of Midler songs. It had been five years since the release of her last all-singing album, *No Frills,* and it was great to have her back in the music business. She had certainly been busy in the interim—having filmed six movies back to back.

Bette had admittedly been so stung by the poor reception that her 1983 *No Frills* album received that she basically stayed out of the recording studio for five years. With the soundtrack album for *Beaches* she was able to return to recording songs without actively chasing that elusive commodity—the hit single. Portraying the role of C.C. Bloom in the film *Beaches* required music to accompany the many phases of the character's career—from jazz, to cabaret, to Broadway, to concert performances—as well as background music to underscore the twists and turns in the film's plot.

The album opens with Bette's version of the Drifters' doo wop classic "Under the Boardwalk," which is played in the film in the opening sequence when the characters of eleven-year-old C.C. and Hillary meet on the boardwalk at Atlantic City—and their lifelong friendship is formed. Her melodic singing of this classic rock & roll song sets the tone for the basis of the album's sound: vibrant, sharp, and fresh.

She was able to record a snappy jazz version of Cole Porter's "I've Still Got My Health," to personify her character's brief jazz and cabaret career. And "The Glory of Love" was very effectively used in the Hollywood Bowl concert sequence as a depiction of the strength and depth of C.C. and Hillary's friendship.

Midler also recorded a pair of contemporary standards: Randy Newman's pensive "I Think It's Going to Rain Today" and her version of the Dean Pitchford/George Merrill/Shannon Rubicam composition "I Know You by Heart." The lilting lullaby "Baby Mine" is used when Hershey's character is expecting to give birth in the film, and the silly brassiere ditty "Otto Titsling" is used in the C. C. Bloom-on-Broadway segment.

One of the best songs on the album is the techno-pop song "Oh Industry." Sounding like it would have fit in very well on the *No Frills* album, it was composed by Bette and noted singer/songwriter Wendy Waldman.

However, the most dramatic and effective song on the *Beaches* soundtrack was Midler's touching interpretation of the song "Wind beneath My Wings." This song of friendship and devotion was the one

that made this album one of the most successful discs of her entire
career. Interestingly enough, it had already been a huge hit for two
other recording acts. In 1983, country star Gary Morris had a hit with
the song on the country music charts. And that same year Gladys
Knight & the Pips had a hit with it on the R&B/Soul charts—under the
title "Hero." The song had also been recorded on albums by a diverse
number of artists, including Sheena Easton, Lou Rawls, and even Willie
Nelson. It seemed an unlikely long shot as a hit single when Bette recorded it and Atlantic Records released it as a single in 1988.

It was the right song at the perfect time for Bette. Her vocal performance on the sentimental song of one friend living in the shadow of
another, flashier one was wonderfully emotional. In June 1989, in
America, Bette's version of "The Wind beneath My Wings" became the
first Number 1 song of her career. In England, the single hit Number
5. The *Beaches* soundtrack album also bounded up the charts to land at
Number 2 in the United States and Number 21 in the U.K.

It had taken her ten years to reclaim the kind of across-the-board
career success that she had in 1979 with *The Rose*—the movie, the
single, and the album. With *Beaches*, she did it all over again. The film
became a popular box-office hit, the single was the biggest of her career,
and the album sold over three million copies in the United States
alone—becoming the best-selling LP of her career to date.

A lot of careful planning went into creating the success of *Beaches*,
especially how it was marketed. Knowing they had a sentimental picture
on their hands, Disney made a preview trailer to run in theaters months
in advance to publicize the film. Originally, they created a trailer that
played up the maudlin aspects of it. Robert John of Disney Pictures
explained, "We cut a very, very emotional and touching trailer. In fact,
we showed it in a marketing meeting to a room full of men. There were
some dewy eyes" (126).

When the trailer was subsequent played before a movie audience, a
woman who was opinion polled afterward gave them the feedback they
needed. According to Robert John, "She said, 'I like to see Bette singing
and laughing and dancing'" (126). With that, they cut a new trailer playing up the fun aspects of the film instead of the sad ending.

The *Washington Post* called it "a bi-coastal crowd pleaser . . . bright-
ened by Bette Midler's sass and sweetened by her songs." The *Hollywood Reporter* called it "Funny, touching and consistently engaging"
(127). And film critic Leonard Maltin found it a "bittersweet saga of a

thirty-year friendship . . . as a vehicle for Midler it's dynamite, with several opportunities for her to sing" (128).

Like *Big Business* before it, Roger Ebert gave *Beaches* only two and a half stars and basically hated the film. He wrote, "Hillary is played in the movie by Barbara Hershey, as a rich WASP to Midler's irreverent Jewish girl. . . . Maybe, in a strange way, one of the problems is Midler herself. She has a reputation for intelligence and irreverence that is mostly deserved, and so when we go to see her in a movie we don't expect her to be portraying a character completely dictated by convention. We expect a little spin on the ball. *Beaches* gives us nothing that can't be spotted coming a mile down the road" (129).

Based on the majority of favorable reviews and a strong word-of-mouth popularity, *Beaches* became a huge box-office hit for Bette when it was released in early 1989. *Beaches* has great pacing, sharp dialogue, and some of the best character-driven material she has ever had on the screen. The juxtapositioning of Midler and Hershey works perfectly. Because of *Beaches*—the movie, the album, and the single it yielded— Bette was back in a big way! However, this time she was behind the steering wheel.

During this same period, Bette Midler had been the subject of a huge lawsuit. Back in 1984 and 1985, the Ford Motor Company had produced and broadcast a series of television commercials to advertise its 1985 Mercury Sable. The song used in the commercials sounded *very* much like Bette Midler singing her first hit, "Do You Want to Dance?" However, it was not Bette Midler at all. In fact, it was her former background singer, Ula Hedwig, who had been paid to go into the recording studio and sing the song identically to the way Miss M did.

Midler didn't just get mad, she got her lawyer involved. She sued the Ford Motor Company for impersonating her and misrepresenting her voice and performance, for $10 million. The trial commenced on September 25, 1989. Finally, on October 31—Halloween, no less—Bette was awarded $400,000 in damages. She didn't just get mad—she got rich! That just goes to show you: Don't fuck with Miss M!

16

FROM A DISTANCE

Bette Midler entered the 1990s with a tidal wave of multimedia creativity. She had three highly varied films in the movie theaters, scored the second biggest hit of her recording career, released a Double Platinum album, won another Grammy Award, was nominated for another Oscar, won another Golden Globe, and, last but not least, she had one of the most harrowingly disappointing film experiences of her career.

Her first project of the new decade found her on the big screen. For Bette's next film, she returned to drama in *Stella.* It was a reworking of a popular Barbara Stanwyck vehicle, 1937's *Stella Dallas,* which was one of the greatest performances of Stanwyck's long and distinguished film career. She was nominated for an Academy Award for her portrayal of Stella, a self-sacrificing mother during the Depression.

According to the producer of this '90s remake, Samuel Goldwyn, Jr., "I wanted to remake this picture because of the astonishing power of its set scenes. We had to make it relevant through the problem of single mothers, but its strength is still the tremendous sympathy we have for Stella as she blunders through life" (130).

Although *Stella* did have some funny Midler moments in it, the film was a somber soap opera of a drama. It was projected that it would tug at the heartstrings in the same way that Midler did when she played C. C. Bloom. Bonnie Bruckheimer said at the time, "I believe people want Bette Midler to be funny, but maybe not as much after *Beaches.* Bette enjoyed that and wanted to do another drama. I've wanted her to do more drama since working with her on *The Rose*. And I think her audience will accept that when it sees the brilliant work she's done here" (130).

The way that Bette portrays the character, Stella is her own worst enemy because of her stubbornness and pride. According to Midler, she instinctively veered toward the soap opera dramatics that the role seemed to beg for. However, the film's director, John Erman, took her into a different direction. "My tendency is to go toward the weepiness of it, but John is always after me to undercut that," she explained at the time. "He's right. No real character is completely humorless. All the single mothers I met had a sense of humor about their situation" (130).

Erman was especially happy to work with Midler. "This is the closest Bette has come to playing a character other than herself," he claimed. "My biggest worry had been whether she would allow herself to dance on that tightrope, but she fully embraced the concept of playing this woman in a very real way—though not without some difficulty" (130).

Bette felt that in many ways she really identified with the role of Stella. "I'm from working-class people," she explained. "I grew up with them, I know them well. A lot of my Stella is based on my mother, who worked hard all her life. Even in the 1950s, mothers were the unsung heroes. This is a kind of hymn to her" (130).

To immerse herself in the part of Stella, Bette even attended bartending classes. "I was surprised by how much stuff I had to learn. I'm quite the housekeeper myself, but I never expected I'd have to get out there and make a tuna casserole," she laughed (130).

Bette was also able to use her own relationship with her daughter Sophie as an inspiration for her interactions with her daughter in the film: "That comes out in the scenes I play with Jenny. There's a depth that's linked to Sophie and the passion I have for her. I wouldn't have known about that without having had a child" (130).

In her efforts to understand Stella's life, Bette did a lot of character research. "There are lots of single mothers out there, and I interviewed a number of them in Niagara, New York," she explained. "I was surprised and devastated by their stories. Many of them live hand to mouth. They work long hours, often for the minimum wage, and none of them were getting child support. They're struggling hard, they've not giving up, and they have positive attitudes" (130).

Stella's coarse personality, low self-esteem, and tragically sad life choices, along with her thick New England accent, were all elements that Bette had to focus on to bring her portrayal to life in a believable way. "The challenge was to strike the right tone, to keep it real," said Midler. Referring to Stella's drab blouses and pants, she explained. "Those weren't made. They came right off the rack. Barbara Stanwyck was very, very endearing, but she was so out-to-lunch with her clothes. Poor people, even if they're sewing, don't have the money to dress like that" (130).

Stella, like *Beaches,* is the kind of film that Bette Davis, or Joan Crawford, or Barbara Stanwyck would be starring in, in the 1930s. Maudlin and old-fashioned, the film is based on *Stella Dallas* by Olive Higgins Prouty. However, this new version was updated to a 1990s context. The most major change in the plot is that Stella chooses not to marry the father of her child.

The Stella Claire whom Bette Midler plays here is a bawdy bar waitress. She plays the role with a very thick Boston/New England accent. Hers is a dismal life. Her father was killed in an accident, and her mother drank herself to death. She has few ambitions and few cares in the world.

Bette's former Harlette buddy Linda Hart plays the part of Linda, who is another waitress in Ed's Bar, where Stella works. Ed, as played here by John Goodman, is a drunken "loser" of a slob—who is one of Stella's closest pals.

The first scene we see Bette in, the patrons at the tavern coerce her into dancing on top of the bar, doing a bump and grind to the bawdy David Rose song "The Stripper." It is 1969 in the film, and Midler is dressed in a pair of patched blue jeans.

In several of the scenes, Bette really gets to let loose and be a bit outrageous. In the striptease scene she is obviously having a blast. She also cuts up in a scene where she stages a food fight. These comic moments enliven her obviously drab and excitement-free life. For the most part, her life is dismal and decidedly lower class. She lives in a slummy apartment and has few goals or ambitions.

While working in the dive bar, she catches the eye of a young medical student named Stephen Dallas (Stephen Collins). With maximum ease, Stephen sweeps her off her feet and seduces her. However, she very quickly realizes that she is outclassed by him. In one of their initial scenes together, she is seen giggling uncontrollably at a classical vocal concert. Clearly, she is more suited for a Lynyrd Skynyrd concert than a recital.

When Stella announces that she is pregnant, Stephen offers her money for an abortion. When he fills a room full of balloons and proposes marriage, Stella turns down both the marriage and the money. Sympathetic to her plight, Ed also offers to marry Stella, but she turns him down as well.

Stella is judgmental and stubbornly proud—to her own detriment. She is also a gloomy and negative character. She would rather do without than accept anything from anyone else. Having just given birth, she even seems to be blasé about seeing her daughter. However, it is maternal love at first sight, as hard-as-nails Stella breaks into tears of love when she finally does lay eyes upon newborn daughter Jenny. Now she finally does have something to focus upon.

When Stephen comes back into her life, again she refuses him. Stephen's world is dining at the Plaza Hotel. Hers is drinking at the local seedy bar with her friends. Bette's best scenes with her daughter come after Jenny (Trini Alvarado) becomes a teenager. That is also the point at which the mother–daughter problems between them escalate.

It is very funny to see working-class Bette running up a dress for her daughter on the sewing machine, so that Jenny can "look like that Madonna girl." There is also a touching sequence with Bette singing "California Dreamin'" a cappella with Trini. These scenes establish the obviously deep-flowing love that Stella feels for her daughter.

At one point in the film, Stella clashes with a snooty member of the local school board (Eileen Brennan). Afterward, Stella says to her, "I think you probably haven't had a good lay in years. I think your legs have been together longer than the Lennon Sisters."

When Stella is arrested in a barroom brawl, the mother she previously clashed with sees her being led to the paddy wagon. It is followed by a sad sequence in which no one comes to Jenny's sixteenth birthday party—a party she had so looked forward to throwing. The only "guests" who do show consist of a carload of teenage boys driving by and "mooning" the apartment. Perceptively, Stella comes to realize that she is ruining her teenage daughter's life.

She then gets a look at the kind of boys Jenny is hanging out with. A pre-stardom Ben Stiller appears here as a punkish older boy—Jim—that Jenny brings home to meet her mother. Stella sees up close how Jenny's fate will be as bad as hers, if she doesn't do something to help.

Desperate for money, Stella hits the streets, selling Nancy Lee cosmetics. One of her more amusing sequences is during this door-to-door saleswoman phase in Stella's forlorn life.

However, Jenny's life is tempered by the kind of existence she experiences while visiting her father in New York City. Stephen Dallas is a successful doctor, and his girlfriend, Janis (Marsha Mason), is a successful editor. When Jenny visits them, she is exposed to a completely different life and a new class of suitors. It becomes an emotional tug-of-war on Christmas Eve for Jenny to have to choose between a night at Mom's slum-like apartment or Dad's truly dazzling party.

One of the most memorable sequences occurs after a credit card shows up in the mail. Stella takes Jenny on a trip to Florida to surprise the aristocratic boy Jenny is in love with. The love affair is undone after Stella makes a fool of herself at a beachside bar, dressed like a crazed floozy. A suddenly blonde Stella proceeds to cause a wild scene, lubricated by *waaaaaay* too many cocktails. In this crazy scene, Stella is dressed in a blue ruffled nightmare of a dress that not even Vicki Eydie would be caught dead wearing.

Later, relaxing by the ocean, Stella overhears two girls laughing to themselves, "You know that 'thing' we saw in the bar this morning? You know who that is? That's Jenny Claire's mother! Can you believe that? I thought it must have been Pee Wee Herman's wife or something!" The scene is largely played off Bette's sinking face.

The World Trade Center is seen in an "establishment" shot, when Jenny goes to New York City to stay with her dad.

Realizing that Jenny would be better off living with her father, Stella launches a plan for the ultimate self-sacrifice. Unexpectedly, she shows up in New York City at Janice's office, and in a woman-to-woman conversation, she plots Jenny's future. One of Bette's best dramatic scenes is with Marsha Mason, where she plans to have Jenny go and live with her father. It is sharp, touching, and emotion-filled.

Naturally, Jenny refuses to consider leaving her mother. So, Stella sets up a scenario to discourage Jenny from staying with her, by embarrassing her and hurting her feelings. By claiming that she is in love with her drunken slob of a boyfriend, Ed, Stella drives Jenny away.

The film ends with a truly tear-jerking scene of Stella watching Jenny's wedding, while standing in the pouring rain outside Tavern on the Green. It is a weepy, melodramatic story of maternal sacrifice. The wedding scene does, however, walk a fine line between being touchingly sentimental and completely sappy. Through it all, *Stella* is a great ensemble film, a well-paced drama, and Bette really did throw herself into becoming the character.

As the credits roll, Bette sings her only song in the film, "One More Cheer." It was produced by Arif Mardin and written by Jay Gurska and Paul Gordon. There was no soundtrack album released.

Bette admitted that she did have her misgivings about doing *Stella* to begin with. However, it was a great deal for her. According to her, "They told me to do it. Jeffrey [Katzenberg] had it in his mind to do it for a long time: he always loved it. He got a wonderful script, and Sam Goldwyn had the rights to it because it was his father's picture. Jeffrey paid buckets for it, so I read it, and it's a good script. I don't exactly do what they tell me without putting up a fight, but I couldn't say 'no' to this because he paid so much money for it" (131).

When it was released in 1990, the critics either loved it or hated it. Mainly, they hated it. Roger Ebert, in the *Chicago Sun Times*, was one of the few reviewers who really liked it, giving it three and a half stars (out of four). According to his review, "Every charge you can make against this movie is probably true—it's cornball, manipulative, unlikely, sentimental and shameless. But once the lights go down and the performances begin, none of those things really matter, because this *Stella* has a quality that many more sophisticated films lack: It makes us really care about its characters. . . . There are scenes here of great difficulty, which Midler plays wonderfully; the scene, for example, where she goes to Marsha Mason's office to ask if Jenny can come to live with Mason and Collins. . . . *Stella* is the kind of movie that works you over and leaves you feeling good, unless you absolutely steel yourself against it. Go to sneer. Stay to weep" (132).

His long-time sparring partner, Gene Siskell, in the *Chicago Tribune*, had the opposite opinion when he wrote, "Bette Midler stars in a laughably bad remake of *Stella Dallas*, the story of a working-class mother who sacrificed her own future for that of her daughter. Stephen Collins is wildly miscast as the man who loves Midler, and Trini Alvarado is too contemporary for the dated character of the daughter. Nothing—absolutely nothing—works here in this shoddy soap opera" (133).

Stanley Kauffman, in the *New Republic*, really ripped into Bette by stating, "Come back, Bette Midler. She is a true original. Why does she spend her time copying others? Especially since she's not doing it very well. She made her reputation, outside singing, as a rude, anticonventional comedienne. But her last film, *Beaches*, and her latest, *Stella*, are mainline tearjerkers. . . . In fact, she once announced plans for a film on the life of Lotte Lenya. Where is it? Where is anything other than her two latest films? They're not only dreadful in themselves, they debase her talent" (134).

Stella was something of a disappointment at the box office. However, Bette didn't take a lot of time to dwell on its outcome. She was busy with several other projects.

While the film was still in theaters across America, on February 21 the song "Wind beneath My Wings" won the Song of the Year at the 32nd Annual Grammy Awards. The award went to the writers of the song, Larry Henley and Jeff Silbar. Bette herself won the Grammy Award for the Record of the Year, marking the fourth time she had one of the trophies. Furthermore, Bette's performance of her winning song was used to close the show that night.

On April 22, 1990, Bette was one of the stars on the ABC-TV broadcast of its *Earth Day Special*. Other stars who appeared on the telecast included Robin Williams, Barbra Streisand, and Quincy Jones.

It had been seven years since Bette Midler had released an album of music that wasn't tied to a movie soundtrack. When it came time for Bette to go into the recording studio to record her twelfth album, *Some People's Lives,* she did so with longtime producer Arif Mardin at the helm.

With regard to her ability to choose the right songs to record, Midler claimed at the time, "I know right away if it moves me, it'll move the public. That has always been my criterion. I have been pressured at points by my label to record this or record that, and I've had terrible, terrible flops . . . so I stopped doing it for the most part. . . . I think that's bullshit" (40).

According to Ahmet Ertegun, the president of Atlantic Records, Midler often derails herself. "She was her own worst enemy when it came to recording, because she had so many doubts about everything," he explained. "The reason for some of her albums not doing well was that there was no real marriage between her and her producers. I think finally we found Arif Mardin, who is the right person to bring out of her what's in her. She's very, very anxious to do her best, and nothing sounds like her best to her, so it has been a very tough procedure" (40).

Some People's Lives is an excellent Bette Midler album. Though it tends to center itself on pop ballads, the diva sounds great, and she can be heard stretching herself into a couple of jazz standards. While the song "Miss Otis Regrets" is presented here as a game bit of fun, there aren't any real Divine Miss M excursions into the outrageous found on this album. Instead, she reaches for touching love songs. Two of the best performances on this album are the ballad "The Girl Is On to You" and the medley of Rogers & Hart's "He Was Too Good to Me" with the contemporary "Since You Stayed Here."

The album opens with a quirky little song that sounds like a rhyme to jump rope to, called "One More Round." It leads into the sentimental Janis Ian ballad "Some People's Lives." On the jazzy side of things, Bette is especially effective on "Spring Can Really Hang You Up the Most," which features a tenor sax solo by Nino Tempo.

However, the album's real masterpiece is Bette's recording of the Julie Gold composition "From a Distance." The song is an emotional epic, which finds Miss M backed up vocally by former Harlette Charlotte Crossley, Cissy Houston of the Sweet Inspirations, and the Radio Choir of New Hope Baptist Church of Newark, New Jersey. "From a Distance" is a song of pacifism; it was unforeseeable that America would get into a Middle Eastern military conflict at the same time that the single version of this song was released.

Swept up into the whole Desert Storm 1990–1991 conflict, Bette's recording of "From a Distance" captured the hearts and minds of radio programmers and record buyers alike. Within weeks, Bette had the second-hottest single recording of her entire career. Between November 1990 and January 1991, the song was in the American Top 10, peaking at Number 2 the week of December 15. The single alone sold over a million copies and was certified Platinum in America. In the United Kingdom it peaked at Number 6.

The album ultimately sold two million copies in America alone. Hot on the heels of what she had done with the *Beaches* soundtrack and "The Wind beneath My Wings" the year before, Bette Midler again had an incredibly hot hit single and a multi-Platinum album. In America, *Some People's Lives* reached Number 6 in America and Number 5 in the U.K.

In February of 1991, Midler was back in movie theaters. Her next screen role was in Paul Mazursky's lunatic comedy *Scenes from a Mall*. The film found her cast as a Beverly Hills relationship counselor, encountering some problems in her own marriage. Starring opposite her was one of her favorite leading men, Woody Allen. According to her, "It was the most fun I ever had in my life. During filming, I'd get up

every day and say, 'I'm going to see Woody,' and I'd jump into makeup
and run out there and wait to hear what he was going to say next. He
was really magical to work with" (27).

She also confessed, "I hadn't had a crush like that since I married my
husband. . . . I love to scream and laugh, and that's why I fell so in love
with Woody. I would laugh and laugh. I would pee! I would have to go
and change my diaper. I swear to God!" (40)

Scenes from a Mall is a very quirky, but highly amusing film, produced and directed by Paul Mazursky of *Down and Out in Beverly Hills*
fame. Bette loved working with Mazursky—who also makes a cameo
appearance—and she had high hopes for the project. This film again
mocks the shallow culture of Los Angeles; this time it's a married couple
at each other's throats at a shopping mall.

The action takes place at the Beverly Center, a shopping mall in the
Beverly Hills area, which—in reality—is an odd conglomeration of
stores. The regular department stores—Macy's and Bloomingdale's—
share mall space with high-end jewelry stores, sushi bars, and designer
boutiques. (*Scenes from a Mall* was filmed at Stamford Town Center in
Stamford, Connecticut, as well as at the Beverly Center.)

Bette plays psychologist Debra Feingold-Fifer. She and her husband,
Nick Fifer (Woody Allen), are about to celebrate their sixteenth wedding anniversary that evening. They drive to the mall to purchase
clothes, food, and gifts for the anniversary party. However, as they find
themselves trapped at the shopping mall, one comic series of mishaps
after another transpires. In addition, a white-faced mime (Bill Irwin)
seems to follow them wherever they go, mocking their misadventures.
The obnoxious mime is played by Bill Irwin, whom Midler had presented on her *Mondo Beyondo* TV special in 1988. He was later to find
fame in the 2000 hit film *The Grinch Who Stole Christmas*, as Cindy
Lou Who's father.

At the mall, after a sushi lunch, Nick admits to his wife that he has
been having affair. It is the Christmas season, and Debra is actively
promoting her new book about marriage, *I Do! I Do! I Do!* In fact, at
the mall's Waldenbooks store, a promotional clip about her book plays
over and over again. True to her marriage therapist stature, at first she
instinctively attempts to digest the news of her husband's infidelity in-
tellectually.

However, when this revelation finally sinks in, Debra knees Nick in
the groin, starts screaming, and throws a very large and expensive box

of sushi at the mime. She manages to make it back to the car, where she breaks down crying. However, the traffic is so thick that she finds herself stuck in the car, unable to escape the snarl of traffic in the parking lot.

Nick finds her in the car, and together they park and return to the mall to discuss this dilemma further. They then argue about which divorce lawyer they should use. He insists that she use him as her divorce lawyer, so they can save the legal fees. Next they start verbally dividing up their community property, over lunch at a Mexican restaurant and several margaritas. Debra manages to get loaded and weepy as the margarita glasses pile up.

Then their argument continues in the mall movie theater— Nick lugging the lime-green surfboard Debra has bought him as an anniversary present, into the theater. The theater scene is hysterical. They begin arguing in whispering tones during an Indian film up on the screen. As he starts experiencing chest pains and has trouble breathing, they somehow rekindle their devotion for one another and then start having sex in the movie theater. Outlandishly, Nick goes down on Debra right there in her seat, and she has a loud orgasm while people on the screen are running down the streets of India. The scene is inspired insanity, to say the least.

After sex, they leave the theater in love and lust. Finally, with the clarity of their sexual reconciliation, she admits that she, too, has been having an extramarital affair. That's it, now he is suddenly all finished with her.

When he attempts to leave Debra stranded at the mall, he returns to the parking structure to find that the car has been towed, as it was erroneously parked in a "handicapped" slot. Next, they run into each other in the painkiller aisle of the mall drugstore. With post–painkiller clarity, they begin discussing their future aspirations for their life.

Then it's off to the mall's blue light–illuminated Maison du Caviar, for champagne and caviar. The opulent caviar makes them romantic again. However, their conversation turns into another argument, this time over which one of their mutual friends they would each like to sleep with.

Throughout the entire film, Debra uses the mall payphone, announcing that the party is "on," "off," "on," "off," and finally "on" again. Suddenly, she wants a new outfit for their anniversary party, which is now back on track. Then, he decides that he, too, wants a new outfit for the evening. As the film ends, they are back together—and still arguing.

This kooky film exploits an old movie theme—*Scenes from a Marriage*—and cleverly takes it shopping. In one scene, they get into the mall elevator and muscleman/romance novel coverboy Fabio is in it.

Although it was not a huge box-office hit, the film is quirky and totally entertaining. Bette's compatriot-in-song Marc Shaiman handled the music for the film, and as the ending credits roll, she sings the standard "You Do Something to Me."

While the reviews for *Stella* had been mixed, the reviews for *Scenes from a Mall* were awful. Roger Ebert, in the *Chicago Sun-Times,* called it "very bad indeed," further dissecting it by stating, "the movie doesn't work, except for a short time at the beginning. . . . Allen and Midler struggle heroically with their characters, but there is nothing in this story for us to believe" (135).

David Denby, in *New York* magazine, claimed, "Both Allen and Midler are required to play the scenes realistically, but as performers, they are inherently too stylized for such a trite, knowing, 'psychological' approach to marital weariness. . . . *Scenes from a Mall* is not a dud—there are a few jokes—but it left me with an almost mournful sense of disappointment" (136). And Leonard Maltin's *Movie Guide* wearily stated, "Fans of the stars should take a look, but this one ranks as a major disappointment" (128).

Coming to her own defense about her latest two films, Bette explained at the time, "I was so slagged for *Stella.* I'm afraid to talk about it even to defend myself. *Stella* wasn't so bad. I guess people just read such terrible reviews that they decided they didn't want to spend their seven dollars. It wasn't that bad. I always cry when I look at it. I believe nobody saw that picture. And the same thing is true for *Scenes from a Mall.* I loved it. I loved making it. I loved being involved with Woody Allen and Paul Mazursky, and I sat in that screening room and I loved it. I was so shocked that people didn't go to see it. I was just dumbfounded. I said, 'Well, you know, you just throw up your hands. What do they want?'" (131).

Regardless of what *Scenes from a Mall* was doing at the box office, Bette was big news in the recording business. On February 20, the 33rd Annual Grammy Awards opened with Midler singing her latest hit, "From a Distance," on the telecast, live from Radio City Music Hall in New York City. Like "Wind beneath My Wings" a year before, the song won the Grammy for Song of the Year, with the trophy going to the song's writer, Julie Gold.

In June of 1991 Bette was in England, where she appeared on the BBC1-TV show *Wogan*. The week of August 29 the Record Industry Association of America announced that the *Beaches* soundtrack had been certified Triple Platinum, making it her biggest-selling album yet.

Meanwhile, Bette's children's song "Blueberry Pie" was revived from the 1980s *Sesame Street* album and was included on the all-star compilation album *For Our Children*, and it reached Number 31 on the American album charts.

On the 15th of September, Bette Midler was honored by AIDS Project Los Angeles, for her charitable work, raising money for AIDS victims. The event, known as "Commitment for Life V," was held at the Universal Amphitheatre.

In 1991, American journalist and TV talkshow host Geraldo Rivera published his memoir *Exposing Myself*. In the text of the book, Rivera wrote about his hot affair with Bette Midler during the 1970s. Bette saw "red" when she read what he had to say about her, and all of a sudden a whole lot of mud was flung!

Wrote Geraldo, "She had great tits and personality to match. We were in the bathroom, preparing for the interview, and at some point I put my hands on her breasts. She loved it, and we fell into a passionate embrace, which segued immediately into a brief and torrid affair. Bette had an enormous sexual appetite in those days" (137).

Midler saw it a little differently. According to her at the time, "You call that little thing an affair? He's such a toad! He has the nerve. . . . he's such a user. Let me tell you my *Geraldo* story. He'd just come off his Willowbrook thing. He was really hot. He wanted to interview me, but I forget what channel it was for. This was twenty years ago! He came to my house, and he and his producer pushed me into the bathroom and—check it out. I'll show him—they broke poppers under my nose and started to grope me. I hadn't even said 'hello.' I was completely shocked. Completely stunned. I didn't know what to do. I didn't know how to behave. I had no idea. Then I recovered from what happened, and when we did the interview he started telling me about Maria Shneider and how he must have jumped on her. This guy was insane. I didn't know what the hell was going on. . . . What was I supposed to say in front of his camera crew, 'Get the hell out of my house?' I don't remember if he apologized. . . . I had gone on the road, and he called

After two incredibly successful albums, Midler fell into a record-sales slump with two LPs, which were largely misunderstood: *Songs for the New Depression* (1976) and *Broken Blossom* (1977). *(Courtesy of Atlantic Records / MJB Photo Archives)*

Bette, with co-star Frederic Forrest, in *The Rose*. She longed to become a movie star, and in her first screen role, she received an Academy Award nomination. She played a self-destructive rock star, fashioned after Janis Joplin. *(Courtesy of 20th Century Fox / MJB Photo Archives)*

Bette at the opening of *The Rose*, Ziegfeld Theatre, New York City, 1979. *(Courtesy of Charles M. Moniz)*

Bette's most famous group of Harlettes (clockwise): Charlotte Crossley, Ula Hedwig, and Sharon Redd. They became so well-known that they ended up with their own recording contract. *(Courtesy of Columbia Records / MJB Photo Archives)*

Bette wears a typewriter hat for a record-breaking 1,500 book–signing appearance in 1980 in New York City. *(Courtesy of Charles M. Moniz)*

In *Divine Madness*, Bette not only sang her ass off, she also told several wry and raunchy Sophie Tucker jokes. She once quipped to a loud audience member, "Shut your hole honey, mine's makin' money." *(Courtesy of The Ladd Corporation / MJB Photo Archives)*

In the 1980 concert film, *Divine Madness*, Bette Midler was able to show off many sides of her musical talents. *(Courtesy of The Ladd Corporation / MJB Photo Archives)*

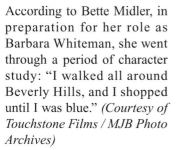

According to Bette Midler, in preparation for her role as Barbara Whiteman, she went through a period of character study: "I walked all around Beverly Hills, and I shopped until I was blue." *(Courtesy of Touchstone Films / MJB Photo Archives)*

Margrit Ramme, Little Richard, Bette Midler and Richard Dreyfus in the comedy hit *Down and Out in Beverly Hills. (Courtesy of Touchstone Films / MJB Photo Archives)*

Born in Honolulu, Hawaii, Bette Midler was always an exotic blossom. Although she has lilies in her hair in this one, it was another flower, the rose, which she is most closely associated with. She starred in a film called *The Rose*, had a huge hit with the song "The Rose," played Madame Rose in *Gypsy*, and even recorded an album called *Bette of Roses. (Courtesy of Atlantic Records / MJB Photo Archives)*

Always considering herself an "*artiste*," and known for her ample bosom, Bette in 1984 starred in the cable television special *Art or Bust*. *(Courtesy of HBO / MJB Photo Archives)*

Singer and record producer Dan Hartman with Bette Midler in 1986. Hartman's song "Waiting to See You" was part of the soundtrack for *Ruthless People*. *(Courtesy of David McGough for Epic Records / MJB Photo Archives)*

Bette gets down on the stage floor in her video for "Beast of Burden." She not only turned the Rolling Stones song into a hit, Mick Jagger made a guest appearance in the video. *(Courtesy of Atlantic Records / MJB Photo Archives)*

Midler, who wrote two hit books in the early 1980s, poses in her pajamas for National Library Week in 1984. The book that she is hugging is her own children's story, *The Saga of Baby Divine*. *(Courtesy of American Library Association / MJB Photo Archives)*

me in Oklahoma, and he wanted to visit me. This is the affair he's talking about? He came to visit me in Oklahoma? I don't get it, but a lot of these conquests of his were sort of unwilling. . . . Date rape? No—interview rape! Well, this was no rape. He didn't rape me, but it was pretty shocking. What a slimeball! I'm really appalled. I can't believe he's doing it. This guy must be really desperate. . . . I'm sure he doesn't give his own measurements. I'll repeat: You call that *little* thing an affair?" (40).

The infuriated Miss M wanted no mistake to be made on her opinion of Geraldo Rivera. "Oh, he was a slimeball!" she exclaimed. "If I had known then that he was going to do this twenty years later, I never would have given him the time of day" (27).

Jeff Erdel, who was identified by *USA Today* as a "Rivera spokesman," said of Midler's efforts to trivialize the so-called "torrid affair" between Bette and Geraldo, "Absurd! He did not drug Bette Midler. . . . This was not a one-night affair or attack. This was the beginning of a torrid, month-long sexual relationship consummated on perhaps twenty different occasions" (138). He also insinuated in the press that Midler's statements were meant as a part of her publicity campaign for her upcoming film *For the Boys*.

Geraldo's rebuttal in the press continued to fan the flames of his controversial book. According to him, "I have no idea why she suddenly turned so mean" (139).

While she was settling scores and clearing up past feuds, Bette also lit into Bruce Springsteen. Apparently, in the 1980s, when she was working with producer Chuck Plotkin, he played the demo of a song Springsteen had written, called "Pink Cadillac." Bruce had yet to record it, and Plotkin was under the impression that it was free for Midler to record first, so she went into the studio and recorded her version of the song. According to Bette, she spent $25,000 recording the song, and, said Bette, "[Springsteen] said I couldn't sing it. . . . it wasn't a girl's song" (140). It seemed that Bruce wanted to record it first, and that Plotkin had no legal right to offer it to Midler. When Natalie Cole recorded the song in 1988 and had a hit with it, Bette was even madder at Bruce than she had been before.

In addition to all of the publicity that was being generated by the Geraldo Rivera–Bette Midler feud, and her gripes about Springsteen, Miss M was in the news in November 1991 for her latest crusade: trash. Well, not the kind of trash that she is usually associated with. This time

around, it was trash alongside the highway, making the American landscape look shabby. According to the press, "Midler was the 236th
Adopt-a-Highway volunteer." A strip of highway in the North Hollywood area was suddenly designated her responsibility, with signs reading, "Litter Removal Next 2 Miles, Bette Midler" (141).

Also in 1991, Bette was part of an all-star public service music video
aired on television and at movie theaters in the United States. The
name of the video was *Yakety Yak: Take It Back.* The video was part
animation and part live action. The animation segments included a cartoon Yak, dancing with music celebrities, delivering a "no littering"
message. Midler appeared in the lively video, which is set to the
Leiber & Stoller song "Yakety Yak (Don't Talk Back)." The Number 1
hit was originally recorded by the Coasters in 1958. Bette is dressed in
a black jacket and skirt with a white blouse, as a school teacher instruct-
ing her students to recycle. The song was slightly rewritten, with the
message "take it back" as the chorus. The video also features Pat Bena-
tar, Queen Latifah, Lita Ford, B. B. King, Kenny Loggins, Natalie Cole,
Charlie Daniels, Stevie Wonder, Tone Loc, Ozzy Osbourne, Quincy
Jones, and the voice of Dr. John as Yakety Yak, the animated Yak.

In a separate public service announcement, Midler is seen on camera
delivering the message: "Listen to me: DO NOT—I repeat—DO NOT
ever throw a bottle or can out of your car window onto the highway. If
you do, I will follow your car. I will come to your house and I will tell
you to your face: 'Take it back! Recycle it!' And, believe me, I can get
very nasty" (142).

Looking stunningly fabulous on the cover of the December 1991
issue of *Vanity Fair* magazine, Miss M began the publicity campaign
that would launch her upcoming movie, *For the Boys.* One of the things
that the *Vanity Fair* piece brought to light was all of Midler's charitable
efforts, especially centering on the AIDS epidemic.

When the AIDS crisis occurred in the early 1980s, Bette Midler was
one of the first Hollywood celebrities to lend unflagging support toward
raising money for AIDS-related charities. It had been going on for a
decade now. The diva said at the time, "The last ten years I have worked
on behalf of people with AIDS because I couldn't stand idly by, twid-
dling my thumbs, pissing and moaning while people I loved shriveled
up and died. I began my career in 1965, and I am not lying, I do not
exaggerate one minute, when I tell you that nearly everyone who I
started out with is dead. . . . I never thought that at such a relatively

young age I would be on such intimate terms with death. My whole adult life I have had gay friends, I've had gay collaborators, I've had gay mentors. And if I live to be a thousand, I could never repay the debt I owe to them. They gave me my vision and they gave me my career" (40).

Among the most significant members of Bette's entourage whom she lost to AIDS was her longtime collaborator and comedy writer Jerry Blatt. On the inside of her 1990 album *Some People's Lives,* Bette wrote her "dedication" in the liner notes: "For Jerry Blatt."

Speaking of Jerry Blatt, Moogy Klingman recalls, "He was a great guy. He was like her best friend. He was a gay bodybuilder type. He was a great guy. I wrote a bunch of songs with him. He was devoted to her" (36).

During this same era, Bette found herself on the threshold of a new era of self-confidence. She had a clear-cut picture of who she was and who her stage persona—the Divine Miss M—was. Regarding her alter ego, Midler explained in 1991: "It used to be confusing. They wanted me to be that. It was like Rita Hayworth—all those guys thought they married [the movie character] Gilda. I didn't want to live like that. I didn't want to put filler in my hair and wear platform shoes my whole life . . . but she [Miss M] wasn't in any agony, psychotic, or . . . well, a little bit, not too much" (40).

When it was suggested that before her association with Disney, her movie career was in the toilet, Midler in her own defense quipped, "It wasn't in the toilet. Oh, maybe I was headed for the bathroom door" (27).

Using a Disney character reference, she claimed that she very often felt like the confused puppet Pinocchio. "Sometimes I'm sorry I got swept up in it," she said about her film career. "Remember when Pinocchio goes to Stromboli, and Stromboli convinces him to be an actor? And Pinocchio performs a little bit, and Stromboli puts him in a cage? Well, that's a lot like what's it's like. You want to do this, and you're completely fascinated by the dream. And you get there. And suddenly you're in a cage" (27).

According to her, she had absorbed a lot of knowledge about the movie business in the last decade of films. "I've learned how to make deals. I've learned how to negotiate and that some things are more important than others. In order to get what you want, you have to choose what's important. You have to find the point past which you would never go. I've learned how to take responsibility for what comes on my watch. You know the old expression, 'It happened on your watch'? Well, you have to take responsibility. And, I've learned where to buy my bras" (27).

Although she was clearly making all of her own decisions in her film career, Bette during this era passed on two very important films. She was offered the starring role in the Stephen King film *Misery* (1990). She claimed that she felt it wasn't right for her. Instead, Kathy Bates took the role of the ultimate crazed fan and won an Academy Award for it. Had she chosen to do the role, it could have been the Demented Miss M who was "hobbling" James Caan, who played the stranded author in the film.

Another film she declined starring in was a vehicle that was developed at Disney just for her: *Sister Act* (1992). It was the comic story of a Las Vegas lounge singer who takes refuge in a convent, when she finds herself being chased by "the mob." Instead, Whoopi Goldberg starred in the movie. The film was such a huge box-office hit that it was followed two years later by *Sister Act 2*. Bette had other ideas.

The Pee Wee Herman scandal was one of the biggest headline-grabbing stories of this era. When the popular children's talkshow host was caught masturbating in an adult theater in Florida, it ruined his TV career. According to Bette Midler at the time, "You know, I wanted so much to do a movie with Pee-Wee Herman. I really ought to. That would be so jive. . . . My character is so broad and so over the top, and his character in its way is over the top, too. His character is quite sly in that he sort of knows what's going on, but he never participates, and I wanted to do a *My Little Chickadee*–type of thing while he falls in love with me in an innocent way and I kind of use him in a nefarious way. Personally, I happen to like Pee-Wee. He's such a sweet guy. He's a big gardener. Big big big. Nobody who is a gardener can be all bad. . . . I don't know what the hell he was doing in that theater. I swear to God! But what's the big deal? That's what those theaters are *for*. You'd think that people had never been to one. How can you be so hypocritical as to have one [adult theater] in your community and then pretend you don't know what's going on in them? It's so stupid! Maybe he should have brought a raincoat—who knows? It's just so jive" (40).

Of all the films Bette had done up to this time, she had the highest hopes for her own production of *For the Boys*. Ever since she first sang the Andrews Sisters' "Boogie Woogie Bugle Boy," it had been a foregone conclusion that one day she would star in a 1940s-era film. Doing such a musical picture had been an idea Bette and her All Girls Productions had been attempting to get off the ground for years.

Ultimately, this was to be the first film that she *didn't* do for Disney Studios in seven years. It wasn't for lack of trying. "We asked them," Bette explains. "We brought it to them. It was one of the things we had to offer them when we first came, and it was not their kind of picture. They didn't want to spend that much money, take that much risk. I've always understood how they feel about their product, so it really didn't bother me. It remains to be seen if the public likes it or not, but they've gotten that it's good. Jeffrey [Katzenberg] was thrilled. I belong to them in a certain sense. If this is a hit, it just enhances me for them" (40).

For the Boys was to be something of a reunion for Bette, as it put her back together with director Mark Rydell, who had also directed her in *The Rose*. Since they had last worked together, Rydell had directed screen legends Henry Fonda and Katherine Hepburn in 1981's *On Golden Pond*. Both veteran actors won Academy Awards for their work in that film.

According to Rydell, "Bette was a more ragged human being during *The Rose*. It served *The Rose*, that kind of emotional skinlessness. She had a kind of hysterical talent during that period. She's not that way anymore. She's learned to function with ease. In *The Rose* I directed a child, now she's a grown-up woman. In the last twenty years I don't know of a deeper, more profound talent than Bette Midler. It's like Katherine Hepburn. Katherine Hepburn is oddly not dissimilar. Their equipment is Ferrari. You're not dealing with a Ford. You're dealing with a Formula One engine" (40).

As the film was about to open in theaters, even the soundtrack of *For the Boys* was highly publicized. The December 6, 1991, issue Tucson's *Arizona Daily Star* carried a feature about the film's supervising music editor, Curt Sobel. According to him, doing the sound editing on the film posed several challenges. "We could expand or compress words and whole sentences. Ordinarily, you record all music ahead of time, the actor practices lip-synching, and then has playback running through earphones and monitors, and they try to match" (143).

He explained, "The whole film, outside of two songs that Bette sings, is all playback." The songs "Come Rain or Come Shine" and "In My Life" were the songs which were filmed and performed live. "In that last song," says Sabel, the final lyric was computer enhanced: ". . . the very last line, where she doesn't quite sing the last note, is a playback line done months earlier" (143).

Sobel says that Midler "was wonderful, very demanding, very opinionated. She knows what she likes and dislikes, and has no hesitation in letting you know" (143).

One of the most fascinating aspects of the *For the Boys* soundtrack is that Bette's first musical number in the film, "Billy-a-Dick," is actually a rare and never-before-recorded song by Hoagy Carmichael and Paul Francis Webster. Finding a genuine 1940s-era Hoagy Carmichael tune, and giving it its debut in this film, was the kind of painstaking attention to detail that distinguishes *For the Boys* as a carefully crafted picture.

One of the most crucial aspects of producing this film was deciding on the right choice of a leading man. Finally, it was decided that James Caan was the prefect actor to bring to life the role of philandering comedian Eddie Sparks. Although he is better known for his tough-guy roles, in films like *Rollerball* and *The Godfather*, Caan was also used to dealing with divas. After all, he did co-star with Barbra Streisand in *Funny Lady* in the 1970s, playing Billie Rose to her Fanny Brice. Bette and James had nearly co-starred together in *Misery*—had she not turned that film down.

Said Caan of Midler, after working with her on *For the Boys:* "Bette is the hardest worker I've ever dealt with" (40).

The film *For the Boys* tells the story of two USO performers, through their career, which spans fifty years and three different wars: World War II, Korea, and Vietnam. Like *Beaches,* it was an All Girls picture, produced by Bette Midler, Bonnie Bruckheimer, and Margaret South.

The premise of the film is that veteran song and comedy stars Dixie Leonard and Eddie Sparks are being honored with a presidential medal on a huge television special, and a production assistant is being dispatched to try and coerce Leonard out of the Hollywood apartment she has been holed up in for years, to appear on the program.

When the production assistant arrives at Dixie's memorabilia-filled apartment, we find Bette in a ton of aging makeup, playing an eighty-year-old. Bette looks something like the comedian Sophie Tucker did in the 1960s, and her character of Dixie Leonard also has the same salty tongue of foul-mouthed "Soph."

While trying to convince the aged singer to participate in the show, the production assistant, Jeff Brooks (Arne Gross), has to sit and listen to Dixie's reflections about the past. It is through those reflections that the action of *For the Boys* unfolds, in a series of flashbacks.

In the first flashback Dixie Leonard is seen in a recording session, recording the song "Billy-a-Dick," with her girlfriends Myra (Pattie D'Arcy) and Colleen (Melissa Manchester) singing harmony vocals. This is one of the film's biggest treats, seeing and hearing Bette with Melissa—her very first Harlette.

When Eddie Sparks's female singer drops out of the show midtour, Dixie is invited to England as her replacement. It would be her job not only to sing on the show for the American troops, but to banter jokes with Eddie Sparks onstage.

While in makeup and waiting in the wings for her first appearance with Eddie, she rips her gown. So, instead of missing her cue, she bounds onstage dressed in an officer's jacket, high-heels, and no skirt or pants. This causes quite a stir. Then she sells an up-tempo song to the troops—the catchy boogie-woogie number "Stuff Like That There." When the lights suddenly go out, she carries on like a seasoned trooper, singing Johnny Mercer's "P.S. I Love You."

Although Dixie's sexually suggestive repartee on stage offends Eddie and almost gets her fired, when he sees how adept she is with a song, he begins to mellow. After a backstage battle and a nightclub reconciliation, an act is born.

The Eddie Sparks and Dixie Leonard duo is such a hit as a wartime act that it blossoms in the next decade, not only in front of the troops in Korea, but on 1950s television as well. Some of the liveliest scenes take place in the TV show sequences.

There is no question that Eddie Sparks is a clone of comedian Bob Hope, who was famous for entertaining troops around the world during the exact eras that *For the Boys* is set in. The same is true for Eddie's theme song "I'll Remember You," which is obviously fashioned from Bob Hope's trademark tune, "Thanks for the Memories."

As Dixie tells her story, she paints Sparks as quite the ladies man. "How they loved him, those boys," reminisces Dixie of Eddie. However, she is always quick to explain, "He screwed everything that moved."

Also crucial to the act is Eddie's longtime gag writer, Art (George Segal). He happens to be Dixie's uncle, who was instrumental in introducing the famous pair to each other. However, in the 1950s, when Art expresses an opinion that sounds decidedly Communist, Eddie is forced to fire him from the show. With that, Dixie starts her own World War III, against Sparks.

Another pivotal relationship that occurs in the film involves Dixie's young son Danny. Since Eddie has a wife and three daughters of his own, he clearly longs to have a son. Instead, he has a bond with thirteen-year-old Danny. Danny is like the son that Eddie never had.

As the film progresses into the late '60s, Eddie convinces Dixie to put the act back together to tour Vietnam. He does this by setting up a meeting with her drafted son, Danny, since they both miss him terribly.

When Eddie and Dixie reunite for a tour of entertaining the troops in Vietnam, *For the Boys* suddenly swings into "Bette Midler does *Apocalypse Now*"–mode. Dixie is in shock when she sees that all the soldiers are tripping out on drugs. One soldier has gone totally nuts and is amassing a collection of dead enemy ears—which he keeps on a string. But when a horrified Dixie offers to pull some strings to get Danny out of there, he declines, because it might break his "uncle" Eddie's heart.

The Vietnam sequences give Bette some of her strongest dramatic moments on screen. One of the high points comes when she sings the sentimental Beatles song "In My Life" to a drug-altered troop of soldiers. Then tragedy suddenly strikes.

In a catastrophic scene, while Dixie and Eddie are in attendance, a vicious enemy strike occurs, and Danny is riddled with bullets. Witnessing the death of the boy they both loved so dearly becomes the event that splits Dixie and Eddie up for twenty-five more years—until the present-day '90s.

After refusing to have anything to do with Sparks or his Presidential Medal, Dixie suddenly decides to show up at the live telecast. However, her motive is not necessarily to appear at the show, but to have a final backstage showdown with Eddie Sparks.

Alone in his dressing room, Dixie asks of Eddie, "Mind if I smoke?"

He shoots back at her: "I don't care if you burn."

This ignites a fight up to the bitter end. After she tells him off, she turns to leave and lets him take the stage alone. With heightened emotional drama, Dixie watches from the wings as Eddie starts to dotteringly "lose it." As he rambles on, visibly upset, Dixie decides to take the stage for one last tearful reunion.

Some of *For the Boys* is tear-jerkingly sentimental. Although it has some very funny moments, it is also highly dramatic. For Midler, it provided her with the most even and emotional drama of her film career. When viewing this film, we have no doubt that Bette has put her heart into it. It is finely crafted and well acted, and it contains some great musical performances.

When the film was released, it was marketed like a big glamorous movie from the 1940s. The Los Angeles debut of the film had the air of an old-time Hollywood premiere. In grand Hedda Hopper style, Jeannie Williams, in *USA Today*, leaked out La Midler's fashion choices for the opening night gala by announcing, "She'll go for the glamour. But with a sensible difference. Designer Robert Turturice *(Beaches)* has remodeled the purple velvet number Bette wore to the Grammy Awards. They got lots of favorable mail on the dress, and it's reappearing calf-length with a V-neck, minus roses, plus beads" (144).

On November 14, 1991, Bette gave a forty-minute live musical performance at the premiere of *For the Boys*. Held at the Academy of Motion Picture Arts and Sciences in Los Angeles, she sang songs from the film for a special invited audience of VIPs and press. And, during her publicity sweep, on November 22 she appeared on *The Tonight Show*.

It's a drama, it's a musical, it's a soap opera, it's political, it's patriotic, and it somehow roundly missed every audience. Yet the really strange thing about *For the Boys* was that it received great reviews. It indeed received some horrible reviews as well, but mainly, the critics seemed to love it. "Don't miss *For the Boys!* A sassy, sensational performance from Bette Midler, the best of her career," claimed Pat Collins of WWOR-TV (145). "Midler struts her best stuff," wrote David Ansen in *Newsweek* (145). "Hilariously funny. Bette's most magnificent movie ever!" Larry Frascella, *US* magazine (145). "Midler is not only divine, she could walk home with the Oscar," said Joel Siegel on TV's *Good Morning America* (145). "The best slambang entertainment of the year!" claimed Bob Thomas for the Associated Press (146).

Renata Polt, in the *Pacific Sun*, proclaimed, "In all, *For the Boys* is a winner, a perfect vehicle for Bette Midler, who carries the show, and has never been in better form. . . . It's a funny, sexy, tuneful, even thoughtful. I can't think of a better way to start off the holiday season" (147). In *USA Today* Mike Clark gave it three stars out of four and proclaimed, "*For the Boys*, which allows Bette Midler to fulfill what is probably her life's dream: to look just like the twilight Sophie

Tucker. . . . Midler may have her career role here; Caan has never been so loose and likable on screen. If you savor moldy show biz sagas with Ethel Merman or Susan Hayward, you may (like me) find *For the Boys* a guilty pleasure that's not for the birds" (148).

A lot of the raves were for Midler herself. The *New York Times* called *For the Boys* "a custom-tailored showcase for [Midler's] talents. . . . Midler has wisely taken the bull by the horns" (98).

And then, there were the press members who loathed the film. According to *Entertainment Weekly*, "For most of the movie she's like a watered-down cross between the Divine Miss M and the long-suffering earth mothers she played in *Beaches* and *Stella*. Dixie isn't a character exactly—she's a walking Bette's greatest hits package. . . . *For the Boys* wants to make you laugh, cry, and everything in between. In the end, though, the movie, with its schematic sentimentality and just-add-water period settings, is a great big empty shell—a reminder that, no, they really *don't* make 'em like they used to" (149).

Amy Dawes, in *Daily Variety*, said, "Fox's song-driven wartime show-biz meller *For the Boys* is a big, creaky balloon of a movie that lumbers along like a dirigible in a Thanksgiving parade, festooned with patriotic sentiment, clumsy but still fitfully likable as a vehicle for the punchy, effervescent Bette Midler. . . . Presented as a wildly popular comedian and legendary ladies' man, he [James Caan] gives evidence of neither. Midler, as spunky singer Dixie Leonard, seems more like a gal enduring a tough job situation than like a woman feeling an attraction to Caan's supposedly seductive Eddie Sparks. . . . pic suffers from the lack of electricity between them" (150).

Detroit's *Orbit* magazine tore into the film by stating, "There are two very frightening things about *For the Boys*. James Caan—Sonny Corleone—with red hair, singing, and Bette Midler as a senior citizen . . . [as Eddie and Dixie] their twenty-five years together entertaining troops and driving each other crazy, while driving viewers of this film to drink. . . . The fact that some critics are praising this mess, is mind-boggling—unless of course they mistook the soundtrack for a quality film" (151).

Well, on the positive side of things, there were several critics who conceded that the film was a "bomb," but declared the coinciding album a big hit. "The soundtrack for the new film starring Bette Midler, is much more of a stand-alone listening experience. However sluggish business is at the box-office, the soundtrack is one of Midler's better albums, reminiscent of her ability to send up a vintage style while giving it new life" (152).

There was no question that Bette Midler excelled at bringing to life the classic big band swing sound of the 1940s. The soundtrack album of *For the Boys* gave her a platform to really delve into the music of this era. With the exception of two brief instrumentals, the *For the Boys* soundtrack is a full Bette Midler album. If one were to name the most prominent songwriter on this album, it would be the great Johnny Mercer. Of the eleven Midler vocal numbers it contains, she performs four Mercer numbers, including "P.S. I Love You," "Come Rain or Come Shine," and two versions of "I Remember You." The only new material included here is the sentimental Diane Warren composition "Every Road Leads Back to You." The aforementioned "Billy-a-Dick" (with Melissa Manchester) opens the album and really sets the tone for this—the ultimate 1940s-style Bette Midler album. Other great musical highlights include Bette's swinging "Stuff Like That There," her version of the ballad "For All We Know," and her touching rendition of the Beatles' "In My Life." With the exception of the production of one Johnny Mercer instrumental, "The Girl Friend of the Whirling Dervish," the album was produced by Arif Mardin.

The *For the Boys* soundtrack album had a nice run on the record charts. It peaked in *Billboard* magazine at Number 22, and it was certified Gold, for selling over 500,000 copies in America. In England, it made it to Number 75 on the album chart. Only one single was released from the album. It was the song "Every Road Leads Back to You," which peaked at Number 78 in America.

She was nominated for a Golden Globe for her role as Dixie Leonard, and at the ceremony, held in Los Angeles, much to her surprise she won it. Accepting the award, she said from the stage, "I want to thank the Foreign Press Association for honoring a film when the American public dismissed it" (131).

And she was again nominated for a "Best Actress" Academy Award, which she did not win. Although Golden Globe-winning and heralded by so many critics, the bottom-line could not be denied: *For the Boys* was a financial disaster. Playing at the height of the Christmas season, it was largely ignored. At cineplexes across America, it was playing to nearly empty theaters.

The night of the 49th Annual Golden Globe Awards, Bette Midler complained to a reporter for *USA Today*, "I've been through a lot in the last couple of months. It's been a lot of stress. All of us thought that it was a picture everybody would adore. We miscalculated. We were so sure we had a winner. That's why it was so disappointing. . . . It was a grown-up picture for grown-up people and they simply did not come. It was so ambitious. Maybe it was too ambitious" (153).

She also claimed at the time, that she would "never" star in another musical, "Because . . . people are [not] interested in them. They want a thrill a minute. They want violence. They want to be overstimulated" (153).

When she was asked what she had going on in her career at the moment, a dramatic Midler shot back: "I have nothing" (153).

According to Bonnie Bruckheimer, "We spent years on that project, and nobody went to see it. That was shocking to me. I thought it was a sure thing. I was catatonic when it failed" (22).

Said Midler, "By the time *For the Boys* came around, I had been through *Jinxed* and so many other storms. I had so much armor around me. I had turned into a . . . man. And you know how they are. They have no feelings" (22).

As she had proved so many times in the past, just when things look the bleakest, it's simply time to stand up, brush yourself off, and start anew. That is exactly what Bette Midler was about to do—again.

17

BETTE OF ROSES

While Bette's feelings may have been hurt by the public's reception toward her *For the Boys* project, she was too much involved in other films, new appearances, and reflecting about her life to dwell on this.

One of the things that Bette most enjoyed between projects was her home life inside her Coldwater Canyon house. Said she at the time: "I really have decided that the outside world doesn't have a lot to offer. You have to make your own heaven in your own home. How many after-hours bars can you go to? How many vodka gimlets can you drink?" (40).

Speaking of her daughter in 1992, Midler claimed, "She's a lot like me. So it's comforting, and also horrifying. She really gets on my nerves sometimes. I love her, but she's really stubborn. If you ask her to apologize, she won't do it" (27).

She was also very comfortable and happy with her marriage to Martin. However, she admitted that whenever the two of them did have an argument, she simply insisted that she win every difference of opinion. "That's one of the main things my husband hates about me—I always have to be right. I tell him, 'I don't have to be right. I simply am right,'" she proclaimed (27).

According to her, "I'm a fabulous cook, and my husband is a fabulous cook. I collect cookbooks. I love good food. I sew. You won't believe it, but I sew. We decorate. We go to flea markets and swap meets. We have a lot of friends who own restaurants, people who like to eat well. I like that. There's a certain quality of life that's missing in this country. People go so fast—everything in this country is about speed, about going faster, having more status, more money. And I find that's not really the way" (27).

On March 23, 1992, the United States Supreme Court made an official ruling on Ford Motor Company's appeal against Midler's 1989 judgment, with regard to the recording of "Do You Want to Dance?" According to *USA Today*, "A $400,000 award was upheld for singer Bette Midler against an ad agency that used a 'soundalike' for a 1986 TV commercial. Midler's former back-up singer was told to sound like Midler in the Ford ads" (154).

That spring, the voice of Bette Midler was heard narrating the children's story "Weird Peanuts." It was telecast on *Shelley Duvall's Bedtime Stories* series for kids on the Showtime network in America.

On May 21, 1992, Bette Midler had the honorable distinction of being Johnny Carson's very last guest on *The Tonight Show*. He had announced his retirement, and he wanted to have her on the final show to help him bid TV audiences "good-bye." Carson had been hosting the late night show on NBC-TV since October 2, 1962.

It was a very touching performance on both of their parts. It was a sentimental event, but Bette kept the program upbeat with her jokes and mugging with Carson. During the program she sang "Dear Mr. Carson" to Johnny, to the tune of "Dear Mr. Gable," which Judy Garland once sang to Clark Gable in *Broadway Melody of 1938*. She made jokes about people at home having sex while watching *The Tonight Show*. She sang Carson a song that he identified as his favorite, "Here's That Rainy Day." Johnny, teary eyed, said the audience, "You people are seeing one hell-uva show." Indeed, they were. However, the biggest highlight of the evening was Midler serenading and saluting Johnny with a special rendition of the Johnny Mercer/Harold Arlan song "One for My Baby (and One More for the Road)."

The show was a huge ratings hit, and everyone seemed to be talking about what a touching and wonderful performance Midler delivered. According to her, she was overwhelmed by receiving "such an outpouring of love and goodwill from vast numbers of people as I did after that show. What I'm trying to say is that people were so thrilled by that evening, and I think they were so glad because they felt that I had given him something that he deserved, what they wanted to give him if they could have, I said 'thank you' for them in the way they wanted. . . . That was great, just great" (155).

For her it was a very special evening, and a magical hour and a half of TV history. Yet, to this day, she refuses to watch a tape of the show. "I did it and I walked away, and I think he did, too. I will always have the memory. . . . I wanted to keep my memory of it the way it is for me. I didn't want to have to look at it and say, 'I shouldn't have done that. I didn't know that happened. Gee, that's not the way I remember it,' which is really truly gorgeous" (155).

On August 30, 1992, at the annual Emmy Awards, Bette's perform-ance on the final episode of *The Tonight Show* was nominated in the category of Best Performance, Variety or Music Program. She won, but was not present to receive the trophy.

Bette, in fact, got so much attention for being Johnny Carson's last guest on the final episode of *The Tonight Show* that she was later to lampoon herself, on TV's animated comedy series *The Simpsons*. How-ever, on *The Simpsons* episode that Midler provided the voice to, she was serenading comically Crusty the Clown on his last TV show.

On September 23, she attended the fashion industry party "Valen-tino: Thirty Years of Magic," with all proceeds going toward AIDS char-ities. On October 3 she was one of the stars at the biannual Children's Diabetes Foundation benefit, which was held at the Beverly Hilton Hotel. And on December 23 she was among the celebrities to appear on CBS-TV celebrating the *HBO 20th Anniversary* special.

When Bill Clinton was inaugurated president of the United States, several huge gala events were held, at which some of the biggest celeb-rities in America performed. Bette was included in the special *A Call for Reunion*, on January 17, 1992.

In the summer of 1992, Bette Midler released the American version of her *Greatest Hits* album, *Experience the Divine*. It contains fourteen of Bette's best, and best-known performances, from her first eleven years on Atlantic Records. Interestingly enough, five of the songs were taken from her *Divine Miss M* album: "Hello in There," "Do You Want to Dance?"; "Chapel of Love;" the Manilow-helmed version of "Friends;" and the single version of "Boogie Woogie Bugle Boy," which Manilow also produced. Naturally, the album included her three biggest hits: "The Rose," "From a Distance," and "Wind beneath My Wings." The album also featured "Only in Miami," "When a Man Loves a Woman," "Miss Otis Regrets," "Shiver Me Timbers," and "In My Life."

The one never-before-released song was Bette's rendition of "One for My Baby (and One More for the Road)," taken from her award-winning performance on *The Tonight Show.*

A very good sampling of Miss M's astonishing career, it also seemed to ignore several of her career highlights. There was nothing from her albums *Bette Midler, Songs for the New Depression, Broken Blossom, Thighs and Whispers,* and *Divine Madness.* Even singles like "In the Mood," "Beast of Burden," "Married Men," and "You're Moving Out Today" were skipped over.

The album was quite successful. Although it only made it as high as Number 50 on the American *Billboard* charts, it sold progressively well, and it eventually sold a million copies and was certified Platinum. In the U.K. it made it to Number 3 on the album charts.

For her next big screen role, Bette chose a trademark Disney film. She played the leader of a trio of witches in the strictly family-fare Halloween spoof *Hocus Pocus.* Sarah Jessica Parker and Kathy Najimy portrayed her spellbinding siblings in this light comedy, clearly aimed at children.

The male lead in the film, Max, is played by teenage Omri Katz, who is most famous for having played the role of young John Ross Ewing in the nighttime TV soap opera *Dallas.* And Thora Birch plays eight-year-old Dani, who ends up wrangling with this trio of kooky witches. Birch is so saccharine sweet that it is hard not to wish that a really nasty spell gets put upon her. But alas, she and Katz end up outwitting the evil threesome by the end of the picture—in good Disney fashion.

Choreographer and video director Kenny Ortega was the director of *Hocus Pocus,* and the film was coproduced with Bette's business partner, Bonnie Bruckheimer.

The beginning sequence starts out suspensefully enough that it looks like it might develop into an adult horror flick. It is 1693, in Salem, Massachusetts, where the three Sanderson sisters are the town terrors. We find them casting a spell to provide themselves with eternal youth. They have the ability to steal the youthful life force from young girls and turn back the hands of time on their own bodies.

When the older brother of their latest victim interferes, the Sanderson sisters simply turn him into a talking black cat—one who has the powers of eternal life. When the townspeople get ready to put the witch trio to death, the women cast another spell, which puts them in some sort of time-warping cosmic suspended animation.

Cut to 1993, when they are brought back to life, only to wrangle with a whole new generation of children and adults—and the same talking black cat who is still hanging around Salem, waiting for vengeance.

Bette obviously had a ball playing the part of Winifred Sanderson. Her clothes and makeup alone are totally over-the-top. As Winny, Midler wears an elaborate, bosom-exposing green velvet Victorian gown. Her hair is a wild mane of carrot orange, her mouth is filled with rat-like teeth, and she has talons for fingernails. Her over-the-top acting is equally as outrageous and scenery-chewing. Throughout, Miss M seems to be doing her best combo impersonation of Edna May Oliver, Margaret Hamilton, and Bette Davis as Baby Jane Hudson.

In fact, all of the witches overact with great delight. Sarah Jessica Parker as Sarah Sanderson is a bit of an airhead, and Kathy Najimy as Mary Sanderson is a ditzy clown. As the Halloween 1993 plot progresses, the supporting characters become more and more cartoonlike. They include a magic spell book that floats through the air, has a winking eyeball on its cover, and possesses the ability to turn its own pages. The witches even bring back to life a ghoul who was buried with his mouth sewn shut.

Although Bette and her evil sisters are the stars of the film, the plot is driven by and centers around the modern-day brother and sister, who are the protagonists to the wicked Sanderson gals. It is October 31—the one night of the year when dead spirits can come to life. When Max and his sister Dani "trick or treat" at the house of a teenage girl he likes at school, Allison (Vinessa Shaw), the three children set out for the Sanderson house—on a day that just happens to be the 300th anniversary of the witches' public lynching. It seems that the witches set their postmortem, time machine of a spell to revive them on exactly that date, whenever a virgin lights the enchanted candle. In this case, much to his embarrassment, it turns out to be Max.

Like events that occurred 300 years previously, the teenage brother attempts to save his little sister from the clutches of the evil sisters, with the help of the three-century-old talking black cat. This is strictly a cartoonish comic adventure, so one has to abandon belief in logic and go with the *Wizard of Oz* sense of reality that this film conjures up.

There are some slapstick comic moments along the way. When the Sanderson sisters travel the streets of Salem on their brooms, goofy Najimy, at a loss for a good broom, grabs the next best thing—a vacuum cleaner.

In one of the silliest sequences comes when the sisters stumble into the household of Garry Marshall and Penny Marshall. Since it is Halloween, the modern Salem citizens don't think anything is odd about the Sandersons' 300-year-old garb. Garry is dressed as Satan, and Bette and her witch sisters mistake him for the real master of the gates of Hell.

The most amusing Midler scene comes when the witches follow the kids to a costume party. Not one to miss a spell-binding musical moment, Bette ends up onstage singing her own wicked version of the Screamin' Jay Hawkins' hit "I Put a Spell on You." The script doesn't miss the chance to use every pun it can get its hands on, including "The witch is back!"

The kids end up being savvy enough to trap the witches in the pottery kiln of the local high school, in an attempt to shake and bake them into oblivion. However, when that plan backfires, Bett and her sister witches come back for another round of battle with the mere mortals. Justifiably, the witches get even with the two bullies who bedeviled Max at the beginning of the film. As this is a Disney children's flick, by the end of the film the kids win, and the witches are exiled to oblivion.

Released in the summer of 1993, *Hocus Pocus* received mixed reviews, but did well at the box office, as "G"-rated family fare. Said Miss M at the time, "I did [*Hocus Pocus*] because I've got a six-year-old kid and there's nothing out there for her to see. It's harmless: it's got no four-letter words—the violence is minimal. It's broad and silly, but I don't have to worry what I look like. . . . It's nice to just romp" (131).

She was also happy to find out that her witch film sold more tickets at the box office than *For the Boys* did. This, especially, was good news to hear. "Well, I'm not disappointed anymore!" she exclaimed at the time, "Because y'know, I got my box office grosses [for *Hocus Pocus*] today and I'm just swimming along. Yes! I have a new hit! I don't have to think about *For the Boys* anymore. So there!" (155).

Bette's next film appearance was both "inspired" and "divine." Ever since she played the Rose in her first film, she had toyed with the idea of portraying Mama Rose in the timeless Broadway classic *Gypsy*.

It was filmed in eight weeks in Los Angeles, California, with an estimated budget of $14 million. CBS-TV paid in excess of $5 million to broadcast it twice. Bette was thrilled to be cast in the role. "I always wanted to play that character," she claimed. "I would have played it in stock if I had had the chance. The score is extraordinary. The writing is just incomparable." She also joked, "Nothing was skimped on. Except my salary" (155).

Filming *Gypsy* reinforced Bette's feelings of frustration at the difficulty of producing movie musicals. According to her, "I feel bad that the whole nation doesn't get to celebrate this tradition more often because it is valuable and it is well-crafted and it is something that we should be proud of. Yet we seem to throw the magical things that we've made aside or tear them down and tramp on them. Maybe it's because we're constantly reinventing ourselves, but personally I think it's a real waste" (155).

She also revealed that she had consciously stayed away from singing Broadway show tunes in her act and on her albums. "It's something I've avoided doing throughout my career, singing show tunes. And I really like show tunes. [They're] such a peculiar thing in American life because most people were interested in rock & roll or popular music or rhythm & blues music, they don't want anyone to know that they're closet show-tune listeners. But I am!" (155).

From the very opening scene, when Mama Rose pushes her daughters onstage at Uncle Jocko's talent show audition, it's clear that Midler—with her bawdy singing style and quipping sense of humor—was made for this role. The character of Rose is aggressive, abrasive, witty, and sharp. These are all qualities that Midler has going for her.

The performances—from those of the stars to the supporting characters—are all exciting and fresh. Bette was obviously able to include a couple of her own favorite people in the cast: Peter Riegert as Mama Rose's love interest, Herbie; and former-Harlette Linda Hart as the hard-talking stripper with a trumpet, Miss Mazeppa.

The fact that Bette and Peter were once romantically involved makes their on-camera chemistry so much more believable. They look like two people who could be in love with each other, and their scenes are all the more natural for this. They look and sound good together, serenading each other with such classic Stephen Sondheim lyrics as "You'll Never Get Away from Me," "Funny," and "Together, Wherever We Go."

The film is based on the memoirs of stripper Gypsy Rose Lee, and the real star of the show is her domineering mother, Rose. Rose is determined that her two daughters have the kind of show business career she would have loved to have had. She relentlessly pushes daughter June, who is backed up by less-talented Louise. When teenage June

(Jennifer Beck) runs off with a boyfriend, Rose is determined to turn Louise (Cynthia Gibb) into a huge star. (In reality, "dainty" June grew up to be real-life film star June Havoc.)

The musical was originally written with Ethel Merman in mind, and she was the star of the original Broadway production in 1959. It was later turned into a film starring Rosalind Russell and Natalie Wood (1962), which is still very popular. Then it was revived on Broadway, by Angela Lansbury in 1971 and by Tyne Daly in 1989. With music by Jule Stein and lyrics by Stephen Sondheim, it was one of the most popular musicals ever written and a show that has stood the test of time. It was truly ripe for the Midler touch.

When Rosalind Russell played the role in the first film, she was not a dynamic singer. Although she sang all of Rose's songs in the film, it wasn't always her voice that was heard—specifically, the song "Rose's Turn." On this vocally demanding number, Russell's voice was "augmented" with the voice of professional behind-the-scenes singer Lisa Kirk. It had been a long time since an actress could really belt out these songs as they were meant to be sung, and Miss Midler was just the right gal to fill Rose's high heels.

Bette had, of course, been in *Fiddler on the Roof* and had headlined Broadway with her concert stage act, but she had never *starred* in a "book" musical like this. By mounting this handsome-looking and very faithful production, it was her chance to give her own indelible interpretation to a classic Broadway show, while capturing her performance on film. Bette's production of *Gypsy* debuted on CBS-TV in America on December 12, 1993. In addition, Atlantic Records released a deluxe soundtrack album to accompany it. In markets outside of the United States, *Gypsy* was released as a theatrical film.

Bette is in her Yenta-esque heyday as the ultimate stage mother. She takes songs like "Some People" and attacks them with determination and spark. The story holds up well and is truly one of Midler's finest filmed performances.

Although a true survivor, Mama Rose is an unsympathetic character, for the most part. In fact, she is so cheap that she steals blankets from hotels to sew into overcoats, and she pockets the silverware from restaurants when no one is looking. She is determined to make ends meet, no matter what she has to do—from petty thievery to selling her own teenage daughter into burlesque.

According to Gypsy Rose Lee herself, "Mother had been many

things, but she had never been nice. Charming, perhaps, and coura-
geous, resourceful, and ambitious, but not nice. Mother, in a feminine
way, was ruthless. She was, in her own words, 'a jungle mother.' The
jungle was vaudeville of the 1920s, and we were her brood" (156).

The scene that erupts into the song "Everything's Coming Up Roses"
is perhaps Midler's most magical screen sequences ever—second only
to the film's last-act tour de force, "Rose's Turn." The bawdy, scenery-
chewing intensity of both numbers plays well with all of Midler's theatrical attributes. This bigger-than-life role and these gutsy songs seem
custom-made for Bette. The scene in the dressing room right after she
tells Herbie to go to Hell is an intense, pivotal point in the movie. The
emotions played off Bette's face are magical. Furthermore, many of
Bette's songs in the film were filmed and recorded "live" as they happened. This is rarely done in film. Usually, the vocal tracks are prere-
corded, and the singer lip-synchs. Here, Midler sings them live and
imbues them with a spontaneous fire that is riveting to watch and to
hear.

Strong acting by a brilliant cast full of supporting characters makes
this film a treat throughout. Andrea Martin as Mr. Grandsinger's prim
secretary, Ed Asner as Rose's stern father, Michael Jeter as a befuddled
Mr. Goldstone, Christine Ebersole as acidic Tessie Tura, and Anna Mc-
Neeley as bubble-headed Miss Electra, all make the most of their
scenes. Cynthia Gibb is especially charming as Louise. Her scenes with
the strippers are priceless—she is the only person on the screen who
can seem to stand up to Mama Rose. And Linda Hart is a scream as the
haughty and vulgar Miss Mazeppa.

The reviews for *Gypsy,* and for Bette, were unanimously glowing.
Ken Tucker, in *Entertainment Weekly,* claimed, "Even if you don't like
musicals, you'll like this one. The primary reason is Bette Midler's hilarious, heartfelt performance as Mama Rose, a star turn that caps a real
comeback of a year for Midler. . . . By the time Midler revs up for
her final curtain showstopper, 'Rose's Turn,' she has convinced us that
Rose—brassy, vulgar, and selfish—is worthy of respect as a woman who
had to live out her dreams through her children because, as she says,
she was 'born too soon and started too late.' Midler builds 'Rose's Turn'
into a spectacular statement of amoral show-business principles" (157).

"Entertaining! Bette Midler is manic as the obsessive, ambitious
Rose!" claimed *Sight and Sound* (98). Mike Duffy, in the *Detroit Free
Press,* wrote, "This three-hour Midler tour de force—based on the

famed Broadway musical—shimmers and soars with vintage show business pizzazz. If ever there was a harmonic convergence of star and role, it is here. Bette Midler was born to play Mama Rose." Rick Kogan, in the *Chicago Tribune,* proclaimed, "Midler's skill and singing, which succeed in redefining and deepening the character. . . . Midler scores knockouts with virtually every number!" (98). Jonathan Taylor, in *Daily Variety,* said, "This new production, headed by Bette Midler in the role she was born to play, succeeds. . . . Midler's Rose is explosive, riveting and impossible, yet impossible not to love" (158), And the list of raves went on and on.

With regard to singing the electrifying show-stopper "Rose's Turn," Bette concedes, "That was a real challenge. It's full of emotion. It's full of those high Bs!" (155).

Gypsy was a huge ratings success when it originally aired on December 12, 1993. The film has subsequently gone on to become successful video and DVD releases. It remains one of her strongest film performances and is a "must see" in her growing cinematic resume.

The one sad note about Bette's triumphant turn in *Gypsy* was that director Emile Ardolino died of AIDS a month before the debut telecast.

Gypsy was such a huge hit for Midler that she won a Golden Globe for her portrayal of Madame Rose, in the category of Best Performance by an Actress in a Motion Picture Made for TV. Made in cooperation with Midler's All- Girls Productions, the executive producer was Bonnie Bruckheimer, and the soundtrack album was coproduced by Arif Mardin, Michael Rafter, and Curt Sobel.

The *Gypsy* album includes all seventeen songs that were used in the film. Although Bette sings only seven of those songs, it is worth the price of the disc just to hear her belt her way through "Some People," "Small World," "Mr. Goldstone," "You'll Never Get Away from Me," "Everything's Coming Up Roses," "Together, Wherever We Go," and the show-stopping "Rose's Turn." The rest of the cast performs excellently here, too, accompanied by a full orchestra, conducted by Michael Rafter.

On December 15, 1993, Radio City Music Hall unveiled it's new "Sidewalk of Stars," resembling the Hollywood Walk of Fame. Fourteen stars who have headlined the classic deco theater include Tina Turner, Liza Minnelli, Frank Sinatra, and Bette Midler.

When the Golden Globe Awards were handed out in Los Angeles on

January 25, 1994, Bette was awarded a trophy for her role as Mama Rose in *Gypsy*. Midler, however, was with her family, vacationing in Hawaii.

On February 16, 1994, Bette appeared in a Los Angeles courtroom to testify with regard to her production of the film *For the Boys*. Singer and actress Martha Raye had in real life made a lifelong career out of appearing on USO shows for the American troops, much like the film's fictional character Dixie Leonard. Raye's suit alleged that her own biography was used as a basis for the film and that she should be paid for damages. Apparently, Raye had personally met with Bette in the mid-1980s to discuss a Midler version of Martha's life. However, both 20th Century-Fox and All Girls Productions declined to purchase the Martha Raye biography—*Maggie*—for the million dollars the veteran comedienne was asking. There was also the ongoing tabloid scandal concerning Raye and her much younger—and allegedly more manipulative—new husband. According to Bette's testimony that day in court, "The stories have no resemblance except for one thing—they both were entertainers during wartime" (131). Ultimately, the court ruled in Bette's favor. Sadly, Martha Raye suffered a heart attack and died later that year.

During the spring and summer of 1994, Bette toured across the American countryside again in her *Experience the Divine* tour. She announced to the *Boston Globe*, "We had a fabulous time last year. And when the season rolled around again, we decided to do it again. There were a whole bunch of places we didn't get to last year, and there were requests to come back to some of the places we did get to, so we strapped on the old harness and here we are again" (131).

On May 13, Bette opened the tour in St. Petersburg, Florida, at the ThunderDome. The tour wove its way across the countryside, and finally, on September 3 and 4, she headlined at the MGM Grand in Las Vegas. This was the first time she had played Vegas since 1976.

About Bette's 1994 tour, Susan Wloszczyna, in *USA Today*, wrote, "It's been a decade since Midler's last major tour, and the faithful aren't just hungry, they're starved. . . . Though the ode to burlesque had it moments, it was little more than a plug for Midler's *Gypsy* TV special. The old material (especially a gospel-charged 'Delta Dawn' and a heart-tugging 'Hello in There') clearly outshone the new. . . . Midler hasn't lost her knack for making expertly choreographed extravaganzas seem like spontaneous combustions. Clinton should just declare her the National Diva!" (159).

Referring to the passage of time since her last tour, Bette commented from the stage, "Ten years! Time flies when you're on Prozac. Well, enough about you, what about me?" (159).

Bette told the *New York Times* that in September of 1994, she officially had moved back to New York City. According to her, "I moved back because of the earthquake. And I needed to get back to a town where I could have a conversation about something other than [film box-office] grosses" (160).

The earthquakes in Los Angeles in 1993 proved to be "the last straw" for Midler's fascination with living permanently on the West Coast. Explained Bette, "My daughter's school was in the valley, just under these homes, and if the earthquake had happened during the day, and the houses had fallen on the school, she would've been killed. We couldn't bear the thought. So we came here" (17).

On September 11, 1994, Bette Midler appeared on the 46th Annual Emmy Awards in Los Angeles. Since *Gypsy* was nominated as the Outstanding Made-for-TV Movie, she performed the show-stopping song "Rose's Turn." The AIDS-themed *And the Band Played On* ending up taking the trophy, but Midler, in her own inimitable fashion, stole the show!

When the Manhattan Transfer recorded its 1994 album *Tonin'*, the group's members invited several guest celebrities into the studio to do duets with them. Since Arif Mardin was producing the album, Bette was a natural choice to join the vocal quartet. Among the other performers on the album are Laura Nyro on "La-La Means I Love You," Smokey Robinson on "I Second That Emotion," James Taylor on "Dream Lover," Frankie Valli on "Let's Hang On," Phil Collins on "Too Busy Thinking about My Baby," Ben E. King on "Save the Last Dance for Me," Chaka Kahn on "Hot Fun in the Summertime," and B. B. King and Ruth Brown on "The Thrill Is Gone." The song that Bette sings with the Manhattan Transfer is "It's Gonna Take a Miracle." Dueting with Transfer singer Janis Siegel and harmonizing with the rest of the quartet, Miss M sounds fabulous on this harmonic and cleverly conceived album.

Bette started the year 1995 in the recording studio, as she commenced work on her sixteenth album for Atlantic Records. It was to be called *Bette of Roses,* and it would prove to be a whole new musical direction for her.

According to Moogy Klingman, during this period he heard from

Bette Midler for the first time in years: "She called me, she wanted to work with Buzzy Linhart. She wanted to do a good deed, get him back on his feet. He was kind of broke and homeless. . . . She was giving me money to give to Buzzy. . . . She was sending Buzzy checks through me" (36).

Midler wanted to hear some of Buzzy Linhart's songs, in hopes that she would like one of them and record it, thus helping him financially. "There was a song called 'Fountain of Youth' . . . mountains of truth," recalled Klingman.

According to Buzzy, "We recorded about eight songs in a month. At one point she was maybe going to record one. She's a real stickler for perfection. It was called 'Dreams of Sand'" (37).

Ultimately, none of the songs that Klingman and Linhart wrote for her during this era were released. According to Moogy, "She called me to tell me how much she didn't like them." The songs, known as "The Buzzy/Moogy Sessions," sung by the two songwriters, ended up being sold on the Internet on Klingman's website. Midler decided to go in a different direction, musically.

In March of 1995, Midler appeared in Washington, D.C., at a White House reception that honored the twenty-fifth anniversary of National Public Radio (NPR). Said Bette that day, "I'm not going to get political. We don't come to the White House for that. We come hoping that there will be embossed towels that we can take home to our family and friends" (131).

On May 18, 1995, Bette guest-starred on the *Seinfeld* TV series. It was an episode called "The Understudy," and Miss M played herself, involved in a theater project cooked up by the stars of the series. In the plot of the show, she ends up in a typical Seinfeldian comedy of errors. Her performance on the show turned out to be a great comic turn for the diva. Bette had never worked on a sitcom before, so this was a whole new experience for her. *Seinfeld*—which starred stand-up comedian Jerry Seinfeld—was a huge ratings success throughout the 1990s, so Midler was fascinated to see the process in action and was happy to participate in it.

According to Bette, "I didn't watch *Seinfeld,* but once I was on it, I said, 'Why are they acting like this? What is this about?' There was all this cereal on the set, and I didn't understand it. On my episode, they had a Korean nail lady, and I thought, 'That's kind of funny. Because I have been to Korean nail ladies, and I kind of got the joke. So I started watching it, and of course I was hooked. [Those characters] were such nasty people—that's what I liked about them, up until the bitter end. And I'd never seen anything like it. Up until then, it was just *[I Love] Lucy* and *The Honeymooners* for me. I'm just old school" (120).

Relocated in New York City, Bette began her famed clean-up campaign in Manhattan. On June 12, 1995, she was joined by several local officials and dozens of schoolchildren under the George Washington Bridge at the Little Red Lighthouse, as she announced the successful clean-up of over seven miles of public land on the Upper West Side.

On June 22 she was one of the honorees at the annual "VH1 Honors" celebration in Los Angeles. Every year the televised video network honors celebrities who have done outstanding charity work. Bette was honored for her long-time charity work with AIDS-related causes and for her environmental clean-up campaign.

On December 22, Bette's beachfront house, which she owned on the Hawaiian island of Kauai, was destroyed in a fire. She was not in the house at the time. The cause of the fire was officially listed as having been started by arson.

For Bette's next film role, she was one of the stars of the 1995 box-office hit *Get Shorty.* The film tells the story of a gangster, Chili Palmer (John Travolta), who leaves Miami to collect an outstanding debt in Hollywood. In the process, he teams up with a grade "B" film director and goes into the movie business. The self-absorbed actor they want to land to give their film prestige is Martin Weir (Danny DeVito), whose bio-pic of Napoleon is a current hit. Dennis Farina is wildly comic as bumbling mobster Ray "Bones" Barboni. The movie is filled with thugs, guns, and the outlandish doings of several actors—billed and unbilled.

Bette plays Doris, a not-so-bereaved widow. In her first scene, Bette comically throws her body at director Harry Zimm (Gene Hackman). In a surprise visit, she shows up in a faux fur coat and makes a pass at him. Thinking she has come to his Hollywood apartment to grieve the death of her dear departed husband, Murray, Harry watches in awe as Doris opens up her fur coat to reveal herself in sexy lingerie.

When Harry begins to eulogize Murray's talent as a screenplay writer, Doris snaps back, "What he was, was a 'hack.' He couldn't get a job working for anyone but you." When Harry attempts to deflect her sexual advances, she reaches down to his crotch and reports, "You seem to feel fine about it."

And what about poor dear departed Murray? Hackman inquires. "Murray's dead," says a nonplused Bette.

Her second scene comes in the hospital where Harry is being treated. It seems that he has had a wrangle with someone to whom he owed money. Showing up in the hospital with Chili and Karen (Rene Russo), Doris is especially friendly with a pair of hunky cops she passes in the hallway. "Goodnight, Todd. Goodnight, Louis," she says as they walk by her.

Although Bette doesn't have any onscreen scenes with her, Linda Hart has a prominent part in *Get Shorty*. She plays the wife of a bungling embezzler who has faked his own death and collected on the insurance policy.

Bette was in another hit film, and the reviews for *Get Shorty* were incredibly strong. According to Michael Wilmington in the *Chicago Tribune*, "*Get Shorty* is one of the sharper, funnier, better-cast, better-written movies around . . . with unbilled actors like Harvey Keitel, Penny Marshall, and Bette Midler" (161). And Janet Maslin in the *New York Times* especially loved "a quick cameo from Bette Midler as one very merry widow" (162).

Also in 1995, Bette Midler released her final album for Atlantic Records, *Bette of Roses*. Bette and her long-time producer Arif Mardin decided that it was time for a musical departure for Miss M. *Bette of Roses* has the distinction of being the first all love ballad album of her career. Furthermore, it contained no jazz songs, no '40s cover tunes, no rock & roll, and no girl group camping.

Explaining her musical vision for *Bette of Roses*, the diva claimed, "The songs are nonjudgmental. I'll stand-by-you types of songs. They're very upbeat, with sweet, positive messages, and the production is very soothing and comforting. In other words: Mom" (160).

Said Arif Mardin at the time, "Bette's voice has improved tremendously. She has a beautifully controlled two-octave range" (160). Indeed, Bette's voice and her range isso much wider on *Bette of Roses* than on any of her previous recordings.

Midler explained at the time, "When I was doing *Gypsy*, I found a singing teacher, Marge Rivinston, who took my voice out of my throat, and put it in my head. She helped me get a new set of vocal abilities that allowed me to choose songs I would never sing before, because I couldn't hit the notes without screeching. I'm not going to say I'm Maria

Callas or anything, but I have made terrific strides. I'm not going to stop until I'm a great singer" (160).

With regard to the dozen songs that they recorded for *Bette of Roses,* Mardin said, "We went through about 50 songs, selecting around 30 of them and going into the studio with just a keyboard player. Out of these we chose 11 for the album plus one for the B side of a single. When Bette sings a song, she lives it. There is always the question of who is singing, this extra investigation into the character in the song" (160).

Bette of Roses created no big hits, and it wasn't everyone's cup of tea. But there is no denying that it is the most focused album she has ever recorded. Anyone who was expecting her alter ego of the Divine Miss M to be anywhere present was sadly disappointed. In that way, *Bette of Roses* struck Midler fans as either a "dream" or a "dud."

First of all, Bette's recording of "To Deserve You" is perhaps—technically—the best song she has ever recorded in her career. In terms of emotionally connecting with her lyrics and really singing, the intensely yearning "To Deserve You" is an undeniable Midler masterpiece. She pours her heart into this song, and she commands your attention with her performance. Another, more subtle classic is the slightly bluesy "To Comfort You," which features Ula Hedwig in the background.

The album opens with this collection's most whimsical song, Cheryl Wheeler's "I Know This Town," which finds Midler singing as a little girl showing a stranger around her hometown.

Showing off the newfound upper register of her voice to full advantage, she sings with herself on multilayered tracks, singing high against her lower voice, turning "The Last Time" into a multi-octave power ballad. Playing on the title of the album, Bette laments about wasted years and wasted tears on this perfect and simple ballad.

The album ends with a bit of the autobiographical pining of a "baby boomer" on "I Believe in You." In the song, Midler sings of the '60s, the Beatles, Häagen Dazs ice cream, and Johnny Carson. It seems custom-fitted to her personality and her own personal perspective.

While the lesser songs on this album emerge as "merely pleasant," the aforementioned high points ultimately buoy the results of this album. *Bette of Roses* has the distinction of being her first album to pick one single mode—in this case, contemporary ballads, some happy and some sad—and adhere to it end to end. Unlike Bette's other releases, *Bette of Roses* is the kind of album that requires several listenings to fully appreciate. For one album, and one album only, it was "Midler light!"

Howard Cohen, in the *Miami Herald*, claimed, "Bette Midler's first album in five years is one of the summer's pleasant surprises. . . . seldom has Midler been so willing to use her full vocal range. . . . *Bette of Roses* isn't perfect. Midler's good-natured vulgarity and delightful brassiness of the olden days are missing . . . and there are too many ballads. But overall, this is the best Bette in some time" (163). And Stephen Holden, in the *New York Times*, remained noncommittal when he wrote, "Ms. Midler's three biggest hit records, 'The Rose,' 'The Wind beneath My Wings' and 'From a Distance,' have all been songs that played on [the] heartstrings. This more serious side dominates *Bette of Roses* . . . made up entirely of contemporary pop ballads, it dispenses completely with the sort of camp nostalgia favored by the Divine Miss M" (160).

In America, the album reached a peak position of Number 45 on the *Billboard* charts. In the U.K., it made it to Number 55. One single, the dramatic "To Deserve You," was released. The cassette single version of "To Deserve You" also featured the rare bonus cut "Up! Up! Up!" which she had recorded with the Manhattan Transfer. There was a CD single version, as well as several dance remixes, of the song. Although it didn't become a hit-making blockbuster of an album, it became known as Bette Midler's "all-ballad" disc, and it steadily sold. In January of 1996 it was certified Gold, and by 2002 it had gone Platinum in the United States.

In 1995, in Australia, a version of *Experience the Divine: Bette Midler's Greatest Hits* was issued with four more "bonus" cuts missing from the American version of the album. The album begins with one of the fantastic remixes of "To Deserve You," and the last cut on the album is the album version of the same song. From the *No Frills* album came "Beast of Burden" and "My Favorite Waste of Time." This eighteen-cut Australian version of the "best of" Bette LP gives an even more rounded and varied sampling of the Divine Miss M's singing talents and more fully spans her entire Atlantic recording career.

As she released *Bette of Roses* in 1995, Bette stopped to look around at the new crop of female singers she was now competing with—both in the record stores and on the airwaves. "The standard of musicianly singing has gone crazy with the Whitney Houstons and Mariah Careys, who have really upped the ante," proclaimed Midler. "Then there's k.d. lang. Oh my God, what a voice! And she has this wonderfully sophisticated sensibility. I think Annie Lennox makes great records. And I have every Nina Simone record ever made. To me, she is like a national treasure" (160). Well, the Modest Miss Midler, you ain't so bad yourself!

For Bette, this was a new era of change. Her work on the film *Hocus Pocus* ended her long streak of working exclusively for Disney. Both *Gypsy* and *Get Shorty* were done for other motion picture companies. From this point forward, Bette was no longer obligated to have her All Girls Productions distributed by Disney either. In 1995 Midler told the *New York Times*, "I had a lot of fun at Disney for the first five pictures. But it got to a point where they wanted to do pictures with their own stamp and didn't want to hire outside writers. They wanted to have their own people, who worked for their prices, reporting to them. That's when things got dicey. And I had a big setback with *For the Boys*. Although I know privately what went wrong, I have no desire to point fingers. I was handsomely paid and did the best work I could, and people chose not to go to it. What can you do? You can't put a gun to people's heads and force them to go to your movie" (160).

Bette Midler claimed in 1995 that she had attained a new level of self-confidence. According to her, "It came after *For the Boys*. We worked like dogs on that and tried so hard. We had a great idea, but we were thwarted every step of the way. When you put that much passion into something and it doesn't work out, sometimes you think it's best not to care quite that much, because the disappointment is so painful. I also think that age has had a lot to do with it. You see the way the world works, and you cannot change the world. It has its own tempo and its own speed and its own motivations. You keep on doing what you do for the people who love what you do" (160).

Well, Bette Midler has never been one to sit still for long. Nor has she been one to be idle and rest on her laurels (or her assets . . . or her ass). Having again revitalized her career with such hits as her incredibly appealing film *Gypsy*, the *Bette of Roses* album, and her hugely popular concert touring, the indefatigable Miss M was about launch onto still another career peak.

FIRST WIVES CLUB

The year 1996 found Bette Midler making the rounds of the TV talk-shows and specials to promote her *Bette of Roses* album. On February 13 she was a guest on *The Late Show with David Letterman.* And Bette even went a little bit country, when she appeared on the CBS-TV special *Wynonna Revelations,* starring Wynonna Judd.

On June 11, the Record Industry Association of America (RIAA) officially certified Bette's *Experience the Divine* album as Platinum. And on June 21, the soundtrack for the Disney animated film *The Hunchback of Notre Dame* was released. On the album, Bette contributed the song "Go Help the Outcasts." All of this activity helped set the stage for her next cinematic adventure—and what an adventure it was to be!

In the past, Bette had a great track record for starring in film hits opposite other strong women, as she had with *Outrageous Fortune, Big Business,* and *Beaches.* Why not cast her with not one, but two equally dynamic female stars? That's exactly what happened with her next screen outing, which became her first number one box-office hit. Teamed with both Goldie Hawn and Diane Keaton, Midler had the biggest film hit of her career: *First Wives Club.*

According to her, it wasn't always a picnic: "That was a really tough movie to make. The script wasn't solid at the beginning. It was the blizzard of '96. There was no lunch. You had to go get your lunch. I mean, it was tough. But I must say, I loved the girls" (164).

First Wives Club opens with a flashback to Middlebury College and four girls from the graduating class of 1969. The quartet of twenty-something college girls is shown graduating with hopes and aspirations, and thanks to one of them—Cynthia—they each have a gift of matching pearl necklaces, for remembrance.

Cut: to the present. An adult Cynthia (Stockard Channing) is seen contemplating suicide by jumping from the balcony of her Central Park–adjacent apartment. Right before she takes the leap of no-faith, she pens notes to her three college buddies to say "good-bye," which she asks her maid to mail for her. In these notes she asks them to actively rekindle and maintain their once-strong friendship. This becomes the reason for the bond between Midler, Hawn, and Keaton, members of a trio who have long ago grown apart from one another.

Annie (Keaton) has a teenage lesbian daughter, and she has broken up with her husband, Aaron (Stephen Collins)—but she still occasionally sleeps with him and lives with the hope that he will eventually return to her. She is the most timorous of the threesome.

Elise (Goldie Hawn) is a Grade B movie star who is obsessed with her youth and her looks and is hooked on plastic surgery. Her funniest scene is in the office of her doctor (Rob Reiner). When she decides she needs her face surgically freshened up, she commands to him, "I want to be young: SCIENCE FICTION YOUNG." When he tells her she is being absurd, she explains to him that there are only three ages in the life of an actress: "Babe, district attorney, and *Driving Miss Daisy!*" She insists on collagen injections on her already-accentuated lips. She instructs the doctor as to the degree of inflated lips she wants: "I want Tina Turner! I want Jagger!"

Hawn's husband, Bill (Victor Garber), is now suing her for half of her production company and assets from the films in which she has starred. His new girlfriend is a beautiful airhead, Phoebe (Elizabeth Berkley), who hopes to become an actress of the magnitude of Elise. Fresh from her starring turn in *Showgirls,* Berkley plays Phoebe with all of the common sense of a Hostess Twinkie.

Bette is Brenda, the brassy but self-suffering member of the triumvirate. At the start of the film she is dressed a bit on the dowdy side, and she is slightly chunky, weight-wise. Her philandering husband, Morty (Dan Hedaya), sells home appliances via awful TV ads in which he stars. The new, younger girlfriend he has traded Brenda for, Shelley, is comically portrayed by a ditzy Sarah Jessica Parker.

Over a girls-only postfuneral lunch, the three women's personalities are defined by the cocktails they order. Keaton has a Virgin Mary, Midler has a Bloody Mary, and Hawn orders vodka on the rocks. In this amusing scene, Bette gets drunk and pressures Goldie about the surreal plastic surgery that is before their eyes.

Hawn's lips are so inhumanly inflated that she can't even light a cigarette she holds in her comically bizarre mouth. With regard to the plastic surgery, Bette pries, "Did you have a little bit, or the full enchilada?" Interestingly enough, in the original film trailer (available on the DVD), the line is "Did you have a little bit, or the full IVANA?"

Bette has some great lines in *First Wives Club*. She describes the emotional valley that has grown between her and Morty. "He starts working out," she explains to her girlfriends. "He grows a mustache, he gets an earring. I said, 'Morty, Morty! What are you a pirate? What's next? A parrot?'"

Dissing Hawn's youth-chasing plastic surgery, Midler proclaims, "And, thanks to Cher's pioneering efforts, you still haven't hit puberty!"

When Bette lights into Goldie about her excessive liquor consumption, Goldie looks down at a garbage pail filled with empty fifths of booze. "I had guests!" claims Goldie in her own defense. Without missing a beat, Bette fires back, "Who? Guns & Roses?"

Naturally, the trio of dumped wives ends up turning the tables on their unfaithful ex-husbands, getting even where it really hurts—the wallet. By the end of the film Goldie regains her perspective, Diane gains her self-confidence, and Bette loses a significant amount of weight—and looks fabulous for the transformation. By the end the triumphant trio emerges from a cocktail party singing an anthem-like version of the Leslie Gore hit "You Don't Own Me."

The film is also filled with a delicious cast full of supporting characters and glittering cameo appearances. Bronson Pinchot is a hoot as an affected gay designer; Maggie Smith is Grunella, a wealthy matron who bonds with the girls; Eileen Heckert is Annie's dry-humored mother; and Heather Locklear is the mistress of Cynthia's widower. The real-life Ivana Trump makes a brief appearance, as do former New York City mayor Ed Koch, comedian Lia DeLaria, Kathie Lee Gifford, and famed feminist Gloria Steinem.

When *First Wives Club* was released, it drew only rave reviews, and audiences loved it. *Rolling Stone* said, "This witty revenge romp is sinfully satisfying. . . . Irresistible fun . . ." *Variety* agreed, "Midler, Hawn and Keaton are a refreshingly cohesive comedy combo with that inde-finable thing known as screen chemistry" (98). *Leonard Martin's Movie & Video Guide* rated it as "entertaining, thanks to three lively stars and an impressive supporting cast" (128).

In *Entertainment Weekly,* Owen Gleiberman wrote of *First Wives Club,* "Paced like a Chris Farley movie and photographed like a den-ture-cream commercial, the *First Wives Club* is the sort of overbright plastic-package comedy that tends to live or die by its jokes. . . . Goldie Hawn, Bette Midler, and Diane Keaton play Manhattanites in their mid-forties who've all been abandoned by their husbands. . . . As soon as you see the actresses bite into their roles, though, you realize that, for them, the film is hitting much closer to home. Who, after all, knows the agony of being passed over for youthful flesh better than Hollywood leading ladies? . . . Hawn, Midler and Keaton luxuriate in the pleasure of their own haughtiness, their proud-to-be-a-bitch venom. . . . Midler, as a housewife too full of rage to worry about vanity . . . If black-widow spiders wrote punchlines, they'd sound like that" (165).

Great pacing, funny one-liners, and excellent performances all around, *First Wives Club* was the biggest box-office smash of Bette Midler's entire career. It was such a widespread hit that it made over $100 million in its theatrical run. According to Bette, "It was incredibly popular. And it really made us think . . . made me think, anyway, how rewarding it is when people love what it is that you do" (164).

In her *Diva Las Vegas* TV special, she later sang about her success in *First Wives Club*—to the tune of "Everything's Coming Up Roses": "One hundred million ain't so hard to do. Honey, everything's coming up grosses for me, so fuck you!"

Richard Corliss, in *Time* magazine, claimed, "*First Wives* is a hit. It has three stars playing to their strengths: Midler the canny yenta, Kea-ton mining lodes of pruney anguish, Hawn a glorious hoot encased in her collagenized lips and sprawling ego . . . Bette Midler, the designated frump in *The First Wives Club,* stares at Goldie Hawn's body with mixed feelings: envy for it's sleekness and disdain for the work needed to maintain it" (166).

In a cover story about the subject matter addressed in the film, writer Elizabeth Gleick, in *Time* magazine, reported, "Women scorned, women afraid of being scorned—and some curious men taken along for the ride—are helping *The First Wives Club* break records. Its $18.9 million opening weekend was the highest ever for a so-called women's film and captured more than one-third of the movie-going market from competition such as Bruce Willis's *Last Man Standing*. The characters played by Goldie Hawn, Diane Keaton, and Bette Midler are like the furies crossed with the Three Stooges—college friends spurned by their husbands in middle age who plan a madcap payback" (167).

Indeed, *The First Wives Club* became the third major film of the 1990s in which women sought and successfully got revenge upon their philandering men. It joined the ranks of enormous box-office popularity alongside the decade's other two top females-even-the-score flicks: *Thelma and Louise* and *Waiting to Exhale.*

One of the most significant things that happened to Bette during the filming of *First Wives Club* was her fiftieth birthday. According to her at the time, "I looked back and I said, 'What happened?' I realized that I had reached a certain point. I have my husband, my daughter, and a pretty good career. I felt that I didn't have to keep doing it in the same way, because I did it. The compulsion is not the same. I'm not so afraid that it's going to be taken away from me. I don't feel like I am on a downward slope. I just feel like I am not so crazed" (17).

This became a time for her to access her life to date. She surveyed not only her career, but her personal life as well. With regard to her charitable nature, at the time she commented, "I never knew my impulse toward goodness was so serious. I think it comes from my parents. They gave to charity, and I remember them saying that no matter how bad things were for us, there were always people who had less. I have confidence that all this stuff will come back to Sophie, because it came back to me" (17).

Speaking of her vanity as a "screen goddess," Midler downplayed the beauty aspect of it. "People don't expect me to be a goddess in the way that Michelle Pfeiffer is considered a goddess. I have more leeway than she does. I never considered myself an artist. Whatever I was doing, I was trying to do it. Singing, acting, dancing. But the learning, that's been the one thing that has been my total entertainment my whole life," she claimed (17).

And then there was her day-to-day role as "domestic goddess." Said Bette, "In a funny way, I'm just a big housekeeper. Martha Stewart has it to a much worse degree, but it's definitely a compulsion. It's my dictator gene—'Let's all live beautiful!'" (17).

While *First Wives Club* was still in the theaters, Midler set off on a short concert tour, which concluded on December 23 and 24 at Universal Amphitheatre in Los Angeles. It was this show that was to become her next TV special. On January 9 and 10, 1997, Bette Midler headlined at the MGM Grand Garden. Those concerts were taped and on January 18 were broadcast on HBO, gloriously uncensored as *Diva Las Vegas*.

Said Miss M of the special: "It's a beautiful show. It's got something for everybody. It's two hours, and it's nonstop, and I'm in all of it. God only knows what's going to happen. God only knows" (164).

Everything about *Diva Las Vegas* was grand, lush, and excitingly fun. Four showgirls with angel wings blowing trumpets to herald the arrival of Bette—who makes her entrance singing "Friends" hovering twenty feet above the stage, from a throne in a cloud. After she descends to the stage, she sings—and raps—a new autobiographical monologue of a song, called "I Look Good." And she does indeed. Or, better yet, as she so eloquently put it, "So rich, so cheap!"

After an energetic performance of Cole Porter's "Miss Otis Regrets," Bette grouses of the venue du jour: "Oy Vegas." Complaining of her own world-weariness, she proclaims, "Sometimes my brain goes on a CD shuffle. You know, when you put a whole bunch of CDs in the machine and press 'random'—any old thing comes up."

She showed off her jazzy side with "Spring Can Really Hang You Up the Most," and she showed off her love ballad side with "Bed of Roses."

One of the funniest moments in this special found her singing an ode to her own sudden box-office success in *First Wives Club*. Lyrically congratulating herself, she sang to the tune of "Everything's Coming Up Roses"—"I'm in a hit! A big fucking hit, BABY!"

Explaining the sudden success of her latest film, she said, "I've never been a first wife before. I was the other woman once or twice." This was her lead into her solo version of "You Don't Own Me" from *First Wives Club*.

She goes off on a whole '70s bent, encompassing the Hues Corporation's hit "Rock the Boat." Continuing on her '70s trip, she made a joke about once knocking over a whole tray of cocaine, only to watch an entire room full of people drop to their knees and try to snort it out of the shag carpeting. And speaking of memories of the "me" decade, her own song "The Rose"—released on album in 1979—still manages to bring down the house

Midshow, she presented her new risqué stripper's segment—her ode to burlesque. As she proclaims, "It was Vaudeville with an X rating"

This leads to Midler and the Harlettes reviving her song "Pretty Legs and Great Big Knockers."

When it comes to "off color," Bette's Sophie Tucker jokes couldn't be far behind. They haven't become any less titillating or decidedly blue: "My boyfriend Ernie said to me, 'Soph—if you could learn to cook, we could fire the chef.' I said, 'Ernie, if you could learn to fuck, we could fire the chauffeur!'"

To turn the spotlight to her recent smash portrayal of Mama Rose in the film *Gypsy*, she performed a passionate version of the show-stopping "Rose's Turn."

Bringing to the stage the one and only Dolores DeLago, Bette restaged "Drinking Again"—which here is sung in a karaoke bar. However, when she emerges from behind the bar, it is "Dolores" in her mermaid tail, erupting into "MacArthur Park." It seems that Dolores has been active since last she hit the stage. She now operates the merchandise hotline 1-800-DOLORES, which she uses to sell her own self-help program, "12 Strokes to Satisfaction."

With the Harlettes as the mermaid fin–wearing, wheelchair-bound DeLago Sisters, Bette and her girls launch into Blondie's disco hit "Call Me." "Stop the insanity!" shouts Bette at the top of her lungs. However, as every good Bette fan knows, when it comes to Midler, the insanity has just begun.

They sang "Boogie Woogie Bugle Boy" in fishtails and performed their Hawaiian ball swinging routine to the Village People's "In the Navy" The half-fish DeLago quartet also swung into "The Greatest Love of All" and finally "New York, New York," with top hats and spinning about the stage in their electronic wheelchairs.

Naturally, Bette's acidic comments throughout the show are classic. Speaking of Joan Rivers selling jewelry on the Home Shopping Network, Midler comically blasts, "Who's buying all that shit?!"

"Ukelele Lady," a 1930s song from Hawaii, was turned into a production number, featuring barefoot Bette in a sarong, singing the song of her native state, with an ensemble. Amid the Hawaiian beach fashion–clad performers was Bette's teenage daughter, Sophie, also singing and playing a ukelele.

Bette, in a spangled brown gown, was forcefully dramatic on the power ballads, including a heartfelt version of "From a Distance."

She also sang "Do You Want to Dance?" and a very effectively torchy

"To Comfort You," which was one of the most memorable perform-ances in a show filled with exciting high points.

For the concert's end, Bette saved "Stay with Me," "Wind beneath My Wings," and a beautiful version of "The Glory of Love" from *For the Boys*. She looked great and sounded great throughout. It was a fresh new twist on the constantly evolving *Bette Midler Show*. A well-balanced evening that combined all of Bette's many musical facets, *Diva Las Vegas* was a huge critical and ratings success.

She rounded up the usual cast of characters for backstage roles as well. The choreography was handled again by Toni Basil, and the show's special musical material was composed and arranged by Marc Shaiman.

Bette's latest special was so popular, and so well-produced, that it became her most highly saluted television outing yet. On September 14, 1997, *Diva Las Vegas* was awarded an Emmy as the year's Best Individual Performance: Variety or Music Program. November 15, at the Cable ACE Awards, held at the Wiltern Theater in Los Angeles, *Diva Las Vegas* won the award as the Best Music Special or Series.

In Midler's film career, *First Wives Club* was a tough act to follow. It was such a huge success that she kept expecting the studio to phone her and propose a *First Wives Club 2*–styled sequel for Hawn, Keaton, and Midler. According to Bette, the studio could never seem to get it to-gether. Frustrated that no one seemed to be offering her a film role, she simply produced and starred in her own vehicle. She chose the broad comedy *That Old Feeling*.

Speaking of *That Old Feeling*, Midler said at the time, "It's funny. It's really funny. It has a lot. . . . it has everything. It has a lot of heart. It has Dennis Farina in it, who is a terrific comic. It was directed by Carl Reiner. We have really high hopes for it, because we know they [audiences] want to laugh. And, there's a lot of laughs" (164).

Bette not only starred in *That Old Feeling*, she also produced it with Bonnie Bruckheimer and All Girls Productions. *That Old Feeling* gave Bette the chance to create the kind of screwball comedy that she always enjoyed. Directed by Carl Reiner (*The Man with Two Brains*, *All of Me*), the film is lighthearted and entertaining and gives Bette some inspired moments on the screen.

That Old Feeling opens with a glittering view of lower Manhattan, with the World Trade Center prominently shown. Then it cuts to a young couple getting engaged in a fancy restaurant. Discussion of wed-ding plans by the betrothed couple—Molly (Paula Marshall) and Jamie

(Keith Marks)—finds the young girl explaining worriedly that her parents hate each other so much that she is scared to have them in the same room. Naturally, with a build-up like that, it is Bette who plays her difficult, volatile, and eccentric mother, Lillian. It also seems that the mother of the bride-to-be is a famous actress, with an immense ego and sharp wit. She is so famous and has such a devoted legion of fans that she is chased by Joey (Danny Nucci), a relentlessly stalking member of the paparazzi.

Having her own company produce the film assured Bette that she would look great in every shot and that she would be provided with juicy one-liners throughout the film—and she launches into them with gusto. Every second she is on the screen, she sizzles with comic energy. Reapplying her makeup for the big wedding, Bette quips to her new husband, Alan (David Rasche), "I'm not neurotic. I'm just a bitch—all right?"

Lillian hasn't spoken to her ex-husband, Dan (Dennis Farina), in fourteen years. When they meet again at their daughter's wedding, predictably they erupt into a screaming cat fight mid-wedding. However, while arguing, Lillian and Dan rediscover the passion that brought them together originally. A physical battle leads to humping on the hood of a limo—and finally sex in a red sports car.

Directed by Carl Reiner, with a screenplay by Leslie Dixon—who had written *Outrageous Fortune*—*That Old Feeling* is a comedy in the tradition of the '30s and '40s screwball classics, and the tone of the film is lighthearted fun. Although the plot of the film starts to lose momentum in the middle, it certainly has its share of comic moments.

Sneaking out on their spouses for "coffee," Dan and Lilly start acting like teenagers tiptoeing off for sexual encounters—to the chagrin of their daughter. Along the way, Dan's confused second wife, Rowena (Gail O'Grady), seems emotionally oblivious to the proceedings. In a sentimental scene in a hotel lounge, Bette sings a beautiful ballad, "Somewhere along the Way" to Farina—which also appears on the soundtrack album. Midler and Farina are a hysterical match on camera, but when the supporting cast is called upon to carry several scenes, the action sags and the laughs cease.

As the farcical film progresses, the other cast members also switch romantic partners, and Midler and Farina begin battling again. As frustrated Lilly, Bette has a humorous food-gorging scene. And in one funny segment, the sleazy paparazzi photographer Joey shows off his file of Midler pix, including a humorously weight-enhanced fat shot of her.

The final sequence—a comic clash at an airport terminal—is cute in sort of a "drawing room comedy" way, with Midler and Farina using their daughter's honeymoon plane tickets to fly away together. *That Old Feeling* comically crackles in several spots. And when Bette is on camera, she is witty, sharp, and laugh-out-loud funny.

When the film was released, the critics seemed to love it. The *New York Times* called it "[A] raucous, high-spirited romantic comedy. . . . Mr. Reiner and Ms. Dixon pack a lot of comic smarts into *That Old Feeling* and their expert cast makes the most of it . . ." (98). *USA Today* said, "Bette Midler flings the usual zingers with fang-baring zeal in a part that plays to her brassy strengths" (98). And in the *Los Angeles Times,* John Anderson claimed, "She's seldom been more Bette than as the brassy, sassy, and lethally theatrical Lilly of *That Old Feeling*, a schticky situational comedy that pays tribute to director Carl Reiner's roots in television while giving some well deserved exposure to a lot of talented people. *That Old Feeling* is a very traditional comedy in a surreal sort of way. [It] is generally fun, thanks to old pros Midler and Farina" (168).

A big and cartoonish film, *That Old Feeling* was a fun screen romp for Midler that seemed to come and go in and out of theaters with little fanfare. It was originally supposed to be released on Valentine's Day, but was later rescheduled for April 1997. The first weekend, the film grossed less than $5 million at the box office and dropped off from there.

On April 30, Bette showed up as a guest star on the Fran Drescher hit comedy *The Nanny*. Again she was dabbling in the TV sitcom arena and obviously testing the waters for future projects.

Along with contributions from two of her prime rivals—Paul Simon and Madonna—Bette in 1997 was heard on the charity album *Carnival! The Rainforest Foundation Tribute.* Bette contributed the song "Sweet and Low" to the LP. It was a song that Midler later explained had special meaning for her, as it was one of her mother's favorites.

On February 6, 1998, Bette performed in New York City at the Theater at Madison Square Garden to launch the National Basketball Association's All-Star Weekend. As off-the-wall as that sounds, there were other rumors afoot that spring. One of them claimed that Midler was considering doing a staged version of the Bette Davis/Joan Crawford horror film *Whatever Happened to Baby Jane?* Who would they have cast to play "Blanche" to her "Jane"? Cher? However, it didn't materialize that season.

What did materialize, however, was her first album for Warner Brothers Records. And it was well worth the wait! Entitled *Bathhouse Betty,* it was the best Midler album since the 1970s. For all of the Midler fans who were waiting for a worthy update of her classic, multi-mood Divine Miss M formula, this was it.

According to Bette, she arrived at the formula of *Bathhouse Betty* from the feedback she received from her last album, *Bette of Roses:* "With the last record, I had friends calling me up saying, 'There's no variety.' Now they say there's too much. The only thing I don't do in this record is sing in Chinese. I want to do what I want to do. I don't want to do what the demographics tell me to do. I'm too old for those games" (169).

To assure the most variety possible, she chose to open up the producing tasks to a new breed of people—and just for safety's sake, to include a couple of cuts by her long-time producer Arif Mardin. Among the new producers she worked with on *Bathhouse Betty* were Ted Templeman, Brock Walsh, David Foster, Chuckii Booker, and her own musical director Marc Shaiman.

According to Bette, the album's peculiar title actually came from the words a crazed fan shouted outside her Manhattan home. "He was outside my house screaming, 'Bathhouse Betty! Bathhouse Betty!' It's funny—I'm the only person who's ever been stalked who was listening. Now there's going to be a million guys coming out of the woodwork, saying, 'It was me! It was me!'" (169).

A wildly mood-swinging album, it opens with the touching Leonard Cohen/Bill Elliott/Jennifer Warnes ballad "Song of Bernadette." It is based on the legend of Bernadette, who once saw the "queen of Heaven," only to have no one believe her story. However, this spiritually driven song has such an optimistic message of faith in love that it comes across as beautifully inspirational.

It was produced by Ted Templeman, who was responsible for all of the great Doobie Brothers albums on Warner Brothers Records in the 1970s—like *Livin' on the Fault Line* and *Takin' It to the Streets.* The background singers on this cut include the longest-running Harlette—Ula Hedwig—and Patty D'Arcy, who was featured in *For the Boys.*

Not lingering in any one mood or mode for more than five minutes;

the next song jacks up the beat, as Bette Midler's first foray into danceable rap. If ever there was a song that was 100 percent ideal for Miss M, this is it: "I'm Beautiful." Loaded with full-of-herself chorus lines like, "I'm beautiful, DAMN IT!" this was the ultimate sign that the Divine Miss M was truly back in full form.

Written by Brinsley Evans and produced by Arif Mardin, this snappy, bitchy rap proved once and for all that Midler was at the top of her game. As she explained it at the time, "I rap lite on 'I'm Beautiful.' I have an excellent sense of time. I was thinking of taking up the bass or drums because I like rhythm. The problem is, I have nothing to say. What am I going to rap about? My hairdresser? My nails? Actually, that could be fun!" (169).

And speaking of hairdressers, that's exactly how she came upon the song to begin with. "My hairdresser tells me what's happening," she admitted. "He brought me 'I'm Beautiful,' I was determined to do it because I really liked the message. Did you know that's Zero Mostel ['sampled' on the song] saying, 'Flaunt it, baby,' from *The Producers*?" (169). The song is laugh-out-loud funny to hear, and Midler clearly projects the joyousness of singing such a fun message of self-deification.

After the goofiness of "I'm Beautiful" comes one of the most touching ballads that Bette has ever sung. "Lullaby in Blue" is about a mother trying to explain her life to the daughter she gave up for adoption several years previously. Sad, bittersweet, touching, and incredibly heartfelt, it is the album's "Hello in There"–styled moment. Written by Brock Walsh and Adam Cohen, and produced by Walsh, "Lullaby in Blue" is perfect for Midler.

Spotlighting her Hawaiian roots, Midler presents a song that was written in 1925 about the fiftieth state, "Ukulele Lady." She had never recorded a Hawaiian-styled ode, and the song conjures up images of grass skirts, flower leis, and brassieres fashioned of coconut shells.

Mark Shaiman's production contribution on *Bathhouse Betty* comes on "I'm Hip," which reprises the formula of "I'm Beautiful" in a '50s jazz mode. With Midler comically singing that she'll do anything to be hip—from narcotics, to meditation and macrobiotics.

One of the 1930s chestnuts that Midler sang back in the days at the Continental Baths was "I Sold My Heart to the Junkman." It was revived in the 1960s when it was recorded by Patti LaBelle & the Bluebelles. Bette was originally going to use this song on the opening of her *Live at Last* album, but changed her mind and did "Oh My, My" instead. It was worth the wait for this one, presented by her like a song suited for a singer in a smoke-filled bar and lounge.

A big and bawdy performance is what Bette gave to the 1955 song "One Monkey Don't Stop No Show." Not to be confused with the hit of the same name by the 1970s trio, Honey Cone, this one has Bette—in the context of the song—getting rid of her lover at three o'clock and having a new man by her side by the time the clock struck "four." A jazzy Ted Templeman production, this song is as big and brassy as Midler herself and shows off her full talents—complete with a wailing horn section.

Other excursions into the bizarre find Bette singing about the life of a boxer on the song "Boxing" and about the relationship between shoe size and penis size on the snappy "Big Socks." "Boxing," which was a Ben Folds Five song, finds Midler singing of her career in the ring. It didn't necessarily suit her, subject-wise, but it was fun to hear her present an off-the-wall story song. "Big Socks" is a lunatic upbeat song in which Bette pokes air in the supposed relationship between "big feet" and "big meat." Unabashedly singing about male sexual organ dimension, Midler tells an underendowed suitor to take his equipment "back to the kiddie section." Only Bette could sing this kind of quirky material with a straight face and musically pull it off.

She finishes off the album in ballad mode with "That's How Love Moves," "My One True Friend," and "Laughing Matters." The best of the three here is "My One True Friend," which was written by a stellar trio of true songwriting pros: David Foster, Carole King, and Carole Bayer Sager. The sentimental number about friendship and devotion "My One True Friend" was used as the theme song for the 1998 Merle Streep film *One True Thing*.

In fact, the whole film heavily features songs by Bette Midler. In addition to hearing "Do You Wanna Dance?" and "Friends" on the soundtrack, Miss M also contributed the brand-new "My One True Friend." According to Bette, "Meryl Streep called me up and said, 'I'm doing this movie, and we want to use your songs.' What do you say to that? 'No?' 'I'll get back to you'? 'My people will call your people'? You say, 'Of course, Meryl! How're things? How're the kids? Of course!'" (169).

The *Bathhouse Betty* album was a huge hit with Midler fans. It really marked a return to the kind of album that first established her recording career. The heavily varied material on this disc and the sincerely devoted performances by Bette make this one of her all-time great albums. Furthermore, the Japanese version of this album features a bonus track, called "Happiness."

The song "I'm Beautiful" was a natural selection for a single—and what a huge hit single it became. Remixed in seven different varieties, and put on a special CD single, "I'm Beautiful" became Midler's first Number 1 single on the Dance charts. Not only was she beautiful; she had a hit, DAMN IT!

Trying to get herself—and her music—some radio air time alongside a whole new generation of stars was proving daunting for Midler. She observed during this era, "People past a certain age have been shut out of the business. I remember when rock came in, Benny Goodman and Frank Sinatra couldn't get on the radio. It must've been painful. Now I know what it feels like" (169).

She also claimed at the time that she was already planning her next album. "I want to sing 'Moonlight in Vermont.' I'd like to sing some true Hawaiian music, and I would like to sing 'I like Bananas because They Have No Bones.'" When she was asked if she had any duets she was considering recording, she replied, "Missy Elliott. I like her a lot. She makes me laugh. She's really musical and kinda sorta fearless. I like the way she looks. I like the way she carries herself" (169).

In December of 1998 Bette was busy promoting her *Bathhouse Betty* album, which hit Number 32 on the *Billboard* pop charts in America. The week of the fifth of December in the U.K., her British single "My One True Friend" appeared on the record charts, at Number 58. On December 7, she was seen on the TV special *The Billboard Music Awards,* which was being broadcast live from the MGM Grand Garden in Las Vegas, Nevada. On the show she was seen in another location—via satellite—at the Las Vegas outpost of the Hard Rock Cafe, singing her song "One Monkey Don't Stop No Show," accompanied by the band the Crown Royal Revue.

On December 11, she appeared in New York City at a concert staged by radio station WKTU. The event was billed as "Miracle of 34th Street," as it took place at the Hammerstein Ballroom, just down that street from Macy's department store. Also on the show was the Swedish group Ace of Base, Deborah Cox, and Cher. Cher was in the middle of her massive international come-back tour, with her huge number one hit "Believe."

The divas hadn't appeared on the same bill in years and had long since fallen out of favor with each other. That night Cher was perform-ing three cuts from her *Believe* album. Since several of the songs on the album—particularly, "Believe"—featured audible postproduction spe-cial effects, Cher chose to lip-synch her three songs to her recordings, instead of singing them live. Bette Midler, on the other hand, was going to perform her songs live.

First of all, Cher went onstage before Bette, which Midler took of-fense to, then Cher kept everyone waiting a half-hour while her makeup went through an emergency retouching. Furthermore, Cher forbid any cameras to be used while she sang, in an edict to the press and the public.

Not one to miss a chance to sling a little mud, Midler supposedly snidely said that night: "I'm a star! I'm not someone who used to be famous and is trying to become famous again." The item was first re-ported in the *New York Daily News* and then was picked up and re-peated in *People* magazine. Although *People* carried the disclaimer "Midler reps deny she made that crack," it was perceived as being accu-rately quoted (170). Pass the Meow Mix!

On December 17, 1998, Bette appeared on *Late Night with David Letterman*, to further promote her album *Bathhouse Betty*. The week of January 16, 1999, the RIAA certified *Bathhouse Betty* as having gone Gold in the United States. Viva la Bette!

Midler was on hand at the 1999 edition of the Rock & Roll Hall of Fame presentation, held at the Waldorf Astoria Hotel in New York City. After the induction ceremony, she got up on stage and boogied with the rock & roll class of 1999.

As the Disney Corporation's favorite leading lady, in 1999 Bette made yet another appearance in one of the company's films. This time around, it was in the long-awaited sequel to the company's most famous experimental classic, *Fantasia* (1940).

The original and renown eight-segment film had teamed state-of-the-art animation with classical music to create a timeless gem. With Leopold Stokowski and the Philadelphia Orchestra providing the soundtrack, in 1940 the Disney animators pulled out all the stops to bring them to life with imaginative hand-illustrated screen images. "Dance of the Hours" was presented with hippos and alligators doing a ballet, "Night on Bald Mountain" presented a confrontation between good and evil, and "Tocotta and Fugue" became an abstract visual mon-tage of colors and shapes. However, the best-known segment found

Disney's leading man, Mickey Mouse, mixing with magic on "The Sorcerer's Apprentice." As the hapless apprentice, the heroic rodent battles against endless buckets of water that enchanted brooms carry—causing a massive flood. The original *Fantasia* film had a single narrator, Deems Taylor, who introduced the individual segments.

It took nearly fifty years to mount a sequel, but the new film is a cinematic masterpiece worthy of bearing the name *Fantasia 2000*. In this fresh version, several of the stars, including Steve Martin, Quincy Jones, Penn & Teller, James Earl Jones, Angela Lansbury, and Bette Midler, are on hand to play host to the new classical segments.

Fantasia 2000 includes several classic pieces and some modern masterpieces as well. George Gershwin's "Rhapsody in Blue" here gets a Manhattanite scenario, artistically inspired by famed caricature artist Al Hirschfeld. And the original centerpiece of the original film, "Sorcerer's Apprentice" is again presented here, immaculately restored with eye-popping colors—starring Mickey Mouse, who looks less grainy and more dazzlingly bright than ever before. Although Donald Duck was missing from the 1940 film, he makes a star turn here on the Sir Edward Elgar march: "Pomp & Circumstance—Marches 1, 2, 3 and 4."

Bette is on hand to introduce "The Steadfast Tin Soldier" by Hans Christian Anderson, set to Dmitri Shostakovich's "Piano Concerto No. 2, Allegro Opus 102." In her brief segment, she looks strikingly glamorous in a black dress and a gold lamé shawl. Her hair is still champagne blonde, but she has an orange spotlight on her, so she is photographed in a warm glow on camera.

Standing on a soundstage against a turquoise blue backdrop, she explains on camera about all of the original *Fantasia* ideas that were scrapped along the way to completing this new animated masterpiece. According to Bette, these included Salvador Dali wanting to do a metaphor of life, comparing it to a baseball game; a darkly illustrated version of Wagner's "Ride of the Valkyries"; a bug ballet; a baby ballet; and even a polka.

In this particular Miss M-introduced segment, it is midnight and all of the toys are coming to life. The whirling music box ballerina and one of the small tin soldiers flirt with one another, while the evil jack-in-the-box jealously looks on and plots to get the soldier out of the picture—and right out of the moonlit room's window. The action that unfolds, traces the soldier's daunting path back to defend the ballerina from jack's advances.

Well, Bette had joked for the last fifteen years that she had been primarily working *for* Mickey Mouse. Now, at long last, here is Bette— literally starring with Mickey Mouse and Donald Duck!

The next film Bette was seen in was a satirical comedy called *Jackie's Back*. It was produced for broadcast on the Lifetime Cable Network and it originally aired June 14, 1999.

Jackie's Back is a mock documentary along the lines of comedy classics *Spinal Tap* and *The Rutles*. However, the act that is getting the whole *Behind-the-Music* routine, in this case, is the fictional Jackie Washington. In this full-length film we meet the host of the show-within-a-show: *Portrait of a Diva*, Edward Whatsett St. John (Tim Curry). He proceeds to present Jackie and several of the people from her eventful career and her colorful past.

Jackie is portrayed by one of Bette's former Harlettes, Jenifer Lewis. As another Harlette to find stardom, Lewis has since been one of the stars of such films as *Corrina Corrina, The Preacher's Wife*, and *What's Love Got to Do with It?* Her Jackie is a diva-out-of-control, and she clearly has a ball with this role.

The over-the-top script presents Washington as something of a walking tabloid headline waiting to happen. Among the skeletons from the closet is an examination of Jackie being accused of stabbing her husband in the head with an "Afro pick" haircomb. When the cameras catch up with the ex-husband, his forehead still has the comb's tooth scars in it. The documentary follows Jackie in her path toward a big comeback performance. Some claim she is a legend, others claim she is little more than a "boozing has-been."

A who's who of Hollywood and the music business are featured in the documentary. Either playing roles or playing themselves, celebrities show up discussing Jackie—mostly in a scandalous way. Ricki Lake, Jackie Collins, Grace Slick, Liza Minnelli, and Taylor Dane were among the dozens of cameo appearances in *Jackie's Back*. Mary Wilson of the Supremes is in the film as Jackie's third-grade teacher, Vesta Crotchley. Said Wilson of Jackie: "She had the largest boobs—breasts, I have ever seen on an eight-year-old child."

Her bitter older sister Ethyl (Whoopi Goldberg) complains loudly about how Jackie's career should have been hers. Julie Haggerty, of *Airplane!* fame, plays Pammy Dunbar, a ditzy pitchwoman, selling "Essence of Jackie" hair relaxer with Washington on a TV infomercial gone bad. It is directly followed by country star Dolly Parton complaining on camera that it was "Essence of Jackie" that nearly killed her dog.

And, amidst it all, along comes Bette. Playing herself, she is interviewed on camera and doesn't miss a chance to "dish" legendary soul singer Jackie. She relates a story about how she had to share a dressing room with Jackie at an industry event. Jackie supposedly recoiled at being hugged by Bette. Midler called her a "racist," who thinks that white people all smell like white potato chips. "A fucking nightmare," is how Miss M describes the dressing room debacle. "I was devastated!" she claimed, "I don't smell like white potato chips. I have always prided myself on, on, on, on smelling flowery." According to Bette, the revenge came when she next ran into Jackie. This time it was Washington who was stinking—drunk, that is—"She was reeking of gin!" proclaimed a gloating Midler.

Jackie's Back was directed by Robert Townsend (*The Five Heartbeats, B.A.P.S.*), and the musical director was Marc Shaiman. It was a funny and amusing film, enlivened by Miss M's presence. *Jackie's Back* originally ran on USA Cable network and was later released on DVD (2002).

In her third 1999 big screen appearance, Bette was one of the stars to be interviewed for the real-life video documentary *Get Bruce.* The film was produced and directed by Andrew J. Kuehn; the subject of the 73-minute video portrait was Bette Midler's long-time joke writer Bruce Vilanch. In the two decades since he first worked with Miss M, he had moved from Chicago to Hollywood, where he wrote scripts for Donny & Marie Osmond's 1970s TV series, *The Brady Bunch*'s musical TV specials, and a host of stars in need of carefully tailored jokes for their live acts, movies, or TV show appearances.

Several of the media stars whom Vilanch has closely worked with appear on camera, chatting, reminiscing, and making jokes to and about Vilanch. In addition to Bette Midler, *Get Bruce* also features a glittering cast of subjects, including Raquel Welch, Nathan Lane, Lily Tomlin, Billy Crystal, Whoopi Goldberg, Rosanne, Shirley MacLaine, and Paul Reiser. Even Ann Margaret gets into the act, as she sings the film's theme song, "Get Bruce."

The premise of the movie is that whenever they are invited to say something witty in public, they all come to the same solution: "Get Bruce!"—he'll write the jokes.

An unlikely star, thanks to his frequent TV appearances on the

Bette played a raving harpy of a wife in the 1986 comedy hit *Ruthless People*. She played Barbara Stone, a woman who is kidnapped. However, her husband doesn't want her back, and she is such a terror that her kidnappers have to keep lowering the ransom. *(Courtesy of Laurel Moore for Touchstone Pictures / MJB Photo Archives)*

When a captive Midler is locked in a basement with gym equipment, she puts herself on an exercise regime, and turns the table on her captors in *Ruthless People*. The 1986 film was part of a cinematic winning streak for the actress. *(Courtesy of Laurel Moore for Touchstone Pictures / MJB Photo Archives)*

Lily Tomlin and Bette Midler teamed up to play two sets of mismatched twins in the 1987 comedy *Big Business*. Two Midlers and two Tomlins spelled double trouble and double laughs for the pair. *(Courtesy of Laurel Moore for Touchstone Pictures / MJB Photo Archives)*

Midler and Woody Allen played a battling husband and wife in the 1991 film *Scenes from a Mall*. While shopping for their anniversary party, they each learn that the other is having an extramarital affair. *(Courtesy of Brian Hamill for Touchstone Pictures / MJB Photo Archives)*

The film *For the Boys* was a dream project for Bette. Starring with James Caan, she was also the producer of the film. Although the role gained her a second Academy Award nomination, the movie was a huge box-office disappointment. *(Courtesy of Francois Duhamel for Twentieth Century Fox / MJB Photo Archives)*

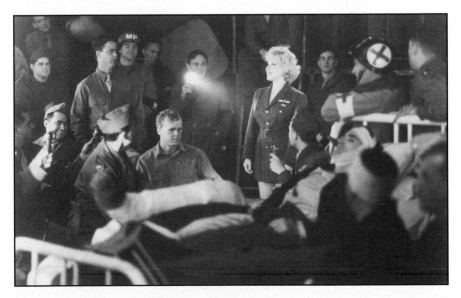

Playing USO entertainer Dixie Leonard in *For the Boys*, Bette really threw herself into the role. It was the perfect movie to let her sing several classic Johnny Mercer songs from the 1940s. She won a Golden Globe for her starring role in the film. *(Courtesy of Francois Duhamel for Twentieth Century Fox / MJB Photo Archives)*

Goldie Hawn, Diane Keaton, and Bette Midler play three women out for revenge when they are each dumped by their husbands in the 1996 comedy hit *The First Wives Club*. *(Courtesy of Andy Schwartz for Paramount Pictures / MJB Photo Archives)*

By the end of *First Wives Club*, the trio of Diane, Goldie, and Bette are triumphant in their plot for revenge against their ex-husbands. All dressed in white, the trio erupts into a self-empowering version of the song "You Don't Own Me." *The First Wives Club* was the biggest hit film in Bette's entire film career, grossing more than $100 million dollars at the box office. When she staged a concert called *Diva Las Vegas* the following year, Midler sang of her screen success in this movie "I'm in a hit, a big fucking hit BABY!" *(Courtesy of Andy Schwartz for Paramount Pictures / MJB Photo Archives)*

Dennis Farina plays Bette's ex-husband in *That Old Feeling*. When they meet again at the wedding of their daughter, they begin arguing, but their altercation somehow rekindles their once-hot lust for each other. *(Courtesy of Takashi Seida for Universal Pictures / MJB Photo Archives)*

In the 2000 film *Isn't She Great*, Bette Midler played *Valley of the Dolls* author Jacqueline Susann, with Nathan Lane as her husband Irving Mansfield. *(Courtesy of Photofest)*

Miss M took a big gamble in 2000 when she starred in her own network TV series, *Bette*—and lost. Milder and her co-stars (left to right): James Dreyfus, Joanna Gleason, Lindsay Lohan, and Kevin Dunn. *(Courtesy of Photofest)*

In the year 2000 Midler was the star of her own weekly television series, starred in two films (*Drowning Mona* and *Isn't She Great*), and released her eighteenth album, entitled *Bette*. To quote the multi-million-selling, award-winning diva herself: "I'm beautiful—DAMN IT!" *(Courtesy of Greg Gorman for Warner Brothers Records / MJB Photo Archives)*

twenty-first-century version of *Hollywood Squares* (produced by Whoopi Goldberg), Vilanch has become a nationally noted media star. For the most part, Bruce looks like a rotund, gay teddy bear with a beard, who has what looks like unkempt and curly mop-like blonde "Tina Turner" hair plopped on his head. In this documentary portrait, he proves to be as good a stand-up comic as he is a writer. Bruce always seems poised and ready to deliver his stream-of-consciousness schtick.

While most of his famous clients have their own trademark "look," Bruce has his own as well. He is never seen in public without being dressed in a T-shirt—one tackier than the next. For formal occasions, Vilanch simply puts a sport coat on over the tacky T-shirt. This amusing documentary is loosely in the vein of "a day in the live of . . ." and it follows Vilanch from his abode, and his wall of T-shirts, to on-camera encounters with his famed clients.

"For years, I never said a word that Bruce didn't charge me for," claims Midler (171). As she explains the evolution of her work with him, "Bruce hitched himself to my wagon." According to her, she met him when she was at Mr. Kelly's in Chicago and instantly said to him, "You got any lines?" He has been writing gag lines for her ever since. It was Bruce who originally introduced Bette to the "blue" comedy of Sophie Tucker and Belle Barth. Tucker and Barth were both grand dames who would tell a filthy joke on stage with flair. Thanks to Vilanch, her "Soph" character was a fusion of these ladies' scandalous acts.

Apparently, Vilanch has been putting words in Midler's mouth ever since. She says on camera here: "Bruce was the first man to put something in my mouth that actually made us both money!"

Explaining the key to Vilanch's talent, Bette says, "He has a great sense of who people are, what their images are in the public."

To demonstrate the point, Bette is seen in various film clips, reciting Vilanch-written gags. From *Diva Las Vegas,* she is seen telling jokes onstage that Vilanch penned for her. She was shown on the final episode of *The Tonight Show with Johnny Carson,* making jokes about people watching the program while having sex in front of the TV. She is also seen singing "Dear Mr. Carson" to Johnny to the tune of "Dear Mr. Gable."

There is some great old footage included in *Get Bruce,* which shows Bette in a grainy black and white film at Mr. Kelly's in Chicago, where she first encountered Vilanch in the early '70s.

In addition to Midler's appearance, her musical director Marc Shaiman is also a part of the documentary, shown working with Bruce on a special musical number. Finally, Bette is seen and heard serenading Vilanch with the song "I Could Write a Book."

Get Bruce, in its limited theatrical run, received great reviews from media insiders. "Fascinating . . . As much an insight into the celebs as it is into this funnyman himself!" said *Entertainment Weekly.* "Some choice scenes . . . how can the movie miss?" wrote *Movieline.* "[A] likable documentary . . . Mr. Vilanch effuses the good-natured canniness of an all-knowing cherub" was the *New York Times'* assessment. And *USA Today* found it "Engagingly funny!" (98).

During 1999, one of Bette's most publicized projects had nothing to do with movies or music. It had to do with trash: the kind that once choked the streets and parks of New York City. Ever since moving back to Manhattan in 1994, Midler had been working with the New York Restoration Project to clean up America's greatest city.

According to her, when she first moved back to New York, she couldn't believe the mess she witnessed there. All of her memories of the city seemed to be littered with trash, strewn about like confetti. "Oh, my God! Look what's on the side of the road! Did a garbage truck explode?!" she exclaimed (1).

Cleaning up a couple of miles of freeway in Los Angeles was one thing, but cleaning up New York City was quite another. However, she felt that she was up for the challenge. "Garbage is my field of expertise. It's shallow, but I'm more interested than most," she says. "I do love the planet. When I look around, and I see all the things that have managed to begin and end their lives on this planet, I just know there's a God. There has to be. It couldn't be this beautiful without one" (1).

According to her, one of Bette's main inspirations in the realm of charity workwas Eugene Lang, a successful businessman. In 1981, when he went to see his old East Harlem elementary school, he pledged a college scholarship to any student who was there that day and who successfully graduated from high school.

According to Bette, "It made me think, 'Wow, one person can make a difference. Here was a guy who didn't just give money. He established a whole network of people to help people" (172).

Bette took to the phones. One of the first people she called was Jan Wenner, the publisher of *Rolling Stone* magazine and a long-time friend. He volunteered office space to Bette for her clean up New York campaign. From there, she started calling more of her friends and acquaintances. She recalls, "It would take a whole day working myself up to make these phone calls. A lot of times, I'd end up talking to their secretaries. They'd say, 'Is that really you?' But then their bosses wouldn't call me back" (172).

Suddenly, abandoned cars, hypodermic-needle-filled parks, and garbage-littered streets became Midler's cause. When she successfully helped to raise money to purchase abandoned lots of property and subsequently turned them into clean and refurbished city parks and gardens, the ball slowly began to roll.

Says Midler, "None of us expected the outpouring of love and gratitude over this gesture. I didn't realize how much emotion had been invested in these gardens. It made me think there's more to be done. I'd like to do more. We would like to begin a community garden movement. We're not exactly sure how" (172). After years of talking trash on stage, Bette Midler was now cleaning up New York City trash as her newfound charitable cause.

According to the diva, in the 1990s she made a switch in causes, from AIDS charities to her famed clean-up campaigns. With regard to her switch in focus, she explained, "All my friends died. I did my part and then I moved on. I wanted to get into an area where there was absolutely nobody" (173). That opened the door to her now famous work with the New York City Preservation Society.

What a divine century the 1900s had been for Bette Midler. And the 1990s had been a great decade for her—more awards, more musical hits, the biggest across-the-board hit film of her career. What was she going to do for an encore? Well, if anyone could come up with one, it was Bette. She was about to blast herself into the 2000s the only way she knew how: explosively divine!

19

ISN'T SHE GREAT?

The year 2000 was one of the most high-profile twelve-month periods of Bette Midler's entire life. She headlined sold-out millennium shows in Las Vegas, she had three new films in the theaters, she released the eighteenth album of her career, and in a daring and unprecedented career move, she starred in her own weekly network television sitcom. Miss M has often been acknowledged as one of the hardest-working divas in all of show business—and that record-breaking year, she literally did it all.

This is not to say that all of this activity was highly successful, but she certainly ran the gamut of well-publicized projects in 2000. It seemed not so much to be the first year of the twenty-first century as it was "The Year of Bette."

As the 1990s came to a close, several singing stars headlined high-ticket-price shows in New York, Los Angeles, and Las Vegas. The Eagles and Linda Ronstadt were at the Staples Center in L.A., Barbra Streisand was charging up to $2,500 a ticket for her New Year's bash, and at the Mandalay Bay Miss M was holding court and breaking in the new century as only she could. Appropriately, she called her Vegas shows "The Divine Miss Millennium."

According to *Las Vegas Sun* reporter Jerry Fink, "'The Divine Miss Millennium' was the best 'Bette' for concert entertainment in Las Vegas as the year-decade-century-millennium drew to a close" (174).

From onstage at the 8,500-seat Mandalay Bay Events Center, Miss

M strutted around the stage before a near-capacity audience. "I can't believe you came to be with me on the last night of planet Earth," she gushed to the crowd who had come to say good-bye to the twentieth century with her.

Midler made several jokes about the Streisand concert, which was taking place in Vegas at that exact same time. At the conclusion of Bette's show, a drag queen dressed as Streisand showed up onstage and announced to Midler and the crowd, "I slipped away from my show early so I could come over here to see my husband. He couldn't afford my show."

Her show included breast jokes, fart jokes, and everything that is divinely taboo. Midler asked of her crowd that night, "What did you expect for 500 bucks—Shakespeare?" Well, they knew what they wanted, and they got it!

In March of 2000, Bette Midler was back in the movie theaters, in the quirky black comedy *Drowning Mona*. As the film opens, the very first thing we learn is that the plot is set in Verplanck, New York, where the Yugo Car Company test-marketed its inexpensive cars. Hence, everyone in the town of Verplanck drives one of the plain-looking, boxy little automobiles. The citizens' cars are Yugos of different colors, as if these were the only automobiles on the market. Even the town's police cruisers are Yugos. The characters' vanity license plates also differentiate the vehicles. The title star's plate reads "UGOMONA."

The first person we meet there is Bette's character, Mona Dearly. She unsuccessfully attempts to start her own Yugo, then she tries the key in her son's Yugo, and away she goes. Mona is killed off in a car accident in the first five minutes of the film. In fact, she doesn't even make it through the credits before she "sleeps with the fishes." It seems that someone has intentionally severed the brake lines to all four wheels on the Yugo Mona drove off a cliff and into a local lake.

Mona is dead, and it seems that everyone in town has a motive. Of all the residents in this small rural town, the only person concerned with finding out who murdered Mona is the local police chief (Danny DeVito). He is dismayed, in fact, by everyone's blasé attitude. Police Deputy Fegee (Peter Dobson) comments on her death as "Ding dong, the witch is dead—end of story." Her own son Jeff (Marcus Thomas) surmises, "I think she had a personality disorder." Neighbor Bobby (Casey Affleck) claims, "She was the worst person I ever knew my entire life."

After fielding a condolence message at a local bar, her husband's Phil's only comment about the death of his wife is "Hey, you snooze, you lose." When someone asks about Mona's funerary wake, son Jeff proclaims, "We're having one of those Wake & Bake services." Instead of flowers, Jeff places donuts on Mona's grave.

Will Farrell of *Saturday Night Live* fame plays the dark and goofy funeral director, Cubby, owner of Cubby's Custom Caskets and Funeral Home. With regard to the non-outpouring of sympathy for Mona's death, Cubby drawls, "I've seen people more upset about losing money in a candy machine."

In a series of detailed flashbacks, we get to see Bette as the ever-charming Mona in her unpopular life: slapping people, insulting people, hitting people, and assaulting their Yugos with a golf club. Wherever she went, it seems, she left her mark—literally.

One of the most unique aspects about *Drowning Mona* is that Bette allows herself to look her all-time frumpiest on film. She does have one scene, at a knife-throwing contest at the local picnic, where she looks lovely, just to let the audience know that most of the time she has no sense of vanity. In fact, the Mona that Bette plays is an obnoxious beer-guzzling Harpy.

Apparently, she didn't have a happy life in Verplanck, and she made sure that no one else around her was happy for long. In one of the many flashbacks featuring the deceased Ms. Mona Dearly, she announces, "Life handed me a whole pile of shit. What am I supposed to make out of that?" Phil, her dim-witted husband (William Finchtner), replies, "Shit salad?"

Jeff, who is the co-owner of a yardwork business, has one of his hands missing. The film shows three filmed scenarios on how Jeff supposedly lost his hand—all of them involving reaching over his beer: across a running chain saw, into a wood chipper . . . and so on. He, however, claims that his own mother, Mona, cut off his hand. We get to see her wielding a meat cleaver that fateful night, as if she were in an episode of TV's *The Iron Chef.*

Mona's husband is cheating on her with Rona (Jamie Lee Curtis), the waitress in the local diner. Mona's way of confronting him with the affair is to ask, "You been playing *Wheel of Fortune* with someone else?" Funny thing is, when we see Phil and Rona together in bed, they have the board game *Wheel of Fortune* with them.

In addition to the frequent sight of Yugo automobiles, the soundtrack of Verplanck consists mainly of Three Dog Night songs like "Shambala," "Never Been to Spain," "Sure As I'm Sitting Here," and "Joy to the World."

The town is also populated with several other bizarre characters, including a lesbian mechanic, a hobo who seems to know more about what is going on in town than anyone else, a hunky but abusive jerk named Murph (Mark Bellegrino), and the police chief's pretty daughter Ellen (Neve Campbell). She spends most of her time onscreen whining or lamenting about one thing or another. When her fiancé asks her who is ringing the doorbell, she snaps back at him, "What am I? Dionne Warwick?"

This slow-moving film has its moments of sheer fun. And Bette certainly gets to overact with great delight as the dastardly Mona. However, when the murder is solved, the film seems to come to an end as abruptly as Mona's death occurred.

While the reviews on *Drowning Mona* were mixed, some of them were downright vicious. In *USA Today,* Susan Wlosczyna didn't beat around the bush in a review headlined: "*Mona* Immersed in Swill." According to Wlosczyna, "If you've never been the same since your mom sold your copy of *Three Dog Night's Greatest Hits* at a garage sale, this dud's for you. . . . No landfill is big enough to hold all the white trash littering the screen. . . . Dirty secrets leak out and who did it is finally revealed, while Midler bobs by now and again in flashback just to remind us how monstrous Mona really was. She and her movie are actually two of a kind: They're stinkers who deserve to sink" (175).

For CNN, reviewer Paul Tatara likewise lit into the film on several levels. "They really should work out a system where famous actors return the money they were paid when they perform in something as thoroughly useless as *Drowning Mona.* . . . this is one of those movies where every character is dumb and mean, and every joke focuses on the hilarity of them saying dumb, mean things. . . . The story consists of unamusing flashbacks in which Mona belittles and attacks her possible killers. Midler gives it a rote run-through at best. She has a couple of hilariously nasty lines of dialogue, but she mostly just grimaces and throws things at her supposed tormentors. You can hardly call it a performance" (176).

Other reviewers really liked it. Bill Zwecker of WMAQ-TV claimed, "It's a wonderful off-beat comedy!" (177). *Leonard Maltin's Movie & Video Guide 2002* nonetheless found it entertaining: "Fairly amusing black comedy about a small town shaken by the drowning of its most reviled citizen—Midler" (178). *The Video Movie Guide 2002* by Mick Martin and Marsha Porter loved it; they exclaimed, "This dark, tasteless and cynical comedy is funny as hell. . . . Peter Steinfeld aptly calls his script 'White trash *Murder on the Orient* Express'" (179).

Regardless of some strong reviews, *Drowning Mona* failed to find an audience in the theaters. It came and went out of the American cineplexes in rapid succession—and, like ill-fated Mona, quickly drowned. It found a wider audience when it was later released on DVD.

To some people, best-selling author Jacqueline Susann represents the cheesiest of novelists. To others, she is the most-exalted high goddess of the divine literary realm. According to the *Guinness Book of World Records,* she still remains the biggest-selling American novelist. From 1966 to 1973 she broke publishing records by becoming the first writer to hit number one three consecutive times, with her enormously successful novels *The Valley of the Dolls, The Love Machine,* and *Once Is Not Enough.*

The very idea of Bette Midler playing the bigger-than-life Susann at first seemed both inspired and outlandish. A tall, commanding woman, Susann was quite the opposite of shorter and curvier Midler. However, their legendary acid-tongued remarks, their lust for life, their love of a good punchline, and a trademark fashion sense made Bette an intelligent choice.

Susann became a literary star as much for her moxie, drive, and self-promotional ability as for her writing. As *Valley of the Dolls* was being shipped from the printing plant, Jackie and her manager/husband, Irving Mansfield, brought coffee and donuts to the drivers of the trucks delivering her volumes. She was on *The Tonight Show* with Johnny Carson the same night Jim Morrison was a guest, and she stole the show.

Her life was also marked with tragedy. She and Mansfield's only child, Guy, was born autistic. And she developed breast cancer prior to finding her calling as a best-selling author. According to Susann herself, she made a pact with God to give her ten more years of life, and she would work her ass off to create a literary masterpiece.

What an incredible life to make a movie about. However, there were two Jacqueline Susann biographical movies being filmed in Hollywood at exactly the same time. Actress Michelle Lee, who is most famous for her long-running role on TV's *Knots Landing,* announced that she was slated to star as Susann in the made-for-television film, based on the book *Lovely Me*. It was played as a drama and was quite touching and accurate to the facts about Jackie's life.

Isn't She Great? was meant to be a comical life story, lived in the face of life-and-death situations. The challenge for the filmmakers here was to balance the comedy and the tragedy.

"It was the funniest script I ever read," said Bette, as the film was in production. She also felt that she was ready for the demanding cancer scenes. According to her, "My mother had breast cancer twice, and eventually she died of liver cancer. But I remember how it [cancer] was a word you only whispered" (17).

For Jacqueline Susann and *Valley of the Dolls* fans, *Isn't She Great?* was both a treat and a disappointment. The look and the fashion of the film was very Pucci-colored '60s, and there were some real accurate touches in the sets and the costumes. In fact, many of the details of Jackie's life are present. In a scene at the Mansfields' apartment, in the background there is a reproduction of the large portrait of Jackie, done in the style of her famous Philadelphia painter father, Robert Susann. However, other details were muddied. Her real-life affair with comedian Eddie Cantor is depicted as an affair with a clownish fictional comedian named Morry (John Laroquette).

Several real gossipy gems about Susann's life aren't even present here. Jackie supposedly fashioned the character of Jennifer in *Valley of the Dolls* after the tragic suicide of her friend, film star Carole Landis. She supposedly had an affair with and an obsession about Ethel Merman. She also finally became a screen actress, by appearing in cameos in the films of her novels. These would be great angles to delve into here, but the script passes by all of these stories and more.

Furthermore, instead of depicting real-life publisher Bernard Geis and giving him due credit for finally buying the much-turned-down *Valley of the Dolls* manuscript, here he is represented by the fictional Henry Marcus. In real life, Jackie used to have boozy, gossipy luncheons with a circle of girlfriends. In *Isn't She Great?* all of her girlfriends have fictionally been rolled into one best buddy, "Flo" (Stockard Channing).

These details aside, this film did give Bette Midler some memorable moments of fun on camera, as she lets loose in her portrayal of Susann. Demonstrating how to make cheese fondue in a department store, Jackie yells "Shit" when her presentation goes awry in front of an audience. "They say I'm too intense!" Bette screams, while standing in the middle of one of the swampy ponds in Central Park—with the Plaza Hotel directly behind her. And there is a delightfully silly scene at a publication party where Jackie is supposedly singing onstage with Steve Lawrence and Eydie Gorme.

One of the best sequences is a episode set at the wacky Mansfield household. Jackie's prissy editor (David Hyde Pierce) shows up to suggest some rewrites to her manuscript. Bette, as Jackie, cannot figure out which loud and colorful Pucci print outfit to wear to edit in, so she presents a dramatic in-home fashion show. Lane prattles on about what to order them for breakfast, and Channing's biggest concern seems to be what liquor to start the day with. It provides the film with its one wonderfully loony, *Absolutely Fabulous*–styled scene. If this whole film had only been equally as irreverent and crazy throughout, it could have been a hit. In fact, it should have been done as Bette Midler playing Jacqueline Susann, who was in turn playing Edina Monsoon in *Absolutely Fabulous*. As an *AbFab*-like best buddy, Channing does her best Patsy to Midler's Edina/Jackie. Supposedly, Susann had a tree in Central Park she spoke to, whenever she wanted to address God. Bette's tree-conversing scenes here seem uncomfortable and forced. Played neither for drama nor for out-and-out comedy, they fall somewhere in-between and somehow miss the target in both arenas.

According to the film's producer, Mike Lobell, "I don't think we've veered away from the actual facts of Jackie's life, as much as we wanted to make the movie funny" (180). Unfortunately, though, *Isn't She Great?* rarely seems to get laugh-out-loud funny.

There a lot of pieces missing from this puzzle of a film. For instance, it sets up the legendary Truman Capote feud on television, then it fails to show us Jackie's famous TV retort. Some of the more dramatic moments are homogenized here as well. Unable to figure out how to present the drama of son Guy's condition, *Isn't She Great?* simply delivers the facts and then moves on uncomfortably.

According to the film's director, Andrew Bregman, Susann was a unique and fascinating character. "The fact of her life is that she was desperate to be famous," he claimed at the time. "So whether or not she's admirable depends on how you see that ambition. I admire the bravery of it. People have children, among other reasons to live forever. But a child who is affectless and doesn't know who you are—it's like she couldn't even get that right. and she just had this incredible desire to be immortal, knowing that she was on a very short string in terms of her life span" (181).

When husband Irving Mansfield suggests that her path to fame might lie in writing about her bigger-than-life knowledge of sex and drugs and show business than in acting, the film finally picks up steam. Talking trash seemed to give Jacqueline Susann a titillating sparkle and a reason to live—whether she was chatting about herself on a TV talk show or turning true stories of show business into blockbuster novels.

Since Dionne Warwick sang all of the theme songs for the original three Susann films, it is fitting that she also sings the newly written theme song—"I'm on My Way"—with music by her old musical director Burt Bacharach. However, instead of using a Vanessa Williams tune at the end of the film, it would have been much more fun to have Midler do her own version of the old Dionne hit "(The Theme from) Valley of the Dolls" to run over the final credits.

Some critics liked the film. According to Karen Durbin in the *New York Times, "Isn't She Great?* captures the fabulosity of Jacqueline Susann, a gutbucket feminist who yearned for fame, and found it. . . . Mr. Rudnick's best lines cannot be repeated in a daily newspaper. It's worth a ticket just to hear Ms. Midler and Ms. Channing's scabrous exchange about *Ozzie and Harriet* (181).

Others did not. In the *Chicago Sun Times,* Roger Ebert recalled, in his review, having met the real Susann when he was just twenty-three. According to him, "Bette Midler would seem to be the right casting choice for Jackie, but not for this Jackie, who is not bright enough, vicious enough, ambitious enough or complicated enough to be the woman who became world famous through sheer exercise of will. Stockard Channing, who plays Jackie's boozy best friend, does a better job of suggesting the Susann spirit. . . . Jackie Susann deserved better than *Isn't She Great? . . .* Here is a movie that needed great trash, great sex and great gossip, and at all the crucial moments Susann is talking to a tree" (182).

Leonard Maltin's Movie & Video Guide 2002 called it an "ill-conceived film about [a] highly-driven actress-turned authoress . . . Not funny enough to succeed as a comedy, nor serious enough to work as a biography" (178). *The Video Movie Guide 2002* by Mick Martin and Marsha Porter was equally as scalding: "Bette Midler, as Susann, goes through an endless parade of flamboyant costumes which are supposed to define her character. Also there is the uncomfortable blending of comedy and tragedy as she deals with her autistic son and breast cancer . . . could have been a better film" (179).

Isn't She Great? appeared and disappeared in movie theaters at a lightening-fast pace. The year was barely half over, and Midler had already had two year 2000 box-office "bombs."

As she had done with *Get Shorty* in the year 2000, Bette Midler chose to make a brief but high-profile appearance in an all-star film—totally unbilled in the credits. The film was the Mel Gibson, Helen Hunt, Marisa Tomei comedy *What Women Want.* Co-starring in the film are Alan Alda, Delta Burke, Valerie Perrine, Ana Gasteyer, Loretta Divine, and Lauren Holly.

The plot of the film deals with a womanizing man, Nick Marshall (Gibson), who falls into a water-filled bathtub with a plugged-in hairdryer in his hand and is knocked out. When he regains consciousness, he finds that he now has an extrasensory power—he can hear what women are thinking.

Bette portrays the role of Dr. J. M. Perkins, Gibson's marriage- and family-counseling psychologist. With her hair red and slicked down in a stylish shoulder-length bob, wearing a tastefully tailored pants suit, Midler turns in a constrained and comically sarcastic portrayal. Although hers is only a one-scene role, she is brilliantly funny here.

When she discovers that Gibson's character actually can read her thoughts, she says, "Mr. Marshall, you might find this a little unorthodox, but would you mind awfully if I smoked?"

When he says, "No, no, no, I understand," she goes over to a side-table in her office, opens up a fancy wood-and-metal cigarette box, lights up a marijuana joint, and takes several deep "tokes"—intent on getting stoned. Looking on, Gibson does a comic double-take.

Although she has only that one brief scene in the whole movie, it is one of the most memorable in the whole film—which became a huge box-office hit. It proved once again that when the material is right, there is no one like Bette Midler.

"There are no movie roles. But I still have a lot to offer," proclaimed Midler in complete frustration (173).

In the year 2000, Bette was completely reviewing her options: "They thought my work in that movie [*The Rose*] was a fluke. At the time, I was devastated. It was staggering. And it just happened to me again with the *First Wives Club.* The movie made a hundred million dollars, and the studio couldn't get a sequel together. They thought it was a fluke. At least now my attitude has gotten better, you always worry that they are going to find out that you're a fraud. But now I'm so old, I don't care. Let them take it" (22).

She was also frustrated with her once-glorious association with the Disney film corporation. According to her, "Even though I was their favorite girl at Disney, I was never the comic lead in one of their movies. I was always the support. Or the co-girls. I was, at the time, I was the highest-paid female in town, and I never even said anything about it because I thought that would be in poor taste. Now I'm ticked off that I didn't say anything. These days, everyone tells their damn salaries, and I never said a word. That's what comes from being a lady" (22).

What she did take the largest amount of pride in was how her daughter was growing up. Said Bette at the time, "Sophie doesn't watch teen shows. She chooses what she wants to watch, and we watch it with her. I make a big fuss. My motherly instinct has told me that this is a good way to train my daughter. There are some things that are completely off the table. Really terrible language, and drugs. And behavior that is uncivilized. Violence. Sex before you're ready for it. Violent sex. Grossness—there are other ways to behave. You just shouldn't let that become part of your soul. They're grotesque. I mean, *There's Something about Mary*—that stuff used to be private. What happened?" (1).

Was teenage Sophie curious about Bette telling tales of her old days at the Continental Baths? Claimed Bette, "She's not even a little bit curious. I think that's better. Let her get her own dirty jokes. She doesn't need any of mine. She wants to know what it was like at Studio 54 and she wants to know all that smarmy stuff that we lived through. Fortunately, there are enormous blank spots. But what I do remember I tell her about. And she's just, 'Oh my goodness, oh my goodness.'. . . Sophie knows the difference between right and wrong, and she knows what's not good for her. She's not judgmental, she's not scandalized by other people's behavior, but she knows it's not for her" (1).

She was also very happy about her marriage to Martin. "The last couple of years have been really great. We don't fight anymore," she explains. "I think you get to a point where you realize, 'I'm never going to change this person. I'd just better accept this person and enjoy what they have to offer. I think I'll just relax.' I don't think anyone who's lived with a person for a long time hasn't wanted to reach over and strangle that person. Fortunately, those things pass. Our life hasn't been a bed of roses by any means, but we stuck it out, and we came through at the other end. All of a sudden things fall into place" (1).

Looking at the way her career has progressed, Bette Midler was satisfied with the choices she had made up to this point. "With age comes wisdom, and that's one of the things that I learned," she claimed. "I can't drink more than two drinks—I'm the cheapest date on earth. I can't smoke reefer. I can't do blow. I cannot do that stuff. I don't have the physical mechanism that allows me to do it. So I don't do it. And I think it's been good for me. Because I'm still here. And if you watch enough *Behind the Music,* you'll see that everybody took a turn from the left. Everybody. And they all wound up in rehab and losing years of momentum and creativity, and that for me is the most boring thing" (120).

Her own sense of independence was something that she had long relied upon. "I have always been on my own," said Midler. "My mom and my dad, who were children of the Depression and World War II, always said, 'It's best not to count on men.' They never told me I wouldn't get married, but they told me I must learn to be independent, that I must support myself, that I must not think that anyone would support me. Maybe they thought I was so unappealing that I would never get married, but for whatever reason, that was their message: You can only count on yourself. And it took" (22).

In 1996 Bette Midler starred in the most successful film of her career: *First Wives Club.* Since that time, she had come up to bat with three new starring projects: *That Old Feeling, Drowning Mona,* and now *Isn't She Great?* Each one of them was less successful that its predecessor. What was she going to do next?

"I've been making movies for many years," she claimed, "and I was always frustrated by the fact that it was a very, very slow process—very slow to develop, very slow to get a green light, very slow to make, very slow to edit. Then if you don't do well that first weekend, all that work is for nothing" (1).

Suddenly, there were no new movies being offered to her. However, while all of this was going on, she was being courted by CBS-TV about launching a new project: her own weekly television show. For years she had insisted that TV was the last thing she would ever get involved in. However, she needed a new outlet for her creativity. Eventually, the idea of doing a television show didn't sound as repugnant as once it had.

According to her, "I never wanted to get out of the movie business.

My way is to find another route. When I'm blocked by people who are not interested, not creative, and want to preserve the status quo, I go around them. They see me in a certain way, and they push me aside. That happens everywhere, not just in the movie business. CBS really listens to me. They seem to value what I have to say" (22).

Bette was tired of beating herself up looking for the right movie role. It was time to concentrate on something new. In the year 2000, she was about to embark on a whole new chapter of her career: on television.

20

BETTE TV

While she decided what to do with her acting career, Bette Midler began work on her album *Bette*. Instead of trying an assortment of producers and musical styles, Midler turned to Don Was to produce this new album, consisting largely of mellow-sounding versions of '70s hits and contemporary tunes. The rest of the album was rounded out with new material. After she was finished with the album, she added an additional cut to the disc, which she wrote and produced with Marc Shaiman—the song "Nobody Else but You."

According to Midler, "I'm happiest when I'm singing. And I can always sing. In a funny way; singing gives me a free ride. Music informs everything. Comedy, for instance, is like music. It's all beats, getting the right rhythm" (22).

The *Bette* album opens with a sultry version of the Baby Washington hit "That's How Heartaches Are Made." Over the years it has been recorded by such varied performers as the Marvelettes and Dusty Springfield. It's a great song to start off the album in a sexy, smooth way. Basically, the song sets the tone for most of the album. On *Bette*, the diva delivers similar smooth "quiet storm" renditions of other sexy R&B hits: "Just My Imagination (Running Away with Me)," "Love TKO," and "Shining Star."

She tackles a couple of contemporary classics, too. "God Give Me Strength" was written by Elvis Costello and Burt Bacharach for the film *Grace of My Heart*. The song was sung in the film by actress Illeana

Douglas. In the film, Douglas plays a singer/songwriter styled after Carole King. On this slow and sexy version of "God Give Me Strength," Bette really pours her heart out.

Another stellar performance by Miss M comes on her version of "When Your Life Was Low," which was written by Will Jennings and Joc Sample of the Jazz Crusaders and originally recorded by Randy Crawford ("Street Life"). This sad song of being left behind by an ex-love is equally as slow and somber, with Midler milking the sensitive lyrics for sultry pathos, effectively weaving a tale about the pain of love lost.

The song that garners the biggest amount of electricity is "In These Shoes," which is the one nod to the wacky side of Bette. The lyrics of the song find Midler being propositioned by different men who want to have sex in rugged settings. Bette sings her protest, asking, "In these shoes?" It is the only song on the album that offers a bit of goofy levity to the mellow-love-song mode of the rest of the album.

The sensitive "Color of Roses" is a perfect "rose" reference for Midler on this album. Attempting a bit of techno-pop, Bette cranks up "Bless You, Child." "Moses" finds her singing to a tropical reggae beat, about diamonds, roses, and a "best friend who is queer." For the most part, producer Don Was chose settings for Midler that showed off her voice quite expressively. There are few poignant sad songs on this album, and only wild and campy excursion.

The inclusion of the song "Nobody Else but You" gives a direct tie-in to the diva's new television series, as it was the program's theme song. It sounds very much like a cheerful TV show theme from the 1960s and is a bit out of place in the middle of all of the mellow ballads on this album.

Her eighteenth album release, and her second one for Warner Brothers Records, the *Bette* album didn't have the kind of crazy magic that *Bathhouse Betty* did. A mellow, "adult contemporary" LP, *Bette* never cracked the Top 40 in America on the *Billboard* charts and seemed to disappear rather quickly. It peaked at number 69 in *Billboard* magazine in the United States. The album certainly received a ton of national exposure, with several of the songs—particularly "Nobody Else but You"—getting introduced to the public on Midler's TV show *Bette*. Somehow, this album seemed to get lost in the shuffle.

Next for the diva came this nagging decision: Should Bette do TV? Should Bette *not* do TV? Should Bette do TV? Should Bette *not* do TV?

According to her, she finally said "yes" to doing a series for CBS during the 2000–2001 season, but she kept secretly hoping that an incredible movie offer would materialize, and she would have to get out of it: "I thought I could set up a movie before committing to a series. But it was really a struggle. My husband and I talked about it and he said, 'Turn a corner and be funny'" (22).

Occasionally, in the past, Midler would say "yes" to one project or another and then wished that she hadn't. Often she would get her business partner Bonnie Bruckheimer to back out of commitments. Bonnie thought that television could be a good move for Bette: "On TV, I told her, she could do everything she wants to do: laugh, cry, sing, do physical comedy, anything. I would talk to her about it endlessly. Bette is always saying 'no,' and then, when she finally says 'yes,' she always tries to get out of it. A week before the final Johnny Carson show, she called and said, 'You have to get me out of this show.' But I convinced her. I thought, 'She's Bette Midler. If this show doesn't work, does that end thirty years of what she's done in her career?' No. And, anyway, they don't write movies for her anymore, whether she's in a TV show or not" (22).

With regard to this TV gamble, Midler claimed at the time, "I always said I'd never watch anything stupider than me. And a lot of TV is really stupid. But movies are over for me. There's nothing there for me. It was so hard to get a picture. My agents could only get me these cameos and I said, 'What am I doing these cameos for?' And I saw that all my compatriots, all the girls I had come up with—I never say women, I always say, 'Girls, we're not doing so good.' So rather than wait for the axe to fall completely, because I like to work and I think I have a lot to offer, I said, 'That's it. Let's try television'" (22).

Martin von Haselberg thought it was a good career move, in an exposure and marketing sort of way. "I felt the films were not the best vehicles for her. I thought TV could be an extension of her live show, where she really gets to show off her talent in a way I don't think she can on film. But the audience for a live show is limited to 25,000 people. On TV, she can reach a lot more," he surmised (120).

Knowing they had a half-hour prime-time situation comedy as the format they were working with, the first decision to be made was what Miss Midler was going to be. All sorts of fictional situations were proposed. She could be a teacher, she could be a judge, she could be a housewife. What did *she* want to be?

Bette started meeting with writers, who bantered around ideas to her. As she explains it, "We took these pitch meetings, and as charming as all those writers were, I kept saying, 'I can't have an adopted daughter. I can't be a ghost. And I don't want to play a high school principal or a real estate agent'" (22).

Jeffrey Lane was used to working with stars and fashioning shows for them. Among his other credits, he had been the executive producer for the show *Mad about You*, which starred Helen Hunt and Paul Reiser. He seemed like the perfect choice to work with Midler.

Bette met Jeffrey Lane for lunch one day at famed Hollywood-area restaurant Spago's, to see if they could come up with any conclusions as to what Bette's character should be on the show. Lane recalls, "When I met Bette at Spago—I was too nervous to eat and took my sandwich home. I said, 'What could be a more interesting character for a television show than Bette Midler?' It was what seemed right, although I knew we'd have to emphasize her family life. She couldn't be too glitzy, but I didn't think that would be a problem, because everybody knows that Bette Midler worked for everything she got. We wanted Bette in real life, with real concerns. On this show, she's a woman who runs a business, and that business is herself. And that's how I think a lot of women see their lives: every day presents its own challenges. Her life and career is all our lives and careers. Bette's experiences are just more heightened" (22).

As Bette tells of the lunch meeting, "When Jeffrey Lane and I had lunch, he was very dour. He didn't seem happy. But somehow we got to talking, and he suggested that I play myself. And that was exactly right" (22).

There had certainly been other television shows semi-based in reality, where real-life comics like Jerry Seinfeld, George Burns, and Jack Benny each played exaggerated versions of themselves. Seinfeld had Elaine, George, and Kramer as his off-the-wall and equally self-centered friends. George Burns had his talented comedienne wife—Gracie Allen—as his foil. Stingy Jack Benny had his butler, Rochester, to banter with and to put Benny in his place. In theory, it could have worked for Bette. However, it was to end up a huge mistake in the long-run.

Hoping that the *Bette* show could have the same kind of kooky supporting characters as the show *Seinfeld*, Midler commented, "Everyone wants me to have a Kramer. I say, "I am Kramer.' I want to have only straight people around me" (22). Unfortunately, it meant that the entire weight of the show was going to rest on her shoulders.

Bette told Lane about her life and her business partner, Bonnie Bruckheimer, and her long-time musical director and occasional producer, Marc Shaiman. She told him about her daughter and her husband.

When Bette and Bonnie Bruckheimer told Lane some of the crazy stories about their working relationship, he took notes, and that relationship became the basis for the TV character named Bette and the one who was to be called Connie—fictional Bette's manager.

They took the character that was Marc Shaiman and developed him into Oscar, fictional Bette's gay musical director. They named the daughter Rose, for good luck, and real-life Martin von Haselberg was morphed into the fictional Roy.

According to Bruckheimer, "It captured an exaggerated version of our lives. I took it to Bette and she laughed out loud" (173). It was Bette Midler's real life—but not really.

At the time, Shaiman thought it was a good idea for Midler to pursue a field in television. "They didn't know what to do with Bette in movies. She's one of the last real entertainers. For her, that's like breathing in and out, but movies want a certain type, doing certain types of roles. That's not Bette. Her talent is limitless, and that's why this show might be great" (22).

What were they going to use as a set? How about Bette Midler's real home? "They took Polaroids," Bette was to explain. "It's very odd. My husband thinks the set is not grand enough. He thinks people don't want to see what my life really looks like, that they want the dream of how a star lives. I say, if they're looking at the set, I'm in deep trouble" (22).

Bette got a big laugh out of von Haselberg's first visit to the TV set. "My husband didn't think it was anything like our house. He keeps saying, 'Where's the staff?'" (173).

Then came casting. It seemed like a natural choice to see if Marc Shaiman could play the musical director in the series, since the role was based on his own life. According to him, "I even auditioned to play myself. But they decided to go another way" (22). Ultimately, they chose James Dreyfus to play Oscar, Joanna Gleason became Connie, Kevin Dunn was cast as husband Roy, and Lindsay Lohan portrayed daughter Rose.

Character actress Joanna Gleason first found fame when she was cast as the Baker's Wife in the Stephen Sondheim hit Broadway musical *Into the Woods* in 1987. Kevin Dunn is most notable for playing a father whose son is embroiled in a murder in *Stir of Echoes* and as a frustrated military officer dealing with innercity anti-lizard duty in *Godzilla*.

And, naturally, Bette played Bette. According to her at the time, "This is the 'me' that I wish I was. I get to wear beautiful clothes. I wear high heels all day long. And I have a really nice bosom line" (22).

Explaining the vague line between the real Bette and the TV Bette, Midler explained, "Oh, it's a complete send-up of my life. There's a little bit of truth in it. But it's a send-up—it's a farce" (120).

The reason that it was a huge mistake for Bette to play herself was that she would play the entire series trying to be the most coiffed, most beautiful version of herself. Instead of just letting herself become a character, like the crass Shelley in *Outrageous Fortune* or even as silly as Lilly in *That Old Feeling*, she chose to play the one character who made her the most self-conscious—herself. The daughter on the series had to be sweet and behaved, or it would reflect unflatteringly on Bette's own daughter. The husband on the series had to be good-natured and centered—or it would reflect poorly on Bette's own husband. They certainly weren't going to portray him as a man who would wear an inner tube around his waist and exploding whipped cream on top of his head—like the real Harry Kipper had in *Mondo Beyondo*. Maybe they should have; it would have been a hell of a lot more interesting than the way it unfolded on this series. Furthermore, the Bette on this show was always well-coiffed, in full makeup, and looking fabulous. This meant that all of her comedy had to be isolated to facial expressions, broad gestures, physical humor, and endless mugging.

Both Midler and Jeffrey Lane defended their decisions. According to Lane, "I told her, 'If you do a show, you really should play yourself because if you do anything else, you're not going to use everything" (173).

Said Midler, "Because it's my life. It's really all I know. I mean, I could play a school teacher, but what's the point? You know, I could play a librarian or a bookstore owner, but what's the point? When do I get to be flamboyant and wear my clothes? When do I get to wear my *shoes!?*" (120).

Regarding the blurry line between fact and fiction, however, she noted, "It isn't exactly like my life, but it's enough like my life that it's very odd." (173).

On the positive side of things, when Bette filmed her television series, she was thinner than she had been in years. According to her, a case of digestive tract disorder—"I had amoebas or parasites"—left her twenty-five pounds lighter (173). She decided that it was a sign and worked diligently to make certain that the weight did not return. As she went before the TV cameras for her new series, she was totally svelte. And once the series started, she worked such long hours that the weight stayed off effectively.

Since Bette now lived in New York City, it was a natural concept to film the show where she lived. When the pilot episode of Bette was produced, it was done there. There was no theme song to the show, and the cast members seemed to be experimenting with their roles.

To assure the kind of attention for the show that it deserved, Midler asked her friend Danny DeVito to be a guest star on the first episode. In the plot of the pilot, we see a nervous and neurotic Bette backstage at one of her concerts. For the concert footage, they used the opening clip from the *Diva Las Vegas* show, with Midler descending from the clouds, singing "Friends." DeVito was in the audience of the show, and at the postconcert party, he is seen meeting with Bette. In the context of their brief scene together, DeVito invites her to appear opposite him on his new—fictional—TV show. Naturally, she agrees. However, she doesn't exactly know what role she has agreed to play.

There were two running gags that became central elements throughout the run of Bette. They were her own vanity and her supposed food addiction. In the backstage sequences, Bette either had her hand in a tray full of trashy cheese curls or was grabbing things off DeVito's plate when he wasn't looking. There is also a running gag on the show that her nemesis is actress Sally Field, since it was Field who took the Academy Award when Midler was nominated for *The Rose*.

As a unified force, Oscar, Connie, Roy, and Rose all try to keep the news from Bette that the role she has agreed to play is DeVito's mom. The night after her concert appearance, husband Roy acts amorous toward wife Bette, then falls asleep before she gets into bed. When Midler suddenly erupts into a frenzy of activity on exercise machines and extreme dieting, the rest of the cast assumes that she is upset by being asked to play an older role in the DeVito project. However, her motivation is her desire to be found more sexy by her husband.

Bette did have some funny lines on the show, especially when she was making fun of her own life. On the pilot the fictional Bette announces, "I just don't know if I should do TV. I'll have my own series and then I might as well kill myself" (22).

What ends up happening in the pilot is that Bette plays a silly slapstick act on some complicated gym equipment. It was a scene that one might expect Lucille Ball to enact in the 1950s in *I Love Lucy*. On this particular episode, Bette was trying so hard to act funny that it was not at all funny, just uncomfortably goofy.

Still, the show had some comic potential. On the pilot, Bette is introduced to her daughter's new boyfriend. When the young teenager claims that he is Midler's biggest fan, she whispers to her daughter, "He's gay!"

Joanna Gleason had some great one-liners here and there, which she delivered in a very deadpan style. Basically, she just volleyed one-liners back at Bette, while Midler neurotically talked about herself, food, sex, and her career. As Oscar, James Dreyfus played the role as if he was scared of his own shadow. Since it was established on the show—mainly by Bette's comments—that Oscar is gay, it gave Midler a top banana to bounce campy jokes and one-liners off and dish with.

However, the absolute weakest link in the show was the character of Roy, fictional Bette's husband. Their scenes together were dull, lifeless, and completely unbelievable. Never, through all of their episodes together, did Kevin Dunn look like he was either comfortable or enjoying himself. There was "zero" chemistry between them. Furthermore, since Bette insisted that she be the funniest character on the series at all times, all four of her supporting cast members had to play it straight. With the exception of Gleason as Connie, none of the other actors was given much to do, so when Bette wasn't on camera, the plot completely sagged. And when Bette was on camera, she was working so hard to be funny every second that she wasn't in the least bit funny.

Based on Bette's star power and the pilot episode, CBS-TV decided to purchase the series for its fall 2000 prime-time line-up. One of the ways that the network introduces the shows to its affiliate stations is to fly CBS broadcasters from around the country to New York or Los Angeles, to preview the new shows and meet some of the stars. This is known as "upfront" in the business. Bette was invited to come to one such presentation at Carnegie Hall, so that the local broadcasters and potential sponsors could see her in action.

As Midler explained this comedy-of-errors, "That announcement is called an 'upfront.' Who knew what an upfront was? It was a crazy day. I said to Bonnie, 'What do you wear to an upfront?' She said, "I don't know. What's an upfront?' We were clueless. I wore pants and a sweater. I was upset because I had to cross a picket line to get to Carnegie Hall. I went out onstage, and it was very nice. But then, when I left, my car was gone, and I had to take a cab home. When I got out of the cab, my pants ripped up the back, and my doorman got a good look at my whole tweeter. If that had happened fifteen minutes earlier, I would have exposed myself to all those 'upfronts' at Carnegie Hall" (22).

When the announcement was made that the *Bette* show was getting picked up for several episodes, Midler called up her friend, actress Candice Bergen, for advice. Bergan had starred for several very successful seasons in the CBS-TV series *Murphy Brown.*

According to Bette, "Candice warned me. She said 'They keep you hopping that first year. This is rough'" (173). She had no clue just how rough it was going to get.

One of the first challenges came right off the bat. CBS-TV insisted that the Bette show be filmed in Los Angeles. Bette and her family lived in New York City. She foolishly agreed to fly back and forth between the two cities to work on her show and still have a family life in Manhattan. This would further tap her energy when the show went into full production. This was a huge mistake.

By relocating the production to Los Angeles, the first casting problem arose. Lindsay Lohan, who played daughter Rose, was in school in New York, so she had to be replaced after the first episode. This was another bad omen. The show aired for one week, and there were already cast changes.

The first episode of *Bette* ran on October 11, 2000, and it did surprisingly well in the ratings. Everyone was encouraged by the viewers that the show drew. However, from that high water mark of the pilot episode, every week that *Bette* ran it drew less and less viewers. One of the problems was that the show started out opposite the Regis Philbin–hosted game show *Who Wants to Be a Millionaire.* Apparently, more people wanted to be a millionaire than wanted to see Midler's moderately amusing show.

Actually, the reviews for the pilot were encouraging. Entertainment industry newspaper *Daily Variety* was optimistic about *Bette,* based on its review of that first episode. According to Laura Fries, "Fitting a talent as big as Bette Midler's onto the small screen is a tough task—it's an instance where you have to be careful not to do too much or risk looking like you're just trying too hard. . . . Produced more like a stage play than a TV series, *Bette* is a show about the performer's life and career—only a fictional family and friends, à la *Seinfeld.* The TV version of Bette, we are led to believe, is neurotic and food-obsessed, vacillating between supreme overconfidence and anxiety. . . . Throughout the episode, Midler hoists her bosoms, rants, cries, shouts and mugs for the camera. It's amusing in small doses, but the jokes that work best play on her film career, including a bit about recycling dialogue from her movies, and an ongoing grudge against Sally Field. . . . Naturally, other actors pale next to Midler, but the star has picked an extremely likable and talented supporting cast" (183).

When Bette saw the script for the second episode, she wasn't thrilled. Throughout the fall of 2000, rumors ran rampant through Hollywood of trouble on the *Bette* set. The first problem Midler had was with the writers of the show. According to her, "My only concern is that the show be funny. After the first episode, I marched into the writers' room and I said, 'I don't want titters. I want guffaws.' They looked at me and said, 'Yes, Ms. Midler,' and I got guffaws" (22).

When the ratings dropped off for episodes #2 and #3, Midler got defensive in the press. Furthermore, she started to distance herself from the blame, if anything should go wrong. In October of 2000, she claimed, "I must emphasize the fact that I know nothing. I know nothing about producing for TV, about how they market it—nothing. So when people say to me, "Oh, do know what your time slot is?' I just look at them blankly, because I have absolutely no idea. Some of them say to me, 'Do you have any idea how lucky you are?' And I just have no idea. Everyone is disappointed in the fact that I know nothing. I'm not a television actor" (120).

After the first three episodes were aired, the network was still encouraged that the series could make it. In the October 31–November 8, 2000, issue of the *Hollywood Reporter,* news of an extension for the *Bette* show was announced. According to the article, "CBS is beginning to trigger its full-season pick-ups. Sources said the eye network has returned nine episode orders to the new Bette Midler sitcom. . . . Columbia Tri-Star TV's *Bette* has delivered CBS' best numbers in years in the unsheltered Wednesday 8 P.M. slot" (184). However, that decision was based mainly on the viewership of the debut episode.

Slowly, the show was losing a ratings battle. "Okay, let me explain to you, I'm up against Regis!" she argued. "If I fall, what does that mean? Regis is an hour. Do the math. Two half-hours per network. There are three other networks. If I go down, there are five other shows with me" (173).

What she did realize, painfully, was that she had gotten herself seriously in over her head. "It's an enormous amount of work. And this stuff is very ambitious—I think. Last week, there was a 10-page scene—and a song and a dance and a wig and an Elizabethan ruff. I thought I was going to die," she claimed (173).

The show was filmed at Culver City Studios on Friday nights in front of a live studio audience. The cameras started rolling around 6:30 P.M., and it would usually end well after midnight. The filming typically went so late that the cast and crew were placing cash bets as to what ungodly hour they would finish up.

According to co-executive producer Janis Hirsch, Midler started insisting on reshooting every scene multiple times: "She always wants to do it one more time because she thinks she can do it better—and she can. I've never seen an actress work so carefully" (173).

When the show went into full production, one of the first things they had to do was cast a Los Angeles–based teenage actress to play the part of Rose. They decided on Marina Malota. The young actress recalls that the audition was a breeze for her: "I was calm and just went in and did my lines—and got a lot of laughs. I've never been nervous performing for people" (185).

Speaking of her portrayal of the character Rose, Marina explained, "[She] loves her mother, but knows that her mom can also be a little silly about things sometimes. They have a really strong relationship. . . . The lines are like a mother/daughter conversation in real life, so it's natural for me. Since Bette is just awesome and has a daughter a year older than me, it does feel like she's a second mom" (185).

The show's executive producer and director, Andrew D. Weyman, explains that in recasting the role of Rose, they were "looking for someone who could go toe-to-toe with Bette Midler[, which] was a difficult order—and Marina can look Bette in the eye and [quickly] respond. She's very real, not overly coached and actor-y" (185).

To erase the audience's memory of the original Rose, on the second show of the series "Rose" is referred to, but is never shown. When the character appears on the third show—the Halloween-themed show—she is played by Marina.

Andrew Weyman is known for having directed TV series with some of the most difficult-to-work-with women in show business: Ellen De-Generes in *Ellen,* Rosanne in *Rosanne,* and Cybill Shepard in *Cybill.* He then graduated to directing Midler in *Bette.* According to him, "My agent told me, 'You have a reputation of being able to work with diffi-cult people.' I said, 'Do me a favor, get me a different reputation'" (173).

Said Weyman of Bette at the time, "She's one of the most interesting blends of insecurity and courage in an actor that I've ever seen" (173).

Filming a new episode every week proved a new kind of working experience for Midler, and a fast-paced one at that. "Making the pilot was so much fun," she claimed. "I hadn't used all these skills in a while. But now that we're on the third show, I can see that it's almost too much. If the script is at 20 percent on Monday, by the time you get to Friday, you have to work 1,000 percent to get the show to work. That is brutal. I find that process really exciting. Up to a point" (22).

When Martin von Haselberg was asked whether or not his relation-ship with the real Bette was anything like the TV version, he replied, "The husband on the show is a calming, objective person who is mar-ried to this tornado—a leveling influence. That does bear some resem-blance to our actual relationship. She is a person with inexhaustible amounts of energy—sometimes I think I can persist in directing that when it's at risk of losing direction. Many people warned against her doing this. They said the format of TV is too small for her. But look at *I Love Lucy*—a huge show on the small screen" (120).

As it often is in network television, very often the show's scripts were being developed as they went along, throughout the week. If a joke or a situation didn't seem to work, it had to be rewritten. "You have to be on your toes. The entire time you're doing it, they're rewriting and they're feeding you lines. If you snooze, you lose. When it's done, you're flying," Midler claimed (1).

One of the biggest challenges of taping this show was that it was performed in front of a live studio audience. Explained Bette of per-forming in this way, "You're not supposed to play to the audience, but you have to be aware of them enough so that you use their laughs for timing" (173).

As the pace of the show's filming schedule picked up, it became more and more difficult for Bette to control the variables. "Some things are hits and some things are misses," she said during the show's production. "You go on. The idea is to last and to do your work. This is the road I took and this is what happened once I got on the path. Maybe another fork in the road will come. That's what it's about. It's not about getting stopped and having nervous breakdowns and slashing your wrists because you didn't get a job" (173).

With regard to the cast and crew, she claimed, "I like everybody in it. I've met lovely, lovely people. But it's a huge, huge machine that is absolutely ruthless and you just have to run to keep up." However, in late 2000 she started admitting, "Oh my God, this is so hard!" (173).

Bette felt that she would also feature a cavalcade of guest stars on her show. Several of them she got to appear on *Bette,* including Olivia Newton-John, Danny DeVito, Dolly Parton, Oprah Winfrey, George Segal, the stars of TV's *The View,* Tim Curry, and Jon Lovitz. There were several others who flatly declined, including Jack Nicholson, Sally Field, and Candice Bergen.

She had come up with a great idea for an episode co-starring Sally Field. Explained Bette, "We've been having this running feud because she won my Oscar, and you know, I've been doing that Adopt-a-Highway thing for years and years. So the Adopt-a-Highway people call me up and say, 'Your mile is just a mess. We can't keep your mile in any order. You'd better go see what's happening. Do you have any enemies?' So, I go up at night and I see that someone is soiling my mile. But I don't know it's Sally because she's got a bag over her head. I only see the license plate, so I have to go to the DMV [Department of Motor Vehicles]. I've never been to the DMV. Go to the DMV and get into the records and find out who it is, and it turns out to be Sally. Isn't that hilarious? How I really wish she'd do it" (120).

When Tim Curry guest-starred on the show, he was baffled by the role he would be playing. "It's very weird," claimed Curry. "They said, 'You'll be playing yourself.' And I said, 'Who is that?'" (173).

Bette also came up with a great scene involving a fart. In the episode, she develops laryngitis and cannot talk. The set-up has her in the elevator with someone famous, who farts. When other people on the elevator make disgusted faces, the celebrity says something to the effect of "Oh, Bette, how could you?" and mute Midler has to take the blame for the flatulence.

Explaining her casting efforts, Midler explained, "I needed a famous person to come and fart. Candice Bergen said, 'I wanted to do it, but I ran it by my people and they didn't embrace the idea.' I wanted to say, 'Well, why not?'" recalled Bette. Determined to find a big-name celebrity to do the fart joke scene, she started thumbing through her own phone book. According to her, she next called up Jack Nicholson. "I called him up and he was very amused, but he wouldn't do it. I said, 'Jack! You're just up the road, come on down!' He said, "I don't do TV.' I said, 'Well, you don't do TV yet, babe!'" (173).

When she couldn't find a celebrity to come on her show and fart, she simply rewrote the scene to include a character actor with the gas problem. It became the character of Bette's analyst, who announces in the elevator that she is on a new vegetarian diet and has a gas problem, just before she farts and then she blames it on Bette.

On the second show Miss M is shown winning an award for a guest-starring role on the military TV show *JAG*. David James Elliot, one of the stars of *JAG*, makes a guest appearance. When Bette accepts another award later in the show, George Segal appears as himself, honoring her in a filmed tribute. There is a running gag in this show that her movies move with rapid succession in and out of theaters, to become Grade-B in-flight film entertainment. On the third show, Dolly Parton appears as herself, taping a TV appearance with Bette.

On the episode with Oprah Winfrey, Bette was invited to participate on an "Oprah's Book Club" segment. When Midler overbooks herself, she neglects to read the book being discussed in the interview and attempts to bluff her way through it—only to make a fool of herself. In another episode, Bette attempts to obtain great seats at an L.A. Lakers basketball game for Roy. She ends up dislocating the finger of star player Kobe Bryant and performs as a cheerleader along with the Laker Girls.

On the episode co-starring Tim Curry, Bette talks her way into a production of *Hamlet*. When she cannot seem to remember the speeches, she turns her performance into an Elizabethan version of the Divine Miss M. One episode co-starred TV journalists Joy Bahar, Lisa Ling, Merideth Vierra, and Star Jones of *The View*. Bette gets caught in a white lie, claiming she saved a drowning boy. When the hostesses of *The View* want her to bring the boy on the show as a guest, Bette is forced to hire a boy to pretend he was rescued by her.

Actually, two of the best episodes came along just before the end of the run of *Bette*. In one called "The Invisible Mom," Bette becomes a

volunteer at Rose's school and wrangles with another of the moms—
Olivia Newton-John. In an episode called "Poltergeist," Jon Lovitz
moves into Bette's house when his is being remodeled. Wanting to appear generous, Midler lets him stay, while he slowly drives her nuts. He
tries to convince Bette that there is a "black cloud" of misfortune over
her house and that she should sell. Lovitz has the best line, basting a
turkey in Bette's kitchen. With turkey baster in hand, he announces,
"Gobbles needs a bath."

Bette also used the series to publicize her new album. It seemed that
every week she was able to insert one song or another from the *Bette*
LP. One particular episode centers around a recording session for the
song "Color of Roses." When Bette invites Oscar to produce a song for
her new album, always-in-control Bette can't decide how to do the song.
Along the way, she performs the song in a disco version, a rap version,
a Jamaican reggae version, and even a gospel version. Finally, she decides to go with Oscar's original concept, the simple ballad version of
the song.

Somewhere along the line, the show went from being "exhilarating"
to "exhausting." On the set of *Bette, Los Angeles Times* reporter Clara
Hall observed Midler up close during a TV taping. In an article called
"Hard Work If You Can Get It," Hall claimed, "Devoid of makeup she
looks like the plain-faced, 54-year-old businesswoman that she is" (173).
Break out the kitty litter!

According to Bette, "It's very fast. I had no idea. I called Candy
Bergen and she said, 'It's a dream job, but you don't go to the bathroom
for the first year.' The other day I said, 'I have no time. I can't go to the
bathroom.' And they said, 'Well, you went yesterday'" (22).

It wasn't long before reports of extreme diva exhaustion began to be
emitted from the set of *Bette.* The show hadn't been on the air a month
when the *National Enquirer* printed the story "Bette Midler's Secret
Agony—Pals Fear She's Heading for a Second Breakdown!" In the publication's November 7, 2000, issue, "a source close to the star" was
quoted as claiming, "Bette's trying to star, produce, direct and design
the entire show herself. . . . One minute she's bursting into tears, the
next she's screaming her head off. . . . Then, if she yells at someone, a
half hour later she's trying to make it up to them by trying to make
them laugh. . . . She's a bundle of nerves. She misses her family desperately and she internalizes everything. She can't take much more of this"
(186).

The article also quoted "a source close to the show," who confirmed Midler's obsession with the series, "She oversees everything right down to the tiniest details—like small props of her TV bedroom. . . . She picks over every scene in every script. If something isn't funny to her, she'll make them rewrite it—right there on the stage" (186). Something was rotten in *Bette* TV land.

In the December 18, 2000, issue of *People* magazine, more serious problems on the set of *Bette* came to light—regarding further cast changes. A color publicity photo of the original cast of the show was depicted, with everyone exuding optimistic smiles. Over the faces of Kevin Dunn and Lindsay Lohan were red circles with slashes through them. Dunn was suddenly out of *Bette*. The article claimed, "CBS rep Beth Haiken calls the split amicable and 'mutual.' Dunn declined comment" (187). The cast of *Bette* was very quickly turning into a dwindling party. With the exit of Kevin Dunn from the cast, clearly the show was also fast becoming a sinking ship, and with Midler at the helm, the good ship *Bette* was taking on more and more water in a choppy ratings sea.

Disparaging remarks from the diva herself were also fanning the flames of disaster. When she went on *The Late Show with David Letterman*, Bette claimed of filming this show, "It's like being a dung beetle pushing this ball of dung up a mountain." She also underscored that comment by calling her show "the lowest thing that ever happened to me." When she appeared on the afternoon talkshow *The View*, she went so far as to intimate that she was so disheartened by *Bette* that she might just go into retirement after this debacle comes to a conclusion. On *The View* she also stated, "It's really much more stressful than I thought" (187).

The reviews in the press were getting progressively worse and worse. In the Los Angeles publication *LA Weekly*, reviewer Robert Lloyd found, "Bette Midler is the star driving the vehicle called *Bette*, and she's pedaling hard to make it go. I like Midler—she's an Ethel Merman for our times. *Brassy* is the good old word for her. She paints in broad strokes, and is not above grabbing her tits for a laugh. . . . As Midler's manager/pal, Joanna Gleason, whom it is always nice to see, plays Ethel to her Lucy, letting loyalty override common sense. . . . The show is funny in bits and in other bits it is not, and on the whole one wishes it were a little funnier a little more often, for Midler's sake as well as ours" (188).

People magazine pointed out, "Would Bette Midler be doing her flamboyant clowning on CBS's *Bette* if 50 years earlier Lucille Ball hadn't gotten tipsy on spoonfuls of Vitameatavegamin or wrestled a grape-stomping Italian woman in a wine vat? Doubtful" (189).

It was clear to everyone that Bette was trying her damnedest to do *I Love Lucy,* year 2000–style. Resorting to slapstick humor to drive this show was a huge mistake. Bette Midler is so sharp, so intelligent, and so funny on her own, she didn't need to stoop to facial mugging and pratfalls. This show should have been on a par with *Murphy Brown* or *Absolutely Fabulous*—instead of with *My Mother the Car.*

There was no question that Bette was trying to make it all work. But it wasn't long before juggling the cross-country commuting and work on the show got to her. "I know I'm going to do the best work I possibly can," she claimed. "And I think I'm going to have a lot of fun. But the workload is just so overwhelming. I don't want to be a bad sport, but it's hard," she complained. "When they say this is a dream job, they lie, lie, lie. I staggered all week. I was dying. I was dead on my feet. I had no idea. No idea. I've worked hard before, but never this hard. I am dumbstruck" (22).

With Kevin Dunn out of the picture, they decided to write Roy out of several of the scripts, concentrating on Bette and Connie in some out-of-town situation. It was the same way they had replaced Rose, only they waited even longer to debut the new Roy. Robert Hayes, who is most famous for the *Airplane!* movies, became Bette's new husband. It was actually a shame that he didn't play Roy from the beginning, because it looked like the two of them were truly having fun together. The chemistry between Midler and Hayes in the "new Roy" episode of *Bette* was quite nice.

It was so ironic that Hays's debut on *Bette* was also the last episode of the series. The show was number 16, appropriately entitled "Brand New Roy." In America, the announcement that *Bette* was over came on Monday; the show's last episode ran on Wednesday. That particular episode amusingly made jokes about Roy's new appearance, likening it to when *Bewitched* changed the actors who played Darrin, during its long television run.

The *Hollywood Reporter* soberly reported the facts: "The Columbia TriStar sitcom starring Bette Midler will have its final airing Wednesday. Production on the show has been shut down after completing 18 episodes of a 22 episode order. *Bette* had been set to be preempted for two weeks this month to make room for *Survivor* and CBS' coverage of the NCAA men's basketball tournament, and eye network brass decided it didn't make much sense to bring the low-rated comedy back after the break" (190). It didn't get much colder than that.

The show's ratings had dropped so low that it wasn't even worth broadcasting the final episodes, which were already "in the can." Furthermore, the show had so few viewers the network chose not to even waste its time broadcasting the reruns of episodes previously shown.

.The last two shows that were filmed were broadcast only outside of the United States. One show, #17, was called "The Grammy Pre-Show." It found Bette scheduled to perform on the Grammy Awards telecast, and the whole family and entourage are invited to join her. Oscar's grandmother is in town visiting, Connie starts a fashion trend with her new earrings, and Bette keeps trying to destroy her diet—and her ability to fit into her gown—by nibbling constantly. The last one, #18, was called "Method to Her Madness." In it, Bette sets out on a quest to find the perfect movie role, by doing some real life research on her own. She ends up in a truck stop.

On behalf of Bette and the All Girls Production company, Bonnie Bruckheimer publicly announced, "Bette and I will miss the very talented group of people whom we had the privilege of working with on a daily basis" (190).

And that was the sudden and abrupt end to Bette Midler's brief foray into network television. For Midler, the cancellation of *Bette* was both a relief and a huge a disappointment.

EXPERIENCE THE DIVINE

In what is perceived as a career "failure" of a year for Bette Midler, 2001 was actually a very high-profile one for the diva. On January 7, she was on hand for the telecast of CBS-TV's annual *People's Choice Awards.* The yearly honors are based on a poll that is tallied by the Gallup organization. Both Midler and her show *Bette* were nominated for awards that evening. Miss M won the trophy as the year's "Favorite Female Performer in a New Television Series." The award had nothing to do with ratings or critical perception of the show, but was based on votes from the public. It was an obvious sign that Bette's personal popularity was—and is—far greater than her highly unpopular TV series.

Two weeks later, on January 21, 2001, Midler was again nominated for an award because of *Bette.* This time around it was the Golden Globe Awards, where she was nominated in the category of "Best Actress in a TV Comedy, Musical, or Variety Series." However, the award went to the star of *Sex and the City,* Sarah Jessica Parker. In her acceptance speech Ms. Parker graciously commented from the podium that she personally thought Midler was going to win the trophy. Parker had been Bette's co-star in both *Hocus Pocus* and *First Wives Club,* and her *Sex* show was truly everything that the *Bette* show was not: brilliantly written, witty, controversial, sharp, and funny.

A month afterward, on February 21, Bette and Stevie Wonder were co-presenters of the award for "Album of the Year" at the 43rd Annual

Grammy Awards, which were broadcast from the Staples Center in Los Angeles. There was quite a bit of controversy in the air that night, due to the number of nominations that misogynist and antigay white rapper Eminem had received—including a nod for the year's best album. Had he taken the award, several human rights groups were expected to verbally protest from the audience. Looking rock & roll chic in a black leather outfit, Bette motioned to Wonder and quipped from the podium, "I was so nervous I brought the most beloved figure in music to hide behind in case some of you want to rush the stage" (191). Ultimately, it was not Eminem's album that won the award, but Steely Dan's comeback disc *Two against Nature.*

During an awards show streak, on February 24, 2001, three days after the Grammys, Bette was at the annual *TV Guide Awards* celebration. Midler and her show *Bette* were up for three separate awards. She ended up being awarded a trophy for "Actress of the Year in a New Series."

Irony of ironies, after personally winning both a People's Choice Award and a *TV Guide* Award, on March 5, 2001, CBS pulled the plug on the *Bette* show. The final episode was broadcast on March 7, and that was the end of the show—no reruns, no big series ending, just the axe. Bette had such high hopes for her TV series. It was a tremendous risk for her to embark upon, and she was crushed when it all came to a dead halt.

According to an article in *Inside* magazine, on March 21, 2001, Midler promptly fired the talent agency she had been signed to, Endeavor. She had been with the firm over the past five years. It had seemed that the agency had steered her into one career blunder after another.

On April 17, 2001, Bette was all smiles when she attended the first anniversary party celebrating the publication of Oprah Winfrey's monthly magazine, *O.* She looked great posing for photos with Winfrey, wearing a tasteful black suit and a blue-patterned silk scarf around her neck.

According to a May 2 Reuters wire service story, the mystery of whom Midler would choose to next professionally represent her was solved when it was announced that she had been signed by International Creative Management (ICM). It would now be handling all of her business affairs and hopefully would steer her into clearer waters than Endeavor had.

At the end of April it had been announced that Bette, together with her business partner Bonnie Bruckheimer, would pen a book about the disastrous *Bette* TV show experience. They were talking with Simon & Schuster Publishers about writing a bitter tome called *Canceled.* However, on May 7, only two weeks later, *Canceled* had also been canceled. Speculation around the project suggested that the reason was that since both Simon & Schuster and CBS-TV were owned by Viacom Inc., it would have been a matter of biting the hand that feeds one, to publish a book bashing the same company by which the publisher was owned.

Midler was one of the stars to appear in New York City on May 22, at a benefit held at the 92nd Street YMCA, called the Spring Gala. Making jokes about her ill-fated TV show, she said snickeringly from the stage, "Los Angeles can be so cold, so cruel, after you've been . . . what's the word? Oh, yes, 'fired.'" She also took time to bash Tom Cruise a bit, pointing out the concurrent tabloid stories questioning his sexuality. Said Miss M, "All these rumors about him being gay. I don't believe it. I don't believe it for one minute. He hasn't been to one of my shows!" (192).

The week of June 15, 2001, Bette's latest single, a disco remix CD of "In These Shoes," reached Number 8 on the *Billboard* magazine's Dance/Club Play charts. The single featured seven different dance remixes of the song. The funniest one is called the "Sound Factory Vox Mix," which has a unique Midler performance. As the rhythm section begins the song, Midler frantically announces, "Gentlemen, gentlemen, gentlemen, please, please, please: SHUT THE FUCK UP! I've got something to say! Why isn't anybody listening to me? This is really starting to get on my nerves. Pay attention!" That Bette, always the lady!

On June 18, 2001, Bette and her husband, Martin, were on hand to attend a screening of the bio-pic *James Dean,* produced by TNT Cable network and co-starring and directed by actor/director Mark Rydell. It was Rydell who had directed Midler in both of her Oscar-nominated roles, *The Rose* (1979) and *For the Boys* (1991).

It was announced on August 31, 2001, that the Record Industry Association of America (RIAA) had officially certified Bette's album *Bette of Roses* as having achieved Platinum status. This marked her fifth album that had logged sales in excess of a million copies in the United States (joining her other Platinum albums: *The Divine Miss M, The Rose, Some People's Lives,* and *Experience the Divine*).

The events of September 11, 2001, were so frighteningly horrific that the whole world—and especially New York City—was in a state of shock. When terrorists hijacked four jet liners on suicide missions and brought down the World Trade Center in a matter of hours, killing thousands, the planet watched in awe. That act, combined with the attack on the Pentagon in Washington, D.C., and the downed plane in Pennsylvania, made that date the single most devastating day in U.S. history in over a century. The site once known as the most architecturally soaring in all of Manhattan was reduced to a twisted pile of rubble, now dubbed "ground zero."

Ten days later, Bette Midler, actress Candice Bergen, boxer Joe Frazier, and promoter Don King were among the famous people who received a guided tour of "ground zero" on the 21st of September. The visit was the idea of New York's most famous recent mayor, Rudolph Giuliani. He felt that the teams of rescue workers at the site could use a morale boost by his inviting some "star" visitors.

On Sunday, September 23, 2001, a crowd gathered at Yankee Stadium in the Bronx to pray, praise, cry, and bid public farewell to the thousands who had lost their lives on September 11. The event was entitled *A Prayer for America,* and it featured prayers from many denominations, including Christian, Muslim, Jewish, Sikh, and Hindu. Hosted by Oprah Winfrey, the performing guests included operatic tenor Placido Domingo, patriotic country singer Lee Greenwood, and Bette Midler. Before a crowd of approximately 30,000 people, the inspiring Miss M sang her song of hope "The Wind beneath My Wings," bringing the crowd to tears.

What strange irony it indeed is, in retrospect. The image of the World Trade Center had very oddly been in so many of Midler's films. It was behind her in the heliport scene in *The Rose* and in films such as *Oliver & Company* and *That Old Feeling,* in what is known as an "establishment" shot of the most famous skyline in the world. Now Bette was called upon to help the public properly mourn its demise—and to salute all of the innocent people killed in this horrific attack.

Three days later, Bette was to deliver a similar emotion-filled memorial performance in Boston, the site of Logan Airport, where the two fatal World Trade Center–bound flights originated. It was her desire that her appearance not be publicized, for fear that celebrity-followers would come to Boston to see her and not to pay their respects to the victims of the tragic flights. However, both the New York and Boston newspapers got wind of her forthcoming appearance and leaked the news to the public. The knowledge of Midler's appearance did not upset the touching effect of her appearance in Massachusetts.

On October 21, 2001, Bette was one of the high-profile acts to perform in Washington, D.C., at RFK Stadium as part of the fundraising concert *United We Stand: What More Can I Give?* Over 48,000 tickets were sold to the all-evening event, ultimately raising over $2 million. What had been intended as an eight-hour event stretched out to twelve hours, and the stadium was not properly stocked to accommodate such a long event. They ran out of food, they ran out of drinks, but they certainly didn't run out of talent that evening. Among the acts on the bill were the Backstreet Boys, James Brown, America, Destiny's Child, Rod Stewart, Mariah Carey, Michael Jackson, and Pink. That night Midler sang her sentimental classic "From a Distance" and her patriotic "Boogie Woogie Bugle Boy." As she was getting ready to sing "The Rose," Miss M said to the crowd, "I want to sing you a song not of sorrow but of hope" (193). A two-hour special was cut from the twelve-hour event and broadcast on November 1, 2001. However, Midler and several of the other older acts were omitted from the ultimate broadcast, in an effort to capture a younger TV-viewing audience. What an insulting and stupid move on the part of that TV network~

Speaking of all the rescue efforts and fundraisers, Midler said at the time, "The number of charities and charitable events has absolutely mushroomed beyond all belief. There's hardly any social life anymore outside of that. In this town, in New York, people go from benefit to benefit to benefit" (194).

On November 24, 2001, it became official that All Girls Productions was no more: Bette and Bonnie Bruckheimer decided to amicably go their separate ways. The company's last film production, *Divine Secrets of the Ya Ya Sisterhood,* would not be affected by this news.

Bette was one of the stars whose voice was used in the HBO holiday television special *'Twas the Night.* She was heard singing the Jewish song "Chanukah, Oh Chanukah," alongside Doris Day's "I'll Be Home for Christmas," Nat King Cole's "The Christmas Song," Los Lobos' "Feliz Navidad," Macy Gray's "Winter Wonderland," and Frank Sinatra's "The Christmas Waltz." The special was largely animated with cartoons, based on classic Grandma Moses paintings, and it combined the celebrations of Christmas, Hanukkah, and Kwanzaa.

January 1, 2002, Bette had the honor of singing "The Star Spangled Banner" to kick off the inauguration of New York City's new mayor,

Michael Blumberg. The event was held outdoors in freezing cold temperatures, on the steps of Manhattan's City Hall, only blocks from "ground zero," before a crowd of 4,000 invited guests that included former mayors Ed Koch and David Dinkins, outgoing mayor Rudy Giuliani, and New York state senators Hillary Clinton and Chuck Schumer. Midler sang the National Anthem in a lower key than usual, giving the song a sense of both sadness and hope, which was apropos, considering what the city had been through in the last several months.

There are so many talented people in the diva's past who have made the Bette Midler saga so full and fascinating. Barry Manilow has naturally gone on to become a hugely successful superstar and as big an international name as Miss M herself. Barry's own multimillion-selling albums have yielded such hits as "Mandy," "Could It Be Magic?" and "Copacabana." Melissa Manchester has also had her own highly successful run in show business and in the recording world. Her catalog of hits includes "Midnight Blue," Whenever I Call You Friend," and "You Don't Know How She Talks about You." Former Harlette Linda Hart holds the record as Bette Midler's most frequent movie co-star. Linda has been in the Midler films *Divine Madness, Stella, Get Shorty,* and *Gypsy.* Katie Sagal found post-Harlette TV fame in the hit series *Married with Children.* Jenifer Lewis had her first move role in *Beaches* and went on to have a varied acting career that included *What's Love Got to Do with It, The Temptations, The Preacher's Wife,* and starring as Jackie Washington in *Jackie's Back*—in which Bette made a guest appearance as herself. Ula Hedwig is Midler's most recurring Harlette in the recording studio, appearing most recently on the *Bathhouse Betty* album. Charlotte Crossley lives in Los Angeles and still shows up on records from time to time. Sharon Redd went on to record several dance hits on her own in the 1980s, including "Beat the Street" and "Can You Handle It?" Her work was compiled on the 1996 album *The Very Best of Sharon Redd.* Sadly, she died of cancer in 1993. Moogy Klingman, who wrote "Friends" and produced most of Bette's *Songs for the New Depression* album, still lives in New York City, is a frequent performer in nightclubs, and has worked on musical projects with Robert Downey, Jr., and Michael Anthony Hall. Musical collaborator Marc Shaiman has become known in Hollywood as a talented songwriter and was nominated for an Oscar for the song "Blame Canada" from the *South Park* film. Bruce Vilanch, who has written jokes for so many stars, became known as a frequent guest on the TV show *Hollywood Squares* in the twenty-first century.

Unlike a lot of divas of Midler's stature, she has not forgotten her friends when they need help. One of the friendships Bette has kept the strongest has been with songwriter Buzzy Linhart.

By the late 1990s, Buzzy had fallen on hard luck, having moved out to Berkeley, California. In 2002 he was confined to a wheelchair. Speaking of Buzzy, Moogy Klingman explained, "He has problems with his bones, he can't really walk. His arms don't work too well. He is still a good singer, but he can't play his guitar anymore" (36).

Describing his predicament, Linhart says, "The problem is that I was injured in a car accident, and then assaulted shortly after, and it really, really hurt my knee and chest. . . . Then it took a MediCal operation that left my knee not functioning even as well as it did before. And I found out to my horror when I tried to tell Social Security and MediCal about it, their response was to call the doctor. And he said, 'Oh, he's fine. I don't know what he said. He's fine. Maybe he's psychiatric'" (37).

Finally, he convinced California social services that he did indeed need a wheelchair. However, he explains, "What MediCal sent was not right for me. First of all, I've got an injured leg. I can't have like a scooter with my foot hanging down all the time. I need one that can lift me up, and lean me back, because it chronically swells. What they sent is not even for my size person. I am a 200-pounder, so that sits in the corner and waits for me to give to someone else" (37).

The wheelchair that he did need, however, he could not afford. "A $10,000 chair that we were able to get, it was slightly used, and we were able to get it for $5,000," explains Linhart (37). However, although a bargain, he didn't have the money to buy it.

Says a deeply touched Linhart, it was Midler who came to the rescue: "When Bette heard that we needed the money, she sent the whole thing about three days later. It was really exciting. It is 'The Bette Midler Chair.' I just feel so closely connected to her" (37).

Of all of the people in Bette's past, one of the most interesting ones is her former manager, Aaron Russo. He now lives in Nevada and has been pursuing a career in politics. In February of 2002 he was written about in the *Las Vegas Sun,* as considering becoming a candidate for governor of that state. In Nevada he had previously run—unsuccessfully—for the U.S. Senate and campaigned for the legalization of marijuana and the creation of a state lottery. Viewing this list of high-profile lives and careers that have spun off from Midler's own creative camp makes her not so much a star as a cottage industry for creative talent.

On April 2, 2002, Bette Midler was one of the stars present at the Boathouse in Central Park in Manhattan, to celebrate the twentieth anniversary of Paul Newman's Own food line, with the proceeds going to charity. Present that night at the event were Michael J. Fox, Rudy Giuliani, Tim Robbins, Tony Randall, and Harry Belefonte. The festivities were kicked off by a performance by Carole King and finished with Bette Midler singing a song written for Newman's Own line of food. How fitting to have Ol' Redhair serenade Ol' Blue-Eyed Newman.

In May of 2002, when TV talkshow hostess Rosie O'Donnell was about to end her six-year run on the air, she had several high-profile guests on the program during her last weeks. As one of the guest stars, Bette serenaded O'Donnell with a song she had never performed publicly before: "I Wish You Love." While chatting with Rosie on camera, she offered her "four words of advice." Comically, they were the profound words "Don't do a sitcom!"

What's next for Bette Midler, musically speaking? It's hard to tell, given the unpredictable nature of her recording career. Many of the producers she has worked with in the past would love to record with her again.

If Brooks Arthur were to go into the studio with her today, what direction would he take? According to him, "Well, you might think I am out of step, but I know I am in step. The first thing that I would do to bring back her record career, and it has to be well coordinated as a two-step kind of a deal. I would do an album of classic standards—a real album of '40s and '50s kinds of tunes. And then I would find songs either from Broadway or something from a movie. The next album after that one would be an album of songs that [have] the depth of 'Wind beneath My Wings.' That's what I would do. Her strength is the ballads, but you've got to have some fun, too. . . . But that is what I would do with Bette right now. I would cut an album of like, 'Love Letters (Straight from Your Heart),' those kinds of tunes. I would cut those kind of 'gems.' And, maybe even have her do a duet with one of her favorite gals from the movies from the '40s or the '30s, or the '50s" (77).

Both Moogy Klingman and Brooks Arthur are dying for Atlantic Records to release some of the songs they cut with Bette while working on the albums *Songs for the New Depression* and *Broken Blossom.* Both of these talented men claim that their best work with Bette is still "in the can" at Atlantic. In fact, there is at least a double-album's worth of recorded Bette Midler material still "in the vaults." In addition to a dozen Klingman-produced songs, there is Brooks Arthur's "Someone That I Used to Love," Ashford & Simpson's tracks with her, and those she did with Hal Davis. There are also several songs that Bette recorded for her films, which have never been released except as part of these films. This list includes "I Put a Spell on You" from *Hocus Pocus,* "One More Cheer" from *Stella,* "You Do Something to Me" from *Scenes from a Mall,* and "A Cowgirl's Dream" from *Jinxed.*

She could also team up with Barry Manilow, and he could produce her singing all of the songs they used to perform together, which she never recorded from her days at the Continental Baths. That list of songs includes "Wheel of Fortune," "Sha-Boom Sha-Boom," "Happiness Is a Thing Called Joe," "Honky Tonk Woman," "Lady Madonna," "What a Difference a Day Makes," "My Forgotten Man," "Ten Cents a Dance," "Come Up and See Me Sometime," "Love Potion Number Nine," and "Great Balls of Fire." Now, there's a hot album idea!

During her four decades as a multimedia star, Bette Midler has had an amazing career. In addition to her artistry as an actress, a singer, and a stage performer, she has also managed to have a rich and full personal life. Her marriage to Martin and life with her daughter Sophie have only added further dimensions to her life experiences.

Bette Midler is someone who totally enjoys her celebrity stature. She also enjoys her privacy from time to time. According to Brooks Arthur, "One day I was at the airport, and I saw a few friends I knew getting off a plane. I ran over and said, 'Hey, Bette!' She said, 'Don't call me "Bette," you're gonna call attention to me. Call me "Dolores."'" (77).

She is also very devoted to her family. She is a dedicated wife and mother, and she does her best to make sure that her daughter Sophie has as normal an upbringing as possible. When you are the Divine Miss M, that isn't always possible, but Bette keeps Sophie grounded.

As for close relatives, the only family Bette has left are her sister Susan and her mentally handicapped brother Danny, who live together in New York City. Susan teaches retarded children, and their relationship works out perfectly. Bette feels that Danny has taught her so much about what is important in life. "Being Danny's sister has made me different from everyone else. I wouldn't trade it in," she stated with conviction and devotion (8).

Would Bette like to rewrite the scenario of her own life story? And, if so, what parts would she like to "edit" or "delete"? According to her, "I'd like to have a little red pencil to scratch out some of the scenes in my life. I always wished . . . that my chest was smaller . . . that my hair was thicker . . . that my eyes were bluer . . . that my IQ was higher . . . that my shoe size was smaller. I never thought I was too pretty most of the time. I used to spend a lot of time turning my nose up in front of the mirror, you know, thinking, 'Well, maybe you should have a nose job.' Now I think I can live with it" (8).

It's hard to believe that Bette Midler was once an "ugly duckling" teenage Jewish girl growing up in the center of a Samoan village. She always felt that she didn't fit in, because she was "different." But she was determined to turn "different" into "special." She dreamed of stardom while she was packing pineapples in Hawaii, so she packed her bags and went after her dreams. In doing so, she has subsequently become an inspiration to many.

She's come a long way from that frightening first night at the Continental Baths—the night when almost no one paid attention to her. By the time she left the "tubs," her ability to transform songs into theatrical vignettes had made her a star. She became known for being brassy, outspoken, and sexually liberated. In the 1940s or 1950s, she would have been the type of woman known as a "broad." And what a talented "broad" she has become! She conquered Broadway, she recorded million-selling hit albums, and she became a movie star.

Despite all of her bawdy behavior and her dirty "Soph" jokes, she has always been a gifted singer who could sing emotional ballads better than anyone in the business. For all of the dozens of songs she has recorded, she will most be identified with "The Rose," "The Wind beneath My Wings," and "From a Distance."

Her stage shows have always been unforgettable—for their outrageous brassiness and for the amazing amount of energy she expends on stage. Indeed, she stops at nothing to please an audience. And she has in the past *really* given her all.

"I think I like singing more than any of that. The singing is the biggest challenge. The rest of it is very, very simple for me. Other people, you know, probably grind their teeth and say, 'Oh, she's so full of it.' But you have to hone that gift constantly—you cannot let it go, otherwise it disappears. That, I think, is the greatest challenge, and I've always liked the challenge" (164).

In her own words, she proclaims, "I think the reason I was put here is to make people happy" (8). Indeed, she's done everything in her power to stand out from the crowd. She's bared her soul in a song, and she's bared her breasts to shock and please an audience. She's mooned Harvard, dropped her dress for St. Louis, flashed Detroit, and performed great feats without fear of convention, taste, or scandal. And, through it all, it has been internationally acknowledged that she *IS* beautiful, *DAMN IT!*

She is unpredictable, and there's no telling what she is going to do next. She is famous for her charitable work as well. Bette Midler has come to be known as a champion of the downtrodden. She's never afraid to stand up for what she believes in—no matter what the odds. She has proved her versatility, and she again has the confidence to take chances. Her ability to look at life and laugh at it, and her talent for bringing to life so many vivid characters, have brought her international fame. She's had several disappointments, but at this point in her career, she has so many irons in the fire and her position in show business is so well established that her star stature is secure. Her legion of loyal fans support her outlandishness, and her critics know what she'll tell them to do if they can't take a joke! Fortunately, the public's love affair with the Divine Miss M has only just begun.

Three decades ago she knew she wanted to get into the movies, and since that time, what an amazingly rich body of filmed work she has created—from dramas like *The Rose, Beaches,* and *Stella* to comedies like *Ruthless People, Down & Out in Beverly Hills,* and *First Wives Club.* She's been a cartoon character in *Oliver & Company,* and often her mere guest appearance in a film brightens up the screen, as it did in *Get Shorty, Jackie's Back,* and *What Women Want.* She has starred in her own TV series, won Emmys for her television specials, and penned best-selling books.

According to her, "I'm very glad I lived the life that I lived. It made me what I am. I'm having a fabulous time" (164).

Books, records, songwriting, television, movie production, motherhood . . . it's clear that Bette Midler and her talent know no boundaries. She isn't easily intimidated by challenge—or by critical or artistic disappointment. As she has been for many years, she is in total control of her career. Who knows? She may even end up playing Lady Macbeth before she's done. To recall the magic word from Baby Divine, there is only one thing better than all of this creativity from Bette, and that is "more!"

SOURCES OF
QUOTED MATERIAL

(1) Jenny Allen, "Bette Midler: The Divine Secrets of Bette Midler," *Good Housekeeping* (October 2000).

(2) "Bette Midler," *Current Biography* (June 1973).

(3) Chris Chase, "Good, Better, Best, Bette," *New York Times,* January 14, 1973.

(4) Charles Michener, "Here Comes Bette!/Bette Midler," *Newsweek* (December 17, 1973).

(5) Robb Baker, *Bette Midler: The Divine Miss M* (Popular Library, 1975).

(6) Cynthia Spector, "Bette Midler: I Want to Be the Most Desired Woman on Earth/Bette: There Is Only One Bette Midler," *Zoo World* (October 25, 1973).

(7) Bette Midler, *Mud Will Be Flung Tonight!* (Atlantic Records, 1985).

(8) Mark Bego, *Bette Midler: Outrageously Divine* (New American Library, 1987).

(9) J. E. Burgoyne, "Midler Liking Home, Hubby," *New Orleans Times Picayune,* July 15, 1986.

(10) "Stargazing," *Kansas City Star,* column item; Kansas City, Missouri; July 3, 1986.

(11) Jan Hodenfield, "Divine Miss Superstar," *New York Post,* December 30, 1972.

(12) May Okon, "Today's Best Bette," *New York Sunday News,* October 28, 1973.

(13) Timothy White, "'The Rose'—Bette Midler Conquers Hollywood/The Homecoming—Bette Midler Outgrows Her Hollywood Dreams in 'The Rose,'" *Rolling Stone* (December 13, 1979).

(14) Patricia Burstein, "Bette Midler: Tender, Tacky and Back on Top/A Showbiz Dropout for 15 Months, Bette Midler Returns in Tacky Triumph," *People* (June 30, 1975).

(15) Dave Hirshey, "Return Engagement: Bette Midler," *Sunday News Magazine, New York Daily News,* November 4, 1979.

(16) James Spada, *The Divine Bette Midler* (Collier Books, 1984).

(17) Melinda Gerosa, "Best Bette," *Ladies' Home Journal* (September 1999).

(18) Mark Morrison, "With a New Husband, Two Hit Movies and a Baby on the Way, Who Wants to Be Ruthless? BETTE MIDLER," *Us* (July 28, 1986).

(19) Al Rudis, "Bette Comes On Strong and Some Can't Take the Heat," *Showcase/Chicago Sun Times,* July 25, 1971.

(20) Richard Corliss, "You Bette! Midler Strikes Again in *Outrageous Fortune*/Bette Steals Hollywood," *Time* (March 2, 1987). Reported by Mary Cronin/New York; Elaine Dutka and Denise Worrell/Los Angeles.

(21) Claudia Dreifus, "Bette Midler: The Outcast Who's Finally 'In'" *Playgirl* (1975).

(22) Lynn Hirschberg, "Bette's Bet/Meta Midler," *New York Times Magazine,* October 8, 2000.

(23) Alan J. Gansberg, "'Tacky' Places and Future Plans Top Divine Miss M Talk," *Herald-News,* Passaic, New Jersey, August 10, 1973.

(24) Judith Stone, "An Even Better Bette," *McCalls* (March 1986).

(25) Patrick and Barbara Salvo, "Bette Midler Had to Kill 'The Divine Miss M,'" *Touch* (July 1974).

(26) "Trash with Flash," *Time* (September 10, 1973).

(27) Marsha Blyth, "Bette Tells All/Bette on Bette," *Ladies' Home Journal* (January 1992).

(28) Radford High School newspaper, Honolulu, Hawaii, 1963.

(29) Kay Holmes, "A Visit to the Pad of the Queen of Camp," *Sunday News Magazine, New York Daily News,* August 5, 1973.

(30) Nancy Collins, "Bette Midler: The Cheese-Bomb American Crapola Dream," *Rolling Stone* (December 9, 1982).

(31) Mark Bego's interview with Baby Jane Dexter, New York City, December 5, 1986.

(32) Mark Bego's interview with a confidential source, New York City, October 15, 1986.

(33) Rex Reed, "That Wacky Little Waif, Bette Midler," *Sunday New York Daily News,* February 20, 1972.

(34) *The Tonight Show,* NBC-TV, October 1970.

(35) Mark Bego's interview with a confidential source, who was once employed by Bette Midler, New York City, October 18, 1986.

(36) Mark Bego's telephone interview with Moogy Klingman, April 9, 2002.

(37) Mark Bego's telephone interview with Buzzy Linhart, April 11, 2002.

(38) Craig Zadan, "Bette's Back!" *New York* (April 14, 1975).

(39) Mark Bego's interview with Marie Morreale, New York City, December 4, 1986.

(40) Kevin Sessums, "Bette's Back/La Belle Bette," *Vanity Fair* (December 1991).

(41) John S. Wilson, review of Bette Midler at Downstairs at the Upstairs, *New York Times,* October 3, 1971.

(42) Gerald Clarke, "Midler: Make Me a Legend!" *Time* (December 31, 1979).

(43) Barry Manilow, *Sweetlife: Adventures on the Way to Paradise* (McGraw Hill, 1986).

(44) Mike Jan, review of *The Divine Miss M, Cue* (1972).

(45) Jim Spada, quoting a 1973 *Rolling Stone* article on Bette Midler, in his book *The Divine Bette Midler* (Collier, 1984).

(46) Bette Midler, *A View from a Broad* (Simon and Schuster, 1980).

(47) A review by Henry Edwards in the *New York Times,* 1972, quoted in a press release from Atlantic Records that was sent out with the *Broken Blossom* album.

(48) Rob Baker, "Above and Beyond the Call of Trash," *Soho Weekly News,* May 5, 1977.

(49) Lillian Roxon, "The Divine Miss M. and Those Rotten Old Days," *Sunday New York Daily News,* January 7, 1973.

(50) Mark Bego's interview with Barry Manilow, 1975.

(51) "Bette Midler," a review of her act at the Palace Theater, New York City, *Variety,* December 5, 1973.

(52) Michael LaChetta, "Not Divine . . . but Miss M Is Very Special," *New York Daily News,* December 4, 1973.

(53) Richie Rothenstein's interview with Melissa Manchester, late 1970s.

(54) Stan Mieses, "Surprise! Bette's Grown Up," *Sunday New York Daily News,* March 7, 1976.

(55) Jon Laudau, review of the album *Bette Midler, Rolling Stone* (1973).

(56) Kay Gardella, "Will Cher Be a Long-Playing Single?" *New York Daily News,* February 9, 1975.

(57) Robert G. Smith, "Cher's TV Clothes Cost Up to $30,000 a Week," *National Enquirer,* June 24, 1975.

(58) Robert Wahls, "The Very Odd Couple," *New York Daily News,* April 13, 1975.

(59) Mike Jahn, "Guaranteed Taste-Free," *Cue* (March 14–20, 1975.

(60) Rex Reed, review of *Bette Midler's Clams on the Half-Shell Revue, New York Daily News,* 1975.

(61) Clive Barnes, Revue: Bette Midler, *New York Times,* April 18, 1975.

(62) Mark Bego, "In Manhattan," *Portland Opera* (May 14, 1975).

(63) Richard Goldstein, "The Dark Side of Bette Midler," *Village Voice,* April 21, 1975.

(64) Victoria Kingston, *Simon & Garfunkel: The Biography* (Fromm International, 1988).

(65) Mark Bego's interview with a confidential source, 2002.

(66) Mark Bego's interview with Gary Herb, New York City, December 4, 1986.

(67) Grover Lewis, "Bette and Aaron: One Sings, the Other Doesn't," *New West* (March 13, 1978).

(68) Steven Gaines, "Top of Pop: 'I'm Real Sorry—But That's Show Biz,'" *New York Daily News*, 1976.

(69) David Tipmore, "Bette Midler Bids for Fame," *Village Voice*, February 9, 1976.

(70) "Bette: Shuffle Off in Buffalo," *New York Post*, February 16, 1978.

(71) Peter Lester, "Bette Midler: Give Me Some Respect—I'm a Screen Goddess Now/After Capturing Janis and Being Compared to Barbara, Nothing's Too Lofty for the Divine Miss M," *People* (January 7, 1980).

(72) Liz Smith, "Publicity, Privacy & Personality," *New York Daily News*, 1977.

(73) A press release bulletin sent out to journalists by Atlantic Records, advertising the album *Live at Last* (*Album Reviews*, 1977).

(74) Frank Rose, "Bette Midler Spreads It Around," *Village Voice*, June 20, 1977.

(75) Bill Sievert, "Dispatch: Marred but Successful 'Star Spangled Night,'" *Advocate* (October 1977).

(76) by Leon MacDonald, "Sharon Redd, Ula Hedwig, Charlotte Crossley," *Routes* (June 1978).

(77) Mark Bego's telephone interview with Brooks Arthur, April 17, 2002.

(78) Arthur Bell, "Bette Midler at $20 a Head," *Village Voice*, January 23, 1978.

(79) Nicolas Yanni, review of the *Bette Midler* TV special, *Soho Weekly News*, December 8, 1977.

(80) *Ol' Red Hair Is Back*, TV special, 1977.

(81) David Shaw, "I've Got All These Characters Living Inside of Me," *TV Guide* (December 3, 1977).

(82) Press release sent out by Rogers & Cowan (1975), "Bette Midler Refuses $3,000,000: Will Do Intimate Tour Instead."

(83) Mark Bego's review notes, the Copacabana, January 20, 1978.

(84) Rex Reed, "Place Your Bettes," *New York Daily News*, January 18, 1978.

(85) Corby Kummer, "Best Bette Yet," *Cue* (November 23, 1978)

(86) "The Midler Touch," *Marquee* (January/February 1980).

(87) Paul Grien, "A Rejected 'Rose' Blooms for Midler, Enhancing Credibility," *Billboard* (February 4, 1981).

(88) Armistead Maupin, "Bette Midler," *Interview* (1982).

(89) Warren Hoge, "Bette Midler Goes Hollywood," *New York Times*, December 10, 1978.

(90) Stephen Holden, review of *Thighs and Whispers*, *Village Voice*, 1979.

(91) "People" page item, *Time* (November 19, 1979).

(92) Judy Klemesrud, "Bette Midler Takes Her Party in Stride," *New York Times*, November 8, 1979.

(93) Frank Rich, "Flashy Trash," a review of *The Rose*, *Time* (November 12, 1979).

(94) *No Frills,* Cinemax special 1983.
(95) Lee Grant, "Midler: In the Hubbub of *Jinxed,*" *Los Angeles Times, Calendar,* September 5, 1982.
(96) Lee Grant, "Trouble on the Set of *Jinxed?* You Can Bet on It," *Los Angeles Times, Calendar,* September 27. 1981.
(97) Thomas O'Connor, "Bette Midler is Up and In in Hollywood," *New York Times,* June 22, 1986.
(98) Tower Records.com, 2002, Internet site, quoting press reviews from various sources, as individually indicated.
(99) Mick Martin and Marsha Porter, *Video Movie Guide 2001* (Ballantine Books, 2000).
(100) Carol Wallace, "Bette Midler: At 40, the Sassiest Mouth in Showbiz Surprises Herself with a Happy Marriage/Happy at Last? You Bette," *People* (February 3, 1986).
(101) Jack Curry, "Bette Is Back: The Refined Miss M," *USA Weekend* (January 31–February 2, 1986).
(102) John Corry, review of *Bette Midler: Art or Bust! New York Times,* 1984.
(103) "Random Notes: The Prime of Miss Bette Midler," *Rolling Stone* (January 30, 1986).
(104) Stephen M. Silverman, "Mazursky Up & At 'Em, Thanks to *Down & Out,*" *New York Post.*
(105) Bruce Cook, "Up and into Beverly Hills," *News,* Van Nuys, California, January 31, 1986.
(106) Roger Ebert, review of *Down and Out in Beverly Hills, Chicago Sun Times,* January 31, 1986.
(107) Richard Shickel, review of his *Down and Out in Beverly Hills, Time,* 1986.
(108) Bill Morrison, review of *Down and Out in Beverly Hills, Raleigh, North Carolina, News and Observer,* February 12, 1986.
(109) Michael Neill, "The Divine Misses M," "Chatter" item, *People,* 1986.
(110) Monica Collins, "Miss M Never Divined She'd Be This Happy," *USA Today* (July 14, 1988).
(111) Cathleen McGuigan, "The Divine Mrs. M," *Newsweek* (June 30, 1986).
(112) "'The Divine Miss M' Plays a Hellish Hostage in *Ruthless People,*" *News,* Armadillo, Texas; August 3, 1986.
(113) Eleanor Ringel, "Dandy DeVito vs. Best Bette," *Atlanta Journal,* June 27, 1986.
(114) "*Ruthless People* at Holiday Cinemas," *Register Citizen,* Torrington, Connecticut; July 1, 1986.
(115) Peter Travers, review of *Outrageous Fortune, People* (February 16, 1987).
(116) David Ansen with Peter McAlevey, "Some Down and Dirty Zingers," *Newsweek* (January 26, 1987).

(117) Richard Corliss, "Femeraderie" a review of *Outrageous Fortune, Time* (February 2, 1987).

(118) Geoprgea Kovanis, "A Few Words with John Schuck," *Detroit Free Press,* July 19, 1988.

(119) "Florida Heiress Doesn't Want Midler Cast in *Palm Beached*," *St. Petersburg Times,* August 22, 1986.

(120) James Kaplan, "The Real Life Drama behind Bette's New Hit Show/Bette Midler's Divine Inspiration," *US* (October 30, 2000).

(121) Marylynn Uricchio, "Comedy Is Proving to Be Bette Midler's Route to Success," *Pittsburgh Post Gazette,* April 22, 1986.

(122) *Big Business,* Touchstone Home Video packaging, quoting reviews from both *Good Morning America* and *People.*

(123) Roger Ebert, review of *Big Business, Chicago Sun Times,* June 10, 1988.

(124) Marvin Kitman, review of *Bette Midler's Mondo Beyondo, Newsday* (1988).

(125) Susan Spillman, "Bette's the Boss: Her Production Team Gets Aggressive," *USA Today* (January 5, 1989).

(126) Susan Spillman, "The Delicate Art of Hooking Moviegoers," *USA Today* (November 21, 1991).

(127) *Beaches,* Touchstone Home Video packaging, quoting reviews from both the *Washington Post* and the *Hollywood Reporter.*

(128) Leonard Maltin, *1998 Movie & Video Guide* (Signet Books, 1997).

(129) Roger Ebert, review of *Beaches, Chicago Sun Times,* January 13, 1989.

(130) Ron Graham, "Stella, Reborn As an Unmarried Mother," *New York Times,* July 16, 1989.

(131) Allison J. Waldman, *The Bette Midler Scrapbook* (Citadel, 1997).

(132) Roger Ebert, review of *Stella, Chicago Sun-Times,* February 2, 1990.

(133) Gene Siskell, review of *Stella, Chicago Tribune,* February 1990.

(134) Stanley Kauffmann, review of *Stella, New Republic* (1990).

(135) Roger Ebert, review of *Scenes from a Mall, Chicago Sun-Times,* 1991.

(136) David Denby, review of *Scenes from a Mall, New York* (1991).

(137) Geraldo Rivera with Daniel Paisner, *Exposing Myself* (Bantam, Doubleday, Dell, 1991).

(138) Ann Trebbe, "Midler's Turn to Expose Geraldo," *USA Today* (November 4, 1991).

(139) John Barry, "Bette Makes Geraldo Squirm with Anguish," *Arizona Daily Star,* from the Knight-Rider Newswire, November 9, 1991.

(140) Mitchell Fink, "The Insider/Cadillac Fracas," *People* (November 25, 1991).

(141) "Singer Bette Midler Joins California Program to Clean Freeway," *Arizona Daily Star,* from the Associated Press Newswire, November 10, 1991.

(142) *Yakety Yak, Take It Back,* video public service tape, 1991.

(143) Judy Gerstel, "Is It Midler? Or Lip-Synched by Computer?" Tucson's *Arizona Daily Star,* from the Knight-Rider newswire, December 6, 1991.

(144) Jeannie Williams, "How Bette Will Dress for Success," *USA Today* (November 13, 1991).

(145) *For the Boys,* Twentieth Century Fox, DVD package, quoting various publications' reviews of the film.

(146) Bob Thomas, review of *For the Boys*, Associated Press, 1991.

(147) Renata Polt, "Holiday Fare/A Musical Comedy Starring the Inimitable Bette Midler," *Pacific Sun,* November 29, 1991.

(148) Mike Clark, "For the Boys, Midler Lets Loose," *USA Today* (November 22, 1991).

(149) "Stars and Gripes," a review of the film *For the Boys, Entertainment Weekly* (November 29, 1991).

(150) Amy Dawes, "Film Reviews/*For the Boys*," *Daily Variety,* November 18, 1991.

(151) "Movieola," review of *For the Boys, Orbit* (December 12, 1991).

(152) David Patrick Sterns, "Movie Soundtracks with Winning Scores," *USA Today* (December 6, 1991).

(153) Ann Trebbe, "The 49th Annual Golden Globe Awards: A Night of Glitter and Congratulations/Midler's Burst Bubble," *USA Today* (January 20, 1992).

(154) "Sound-Alike Ads," *USA Today* (March 24, 1992).

(155) Matt Roush, "Bringing Out the *Gypsy* in Midler/Her Happiest Night with Johnny," *USA Today* (July 20, 1993).

(156) *Gypsy,* album liner notes, Atlantic Records, 1993.

(157) Ken Tucker, "Sure Bette," a review of *Gypsy, Entertainment Weekly* (December 10, 1993).

(158) Jonathan Taylor, review of *Gypsy, Daily Variety,* December 8, 1993.

(159) Susan Wloszczyna, "Midler, As Divine As Ever," *USA Today* (August 27, 1993).

(160) Stephen Holden, "The Two Sides of Bette Midler, Mushy and Divine," *New York Times,* July 16, 1995.

(161) Michael Wilmington, review of *Get Shorty, Chicago Tribune,* 1995.

(162) Janet Maslin, review of *Get Shorty, New York Times,* 1995.

(163) Howard Cohen, review of *Bette of Roses, Miami Herald,* 1995.

(164) Home Box Office, 1997, promo-interview regarding the HBO special *Diva Las Vegas.*

(165) Owen Gleiberman, "Ms. Guided Effort," *Entertainment Weekly* (September 27, 1996).

(166) Richard Corliss, "The Ladies Who Lunge," *Time* (October 7, 1996).

(167) Elizabeth Gleick, "Hell Hath No Fury," *Time* (October 7, 1996).

(168) John Anderson, review of *That Old Feeling, Los Angeles Times,* 1997.

(169) Jessica Shaw, "Dial M for Midler," *Entertainment Weekly* (September 18, 1998).

(170) *People,* 1998, a gossip item from the magazine's website.

(171) Sherri Sylvester, "*Get Bruce* Documents Career of Joke-Writing King," CNN (from CNN.com website), August 11, 1999.

(172) Jonathan Mandell, "Always Divine, Now Garbage Has Made Her a Saint," *New York Times,* November 17, 1999.

(173) Clara Hall, "Hard Work If You Can Get It," *Los Angeles Times, Calendar,* 2000.

(174) Jerry Fink, "Midler Divine for Her Globe-Hopping Followers," *Las Vegas Sun,* January 3, 2000.

(175) Susan Wlosczyna, "'Mona Immersed in Swill," *USA Today* (March 3, 2000).

(176) Paul Tatara, "*Drowning Mona* Has That Sinking Feeling," CNN (from CNN.com website), March 14, 2000.

(177) Bill Zwecker, review of *Drowning Mona,* WMAQ-TV, 2000, as quoted on the DVD package of the film.

(178) Leonard Maltin, *Leonard Maltin's Movie & Video Guide 2002* (Signet, 2001).

(179) Mick Martin and Marsha Porter, *The Video Movie Guide 2002* (Ballantine, 2001).

(180) *Isn't She Great?* Universal Pictures 2000, DVD package production notes.

(181) Karen Durbin, "A Princess of Pulp Returns to Even the Score," *New York Times,* January 16, 2000.

(182) Roger Ebert, review of *Isn't She Great? Chicago Sun Times,* 2000.

(183) Laura Fries, "Bette," a television review, *Daily Variety,* October 10, 2000.

(184) Cynthia Littleton, "CBS 3-Peat: Bette, Dear, Fugitive," *Hollywood Reporter,* October 31–November 6, 2000.

(185) Rachel Fischer, "Divine Comedy," *Hollywood Reporter,* Show Biz Kids Special Issue, December 2000.

(186) Marc Cetner, Michael Glynn, Patricia Towle, and Nim Nelson, "Bette Midler's Secret Agony—Pals Fear She's Heading for a Second Breakdown," *National Enquirer,* November 7, 2000.

(187) "Bette's Castoffs," *People* (December 18, 2000).

(188) Robert Lloyd, "Cruise Control," *LA Weekly* (November 3–9, 2000).

(189) Tom Gliatoo, "Tube" column, "Finding Lucy," *People* (December 4, 2000).

(190) Cynthia Littleton, "Bette Doesn't Pay Off for CBS," *Hollywood Reporter,* March 6–12, 2001.

(191) *The 43rd Annual Grammy Awards,* CBS-TV, February 21, 2001.
(192) Spring Gala, a benefit held in New York City, to benefit the YMCA, May 22, 2001.
(193) "Response to Terror: The Air War/Fund Raising," *Los Angeles Times,* October 22, 2001.
(194) Ann Aldenburg, "Celebs Have Helped Raise $200M in Past 3 Months," *USA Today* (December 18, 2001).

BIBLIOGRAPHY

Baker, Robb. *Bette Midler: The Divine Miss M.* Popular Library, 1975.

Bego, Mark. *Bette Midler: Outrageously Divine.* New American Library, 1987.

———. *Cher: If You Believe.* Cooper Square, 2001.

Halliwell, Leslie. *Halliwell's Filmgoer's Companion, Ninth Edition.* Charles Scribner's Sons, 1988.

Kingston, Victoria. *Simon & Garfunkel: The Biography.* Fromm International, 1998.

Mair, George. *Bette: An Intimate Biography of Bette Midler.* Birch Lane, 1995.

Maltin, Leonard *1998 Movie & Video Guide.* Signet, 1997.

———. *Leonard Maltin's Movie & Video Guide 2002.* Signet, 2001.

Martin, Mick, and Marsha Porter. *Video Movie Guide 2001.* Ballantine, 2000.

———. *Video Movie Guide 2002.* Ballantine, 2001.

Manilow, Berry. *Sweetlife: Adventures on the Way to Paradise.* McGraw Hill, 1986.

McAleer, Dave. *The Book of Hit Singles.* Miller Freeman, 1999.

Midler, Bette. *A View from a Broad.* Simon and Schuster, 1980.

Rees, Dafydd, and Luke Crampton. *VH1 Rock Stars Encyclopedia.* DK Publishing, 1999.

Rivera, Geraldo, with Daniel Paisner. *Exposing Myself.* Bantam, Doubleday, Dell, 1991.

Seaman, Barbara. *Lovely Me: The Life of Jacqueline Susann.* Morrow, 1987.

Spada, James. *The Divine Bette Midler.* Collier, 1984.

Waldman, Allison J. *The Bette Midler Scrapbook.* Citadel, 1997.

Whitburn, Joel. *Top Pop 1955–1982.* Record Research Inc., 1983.

———. *Top 40 Albums.* Record Research Inc., 1995.

———. *Top Pop Albums 1955–1985.* Record Research Inc., 1985.

———. *Top 10 Singles Charts.* Record Research Inc., 2001.

DISCOGRAPHY

Bette Midler—Solo Albums

1. *"THE DIVINE MISS M"* (Atlantic Records) 1972
    1. "Do You Want to Dance?" (Bobby Freeman) 2:56
       Producer: Joel Dorn
    2. "Chapel of Love" (Jeff Barry, Ellie Greenwich, and Phil Spector) 2:52
       Producers: Barry Manilow, Geoffrey Haslam, and Ahmet Ertegun
    3. "Superstar" (Leon Russell and Bonnie Bramlet) 5:09
       Producers: Barry Manilow, Geoffrey Haslam, and Ahmet Ertegun
    4. "Daytime Hustler" (Jeff Kent) 3:29
       Producers: Barry Manilow, Geoffrey Haslam, and Ahmet Ertegun
    5. "Am I Blue?" (Grant Clarke and Harry Akst) 5:21
       Producer: Joel Dorn
    6. "Friends" (Mark Klingman and Buzzy Linhart) 2:49
       Producers: Joel Dorn
    7. "Hello in There" (John Prine)
       Producer: Joel Dorn
    8. "Leader of the Pack" (Jeff Barry, Ellie Greenwich, and George Morton) 3:41
       Producers: Barry Manilow, Geoffrey Haslam, and Ahmet Ertegun
    9. "Delta Dawn" (Alex Harvey and Larry Collins) 5:16
       Producers: Barry Manilow, Geoffrey Haslam, and Ahmet Ertegun
    10. "Boogie Woogie Bugle Boy" (Don Raye and Hughie Prince) 2:26
        Producer: Joel Dorn
    11. "Friends" (Mark Klingman and Buzzy Linhart) 2:50
        Producers: Barry Manilow, Geoffrey Haslam, and Ahmet Ertegun

2. *"BETTE MIDLER"* (Atlantic Records) 1973
    1. "Skylark" (Hoagy Carmichael and Johnny Mercer) 3:02
       Producers: Arif Mardin and Barry Manilow
    2. "Drinking Again" (Doris Tauber and Johnny Mercer) 2:46
       Producers: Arif Mardin and Barry Manilow
    3. "Breaking Up Somebody's Home" (Denise LaSalle) 3:47
       Producers: Arif Mardin and Barry Manilow

    4. "Surabaya Johnny" (Kurt Weill, Bertolt Brecht, and Herbert Hartig) 4:52
       Producers: Arif Mardin and Barry Manilow
    5. "I Shall Be Released" (Bob Dylan) 4:55
       Producers: Arif Mardin and Barry Manilow
    6. "Optimistic Voices" (E. Y. Harburg, Harold Arlen, and Herbert Stothart)
       "Lullaby of Broadway" (Al Durbin and Harry Warren) 2:26
       Producers: Arif Mardin and Barry Manilow
    7. "In the Mood" (Joe Garland and Andy Razaf) 2:37
       Producers: Arif Mardin and Barry Manilow
    8. "Uptown" (Thomas McKinney)
       "Da Doo Run Run" (Phil Spector, Ellie Greenwich, and Jeff Barry) 3:22
       Producers: Arif Mardin and Barry Manilow
    9. "Twisted" (Wardell Gray and Annie Ross) 2:23
       Producers: Arif Mardin and Barry Manilow
   10. "Higher and Higher (Your Love Keeps Lifting Me)" (Gary Lee Jackson, Carl W. Smith, and Raynard Miner) 4:08
       Producers: Arif Mardin and Barry Manilow

3. *"SONGS FOR THE NEW DEPRESSION"* (Atlantic Records) 1976
    1. "Strangers in the Night"
       (Charles Singleton, Eddie Snyder, and Bert Kaempfert) 3:17
       Producer: Arif Mardin
    2. "I Don't Want the Night to End" (Phoebe Snow) 3:46
       Producer: Moogy Klingman
    3. "Mr. Rockefeller" (Bette Midler and Jerry Blatt) 4:02
       Producer: Moogy Klingman
    4. "Old Cape Cod" (Claire Rothrock, Allan Jeffrey, and Milt Yakus) 2:47
       Producers: Joel Dorn and Bette Midler
    5. "Buckets of Rain" duet: Bette Midler and Bob Dylan (Bob Dylan) 3:54
       Producer: Moogy Klingman
    6. "Love Says It's Waiting" (Nick Holmes) 1:37
       Producer: Moogy Klingman
    7. "Shiver Me Timbers" (Tom Waits)
       "Samedi et Vendredi" (Bette Midler and Moogy Klingman) 6:20
       Producer: Moogy Klingman
    8. "No Jestering" (Carlton Malcolm) 3:57
       Producer: Moogy Klingman
    9. "Tragedy" (Gerald Nelson and Fred Burch) 3:03
       Producer: Moody Klingman

10. "Marahuana" (Arthur Johnston and Sam Coslow) 2:27
    Producers: Joel Dorn and Bette Midler
11. "Let Me Just Follow Behind" (Moogy Klingman) 3:30
    Producer: Moogy Klingman

4. *"LIVE AT LAST"* (Atlantic Records) 1977
   1. "Backstage" (dialogue) 0:18
      Producer: Lew Hahn
   2. "Friends" (Moogy Klingman and Buzzy Linhart)
      "Oh, My, My" (Richard Starkey and Vincent Poncia) 2:28
      Producer: Lew Hahn
   3. "Bang, You're Dead" (Valerie Simpson and Nicholas Ashford) 3:15
      Producer: Lew Hahn
   4. "Birds" (Neil Young) 4:39
      Producer: Lew Hahn
   5. "Comic Relief" (dialogue) 2:38
      Producer: Lew Hahn
   6. "In the Mood" (Joe Garland and Andy Razaf) 2:09
      Producer: Lew Hahn
   7. "Hurry On Down" (Nellie Lutcher) 2:07
      Producer: Lew Hahn
   8. "Shiver Me Timbers" (Tom Waits) 4:00
      Producer: Lew Hahn
   9. "The Vicki Eydie Show" 13:37 total time
      a. "Around the World" (Victor Young and Harold Admanson) 0:23
      b. "Istanbul" (Jimmy Kennedy and Nat Simon) 0:55
      c. "Fiesta in Rio" (Bette Midler and Jerry Blatt) 1:52
      d. "South Seas Scene" (Rik Carlok)
          "Hawaiian War Chant" (Freed/Lileiohaku/Noble) 5:13 combined
          time
      e. "Lullaby of Broadway" (Al Dubin and Harry Warren) 2:00
      Producer: Lew Hahn
   10. "You're Moving Out Today"
       (Bette Midler, Carol Bayer Sager, and Bruce Roberts) 2:56
       Producer: Tom Dowd
   11. "Delta Dawn" (Alex Harvey and Larry Collins) 5:54
       Producer: Lew Hahn
   12. "Long John Blues" (Tommy George) 2:36
       Producer: Lew Hahn
   13. "Those Wonderful Sophie Tucker Jokes" (dialogue) 2:38
       Producer: Lew Hahn
   14. "Story of Nanette"
       a. "Nanette" (Howard Ditz and Arthur Schwartz) 0:54

    b. "Alabama Song" (Bertolt Brecht and Kurt Weill)

    c. "Mr. Rockefeller" (Bette Midler and Jerry Blatt)

    d. "Ready to Begin Again" (Jerry Leiber and Mike Stoller)
       "Do You Want to Dance?" (Bobby Freeman) 3:23

    Producer: Lew Hahn

15. "Fried Eggs" (dialogue) 2:37
    Producer: Lew Hahn

16. "Hello in There" (John Prine) 3:16
    Producer: Lew Hahn

17. "Finale"

    a. "Up the Ladder to the Roof" (Vincent DiMirco and Frank Wilson) 2:45

    b. "Boogie Woogie Bugle Boy" (Don Raye and Hughie Prince) 3:40

    c. "Friends" (Moogy Klingman and Buzzy Linhart) 3:04

    Producer: Lew Hahn

    NOTE: Entire Album's "Remote Producer": Arif Mardin

5. *"BROKEN BLOSSOM"* (Atlantic Records) 1977

    1. "Make Yourself Comfortable" (B. Merrill) 3:59
       Producer: Brooks Arthur

    2. "You Don't Know Me" (Eddie Arnold and Cindy Walker) 3:39
       Producer: Brooks Arthur

    3. "Say Goodbye to Hollywood" (Billy Joel) 3:02
       Producer: Brooks Arthur

    4. "I Never Talk to Strangers" duet: Bette Midler and Tom Waits
       (Tom Waits) 3:39
       Producer: Bones Howe

    5. "Storybook Children" (David Pomeranz and Spencer Proffer) 3:40
       Producer: Brooks Arthur

    6. "Red" (John Carter and Sammy Hagar) 3:17
       Producer: Brooks Arthur

    7. "Empty Bed Blues" (J. C. Johnson) 3:19
       Producer: Brooks Arthur

    8. "A Dream Is a Wish Your Heart Makes"
       (Mack David, Al Hoffman, and Jerry Livingston) 3:09
       Producer: Brooks Arthur

    9. "Paradise" (Perry Botkin Jr., Gil Garfield, and Harry Nilsson) 4:15
       Producer: Brooks Arthur

    10. "Yellow Beach Umbrella" (Craig Doerge and Judy Henske) 4:24
       Producer: Brooks Arthur

    11. "La Vie en Rose" (Mack David, Louiguy, and Edith Piaf) 2:59
       Producer: Brooks Arthur

6. *"THIGHS AND WHISPERS"* (Atlantic Records) 1979
    1. "Big Noise from Winnetka"
      (Gil Rodin, Bob Crosby, Bob Haggart, and Ray Bauduc) 6:56
      Producer: Arif Mardin
    2. "Millworker" (James Taylor) 4:06
      Producer: Arif Mardin
    3. "Cradle Days" (Aaron Neville and Tony Berg) 5:00
      Producer: Arif Mardin
    4. "My Knight in Black Leather" (Jerry Ragovoy and Estelle Levitt) 4:53
      Producers: Arif Mardin and Jerry Ragovoy
    5. "Hang On in There Baby" (Johnny Bristol) 6:07
      Producer: Arif Mardin
    6. "Hurricane" (Bette Midler and Randy Kerber) 7:21
      Producer: Arif Mardin
    7. "Rain" (Mack Debennack) 3:41
      Producer: Arif Mardin
    8. "Married Men" (Dominic Bugatti and Frank Musker) 4:01
      Producer: Arif Mardin

7. *"THE ROSE"* Original Soundtrack Album (Atlantic Records) 1979
    1. "Whose Side Are You On?" (Kenny Hopkins and Charley Williams)
      3:38
      Producer: Paul A. Rothchild
    2. "Midnight in Memphis" (Tony Johnson) 3:23
      Producer: Paul A. Rothchild
    3. "Concert Monologue" (monologue) 2:42
      Producer: Paul A. Rothchild
    4. "When a Man Loves a Woman" (Calvin Lewis and Andrew Wright)
      4:32
      Producer: Paul A. Rothchild
    5. "Sold My Soul to Rock 'n' Roll" (Gene Pistilli) 3:23
      Producer: Paul A. Rothchild
    6. "Keep On Rockin'" (Sam Hagar and John Carter) 3:02
      Producer: Paul A. Rothchild
    7. "Love Me with a Feeling" (Hudson Whittaker) 3:38
      Producer: Paul A. Rothchild
    8. "Homecoming Monologue" (monologue) 1:22
      Producer: Paul A. Rothchild
    9. "Stay with Me" (Jerry Ragavoy and George Weiss) 5:00
      Producer: Paul A. Rothchild
   10. "Let Me Call You Sweetheart" (Beth Slater Whitson and Lou Friedman) 1:30
      Producer: Paul A. Rothchild

11. "The Rose" (Amanda McBroom) 3:40
    Producer: Paul A. Rothchild

8. *"DIVINE MADNESS"* Original Soundtrack Album (Atlantic Records)
   1980
   1. "Big Noise from Winnetka"
      (Gil Rodin Bob Crosby, Bog Haggart, and Ray Baudue) 3:52
      Producer: Dennis Kirk
   2. "Paradise" (Harry Nilsson, Gil Garfield, and Barry Botkin Jr.) 4:09
      Producer: Dennis Kirk
   3. "Shiver Me Timbers" (Tom Waits) 3:56
      Producer: Dennis Kirk
   4. "Fire Down Below" (Bob Seger) 3:05
      Producer: Dennis Kirk
   5. "Stay with Me" (Jerry Ragovoy and George Weiss) 6:24
      Producer: Dennis Kirk
   6. "My Mother's Eyes" (Tom Jans) 2:29
      Producer: Dennis Kirk
   7. a. "Chapel of Love" (Jerry Barry, Ellie Greenwich, and Phil
          Spector)
      b. "Boogie Woogie Bugle Boy"
          (Don Raye and Hughie Prince) 4:02 combined time
          Producer: Dennis Kirk
   8. a. "E Street Shuffle" (Bruce Springsteen)
      b. "Summer (the First Time)" (Bobby Goldsboro)
      c. "Leader of the Pack"
      (Jeff Barry, Ellie Greenwich, and George Morton) 9:42 combined
      time
      Producer: Dennis Kirk
   9. a. "You Can't Always Get What You Want" (Mick Jagger and Keith
          Richards)
      b. "I Shall Be Released" (Bob Dylan) 5:56 combined time
          Producer: Dennis Kirk

9. *"NO FRILLS"* (Atlantic Records) 1983
   1. "Is It Love?" (Nick Giulder and Jimmy McCulloch) 4:43
      Producer: Chuck Plotkin
   2. "My Favorite Waste of Time" (Marshall Crenshaw) 2:43
      Producer: Chuck Plotkin
   3. "All I Need to Know" (Barry Mann, Cynthia Weil, and Tom Snow)
      4:08
      Producer: Chuck Plotkin

4. "Only in Miami" (Max Gronenthal) 4:35
   Producer: Chuck Plotkin

5. "Heart Over Head" (Andy Goldmark, Robin Bartteau, and Brock Walsh) 2:52
   Producer: Chuck Plotkin

6. "Let Me Drive" (Gregg Prestopino and Matthew Wilde) 4:02
   Producer: Chuck Plotkin

7. "My Eye on You" (Moon Martin and Bill House) 4:03
   Producer: Chuck Plotkin

8. "Beast of Burden" (Mick Jagger and Keith Richards) 3:48
   Producer: Chuck Plotkin

9. "Soda and a Souvenir" (Jessica Harper) 3:23
   Producer: Chuck Plotkin

10. "Come Back, Jimmy Dean" (Bette Midler, Jerry Blatt, and Brock Walsh) 3:51
    Producer: Chuck Plotkin

10. *"MUD WILL BE FLUNG TONIGHT!"* (Atlantic Records) 1985
    1. "Taking Aim" (Bette Midler) 5:09
       Producers: Bette Midler, Bob Kiminsky, and Jerry Blatt
    2. a. "Fit or Fat" (Bette Midler)
       b. "Fat As I Am"
       (Bette Midler, Jerry Blatt, and Marc Shaiman) 3:10 combined time
       Producers: Bette Midler, Bob Kiminsky, and Jerry Blatt
    3. "Marriage, Movies, Madonna and Mick" (Bette Midler) 6:39
       Producers: Bette Midler, Bob Kiminsky, and Jerry Blatt
    4. a. "Vickie Eydie" (Bette Midler)
       b. "I'm Singing Broadway" (Bette Midler and Jerry Blatt) 4:44 combined time
       Producers: Bette Midler, Bob Kiminsky, and Jerry Blatt
    5. "Coping" (Bette Midler)
       Producers: Bette Midler, Bob Kiminsky, and Jerry Blatt
    6. "The Unfettered Boob" (Bette Midler) 2:58
       Producers: Bette Midler, Bob Kiminsky, and Jerry Blatt
    7. "Otto Titsling" (Bette Midler, Jerry Blatt, and Charlene Seeger) 4:20
       Producers: Bette Midler, Bob Kiminsky, and Jerry Blatt
    8. "Why Bother?" (Bette Midler) 6:44
       Producers: Bette Midler, Bob Kiminsky, and Jerry Blatt
    9. "Soph" (Bette Midler) 4:32
       Producers: Bette Midler, Bob Kiminsky, and Jerry Blatt

11. *"BEACHES"* Original Soundtrack Album (Atlantic Records) 1988
    1. "Under the Boardwalk" (Arthur Resnick and Kenny Young) 4:19
       Producer: Arif Mardin

2. "Wind beneath My Wings" (Larry Henley and Jeff Silbar) 4:53
Producer: Arif Mardin

3. "I've Still Got My Health" (Cole Porter) 1:29
Producer: Arif Mardin

4. "I Think It's Going to Rain Today" (Randy Newman) 3:30
Producer: Arif Mardin

5. "Otto Titsling"
(Bette Midler, Jerry Blatt, Charlene Seeger, and Marc Shaiman) 3:12
Producer: Arif Mardin

6. "I Know You by Heart"
(Dean Pitchford, George Merrill, and Shannon Rubicam) 4:39
Producer: Arif Mardin

7. "The Glory of Love" (Billy Hill) 3:14
Producer: Arif Mardin

8. "Baby Mine" (Ned Washington and Frank Churchill) 2:06
Producer: Arif Mardin

9. "Oh Industry" (Bette Midler and Wendy Waldman) 4:05
Producer: Arif Mardin

10. "The Friendship Theme" instrumental (Georges DeLerue) 1:58
Producer: Arif Mardin

12. *"SOME PEOPLE'S LIVES"* (Atlantic Records) 1990

1. "One More Round" (Jessica Harper, Allee Willis, and Danny Sembe-llo) 1:59
Producer: Arif Mardin

2. "Some People's Lives" (Janis Ian and Rhonda Fleming) 3:26
Producer: Arif Mardin

3. "Miss Otis Regrets" (Cole Porter) 2:49
Producer: Arif Mardin

4. "Spring Can Really Hang You Up the Most"
(Fran Landesman and Tommy Wolfe) 5:30
Producer: Arif Mardin

5. "Night and Day" (Roxanne Seeman and Billie Hughes) 5:29
Producer: Arif Mardin

6. "The Girl Is On to You" (Jude Johnstone) 4:06
Producer: Arif Mardin

7. "From a Distance" (Julie Gold) 4:37
Producer: Arif Mardin

8. "Moonlight Dancing" (Diane Warren)
Producer: Arif Mardin

9. a.   "He Was Too Good to Me" (Richard Rogers and Lorenz Hart)
   b.   "Since You Stayed Here" (Peter Larson and Josh Rubins) 4:09
        combined time
Producer: Arif Mardin

10. "All of a Sudden" (Nathalie Archangel and Scott Wilk) 4:32
    Producer: Arif Mardin
11. "The Gift of Love" (Billy Steinberg, Tom Kelly, and Suzanna Hoffs) 4:03
    Producer: Arif Mardin

13. *"FOR THE BOYS"* Original Soundtrack Album (Atlantic Records) 1991
    1. "Billy-a-Dick" (Hoagy Carmichael and Paul Francis Webster) 1:35
       Producer: Arif Mardin
    2. "Stuff Like That There" (Jay Livingston and Ray Evans) 2:50
       Producer: Arif Mardin
    3. "P.S. I Love You" (Johnny Mercer and Gordon Jenkins) 3:31
       Producer: Arif Mardin
    4. "The Girl Friend of the Whirling Dervish" instrumental
       (Al Dubin, Johnny Mercer, and Harry Warren) 1:15
       Producer: Marc Shaiman
    5. a.   "I Remember You" (Johnny Mercer and Victor Schertzinger) 2:21
             combined
       b.   "Dixie's Dream"
       Producer: Arif Mardin
    6. "Baby, It's Cold Outside" duet: Bette Midler and James Caan
       (Frank Loesser) 1:28
       Producer: Arif Mardin
    7. "Dreamland" (Dave Grusin, Alan and Marilyn Bergman) 3:13
       Producer: Arif Mardin
    8. "Vickie and Mr. Valves" instrumental (Lenny LaCroix) 2:27
       Producer: Arif Mardin
    9. "For All We Know" (J. Fred Coots and Sam M. Lewis) 4:00
       Producer: Arif Mardin
    10. "Come Rain or Come Shine" (Johnny Mercer) 3:29
        Producer: Arif Mardin
    11. "In My Life" (John Lennon and Paul McCartney) 2:25
        Producer: Arif Mardin
    12. "I Remember You" (Johnny Mercer and Victor Schertzinger) 3:33
        Producer: Arif Mardin
    13. "Every Road Leads Back to You" (Diane Warren) 3:47
        Producer: Arif Mardin

14. *"EXPERIENCE THE DIVINE: BETTE MIDLER / GREATEST HITS"*
    (Atlantic Records) 1993
    1. "Hello in There" (John Prine) 4:16
       Producer: Joel Dorn

2. "Do You Want to Dance?" (Bobby Freeman) 2:43
   Producer: Joel Dorn
3. "From a Distance" (Julie Gold) 4:37
   Producer: Arif Mardin
4. "Chapel of Love" (Jeff Barry, Ellie Greenwich, and Phil Spector) 2:53
   Producer: Barry Manilow, Geoffrey Haslam, and Ahmet Ertegun
5. "Only in Miami" (Max Gronenthal) 3:54
   Producer: Chuck Plotkin
6. "When a Man Loves a Woman" (Calvin Lewis and Andrew Wright) 4:53
   Producer: Paul A. Rothchild
7. "The Rose" (Amanda McBroom) 3:33
   Producer: Paul A. Rothchild
8. "Miss Otis Regrets" (Cole Porter) 2:37
   Producer: Arif Mardin
9. "Shiver Me Timbers" (Tom Waits) 4:41
   Producer: Lew Hahn
10. "Wind beneath My Wings" (Larry Henley and Jeff Silbar) 4:52
    Producer: Arif Mardin
11. "Boogie Woogie Bugle Boy" (Don Raye and Hughie Prince) 2:16
    Producer: Barry Manilow
12. "One for My Baby (and One More for the Road)"
    (Johnny Mercer and Harold Arlen) 4:05
    Producers: Bette Midler and Marc Shaiman
13. "Friends" (Mark "Moogy" Klingman and Buzzy Linhart) 2:54
    Producers: Barry Manilow, Geoffrey Haslam, and Ahmet Ertegun
14. "In My Life" (John Lennon and Paul McCartney) 3:12
    Producer: Arif Mardin

(NOTE: Australian 1995 version of this album contains four bonus cuts: a remixed version of "To Deserve You," the album version of "To Deserve You," "Beast of Burden," and "My Favorite Waste of Time")

15. *"GYPSY"* Original Soundtrack Album (Atlantic Records) 1993
    1. "Overture" instrumental (Jules Styne and Stephen Sondheim) 4:56
       Producers: Arif Mardin, Michael Rafter, and Curt Sobel
    2. "May We Entertain You" Lacey Chabert, Elisabeth Moss
       (Jules Styne and Stephen Sondheim) 0:51
       Producers: Arif Mardin, Michael Rafter, and Curt Sobel
    3. "Some People" BETTE MIDLER (Jules Styne and Stephen Sondheim) 3:15
       Producers: Arif Mardin, Michael Rafter, and Curt Sobel
    4. "Small World" BETTE MIDLER and Peter Riegert
       (Jules Styne and Stephen Sondheim) 3:22
       Producers: Arif Mardin, Michael Rafter, and Curt Sobel

5. "Baby June and Her Newsboys" Lacey Chabert, Elisabeth Moss, Joey Cee, Blake
   Armstrong, Teo Weiner
   (Jules Styne and Stephen Sondheim) 2:07
   Producers: Arif Mardin, Michael Rafter, and Curt Sobel
6. "Mr. Goldstone" BETTE MIDLER, Peter Riegert, Jennifer Beck,
   Jeffrey Broadhurst, Peter Lodkyer, Michael Moore, Patrick Boyd
   (Jules Styne and Stephen Sondheim) 2:26
   Producers: Arif Mardin, Michael Rafter, and Curt Sobel
7. "Little Lamb" Cynthia Gibb (Jules Styne and Stephen Sondheim)
   2:20
   Producers: Arif Mardin, Michael Rafter and Curt Sobel
8. "You'll Never Get Away from Me" BETTE MIDLER and Peter Riegert
   (Jules Styne and Stephen Sondheim) 2:57
   Producers: Arif Mardin, Michael Rafter, and Curt Sobel
9. "Dainty June and Her Farmboys" Jennifer Beck, Jeffrey Broadhurst,
   Peter Lockyer, Michael Moore, Patrick Boyd, Terry Lindholm, Gregg Russell,
   Cynthia Gibb
   (Jules Styne and Stephen Sondheim) 4:34
   Producers: Arif Mardin, Michael Rafter and Curt Sobel
10. "If Momma Was Married" Cynthia Gibb, Jennifer Beck
    (Jules Styne and Stephen Sondheim) 2:56
    Producers: Arif Mardin, Michael Rafter, and Curt Sobel
11. "All I Need Is the Girl" Jeffrey Broadhurst
    (Jules Styne and Stephen Sondheim) 4:57
    Producers: Arif Mardin, Michael Rafter, and Curt Sobel
12. "Everything's Coming Up Roses" BETTE MIDLER
    (Jules Styne and Stephen Sondheim) 2:50
    Producers: Arif Mardin, Michael Rafter, and Curt Sobel
13. "Together, Wherever We Go" BETTE MIDLER, Peter Riegert, Cynthia Gibb
    (Jules Styne and Stephen Sondheim) 2:58
    Producers: Arif Mardin, Michael Rafter, and Curt Sobel
14. "You Gotta Have a Gimmick" Linda Hart, Anna McNeely, Christine Ebersole
    (Jules Styne and Stephen Sondheim) 4:07
    Producers: Arif Mardin, Michael Rafter, and Curt Sobel
15. "Let Me Entertain You" Cynthia Gibb
    (Jules Styne and Stephen Sondheim) 2:32
    Producers: Arif Mardin, Michael Rafter and Curt Sobe
16. "Rose's Turn" BETTE MIDLER (Jules Styne and Stephen Sondheim) 4:04
    Producers: Arif Mardin, Michael Rafter, and Curt Sobel

17. "End Credits" instrumental (Jules Styne and Stephen Sondheim) 3:10
    Producers: Arif Mardin, Michael Rafter, and Curt Sobel

16. *"BETTE OF ROSES"* (Atlantic Records) 1995
    1. "I Know This Town" (Cheryl Wheeler) 3:53
       Producer: Arif Mardin
    2. "In This Life" (Mike Reed and Allen Shamblin) 4:11
       Producer: Arif Mardin
    3. "Bottomless" (Bonnie Hayes) 5:18
       Producer: Arif Mardin
    4. "To Comfort You" (Ian Thomas) 4:44
       Producer: Arif Mardin
    5. "To Deserve You" (Marie McKee) 5:15
       Producer: Arif Mardin
    6. "The Last Time" (Maria McKee) 4:52
       Producer: Arif Mardin
    7. "Bed of Roses" (Bonnie Hayes) 4:12
       Producer: Arif Mardin
    8. "The Perfect Kiss" (Scott Tibbs and Marc Jordan) 3:42
       Producer: Arif Mardin
    9. "As Dreams Go By" (Andy Hill and Pete Sinfield) 5:08
       Producer: Arif Mardin
    10. "It's Too Late" (Bob Thiele, Tonio K., and Bonnie Hayes) 4:42
        Producer: Arif Mardin
    11. "I Believe in You" (Sam Hagin and Roger Cook) 4:33
        Producer: Arif Mardin

17. *"BATHHOUSE BETTY"* (Warner Brothers Records) 1998
    1. "Song of Bernadette" (Leonard Cohen, Bill Elliot, and Jennifer Warnes) 3:46
       Producer: Ted Templeman
    2. "I'm Beautiful" (Brinsley Evans) 3:55
       Producer: Arif Mardin
    3. "Lullaby in Blue" (Brock Walsh and Adam Cohen) 5:09
       Producer: Brock Walsh
    4. "Ukulele Lady" (Richard A. Whiting and Gus Kahn) 3:34
       Producer: Arif Mardin
    5. "I'm Hip" (David Frishberg and Bob Dorough) 2:44
       Producer: Marc Shaiman
    6. "I Sold My Heart to the Junkman" (Leon Rene and Otis Rene, Jr.) 3:10
       Producer: Arif Mardin

7. "One Monkey Don't Stop No Show"
(Rose Marie McCoy and Charles Singleton) 2:46
Producer: Ted Templeman
8. "Boxing" (Ben Fields) 4:26
Producer: Ted Templeman
9. "Big Socks" (Chuckii Booker) 3:51
Producer: Chuckii Booker
10. "That's How Love Moves"
(Fitzgerald Scott, Ty Lacy, and Jennifer Kimball) 3:54
Producer: Arif Mardin
11. "My One True Friend"
(David Foster, Carole King, and Carole Bayer Sager) 3:49
Producer: David Foster
12. "Laughing Matters" (Mark Waldrop and Dick Gallagher) 3:54
Producer: Marc Shaiman

(NOTE: Japanese version of this album contains the bonus cut "Happiness.")

18. *"BETTE"* (Warner Brothers Records) 2000
1. "That's How Heartaches Are Made" (Ben Raleigh and Bob Haley)
3:07
Producer: Don Was
2. "In These Shoes" (Kristy MacColl and Pete Glenister) 3:41
Producer: Don Was
3. "God Give Me Strength" (Elvis Costello and Burt Bacharach) 6:31
Producer: Don Was
4. "Just My Imagination (Running Away with Me)"
(Norman Whitfield and Barrett Strong) 3:53
Producer: Don Was
5. "Love TKO" (Cecil Womack, Gil Noble, Jr., and Linda Womack) 4:47
Producer: Don Was
6. "Moses" (Patty Griffin) 4:30
Producer: Don Was
7. "Nobody Else but You" (Bette Midler and Marc Shaiman) 2:51
Producers: Marc Shaiman and Don Was
8. "Color of Roses" (Beth Nielsen Chapman and Matt Rollings) 4:40
Producer: Don Was
9. "Bless You, Child"
(Billy Steinberg, Rick Nowles, and Marie Claire Cremers) 4:33
Producer: Don Was and Rick Nowles
10. "When Your Life Was Low" (Will Jennings and Joe Sample) 3:54
Producer: Don Was

11. "Shining Star" (Leo Graham Jr. and Paul Richmond) 4:49
Producer: Don Was

Bette Midler—On Other Albums

1. *"HERE'S JOHNNY: MAGIC MOMENTS FROM 'THE TONIGHT SHOW'"*
by Johnny Carson and Various Artists (Casablanca Records) 1974
—BETTE MIDLER
   a.   "Lullaby of Broadway" (Al Durbin and Harry Warren)
   b.   "Boogie Woogie Bugle Boy" (Don Raye, Hughie Prince) 5:17 combined total

2. *"RINGO THE 4TH"* by Ringo Starr (Atlantic Records) 1977
—Ringo Starr, backgrounds by BETTE MIDLER
   "Tango All Night" (Tom Seufert, Steve Hague) 2:55
   Producer: Arif Mardin

3. *"CAROLE BAYER SAGER"* by Carole Bayer Sager (Elektra Records) 1977
—Carole Bayer Sager, "harmony" vocal and solo by BETTE MIDLER
   "Shy as a Violet" (Carole Bayer Sager, Peter Allen) 3:06

4. *"IN HARMONY"* by Various Artists (Sesame Street/Warner Brothers Records) 1980
—BETTE MIDLER
   "Blueberry Pie" (Bette Midler, Bruce Roberts, and Carole Bayer Sager) 2:57
   Producers: Lucy Simon and David Levine

5. *"WE ARE THE WORLD"* by Various Artists (Columbia Records) 1985—Dan Aykroyd, Harry Belafonte, Lindsey Buckingham, Kim Carnes, Ray Charles, Bob Dylan, Sheila E., Bob Geldof, Hall and Oates, James Ingram, Jackie Jackson, LaToya Jackson, Marlon Jackson, Michael Jackson, Randy Jackson, Tito Jackson, Al Jarreau, Waylon Jennings, Billy Joel, Cyndi Lauper, Huey Lewis and The News, Kenny Loggins, BETTE MIDLER, Willie Nelson, Jeffrey Osborne, Steve Perry, the Pointer Sisters, Lionel Richie, Smokey Robinson, Kenny Rogers, Diana Ross, Paul Simon, Bruce Springsteen, Tina Turner, Dionne Warwick, and Stevie Wonder (all performing under the name: USA for Africa)
   "We Are the World" (Michael Jackson and Lionel Richie) 7:02
   Producer: Quincy Jones

6. *"HOME ALONE 2"* Original Soundtrack (Arista Records) 1992
   —BETTE MIDLER
     "Somewhere in My Memory" (Bricusse/Williams) 3:58
     Producer: Arif Mardin

7. *"FOR YOUR CHILDREN"* by Various Artists (Kid Rhino Records)
   —BETTE MIDLER
     "Blueberry Pie" (Bette Midler, Bruce Roberts, and Carole Bayer
     Sager) 2:57
     Producers: Lucy Simon and David Levine

8. *"FIRST WIVES CLUB"* Original Soundtrack Album
   —BETTE MIDLER, Goldie Hawn, and Diane Keaton
     "You Don't Own Me" (Marara/White)
     Producer: Marc Shaiman

9. *"TONIN' "* by the Manhattan Transfer (Atlantic Records) 1995)
   —Manhattan Transfer and BETTE MIDLER
     "It's Gonna Take a Miracle"
     (Teddy Randazzo, Lou Stallman, and Bobby Weinstein) 3:56
     Producer: Arif Mardin

10. *"THAT OLD FEELING"* Original Soundtrack Album
    —BETTE MIDLER and Tommy Flanagan
      "Somewhere along the Way" (Adams/Gallop)
      Producer: Marc Shaiman

11. *"CARNIVAL! THE RAINFOREST FOUNDATION TRIBUTE"* (RCA Records) 1997
    —BETTE MIDLER
      "Sweet and Low" (Barnaby)
      Producer: Arif Mardin

12. *"THE HUNCHBACK OF NOTRE DAME"* Original Soundtrack (Disney Records) 1996
    —BETTE MIDLER
      "God Help the Outcasts" (Alan Menken and Stephen Schwartz)
      Producers: Alan Menken and Stephen Schwartz

13. *"ATLANTIC RECORDS 50 YEARS"* (Atlantic Records) 1998
    —BETTE MIDLER
      "Wind beneath My Wings" (Larry Henley and Jeff Silbar) 4:53
      Producer: Arif Mardin

14. 'BEATIN' THE HEAT" by Dan Hicks and His Hot Licks (Surfdog Records) (2000)
    —Dan Hicks with BETTE MIDLER
       "Strike It while It's Hot!" (Hicks) 4:10
       Producer: David Darling

15. *"SEX AND THE CITY"* Television Soundtrack (London/Sire Records) 2000
    —BETTE MIDLER
       "Love TKO" (Cecil Womack) 4:56
       Producer: Don Was

Bette Midler—Singles

1. "Friends"
   b/w "Chapel of Love" (Atlantic Records) 1973

2. "Boogie Woogie Bugle Boy"
   b/w "Delta Dawn" (Atlantic Records) 1973

3. "Friends"
   b/w "Chapel of Love" (Atlantic Records) 1973

4. "In the Mood"
   b/w "Drinking Again" (Atlantic Records) 1974

5. "Strangers in the Night"
   b/w "Samedi et Vendredi" (Atlantic Records) 1976

6. "Old Cape Cod"
   b/w "Tragedy" (Atlantic Records) 1976

7. "You're Movin' Out Today"
   b/w "Let Me Just Follow Behind" (Atlantic Records) 1977

8. "Storybook Children"
   b/w "Empty Bed Blues" (Atlantic Records) 1977

9. "Married Men"
   b/w "Bang, You're Dead" (Atlantic Records) 1979

10. "When a Man Loves a Woman"
    b/w "Love Me with a Feeling" (Atlantic Records) 1980

11. "The Rose"
    b/w "Stay with Me" (Atlantic Records) 1980

12. "My Mother's Eyes"
    b/w "Chapel of Love" (Atlantic Records) 1980

13. "All I Need to Know"
    b/w "My Eye on You" (Atlantic Records) 1983

14. "Favorite Waste of Time"
    b/w "My Eye on You" (Atlantic Records) 1983

15. "Beast of Burden"
    b/w "Come Back, Jimmy Dean" (Atlantic Records) 1983

16. "All I Need To Know"
    b/w "My Eye on You" (Atlantic Records) 1983

17. "Favorite Waste of Time"
    b/w "My Eye on You" (Atlantic Records) 1983

18. "We Are the World" as part of USA for Africa (XXX Records) 1985

19. "Under the Boardwalk"
    b/w "The Friendship Theme" (Atlantic Records) 1988

20. "Wind beneath My Wings"
    b/w "Oh Industry" (Atlantic Records) 1988

21. "From a Distance"
    b/w "One More Round" (Atlantic Records) 1990

22. "Night and Day"
    b/w "The Girl Is On to You" (Atlantic Records) 1990

23. "Moonlight Dancing"
    b/w "Some People's Lives" (Atlantic Records) 1990

24. "The Gift of Love"
    b/w "Some People's Lives" (Atlantic Records) 1990

25. "The Gift of Love" (UK Only)
    b/w "Moonlight Dancing" (Atlantic Records) 1991

26. "Every Road Leads Back to You"
    b/w "I Remember You"/"Dixie's Dream" (Atlantic Records) 1991

27. "In My Life"
    b/w "Billie-a-Dick" (Atlantic Records) 1991

28. "Yakety Yak, Take It Back" as part of an all-star ensemble
    b/w Public Service Announcements

29. "To Deserve You"
    b/w "Up, Up, Up" with the Manhattan Transfer (Atlantic Records) 1995

30. "In This Life"
    b/w "Bottomless" (Atlantic Records) 1995

31. "My One True Friend"
    Promotional and British commercial single (Warner Brothers Records)
    1998

32. "I'm Beautiful" (Warner Brothers Records) 1999

33. "In These Shoes" (Warner Brothers Records) 2000

Bette Midler—12″ Vinyl Promotional Singles

1. "Married Men" (Long Version) 7:58
   b/w "Married Men" (Short Version) 5:32
   (Atlantic Records) 1979

2. "Hang On in There Baby" 5:36
   b/w "My Knight in Black Leather" 6:57
   (Atlantic Records) 1979

3. "Big Noise from Winnetka" 6:56
   b/w "Big Noise from Winnetka" 6:56
   (Atlantic Records) 1979

4. "Beast of Burden"
   b/w "Beast of Burden"
   (Atlantic Records) 1983

Bette Midler—CD Dance Remixed Singles

1. "I'm Beautiful" (Warner Brothers Records) 1999
    1. "Album Version" 3:55
    2. "Danny Tenaglia Continental Club Mix" 8:24
    3. "Victor Calderone Main Vocal Mix" 7:59
    4. "Brinsley Evans Back to the Scene of the Crime Mix" 4:20
    5. "Danny's D-Tour Dub" 9:33
    6. "Victor Calderone Dub" 7:59
    7. "Lil' D-Tour Groove" 4:16
    8. "Victor Calderone Drum Dub" 7:59

2. "In These Shoes" (Warner Brothers Records) 2001
    1. "Radio Mix" 4:10
    2. "Sound Factory Vox Mix" 9:07
    3. "Mark's Heels to Platforms Vocal Mix" 8:35
    4. "Other Side Mix" 7:57
    5. "Extended Radio Mix" 7:17
    6. "Sound Factory Dub Mix" 8:50
    7. "Mark's Sole Dub" 8:23

Unreleased Bette Midler Songs

Produced by Joel Dorn
—"Blue"

Produced by Moogy Klingman
—"Blue Rondo Ala Turk"
—"Young Americans"
—"Oh Jerusalem"
—"Hey Bobby"
—"Vacation in Rio"
—"I Had to Resort to Beauty"
—"I Don't Want the Night to End" (unedited version)

Produced by Brooks Arthur
—"Someone That I Used to Love"

Grammy Awards

—1974, Best New Artist
—1981, Best Pop Vocal Performance—Female, "The Rose"
—1982, Best Children's Recording, "In Harmony" by Various Artists, including Bette Midler's recording of "Blueberry Pie"
—1990, Record of the Year, "The Wind beneath My Wings"

Bette Midler's "Gold" and "Platinum" Albums and Singles

Albums

(NOTE: In America, Gold = 500,000 album copies sold; Platinum = one million album copies sold; Double Platinum = two million album copies sold.)

The Divine Miss M (Gold, Platinum)
Bette Midler (Gold)
The Rose (Gold, Platinum, Double Platinum)
Some People's Lives (Gold, Platinum, Double Platinum)
For the Boys (Gold)
Experience the Divine (Gold, Platinum)
Bette of Roses (Gold, Platinum)
Bathhouse Betty (Gold)

Singles

(NOTE: In America, Gold = one million single copies sold; Platinum = two million single copies sold.)

"The Rose" (Gold)
"From a Distance" (Gold, Platinum)

FILMOGRAPHY

1. *Hawaii* (1966)
   Director: George Roy Hill
   Cast: Julie Andrews, Max von Sydow, Richard Harris, Gene Hackman, Carroll
   O'Connor, Bette Midler (an unbilled extra)

2. *The Thorn,* also known as *The Divine Mr. J* (1974)
   Director: Peter Alexander (McWilliams)
   Cast: Bette Midler

3. *The Rose* (1979)
   Director: Mark Rydell
   Cast: Bette Midler, Alan Bates, Frederic Forrest, Harry Dean Stanton, Barry Primus,
   David Keith, Sandra McCabe

4. *Divine Madness* (1980)
   Director: Michael Ritchie
   Cast: Bette Midler, Jocelyn Brown, Ula Hedwig, Diva Gray

5. *Jinxed* (1982)
   Director: Don Siegel
   Cast: Bette Midler, Ken Wahl, Rip Torn, Jack Elam, Val Avery, Benson Fong

6. *Down and Out in Beverly Hills* (1986)
   Director: Paul Mazursky
   Cast: Bette Midler, Richard Dreyfus, Nick Nolte, Little Richard, Tracy Nelson, Elizabeth
   Pena

7. *Ruthless People* (1986)
   Directors: Jim Abrahams, David Zucker, and Jerry Zucker
   Cast: Danny DeVito, Bette Midler, Judge Reinhold, Helen Slater, Bill Pullman, Anita
   Morris

8. *Outrageous Fortune* (1987)
Director: Arthur Hiller
Cast: Bette Midler, Shelley Long, Peter Coyote, Robert Perosky, John Schuck, George
Carlin

9. *Oliver and Company* (1988)—Animated Feature
Director: George Scibner
Cast: Joey Lawrence, Bette Midler, Billy Joel, Cheech Marin, Richard Mulligan, Roscoe
Lee Brown, Sheryl Lee Ralph

10. *Big Business* (1988)
Director: Jim Abrahams
Cast: Bette Midler, Lily Tomlin, Fred Ward, Barry Primus, Michael Gross, Michele
Rlacido, John Vickery

11. *Beaches* (1989)
Director: Garry Marshall
Cast: Bette Midler, Barbara Hershey, John Heard, Spalding Gray, Lanie Kazan, Mayim
Baalik, Marcy Leeds

12. *Stella* (1990)
Director: John Erman
Cast: Bette Midler, Trini Alvarado, John Goodman, Stephen Collins, Marsha Mason,
Eileen Brennen, Linda Hart, Ben Stiller

13. *Scenes from a Mall* (1991)
Director: Paul Mazursky
Cast: Bette Midler, Woody Allen, Bill Irwin, Paul Mazursky

14. *For the Boys* (1991)
Director: Mark Rydell
Cast: Bette Midler, James Caan, George Segal, Patrick O'Neal, Arye Gross, Norman Fell,
Melissa Manchester

15. *Hocus Pocus* (1993)
Director: Kenny Ortega
Cast: Bette Midler, Kathy Najimy, Sarah Jessica Parker, Omri Katz, Thora Birch,
Amanda Shepherd, Vinessa Shaw, Penny Marshall, Garry Marshall

16. *Gypsy* (1993)
Director: Emilio Ardolino

Cast: Bette Midler, Cynthia Gibb, Peter Riegert, Ed Asner, Jennifer Beck, Lacey Chabert,
Elizabeth Moss, Linda Hart, Christine Ebersole, Andrea Martin, Michael Jeter

17. *Get Shorty* (1995)
Director: Barry Sonnenfeld
Cast: John Travolta, Gene Hackman, Rene Russo, Danny DeVito, Dennis Farina, Linda
Hart, Bette Midler (unbilled)

18. *First Wives Club* (1996)
Director: Hugh Wilson
Cast: Bette Midler, Goldie Hawn, Diane Keaton, Stephen Collins, Maggie Smith, Sarah
Jessica Parker, Elizabeth Berkley, Victor Gerber, Marcia Gay Hardin, Bronson Pinchot,
Stockard Channing, Ivana Trump

19. *That Old Feeling* (1997)
Director: Carl Reiner
Cast: Bette Midler, Dennis Farina, Danny Nucci, Gail O'Grady, David Rasche, Jamie
Denton, Paula Marshall

20. *Fantasia 2000* (1999)
Directors: James Algar, Gaetan Brizzi, Paul Brizzi, Hendel Butoy, Eric Goldberg, Pixote
Hunt, Francis Glebas, Hendel Butoy
Cast: Bette Midler, Steve Martin, Quincy Jones, Penn and Teller

21. *Get Bruce* (1999)
Director: Andrew Kuehn
Cast: Bruce Vilanch, Robin Williams, Whoopi Goldberg, Bette Midler, Raquel Welch,
Billy Crystal

22. *Jackie's Back* (1999)
Director: Robert Townsend
Cast: Jenifer Lewis, Tim Curry, Whoopi Goldberg, TV Blake, Tangie Ambrose
Liza Minnelli, Taylor Dane, Dolly Parton, Diahann Carroll, Mary Wilson, Bette Midler

23. *Drowning Mona* (2000)
Director: Nick Gomez

Cast: Bette Midler, Danny DeVito, Jamie Lee Curtis, Casey Affleck, Neve Campbell,
William Fichter, Marcus Thomas, Peter Dobson

24. *Isn't She Great?* (2000)
    Director: Andrew Bergman
    Cast: Bette Midler, Nathan Lane, Stockard Channing, David Hyde Pierce, John Cleese

25. *What Women Want* (2000)
    Director: Nancy Meyers
    Cast: Mel Gibson, Helen Hunt, Marisa Tomei, Valerie Perrine, Bette Midler (unbilled)

Bette Midler's Film Roles

Hawaii (1966)
A seasick missionary's wife (extra)

The Thorn, also known as *The Divine Mr. J* (1974)
The Virgin Mary

The Rose (1979)
Mary Rose Foster (alias, "The Rose")

Divine Madness! (1980)
Herself, Soph, Dolores DeLago

Jinxed (1982)
Bonita

Down and Out in Beverly Hills (1986)
Barbara Whiteman

Ruthless People (1986)
Barbara Stone

Outrageous Fortune (1986)
Sandy Brozinsky

Big Business (1988)
Sadie Shelton/Sadie Ratliff

Oliver and Company (1988) (Animated)
Voice of Georgette

Beaches (1989)
Cecilia Carol Bloom ("C. C. Bloom")

Stella (1990)
Stella Claire

Scenes from a Mall (1991)
Deborah Fifer

For the Boys (1991)
Dixie Leonard

Hocus Pocus (1993)
Winifred Sanderson ("Winnie")

Gypsy (1993) (U.S. TV movie/worldwide theatrical)
Mama Rose

Get Shorty (1995)
Doris (unbilled)

The First Wives Club (1996)
Brenda Morelli Cushman

That Old Feeling (1997)
Lilly Leonard

Jackie's Back (1999) (TV Movie)
Herself

Get Bruce (2000)
Herself

Isn't She Great? (2000)
Jacqueline Susann

Drowning Mona (2000)
Mona Dearly

What Women Want (2000)
Dr. Perkins (unbilled role)

Bette Midler's Movie Quotes

Beaches

CC: "Enough about me, let's talk about you. What do *you* think about me?"

———————

CC: "Oh, Harry, you're an angel. If your mother hadn't been such a bitch, we
        could've
shared something important."

———————

CC: "How's college life? . . . aren't you done YET?!?"

CC: "What I did? You and your lousy letters. Just to get one of them made me special even
before I opened it. All your crappy stories, all your big dreams."
Hillary: "I didn't know that."
CC:" Well, what the hell did you know? Did you know how bad things were for me? No,
because you wouldn't even open my letters. If you had even answered one, just one!
Told me what a jerk I was, anything! But you didn't. You took your friendship away
without even discussing it with me. So, thank you very much for forgiving me. But I
don't forgive you."
Hillary: "I was jealous. I was so jealous of you I couldn't see straight! You did everything you
said you were going to do, everything! And your talent, this incredible talent! I can't even
yodel!"
CC: "Hillary . . . what's yodeling got to do with it?"

CC: "Wait till I get my hands on that agent. I'll kill him. The toad. He told me this was a nightclub with leather banquettes, and a dressing room with a door on it! It looks like a flamingo threw up in here!"

CC: "Are you ready for your radar, dear?"

CC: "Dear Hillary, if you're still mad at me, you're gonna love this letter. My career is officially approaching oblivion. My agent had a brilliant idea: he thinks I should be a disco queen."

Hillary: "I'm not stubborn, I'm . . . right."
CC: "OK, stay in. But will you at least get out of those pajamas? You've been in them for
over a week!"
Hillary: "So what? Who the hell are you, the clothes police?"
CC: "You're not dead yet: so stop living as if you are!"

CC: "I was so wrecked, they had to shut down my first picture. It was horrible. I was terribly edgy. . . . I wasn't comfortable in the medium, you know? So I broke the director's jaw."

CC: "I'm doing what I set out to do, remember? I'm living the life you didn't have the courage to live. So don't give me you're not jealous. You're so jealous you can hardly breathe."

CC: "Listen. I know everything there is to know about you. And my memory is long. My memory is very, very long."

Big Business

Sadie Ratliff: "I hate men who smell like beer and bean dip . . . and makin' love in the back of recreational vehicles!"

Sadie Shelton: "I don't see how is it that you, my own sister, can stuff your face and nothing happens and I subsist on 60 calories a day or else blow up like a Macy's Day float!"

Sadie Ratliff: "Whoa . . . I've tied hogs slipperier 'n you!"

Sadie Ratliff: "Mmm! Friendly men in this town!"

Sadie Ratliff: "I find myself just praying for a UFO sighting! I stand here and I say, come and get me, come and get me!"

Sadie Ratliff: "Not with a man covered in pig poop, no sir, I don't."

Sadie Ratliff: "I'm not gonna stick around here like a clove on a baked ham, I'm gonna kick up my heels!"

Sadie Shelton: "Is this how we come dressed to the office? You look like a blood clot."

Sadie Shelton: "What's this, are we hearing voices now . . . like Joan of Ark?"

Sadie Shelton: "I know your plans, sit up in that room and pretend you're wafting through a field of daisies while you make love to the pastry cart— now PUT DOWN THAT ECLAIR and get down here and help me find these RATLIFF people!"

Sadie Shelton: "Oh, god! It's me with a bad haircut!"
Sadie Ratliff: "Bad?! I paid twelve bucks for this!"

Sadie Ratliff: "It's pod people! I saw that movie!"
Sadie Shelton: "I was at the premier!"

Sadie Ratliff: "They're robots! They wanna kill us a-and take our places! There's UFO written all over this thang!"

Sadie Ratliff: "These press-on nails . . . think I shoulda pressed harder, Rose?"

Divine Madness

Bette: "The question before us is where's her clitoris?"

Bette: "Oh, my girls! When I first saw these girls, they were peddling their papayas on 42nd street, so flushed, so filthy. The astonishing verbal abuse they heaped upon me made me certain that we were destined to share the stage someday. Not only are my girls fine singers and dancers, not only are they gorgeous and talented, but they also think I'm GOD!"

Bette: "How 'bout a spotlight up here, huh? How 'bout a nice white spotlight for the Diva who's sweating her guts out up here, huh?!"

Bette: "And then a wee voice called out to me in the night and reminded me of the motto by which I've always tried to live my life: F°@k 'em if they can't take a joke!"

Down and Out in Beverly Hills
Barbara: "It's true. I am a vegetarian. But I hear that vodka comes from a potato!"

Barbara: "Guilt is useless."

Barbara: "He's going to give that dog fleas, and it's going to be YOUR fault."

Barbara: "I think I see your aura."

Drowning Mona

Mona:"You've been playing *Wheel of Fortune* with someone else!"

Mona: "Well, life handed me a whole pile of shit. What am I supposed to make out of that?"
Phil: "Shit salad?"

Mona: "Fun? I lost Wyatt. I'm a loser. Does that sound like fun to you?"

Mona: "Why don't you take that trophy and shove it up your ass, Calzone!"

Mona: "I don't wanna hurt someone. I wanna hurt you!"

First Wives Club

Brenda: "Now, I ask you, Duarto, who's supposed to wear that? Some anorexic teenager? Some fetus? It's a conspiracy, I know it is! I've had enough. I'm leading a protest. I'm not buying another article of clothing until these designers come to their senses!"

_____

Brenda: "What's the matter, Morty? Can't you buy her a whole dress?"

_____

Brenda: "Bye Bye, love. . . . hello, Pop-Tarts"

_____

Brenda: "My Morty became this big shot on TV. Then it hits: midlife crisis. Major. He starts
working out. He grows a mustache. He gets an earring! I said, "Morty, what are you, a pirate? What's next, a parrot?"

_____

Brenda: "There she is. Princess Pelvis!"

_____

Brenda: "My, my, the bulimia has certainly paid off."

_____

Brenda: "Let's examine the evidence. Look! Nothing but bottles and gallon jugs!"
Elise: "I had guests!"
Brenda: "Who? Guns N Roses?"

_____

Elise: "I drink because I am a sensitive and highly strung person."
Brenda: "No, that's why your co-stars drink."

_____

Brenda: "This is just like *Mission: Impossible!*"
Elise: "Oh! That was a big hit!"

For the Boys

Dixie: "It was purple alright . . . but I don't think it was his heart"

_____

Dixie: "The thing you wanna avoid is outlasting everybody. Can you remember that?"

_____

Dixie: Mind if I smoke?
Eddie: I don't care if you burn.
Dixie: What a prince.

_____

Dixie: "Well . . . alone in the dark with thousands of men. There is a God after all!"

_____

Eddie: "Why don't you put a dress on him and forget about it?"
Dixie: "I would, but then you'd probably make a pass at him!"

Eddie: "Just relax and follow my lead."
Dixie: "Yeah. Right off a cliff."

Dixie: "And how they loved him, those boys. He was generous . . . stingy.
Brilliant . . . infuriating. And a world-class, solid-gold, son-of-a-bitch."

Dixie: "Oh my god! Eddie, look. Up there, in the fish tank! It's . . . the sponsors! Gentlemen, may I say, your coffee, I can't live without it. Because it
isn't just coffee. It's nectar, it's ambrosia, it's really more like a drug, isn't
it? I mean, I'm sure you do put a little narcotic in it because I can't seem
to get enough of it. I've, I've, I've got to have that coffee!!!"

Dixie:"Who's next? Rudolph? He's got a red nose, too. . . . we can't be too
careful!"

Gypsy

Rose: "If I coulda been, I woulda been. And that's show business."

Rose: "What do they mean, can't I read signs? If I can read the fine print on
our contracts, I can certainly read letters two feet high. 'The mother of
Miss Gypsy Rose Lee is not allowed backstage at this theater.' Hummph.
Know what I did with that sign? I laid it out on the ground and sent
Chowsy III down on it. That dog's a trooper. She knew what to do!"

Rose: "We got Herbie for brains, you for talent, and ya both got me . . . to yell
at."

Rose:"If that cow goes, I go!"

Rose: "It ain't bunk! Maybe nothin' wonderful'll happen to me, but they're
gonna have a
marvelous time!"

Hocus Pocus

Winnifred: "You know, I've always wanted a child. And now I think I'll have
one . . . on toast!"

Billy: "Go to hell!"
Winnifred: "Oh! I've been there, thank you. I found it quite lovely."

Winnifred: "Oh Look another Gloooorious morning. . . . IT MAKES ME SICK!"

Winnifred: "Booooooooook, come to mommy!"

Winnifred: "Hello, I want my book. . . . Bonjour, je veux mon livre."

Jinxed

Bonita: "There's no vowels. This isn't funny, Harold. This isn't funny."

Bonita: "Harold! You look just like Frank Sinatra!"

Bonita: "Remember that outfit you said you wouldn't be caught dead in? Well, guess what, Harold. This . . . is it!"

Bonita: "You came in like a shit-kicker, honey, but you're not going out like one."

Bonita: "Talk to my ass, my head's had enough."

Isn't She Great?

Editor: "You can't call the male part a dingle."
Jackie: "Why not?"
Editor: "You just can't."
Jackie: "Dingle, dingle, dingle! What do you call it? A butter-churn?"

Oliver and Company

Georgette: "Perfect isn't easy, but it's me."

Georgette: "I'd like to play with him all right—the little furball!"

Outrageous Fortune

Sandy: "Every guy I have ever slept with . . . and we are way into double digits here, has come back for more, every single one."

Lauren: "They've been HERE!"
Sandy: "Wait a second, no one has been here, it always looks like this!"

Sandy: "I'm supposed to have them unhook my IV so I can pay my bills, is that the routine?"

Sandy: "You know and I know I'm never gonna get another cab to come out here to Vietnam, okay, cue ball?"

Lauren: "I haven't seen a single white person on the street."
Sandy: "There's one. Oops, they got him!"

Sandy: "Oh, like that's really a call he's gonna take: 'hello, we're two starving actresses trying to save the world.' . . . GET REAL!!!!!!!!!!!!!"

Ruthless People

Barbara: "Am I to understand that I am being MARKED DOWN?!!? I've been kidnapped by K-MART!"

Barbara: "Oh my God! I've been kidnapped by Huey and Dewey!"

Barbara: "So, if I look like his mother and you look like his father, this is what our son would look like. Pretty strong argument for birth control."

Barbara: "My husband worships the ground I walk on!!! When he hears about this, he will explooooode!"

Barbara: "Nice butt, that's what they'll say on your first day at the men's club. The San Quentin Country Club. With a cute little rear-end like that, you'll be the belle of the ball. Your dance card will be full every day! You'll be making all kinds of new, close, personal friends. Big, ugly, hairy friends. Not that you'll ever see what they look like. Because you'll be facing the other way."

Barbara: "Sometimes, if it's a firing squad, they miss all the major arteries. BANG! And you don't die right away. . . . you just kind of hang on . . . bleeding, bleeding . . . endlessly!"

Barbara: "You miserable scum-sucking pig! Oh, I'm sorry, dear! They made me say that!"

Barbara: "Help, police, I've been kidnapped! Oh, how the hell do I know where I am?!"

Stella

Stella: "You can buy a girl a book . . . but then when she gets home . . . who she gonna talk about it to?"

Stella: "I wish I knew stuff . . . stuff that'll make her happy. . . . I wanna her happy."

Stella: "A person's happiness is as good as shows in their FACE. . . ."

Stella: "I've got two hands. . . . I can do it myself."

Stella: "I love yah Jenny-girl."

That Old Feeling

Lilly:"I'm not neurotic, I'm just a bitch."

Lilly: "A metaphor! Are WE literary!"

Lilly: "Your twenties are for having sex with all the wrong people."

Lilly: "I haven't been this happy since it was OK to take drugs."

Lilly: "You have more hair. Rogaine? Hair Club for Men? Is it rug?"

Lilly: I hope she's getting those lines above her lips right here, ya know. She's always had that
fabulous tan. I hope she's a fucking raisin!"

The Rose

The Rose: "I am not a hoochie-koochie woman!"

The Rose: "Well, that's okay, cause we don't eat 'em, neither." (in reply to "We don't serve hippies.")

The Rose: "Someone's spreading a rumor that being rich is a drag, but I tell you whoever's spreading that rumor is dead-ass broke!"

The Rose: "I don't even know where the °°°° I am! All these clouds look the same!"

The Rose: "Colonel! Yoo-hoo! Oh, you know I'm talking to you. Air-borne, Houston, air-borne!"

The Rose: "People say to me, 'Rose, when's the first time you heard the blues?' You know what I tell 'em? I tell 'em, 'The day I was born!' "

The Rose: "Where ya goin'? Where's everybody goin'?"

The Rose: "Honey, if you had to work for a living, your ass would be draggin', too!"

The Rose: "Oh my God! That drag queen's doin' me!"

The Rose: "Are you trying to get in my bloomers, sonny?"
Huston: "Working on it."
The Rose: "Oh you brown eyed motherfucker, where you been all my life?"

TV SPECIALS AND SERIES

1. *The Fabulous Bette Midler*   HBO
   First broadcast: June 19, 1976

2. *Ol' Redhair Is Back*   NBC-TV
   Guest Stars: Dustin Hoffman, Emmett Kelly
   First broadcast: December 7, 1977

3. *Bette Midler: Art or Bust*   HBO
   First broadcast: August 20, 1984

4. *Bette Midler's Mondo Beyondo*   HBO
   Guest Stars: Bill Irwin, Paul Zaloom, the Kipper Kids (Martin von Hasselberg and Brian Routh)
   First broadcast: March 19, 1988

5. *Diva Las Vegas*   HBO
   First broadcast: January 18, 1997

6. *Bette*   CBS-TV series
   Broadcast dates: 2000–2001

CONCERT TOURS

Continental Baths (1970–1972)
Carnegie Hall (1972)
Philharmonic Hall at Lincoln Center (1972)
The Divine Miss M Tour (1973)
Bette at the Palace (1973)
Clams on the Half Shell Revue (1975)
The Depression Tour (1975)
The Club Tour (1977)
The World Tour (1978)
Divine Madness! (1979)
De Tour (1982)
Experience the Divine (1993–1994)
Diva Las Vegas (1996–1997)
Divine Miss Millennium Concerts, Las Vegas (1999–2000)

WEBSITES

1. Bette Midler Webpage
   http://www.experiencethedivine.com/
   This is a well-maintained website, full of information and links. There is an outline of her career, news of her family, and even a listing of her movies currently running on television.

2. lerenti.com: Bette Midler Lyrics
   http://digilander.iol.it/lerenti/lyrics/full/m/midler_bette.htm
   This is literally a website devoted to the recorded lyrics of Bette Midler, from *The Divine Miss M* up to *Bathhouse Betty*. In the instance of *Mud Will Be Flung Tonight!* only the song lyrics are transcribed, not the comedy routines.

3. My One True Bette
   http://www.crosswinds.net/~myonetruebette/
   This site contains an album list, movie list, photos, downloadable computer wallpaper, puzzles, lyrics, and various website links.

4. Best of Bette
   http://www.geocities.com/Hollywood/Academy/6179/
   An informative site with separate sections of Bette's TV specials, films, albums, and a musical jukebox on which you can play several of Bette's songs.

5. Bettechive
   http://www.bettechive.com/
   This site contains an interesting overview of Bette's life and career with trivia quiz, bibliography, and more. There is also an interesting timeline of recent events, especially of Midler's events in 2001 and 2002—complete with photos.

6. Delve into the Divine
   http://www.delveintothedivine.cjb.net/
   A well arranged overview of Bette's life and career, with separate sections on television, films, music, multimedia, news, quotes, and more.

7. New York Restoration Project
   http://www.nyrp.org/
   This is the official site of Bette's pet project, responsible for cleaning up New York City's parks and other public places. She can be found on a couple of the site's pages.

8. Klingman, Moogy
   http://www.moogymusic.com/
   This is the site of singer, songwriter, and keyboard player Moogy Klingman. Moogy wrote Bette's signature song, "Friends," and was the producer of her *Songs for the New Depression* album. He was also a member of Utopia and has worked with Todd Rundgren, Bette Midler, Johnny Winter, and more. The site contains a page devoted to Bette.

BETTE MIDLER FACTS

Name: Bette Midler
Namesake: Bette Davis
Childhood nicknames: The Librarian, "Harriet Craig"
Alter Egos: The Divine Miss M, Baby Divine, Delores DeLago, Soph, Nanette
Occupations: Actress, singer, author, songwriter, producer, and diva extraordinaire
Height: 5'1½"
Hair: Presently champagne blonde, occasionally red-orange, and sometimes a dark brown
Eyes: Brown
Date of Birth: December 1, 1945
Place of Birth: Honolulu, Hawaii
Father: Fred Midler
Mother: Ruth Schindel
Siblings: Judith (deceased), Susan, Daniel
Religion: Judaism
First Job: Working at a pineapple factory
Marital Status: Married Martin von Hasselberg, December 16, 1984, at the Candlelight Wedding Chapel in Las Vegas, Nevada
Child: Sophie Frederica Alohilani von Haselberg (born November 14, 1986)
Pet: A Jack Russell terrier named Puddles (a.k.a. Queen Puddles)
Charities: Adopt-a-Highway, Get Out the Vote, the Manhattan Restoration Project, and AIDS Project Los Angeles

MEMBERS OF THE HARLETTES

Melissa Manchester, Robin Grean, Merle Miller, Charlotte Crossley, Sharon Redd, Ula Hedwig, Diva Gray, Jocelyn Brown, Katie Sagal, Linda Hart, Jenifer Lewis, Siobhan O'Carroll, Helena Springs, Carol Hatchett, Melanie Taylor, Rhae Ann Theriault

MARK BEGO'S IDEA FOR A BETTE MIDLER ALBUM, PRODUCED BY BARRY MANILOW: *WELCOME TO THE CONTINENTAL BATHS*

"Wheel of Fortune"
"Sha-Boom Sha-Boom"
"Happiness Is a Thing Called Joe"
"Honky Tonk Woman"
"Lady Madonna"
"What a Difference a Day Makes"
"My Forgotten Man"
"Ten Cents a Dance"
"Come Up and See Me Sometime"
"Love Potion Number Nine"
"Great Balls of Fire"

AWARDS AND DISTINCTIONS

1972—Bette releases her first album, *The Divine Miss M.*

1972—*After Dark* magazine Ruby Award as "Entertainer of the Year."

1973—Grammy for "Best New Artist of the Year."

1973—Bette set a Broadway Box Office Record for her Palace show, which sold out three weeks running.

1974—Special-category Tony Award for her Palace Show.

1975—Bette's hit Broadway show *Clams on the Halfshell* runs for eight months.

1976—Harvard's "Hasty Pudding Award" for woman of the year.

1978—Emmy for "Outstanding Comedy or Variety Special" for *Ol' Red Hair Is Back.*

1979—Bette stars in her first motion picture, *The Rose.*

1979—Academy Award nomination for "Best Actress" in *The Rose* (Sally Field won for *Norma Rae*).

1979—Golden Globe for "Best Actress" in *The Rose.*

1979—Golden Globe for "Best Newcomer to Film" for *The Rose.*

1980—"Entertainer of the Year" from Conference of Personal Managers West.

1980—Grammy for "Best Female Pop Vocal Performance" for "The Rose."

1980—Golden Globe for best original song in a motion picture for "The Rose" (this award actually went to the songwriter, Amanda McBroom).

1982—Grammy for "Best Recording for Children" from *In Harmony* (A Sesame Street Record).

1983—Bette's first music video, "Beast of Burden" with Mick Jagger, premieres on MTV.

1984—Bette hosts the first ever *MTV Video Music Awards* with Dan Aykroyd, live from Radio City Music Hall.

1986—Bette receives her own star on Hollywood Boulevard.

1986—Bette becomes a producer and forms her own production company, All Girls Productions.

1987—American Comedy Award for "Funniest Female in a Motion Picture" for *Ruthless People.*

1987—American Comedy Award for funniest performance on a record for *Mud Will Be Flung Tonight!*

1987—American Comedy Award for "Funniest Female of the Year."

1987—American Comedy Award for a lifetime achievement award for a female.

1988—American Comedy Award for funniest female in a motion picture for *Outrageous Fortune.*

1988—Acknowledged by ShoWest as box office star of the year.

1989—American Comedy Award for funniest female in a motion picture for *Big Business.*

1988—Bette's first #1 song—"Wind beneath My Wings."

1989—Grammy for Record of the Year for "Wind beneath My Wings."

1989—Grammy for "Song of the Year" for "Wind beneath My Wings." (this Grammy actually went to the songwriters, Larry Henley and Jeff Silbar).

1991—Grammy for "Song of the Year" for "From a Distance" (this Grammy actually went to the songwriter, Julie Gold).

1991—Academy Award nomination for Best Actress in *For the Boys* (Jodie Foster won for *Silence of the Lambs*).

1991—Golden Globe for "Best Actress" in *For the Boys.*

1991—Bette receives a Lifetime Achievement/Commitment Award from (APLA) AIDS Project Los Angeles.

1992—Emmy for outstanding individual performance for being the last guest on *The Tonight Show* with Johnny Carson.

1993—American Comedy Award for funniest female in a television special for her appearance as Johnny Carson's final guest on *The Tonight Show.*

1993—Bette returns to the concert stage after ten years with her "Experience the Divine" tour. The show had a record-breaking sold-out thirty nights at Radio City Music Hall.

1995—Bette founded the New York Restoration Project.

1996—American Comedy Award for funniest supporting role in a motion picture for *Get Shorty.*

1996—Bette stars in *The First Wives Club,* her first movie to break $100 million at the box office.

1997—Women in Film Crystal Awards (trio of *The First Wives Club* received this award).

1997—Honored by the United Nations as an "Influential Woman Leader in the Environment.

1997—Emmy for Outstanding Performance in a Musical/Variety Program for *Diva Las Vegas.*

1997—Cable Ace Award for Best Performance in a Musical/Variety Program for *Diva Las Vegas.*

1998—American Comedy Award for funniest female in a television special for *Diva Las Vegas.*

2000—Bette's CBS sitcom, *Bette,* premieres; it's canceled after 18 episodes were filmed, and 16 were aired in America.

2001—*TV Guide* Award for "Actress of the Year in a New Television Series" for *Bette.*

2001—People's Choice Award for "Favorite Female Performer in a New Television Series" for *Bette.*

GUIDE TO THE EPISODES OF THE TV SERIES *BETTE,* 2000–2001

1. "The Pilot"
   Co-starring: Danny DeVito
   First Broadcast in America: October 11, 2000
   Synopsis: Bette is established as a sitcom replica of the Bette Midler the
   public has come to know over the past four decades. When her fictional
   husband, Roy (Kevin Dunn), falls asleep in bed before making love to her,
   Bette does a Lucy-like meltdown in the self-confidence department. She
   consults a plastic surgeon and invests in a sophisticated exercise machine
   that she can't seem to figure out how to use. Bette further loses her grip
   on her family life when she tries in vain to act "hip" in front of her thirteen-year-old daughter Rose (Lindsay Lohan).

2. "And the Winner Is . . ."
   Co-starring: David James Elliot, George Segal, Sharon Lawrence
   First Broadcast in America: October 18, 2000
   Synopsis: When Bette wins an award, she thanks everyone BUT her husband, Roy. Roy couldn't care less, but Bette obsesses of ways to make it
   up to him. Finally, she drives her manager, Connie (Joanna Gleason), to
   seek out ANY sort of award that can be presented to her, so that she can
   thank Roy. She thinks she is getting an award from the American Film
   Institute, but she is getting something quite different at the end of the
   show.

3. "Halloween"
   Co-starring: Dolly Parton
   First Broadcast in America: October 25, 2000
   Synopsis: Bette guest stars on Dolly Parton's TV special, and she is thrilled
   with how well they both get along together. However, her feelings are hurt
   when she finds that Dolly has lavished wonderful gifts on Midler's family,
   manager, and accompanist, Oscar (James Dreyfus). Simultaneously, it is
   the Halloween season, and Bette is dismayed that her daughter Rose (Marina Malota) feels she is too old to trick or treat. As a joke, Bette dresses

up as Dolly and does some devilish pranks in the neighborhood. When her prank gets the real-life Dolly in trouble, Bette repeats the ploy—this time dressed as Barbra Streisand.

4. "Silent but Deadly"
   First Broadcast in America: November 1, 2000
   Synopsis: Stricken with a problem concerning her vocal cords, Bette is rendered speechless for twenty-four hours. Bette is determined not to let her mute condition disrupt her day. Roy thinks that she is mad at him and giving him the silent treatment to get even. This is the episode with the famous fart joke that neither Jack Nicholson nor Candice Bergan would perform. In the set-up gag, Bette takes the blame for someone else "cutting the cheese."

5. "Two Days at a Time"
   Co-starring: Oprah Winfrey
   First Broadcast in America: November 8, 2000
   Synopsis: Bette is invited to be part of one of Oprah's televised book club discussion groups. It seems that Bette has overbooked herself for personal appearances that particular week. She shows up for Oprah's book club and tries to mask the fact that she hasn't read a single word of the book and has no clue what anyone is talking about.

6. "Color of Roses"
   Co-starring: The Harlettes
   First Broadcast in America: November 16, 2000
   Synopsis: Bette invites her faithful accompanist, Oscar, to produce a song for her new album. However, always-in-control Bette won't quit insisting on changing the proceedings. The song she is recording is the cut from her current Bette album, *The Color of Roses*. Along the way, she performs the song in a disco version, a rap version, a Jamaican reggae version, and even a gospel version. Finally, she decides to go with Oscar's original concept, the simple ballad version of the song.

7. "In My Life"
   First Broadcast in America: November 22, 2000
   Synopsis: Bette presents several flashbacks of her fictionalized TV life, including how she and Connie met, how she and Oscar met, how she and Roy met, and the birth of her daughter Rose.

8. "I Love This Game"
   Co-starring: Kobe Bryant, the Laker Girls
   First Broadcast in America: November 29, 2000
   Synopsis: Bette promises Roy floor seats to a Los Angeles Lakers basketball game at the Staples Center. She has to scramble to get the seats and finally gets her hands on them through star player Kobe Bryant. However, when she gets to the seats, Bette finds that she doesn't like their position-

ing in the audience. In a comedy of errors, Bette dislocates Bryant's finger and ends up swept into formation with the team's cheerleading squad, the Laker Girls.

9. " . . . Or Not to Be"
   Co-starring: Tim Curry, the Harlettes
   First Broadcast in America: December 13, 2000
   Synopsis: Bette wrangles her way into a production of *Hamlet,* starring Tim Curry. However, she has an anxiety attack, worried that she doesn't have what it takes to cut the mustard with Shakespeare. Once she has the confidence, she turns her Shakespearean debut into a Divine Miss M production, complete with Harlettes.

10. "Diva Interrupted"
    Co-starring: The Harlettes
    First Broadcast in America: December 20, 2000
    Synopsis: When *US* magazine announces its special issue, "The 50 Most Powerful People in Hollywood," Bette is aghast to find that she is not on the list. She hires a new publicist to get her some press. Everything backfires in her face when she tries to stage a fake nervous breakdown, so that she can make a miraculous recovery.

11. "True Story"
    Co-starring: Joy Bahar, Lisa Ling, Merideth Vierra, and Star Jones
    First Broadcast in America: January 9, 2001
    Synopsis: Bette gets caught in a little white lie, which mushrooms into a nightmare, when she claims that she saved a drowning boy. The four hostesses of *The View* TV show want to have Bette on their show as a guest, along with the saved boy. Bette has to "cast" a boy into the role of the rescued lad, and neither Bette nor the kid can keep the story straight.

12. "Of Men and Meatballs"
    Co-starring: Tony Danza
    First Broadcast in America: January 10, 2001
    Synopsis: Bette and her manager, Connie, leave town to have some fun. Bette wants to hook Connie up with a nice single guy, but they end up with twenty-something boys instead of men. Connie has her pick of a "Mama's boy" and an overanxious stuntman.

13. "Big Business"
    Co-starring: Fred Willard
    First Broadcast in America: January 24, 2001
    Synopsis: Caught up in the idea of having a product to sell on one of the home shopping TV networks, Bette decides to design an outfit to sell on the air. She insists on doing the designs herself, and the result is a hideous disaster of bad taste, which no one wants to purchase.

14. "The Invisible Mom"
    Co-starring: Olivia Newton-John and her daughter Chloe Rose
    First Broadcast in America: February 7, 2001
    Synopsis: Bette decides to volunteer at daughter Rose's school. However, when she is snubbed by another mom (Olivia Newton-John), she does everything she can to endear herself. Connie, meanwhile, stakes herself out in the girl's lavatory, where she ends up giving relationship advice and talking frankly about boys.

15. "Poltergeist"
    Co-starring: Jon Lovitz
    First Broadcast in America: February 28, 2001
    Synopsis: Bette's new neighbor is comedian Jon Lovitz. However, his house is being remodeled, and he asks if he can stay with Bette. Wanting to appear generous, Midler lets him stay, while he slowly drives her nuts. He tries to convince Bette that there is a "black cloud" of misfortune over her house, and that she should sell. Lovitz has the best line; basting a turkey in Bette's kitchen, with turkey baster in hand he announces, "Gobbles needs a bath."

16. "Brand New Roy"
    Co-starring: Robert Hays
    First Broadcast in America: March 7, 2001
    Synopsis: Roy seems to be acting odd, and he actually seems to have some comic chemistry with Bette, unlike Kevin Dunn. Could the reason be that Roy is now portrayed by a brand new actor? Robert Hayes, of *Airplane!* fame, takes over as Bette's fictional husband—in his first and only episode of the series. New Roy and Bette try to leave Los Angeles for a romantic trip to Paris; however, they cause havoc at the airport, and never get off the ground.

NOTE: The previous episodes were broadcast in America on the dates noted. CBS-TV pulled the plug right before the last show was broadcast. The ratings were so low on the show that the network never put the show in "reruns." However, two more episodes were filmed, which ran in several overseas markets. They are as follows:

17. "The Grammy Pre-Show"
    Synopsis: Bette is scheduled to perform on the Grammys, and the whole family is invited to join her. Oscar's grandmother is in town visiting, Connie starts a fashion trend with her new earrings, and Bette keeps trying to destroy her diet—and her ability to fit into her gown—by nibbling constantly.

18. "Method to Her Madness"
    Synopsis: Bette sets out on a quest to find the perfect movie role, by doing some real-life research. She ends up in a truckstop, doing her research.

INDEX

ABOUT THE AUTHOR

Mark Bego is the author of several best-selling books on rock & roll and show business. With forty books published and over ten million books in print, he is acknowledged as the best-selling biographer in the rock and pop music field. His biographies have included the life stories of some of the biggest stars of rock, soul, pop, and country. His first Top Ten *New York Times* best-seller was *Michael!* about Michael Jackson (1984). Since that time, he has written about the lives of *Cher!* (2001), *Rock Hudson: Public & Private* (1986), *Aretha Franklin: Queen of Soul* (1989), *Bonnie Raitt: Just in the Nick of Time* (1996), *Jewel* (1998), and *Madonna: Blonde Ambition* (2000).

In the 1990s Bego has branched out into country music books, writing *Country Hunks* (1994), *Country Gals* (1995), *I Fall to Pieces: The Music and the Life of Patsy Cline* (1995), *Alan Jackson: Gone Country* (1996), *George Strait: The Story of Country's Living Legend* (1997), *LeAnn Rimes* (1998), and *Vince Gill* (2000).

Bego has coauthored books with several rock stars, including Martha Reeves: *Dancing in the Street, Confessions of a Motown Diva*, which spent five weeks on the *Chicago Tribune* Best-Seller list in 1994. He worked with Micky Dolenz of the Monkees (*I'm a Believer*, 1993), Jimmy Greenspoon of Three Dog Night (*One Is the Loneliest Number*, 1991), and Mary Wilson (*Dreamgirl: My Life As a Supreme*, 2000 edition).

His writing has also been featured in several record albums and compact discs. In 1982 he wrote the interior notes to the Columbia House five-record boxed set *The Motown Collection*. His liner notes can also be found in the CD *Mary Wilson, Walk the Line* (1992).

In 1998 Mark wrote books about three of the hottest leading men in late '90s cinema. His *Leonardo DiCaprio: Romantic Hero* spent six weeks on the *New York Times* best-seller list. He followed it up with *Matt Damon: Chasing a Dream* and *Will Smith: The Freshest Prince*.

In 1998 Melitta Coffee launched *Mark Bego: Romantic Hero* blend coffee as part of its Celebrity Series. He is currently developing his book *Rock and Roll Almanac* (1995) into a television series and writing a novel called *Motor City*. Mark divides his time among New York City, Los Angeles, and Tucson, Arizona.

Visit his website: www.markbego.com.